EX LIBRIS

BOOKS BY PAUL TOUGH

*Whatever It Takes: Geoffrey Canada's Quest
to Change Harlem and America*

*How Children Succeed: Confidence, Curiosity,
and the Hidden Power of Character*

Helping Children Succeed: What Works and Why

The Years That Matter Most: How College Makes or Breaks Us

The Years That
MATTER
MOST

How College Makes or Breaks Us

PAUL TOUGH

HUTCHINSON
LONDON

1 3 5 7 9 10 8 6 4 2

Hutchinson
20 Vauxhall Bridge Road
London SW1V 2SA

Hutchinson is part of the Penguin Random House group of companies
whose addresses can be found at global.penguinrandomhouse.com.

First published in the United Kingdom by Hutchinson in 2019
First published in the United States by Houghton Mifflin Harcourt in 2019

www.penguin.co.uk

A CIP catalogue record for this book is available from the British Library.

ISBN 9781847947970

Printed and bound in Great Britain by Clays Ltd, Elcograf S.p.A.

Penguin Random House is committed to a sustainable future
for our business, our readers and our planet. This book is made
from Forest Stewardship Council® certified paper.

For Paula

Contents

I

WANTING IN

---

1. Decision Day

When I walked up out of the subway on that cold spring afternoon, Shannen Torres was nowhere to be seen. We had arranged to meet at 4:15 p.m. in St. Nicholas Park in West Harlem, just down the hill from A. Philip Randolph Campus High School, where she was a senior, a few months away from graduation. But when I got to the park, I couldn't see her anywhere.

My phone buzzed. It was a text from Shannen: "I'm to your left."

I looked up the path and spotted her, sitting huddled over her phone on a bench about fifty yards away. She was dressed in layers against the chill, a beige barn jacket over two dark hoodies. Everything else she wore was black: black sweatpants, big black high-top sneakers, black chunky glasses, and a black backward Nike baseball cap, into which she'd stuffed her long, thick dark hair. I walked over and sat down next to her.

"Hi," she said. "I'm hiding here because I don't want anyone to see me."

I had met Shannen only a couple of times before, so it was hard for me to say for sure if this constituted strange behavior for her. But it definitely seemed a little odd.

Then she explained the situation. It was March 30. At exactly 5:00 p.m. that afternoon, every college in the Ivy League would simultaneously release their acceptance and rejection letters for next year's freshman class. I had dimly understood that the decisions were going out at some point that week, but I hadn't realized they would be arriving at the very moment Shannen and I had planned to meet.

Shannen had applied to two Ivy League colleges: Princeton and the University of Pennsylvania. She wanted to get into Princeton, but she really, really wanted to get into the University of Pennsylvania. It had been her "dream school," she told me, since seventh grade. And in less than an hour, either her dream would come true, or it wouldn't.

That fact was overwhelming her. When I'd interviewed her before, she had always seemed pretty cool — a Bronx girl, a streetwise Dominicana — but here on this bench in St. Nicholas Park, she was coming undone right before my eyes. "I'm the nervousest I've ever been," she said. Her hands were trembling. She looked like she was about to cry.

"I think it's just, like, I've been working my entire life for this one thing," she explained. "It feels like everything is depending on this. Which sounds dramatic, I know. But it's true."

Shannen was born in New York City in 1999 to parents who had emigrated from the Dominican Republic. When she was two, with her parents' relationship crumbling, her mother took her and her older brother to New Bedford, Massachusetts. They stayed with some relatives at first, but that arrangement soon crumbled, too, and they moved next into a shelter run by Catholic nuns, and then, after a few months, into an apartment of their own in the projects.

Shannen started elementary school in Massachusetts, and she was a good student from the beginning. School wasn't stressful in those early years, but once her mother moved the family back to New York, to the Bronx, the pressure started to build. In sixth grade Shannen entered Junior High School 22, a struggling school in a hulking building on 167th Street. There were fights in the hallway every day, and she was bullied by new arrivals from the Dominican Republic who made fun of her for not being Dominican enough. Shannen was proud of her roots and her race, but there were elements of other cultures she was coming to appreciate as well: Coldplay, pasta, Harry Potter novels. She retreated into her schoolwork, studying harder, doing more. And when she got to high school, she worked harder still.

In the entrance hall of Randolph High, on a bright yellow bulletin board on the wall, the administration posts, each semester, the honor roll for each grade, all the top scholars from a school of almost fifteen hundred students, listed in order of their grade point average. In the first semester of her freshman year, Shannen's name appeared at the very top of the list, and her name had stayed at the top ever since. Now, as graduation approached, her academic average was 97.7 percent, which would almost certainly make her valedictorian. In three and a half years, she had not missed a single day of high school.

But remaining number one took an enormous effort. Each night, Shannen stayed up until her homework was done perfectly, sometimes till four or five in the morning, ignoring her mother's admonitions to close the books and go to bed. The previous year, her junior year, was the most grueling. She took three AP courses, and she studied so relentlessly in the first semester that by Christmas she had lost eleven pounds off her already small frame. She got used to sleeping three hours a night. She drank so much coffee that she became immune to its effects.

The harder she worked, the greater people's expectations for her grew. And the more she felt the weight of those expectations, the harder she felt she had to work. Where it was all leading, in Shannen's mind, was college. And not just any college. When she was little, teachers and family members saw her intelligence and intense determination and predicted that she would make it into an Ivy League school. At first it was just one of those crazy things people say to a smart kid, but as time went on, this recurring prophecy began to seem more plausible.

Beginning in sophomore year, Shannen took free SAT-prep classes at Columbia University, and each time she visited, she felt a bit more at home surrounded by neoclassical architecture and great books. In the spring of junior year, she was accepted into a highly selective and demanding college-prep summer program for low-income students called Leadership Enterprise for a Diverse America; historically, more than half of each year's LEDA class was admitted to an Ivy League college. Then four students from the class above hers at Randolph — which is not, on average, a high-achieving school — were admitted to Ivy League–level colleges: Penn, Stanford, Dartmouth, Columbia. They all got full-ride scholarships, and Shannen knew, given her family's limited income, that if she were admitted, she would probably be offered the same. Suddenly the idea that she might aspire to a place like Penn or Princeton didn't seem crazy at all.

BUT THE MORE realistic the prospect of the Ivy League became, the more pressure Shannen felt to deliver. As we sat and waited for the admissions verdict, that was what was weighing on her the most: the reactions of everyone in her life to the news she was about to receive. She visualized herself walking in the door of her family's small apartment uptown and telling her mother that she had been accepted to Penn. She could picture her mother's exact expression. She could almost see the tears of happiness.

And then she pictured herself walking in and having to tell her mom that she had been rejected. The tears of disappointment. And then tomorrow, having to go into school and break the news to her teachers and friends, everyone who had been counting on her to succeed. Hearing "Oh, I'm so sorry," over and over. The pats on the back and the sympathetic hugs, all day long. It was unbearable even to imagine.

That was why she was hiding out on this bench, she told me. She didn't want to be with friends or family that afternoon, or with anyone she knew well; at one point, when she saw a group of her friends walking down the hill behind me, she ducked her head down out of their sight. For some reason, she had decided that being with a reporter was a good alternative. She said she trusted that I was on her side, but she also felt like I was "neutral," that I didn't really expect anything from her. I wasn't invested in her success the way everyone else in her life seemed to be. I wouldn't be disappointed in her if she didn't make the cut.

I was, that afternoon, more than a year into a sprawling reporting project that had already taken me back and forth across the country several times, to rural high schools in Louisiana and inner-city community colleges in Chicago and verdant university campuses in California and South Carolina and Texas and New Jersey. I had interviewed plenty of educators and researchers and administrators. But mostly, on these journeys, I was talking to students like Shannen, young people in high school or college who were trying to make sense, as I was, of the changing landscape of American higher education.

Shannen was clutching her phone as we talked, checking the time, her hands still trembling, counting down the minutes, growing more and more anxious. It was Penn she kept thinking about as we sat there, not Princeton. She liked that Penn was urban and not too far from home. She had visited Penn's campus the previous summer with her LEDA group, and everything about the place had seemed perfect. She bought a sweater with the Penn logo, which she loved wearing. She had spent forever writing her Penn application essay, trying to get it just right. Her dream was to double-major in paleontology and business, taking classes in the archaeology department and at the Wharton School. Her best friend from LEDA, a girl from Tennessee named Tess, was applying to Penn as well, and they had already agreed that if they both got in, they would be roommates.

Shannen had begun crying for real now, quietly, swiping her fingers up under her glasses to catch the tears before they fell. I asked her why she was so upset even before she had received any news, good or bad, and she said she wasn't sure. But she tried to explain.

"School has always been my thing," she said slowly. "I've been working so hard for the past — how long have I been in school? I've been in school since I was three." She rubbed her nose on the sleeve of her hoodie. "So you take the thing that you've been best at your entire life. And you have someone, or in this case a group of people, sitting in a circle, who have not met you personally, who are determining if you're deserving." Shannen could picture them there in the Penn admissions department, paging through her application — her grades and her test scores and her essay and her recommendation letters — and rendering a judgment on who they thought she really was.

"And then they tell you that it's not enough, or that it's not good enough," she said. "Or that someone's score on a test could possibly measure up to all those years of hard work that you put yourself through. That you *chose* to put yourself through." Now she was crying harder. "And I did choose it. I love school. I love what I do. It's something that I don't force myself to do. I come to school because it's me. It's just who I am."

Five p.m. arrived. Shannen picked up her phone. The lockscreen displayed a black-and-white photo of Malcolm X. On the back of the phone was a sticker showing the flaming logo of *Thrasher,* the skateboard magazine. She opened up her mail app, pulled down on her in-box and let it snap back up. Nothing.

"God, I'm so scared," she said, whispering now.

She checked again. Still nothing.

After a few more minutes of pulling and snapping, she went back and read an old message from Penn and realized that she was doing it wrong. They weren't going to send an email after all. She was supposed to log into her account on Penn's applicant portal; the decision would be waiting for her there.

But then she couldn't remember her password.

"Come on, Shannen, you know the password," she said, her thumbs flying across the surface of her phone. "For the first time in six months, I cannot get this password right." She let out a little laugh. "Come on," she said to her phone, "don't do this to me."

Shannen went through the absurd modern dance of online security, secret questions and nine-digit phone codes and temporary
passwords. She finally made it into the portal and found the letter
from Penn. She read it quickly and then, closing her eyes and low-
ering her head, she tilted the screen of her phone in my direction.
All I could make out were the words "sincerely regret," but that was
enough.

Princeton was next, and it was more bad news: she was wait-listed,
and she knew almost no one gets off the wait list at Princeton. Shannen put down her phone and stared at the ground.

WE SAT THERE on the bench as it got colder and the sky began to
grow dark. Shannen was in no hurry to go home and see her mom's
sad face. Couples walked by with strollers and dogs; on St. Nicholas
Avenue, car horns sounded. The green globe lights over the subway
entrance flickered on. An ambulance sped uptown, its siren bleating.

Shannen knew, logically, that this should not feel like the end of the
world. Penn accepts just 9 percent of its freshman applicants. Princeton accepts 6 percent. Statistically, rejection is the likely outcome for
any applicant, even a valedictorian. There was also the mitigating fact
that, two weeks earlier, Shannen had been admitted to Davidson, a
very good liberal arts college near Charlotte, North Carolina, which
had offered her an amazingly generous financial-aid package. The
list price to attend Davidson for four years was about $260,000, but
Shannen, if she went, would pay a total of twelve dollars. Not twelve
dollars a year; twelve dollars for four years. The previous October,
Davidson had flown her down to campus for a visit, and she'd liked it
a lot. She'd be fine there, she knew. But Davidson was a long way from
her mom. And it didn't offer courses in paleontology. And it wasn't
her dream school. It wasn't what everyone was expecting.

That was what made this moment so hard for Shannen. It wasn't
just the practical fact of where she would be spending the next four
years of her life. It was the process of being judged and evaluated. It

was knowing that an institution into which she had poured so much of herself had suddenly decided she was unworthy.

"I just wish they could have at least—I wish it were possible for them to meet me," she said, still teary. "I wish they had a chance to see where I go to school. I wish they had a chance to meet my mom."

I asked her what she thought Penn's admissions officers would see if they visited her school in Harlem or her home in the Bronx.

"They'd see *me*," she said. "They wouldn't see my application. They'd see me. They'd see how much I love my high school. How much I care about what I do. How much I appreciate what I do. How I'm not who they think I am."

I asked her who she thought they thought she was.

"They think I'm an essay," she said. "They think I'm a test score."

There was one representative from Penn whom she had met in person. It was the Penn alumnus who had been assigned to interview her as part of the application process. He was a doctor who worked in Midtown Manhattan, and one day that winter, Shannen had taken the subway down to his office for a conversation. She knew that alumni interviews rarely had an effect on college-admissions decisions. But even if the experience didn't mean much to Penn, it meant a lot to her.

"It was supposed to last thirty minutes," she told me. "But I sat there and spoke with him for two hours. We spoke about everything. He asked me about what I'm interested in. And he asked me about my favorite movie. And we made jokes. He asked me about my favorite food. And I asked him about his favorite food."

I could imagine how the doctor felt, conversing with Shannen. Her enthusiasms were as infectious as they were idiosyncratic: the novels of David Foster Wallace, the latest theory on dinosaur extinction, the Black Lives Matter movement. She started crying again, and I asked her why the story about her conversation with the doctor made her sad.

"Because he just saw who I was," she said. "He was able to witness someone other than 'School Shannen.' Someone other than the person that everyone expects me to be." She took a deep breath. "At least I *think* he saw me that way."

She looked down at her phone. There was a text from Tess, the friend from Tennessee she had been hoping to room with.

"Did you hear from Penn?" Tess wrote.

Shannen texted her back: "Yes. It's a no."

Tess replied with a quick string of texts saying the kind of things you say: They're so stupid. I'm sorry. You totally deserved to get in.

Shannen wrote back: "Did you get in?"

And then there was a long pause, long enough that we both knew what the answer was going to be. Finally the text popped up on Shannen's phone:

"Yes :-/ It's such a crapshoot. It's all about luck."

Shannen and I sat in the twilight for a little longer, watching the cars and buses pass, and then she told me one more story about her alumni interview, the one with the doctor downtown. He'd had a recommendation for her, for the next time she visited Penn — a restaurant he thought she might like, right across the street from campus. "There was this one specific thing that he suggested I order, and I wrote it down," she said. "I still have that piece of paper in my book bag. And the first thing I was going to do in the summer when I got to Philadelphia was go there and order the thing that he suggested I order. And I was going to sit there and eat the food, and I was going to look out the window at the campus. And I expected to have the feeling: I belong there. That if I just crossed the street, that could be my second home."

THE FIRST TIME I met Shannen, the previous summer, she told me that on weekends during high school, when she didn't have too much homework, she would take the B train down to the Museum of Natural History and wander around on her own, looking at the dinosaurs, soaking up the science. Being at the museum gave her a certain feeling, she told me, the same one she had when she would walk across the Columbia campus: a hope that she might someday be able to find her true home in a place like this, a place of prestige and culture and privilege and learning. But for Shannen, that hope was always tempered by a small, stubborn fear that a girl like her might never be fully welcome in such a place. It was a little like the feeling of sitting right across the street from the University of Pennsylvania, yearning for what you could see on the other side, but not being sure if you would ever be invited to cross over.

Economists and sociologists have a name for the process of finding a new place in society, this phenomenon Shannen was dreaming of: social mobility. In its most basic definition, it means moving from one social or economic class to another. Economists can measure how mobile a society is by calculating how likely it is that a child born into any given rank of family income will rise or fall from that station as an adult, and while they differ on exactly what degree of mobility is best, they generally concur that a certain amount is a positive force in a nation's overall health. A society in which people can aspire to rise above their birth is a productive and ambitious one.

But while upward mobility may be good for a nation, it is rarely a smooth and straightforward experience for an individual. Upward mobility is not simply a question of earning more money than one's parents. It is also, for many people, a process of cultural disruption: leaving behind one set of values and assumptions and plunging into a new and foreign one. It can be disorienting and emotionally wrenching, shattering family ties and challenging deeply held notions of identity and purpose.

Mobility is a subject that has always pulled at me as a journalist. Its motivating questions seem so elemental, so essential to our understanding of who we are. What does it take for any of us to alter the conditions of our lives? What gets in people's way when they try? And how do they feel when they succeed? These questions hovered in the background of my three previous books. But a few years ago, I decided to investigate them more directly. And as I did, I encountered an unexpected and unique fact of contemporary American life: in sharp contrast to other ages and other cultures, mobility in the United States today depends, in large part, on what happens to individuals during a relatively brief period in late adolescence and early adulthood. If you are a young American like Shannen Torres, the decisions you make about higher education — and the decisions that are made for you — play a critical role in determining the course of the rest of your life.

That was true not just for superachievers like Shannen. I had spoken with several of Shannen's classmates at Randolph, young people who shared her economic status but not her academic accomplishments, and the choices they faced after senior year seemed just as fraught as Shannen's, but far more constrained: work or the military or college; a two-year or a four-year school; stay in the city or go to school upstate? These students were hearing a variety of messages from school and home and their peers, conflicting stories about how to achieve success and how to ward off failure. It wasn't at all clear to me which choices they should make — and it didn't seem clear to them, either. But those choices, I knew, would likely resonate in their lives for years to come.

MOBILITY HAS ALWAYS been a defining feature of the United States. In 1831 a young French aristocrat named Alexis de Tocqueville visited the country, then still a young nation, to study its political institutions and civic traditions. When he returned home, he recounted his travels in his book *Democracy in America,* now considered one of the classic works of political science. Tocqueville found much to admire in the United States, but he was puzzled by Americans' embrace of the idea that social class should be fluid.

In his book, Tocqueville largely ignored the glaring fact of slavery in the United States, which was an obvious obstacle to mobility at the time for Americans of African descent. Among the white Americans he studied, though, Tocqueville observed a social order that, in contrast to the comfortable stability of Europe's class system, was always in flux. Fortunes were made, and fortunes were lost. "Wealth circulates with inconceivable rapidity, and experience shows that it is rare to find two succeeding generations in the full enjoyment of it," he wrote. "New families are constantly springing up, others are constantly falling away."

The relative chaos of the American class system was disorienting to Tocqueville. If the rich could so easily become poor and the poor could so easily become rich, how could anyone know where he stood? In European nations, "aristocracy had made a chain of all the members of the community, from the peasant to the king," Tocqueville wrote. And that chain, he believed, was a good thing. It kept a society bound together. The United States had lost the cohesion that comes with an aristocratic tradition, he warned: "Democracy breaks that chain, and severs every link of it."

As threatening as this idea may have been to Tocqueville, most Americans in the early nineteenth century were content, even eager, to have those chains severed. What the new nation might be losing in stability, it was gaining in opportunity. "In America," Tocqueville wrote, "most of the rich men were formerly poor," and this remarkable fact, so shocking to a European, remained true throughout the rest of the nineteenth century and into the twentieth. Cornelius Vanderbilt's father was a lowly ferryboat captain. John D. Rockefeller was the son of a traveling salesman. Andrew Carnegie was the son of a poor millworker. Henry Ford grew up on a small farm. The emerging American ideal of the self-made man extended beyond these titans of industry to include western settlers, California gold miners, Texas wildcatters, and all manner of merchants and inventors and entrepreneurs. They embraced the idea that in the United States, upward mobility was available to all, the natural product of a person's ingenuity, appetite for risk, and willingness to work hard.

In the second half of the twentieth century, though, as the animal spirits of the frontier economy were tamed, the nature of American

mobility began to shift. The nation's system of higher education expanded rapidly after World War II, partly because of the millions of
returning veterans who went to college on the GI Bill, and as it grew,
it produced a new economic reality in the United States, one in which
class mobility became tightly linked not with entrepreneurship but
with educational attainment. In prewar America, it may have taken
pluck and elbow grease to rise above your birth, but in postwar
America, what it usually took was a college degree.

And for young Americans in Shannen's generation, the national
statistics were now painting a darker picture, one in which a college
degree was no longer just a tool for upward mobility; it had also become a shield against downward mobility. Young adults who didn't
have a college degree were almost four times as likely to be living in
poverty as those who did. The unemployment rate for Americans
with only a high school degree was double the rate for Americans
with a bachelor's degree. And the disparities went beyond economics: Well-educated white men were now living thirteen years longer
than their less-educated counterparts. Women without college degrees were less likely to get married than women with degrees, and
they were more than twice as likely to divorce or separate if they did
marry. It sometimes felt as though the country was splitting into two
separate and unequal nations, with a college diploma the boundary
that divided them.

That was the reality that Shannen felt she inhabited. If she wanted
to transcend the economic hardships she was born into, she needed
to find her way to the right side of that divide. "That's just what
America intends for you to do," she told me when we first met. "Not
only is there an obstacle course to get into college, there's an obstacle
course to get to the college with the name that lets you get the job you
want." For someone like Shannen, without family money or influential connections, a degree from a prestigious college seemed to be the
only available path to a better future. That was part of what made our
afternoon in St. Nicholas Park so painful for her: as far as she could
tell, there was no room for error in the new system of American class

mobility. Young people from her corner of the Bronx didn't often get second chances.

2. The Mobility Equation

A few days before my vigil in the park with Shannen Torres, I traveled to Palo Alto, California, to spend some time with a young economist named Raj Chetty, who has emerged in recent years as the leading empirical scholar of mobility in the United States today. (He was a professor at Stanford at the time, but in 2018, he was hired away by Harvard.) Chetty, who emigrated from India at the age of nine, has always been a ridiculous overachiever, conducting advanced scientific research while still in high school, earning his PhD in economics from Harvard at twenty-three, and becoming a tenured professor at twenty-seven. He went on to win a MacArthur "genius" award and the John Bates Clark Medal, awarded annually to the best young economist in the country, and most likely the only reason he doesn't yet have a Nobel Prize in Economics is that he's only forty, and the prize has never been given to anyone younger than fifty.

Chetty is a leading figure in a relatively new movement in economic research known as big data, in which increasingly powerful computers employ nimble analytical tools to carve up massive amounts of information. The results of the big data revolution have, over the last decade or two, transformed everything from gene sequencing to baseball scouting to presidential campaigns. Chetty's mission for most of his professional career has been to find ways to use big data to better understand American social mobility: how it works, whom it benefits, and how its machinery has changed and evolved over time.

Early on, Chetty's project was hampered by a lack of good data. When he was a student at Harvard in the early 2000s, researchers studying American economic and social mobility had only a handful of data sets to work with, and those were mostly surveys and samples that tracked just a few hundred or a few thousand people. In Europe, by contrast, researchers had access to much larger stockpiles of government data. Chetty was able to analyze a database on savings behavior in Denmark that included forty-one million observations. He discovered a registry containing complete employment and earnings data for every private-sector worker in Austria over the course of two decades. But at home in the United States, there was nothing that even came close.

In his more fanciful moments, Chetty daydreamed about the data held by the Internal Revenue Service. Now *there* was some big data: decades of records on hundreds of millions of Americans, with individuals linked via their Social Security numbers to their children and grandchildren and parents and grandparents. It was the holy grail for anyone studying economic mobility in the United States. But for years, the word from the IRS was that those records were not available to researchers like Chetty, no way, not ever.

Then, in the spring of 2009, Chetty was looking through a mailing from the *National Tax Journal*, an obscure economics quarterly, when he saw an ad placed by the IRS seeking contractors to help manage its databases. This is something the IRS does from time to time: its stores of data are so enormous and sprawling that it needs help to organize them, and when it does, it invites outside contractors to submit bids to do the work. Chetty had a sudden epiphany. The IRS was planning to pay someone else to do exactly what Chetty had been dying to do: dive deep into its data and try to make sense of it. Why couldn't Chetty bid on the contract himself?

He contacted John Friedman, a friend and colleague then at the Kennedy School of Government at Harvard, and together they worked up a formal bid and submitted it to the IRS. It was rejected. They decided to try again, this time adding to their team another top young economist interested in mobility: Emmanuel Saez, who was at Berkeley. And this time they made an innovative sales pitch: their bid for the job was $0; they essentially told the IRS they would do its work for free.

It was an offer the IRS couldn't refuse. Its administrators said yes, and with that decision, the agency began a remarkably fruitful collaboration with Chetty and his colleagues, one that has, over the past decade, expanded our understanding of the complex interactions among income, geography, race, and education in the United States. The IRS data has allowed Chetty to illuminate in new ways how an American's opportunities for mobility are affected by the neighborhood she grew up in and by the color of her skin — and, perhaps most centrally, by whether and where she goes to college.

Before Chetty started working with the IRS, economists were limited in their ability to understand the effect going to college had on mobility for Americans. They knew that a person with a BA earned more money, on average, than a person without a BA. But it was difficult to say much more than that, to trace exactly who benefited from going to college and how much they gained. Then Chetty discovered, deep in the IRS data, a form called the 1098-T, which American colleges and universities were required to file each year for each student who paid tuition. Each completed copy of the 1098-T included the Social Security number of the college-going student, plus a unique code that identified the particular college the student was attending.

The IRS partially masked the data so that Chetty and his colleagues couldn't view individual 1098-T forms or tax returns, but they were still able to see patterns and trace connections. Each student's Social Security number could be linked to the tax data of that student's parents, going back decades. Which meant that the 1098-T could unlock some of the lingering, unsolved questions about the economic effects of higher education. Consider a student who attended college in, say, 1999. First, Chetty could find in the IRS's database the 1098-T form filed for her that year. Then he could use her parents' data, looking backward, to establish her financial situation during childhood. Then he could use the student's data, looking forward, to find out how much she earned as an adult, a decade or more after leaving college. And finally, he could use the unique code for her college to factor in where she went to school. Repeat this operation enough times,

Chetty believed, and he would be able to identify the precise effect that individual American colleges had on the financial trajectory of students from different economic backgrounds. How did poor students (or rich ones, for that matter) fare a decade after leaving Penn, or Davidson, or Bronx Community College? Thanks to the 1098-T, Chetty believed he could answer that question down to the dollar.

Chetty by this time was a professor at Stanford, and he dispatched a group of young researchers to the IRS office in San Mateo, a bland Silicon Valley suburb fifteen miles north of Palo Alto. Chetty's students were granted a special security clearance that enabled them to access federal tax data — but only while they were physically sitting in the office in San Mateo. For years, they shuttled data requests and data reports back and forth between the IRS terminals in San Mateo and Chetty and his research colleagues in Palo Alto (and at Brown and Harvard and Berkeley). Several billion calculations later, Chetty and Friedman and their colleagues published, in 2017, the initial results of their higher education research in an academic paper and a collection of supporting documents, including what they called "Mobility Report Cards" for thousands of colleges in the United States.

The report was centered around four important discoveries. First, using the IRS data, Chetty and his team found that students who attend ultraselective colleges in the United States are much more likely than other students to become very rich as adults. Young people who attend "Ivy Plus" institutions — meaning the Ivy League colleges plus a handful of other institutions with similarly elevated selectivity rates, like the Massachusetts Institute of Technology, the University of Chicago, and Stanford — have about a one in five chance of landing, in their midthirties, among the top 1 percent of American earners, with incomes over $630,000. People who attend "other elite" four-year colleges (including Davidson) have about a one in eleven chance of hitting the top 1 percent. Students at community colleges, meanwhile, have about a one in three hundred chance. (Students who don't attend college at all have about a one in a thousand chance.) The kind of college you attend, in other words, correlates strongly with what you'll earn later on.

Second, Chetty and his collaborators found that outcomes for poor kids and rich kids who attend the same institution are remarkably similar (the definition of "poor" here being that your family's income is in the bottom quintile, or bottom fifth, of all families nationwide, and the definition of "rich" being that your family's income is in the top quintile). Poor students who attend Ivy Plus colleges wind up with household incomes of about $76,000 a year, on average, as young adults. Rich students who attend Ivy Plus colleges wind up earning about $88,000. That's more than the kids who grew up poor, but not a ton more. There is a similar effect at almost every college: kids who grow up rich earn only a bit more than their college classmates who grow up poor. Attending the same college eliminates almost all the advantages that those who grow up with family wealth have over those who grow up in poverty.

Third, the researchers found that attending an elite college seems to produce a greater economic benefit for students who grow up poor than it does for students who grow up rich. If you're a rich kid, attending an Ivy Plus college rather than no college at all increases your odds of making it into the top income quintile as an adult earner by a factor of four. So you do get an economic boost from your college education, but it's not a huge one. If you're a poor kid, though, attending an Ivy Plus college rather than no college is truly life-changing. It increases your odds of making it into the top income quintile by a factor of *fourteen*.

So far, these results suggest a pretty happy story for fans of economic mobility. Higher education actually works! It can propel students from all backgrounds into the upper reaches of the American economy. Sending poor students to elite colleges is an especially good investment — they benefit more than their wealthy peers do. And when rich and poor students attend the same college, the education they receive there actually does create a fairly level playing field for them as they head off together into the job market.

But that is where the happy story ends. Because the fourth major discovery made by Chetty and his colleagues was that rich and poor students are *not* attending the same colleges. Not at all. At Ivy Plus colleges, on average, more than two-thirds of undergraduates grew up rich, and fewer than 4 percent of students grew up poor. Elite college campuses are almost entirely populated by the students who benefit the least from the education they receive there: the ones who were already wealthy when they arrived on campus.

Using the IRS data, Chetty's team was able to produce Mobility Report Cards not just for each broad category of college, but for each individual institution. What they found was that while every selective college was tilted in favor of wealthy students, some were tilted more sharply than others. And two of the colleges where the tilt was most extreme were Princeton and Penn, the two colleges that rejected Shannen Torres.

Of all the colleges in the Ivy League, Princeton has the highest percentage of students from the top income quintile (72 percent), and Penn has the second-highest (71 percent). And those two colleges educate a smaller proportion of poor students than almost any institution in the nation. Just 3.3 percent of Penn's student body comes from the bottom quintile, according to Chetty's data. At Princeton, poor students are even more of an endangered species: just 2.2 percent of the student body comes from the bottom fifth of the income distribution. That's one student in every forty-five.

CHETTY'S WORK ILLUMINATES the big paradox at the center of the experience of economic mobility in the United States, and it is the same paradox that was eating away at Shannen as she sat in the park that afternoon waiting for news from Penn. The American system of higher education has the potential to be a powerful engine of mobility, able to reliably lift young people from poverty to the middle class, and from the middle class to affluence. But in reality, for many young Americans, it functions as something closer to the opposite:

an obstacle to mobility, an instrument that reinforces a rigid social hierarchy and prevents them from moving beyond the circumstances of their birth.

In contrast to the nineteenth-century mobility that Alexis de Tocqueville described, opportunity in America today does not seem to be open to all, or even open to most. Instead, through our current system of higher education, we seem to have reconstructed, in the guise of openness and equality, an old and established aristocracy, one in which money begets money, wealthy families remain wealthy for generations, and young people like Shannen, born without privilege and power, stay stuck at the bottom.

Over the last few years, I've traveled back and forth between conversations with students like Shannen Torres and encounters with researchers like Raj Chetty, trying to understand this new system — why it exists, where it came from, and what it feels like to be a young person trying to negotiate it. It is the odd reality of this particular moment in American economic history: many of the most fundamental questions about what kind of country the United States will become — like whether it will be a land of opportunity for all, or a land of privilege for a few — are playing out in the lives and decisions of the nation's college students. Every day, on campuses across the country, the vast structural economic forces that Chetty and other economists are tracing meet up with the fragile and unpredictable psyches of American seventeen- to twenty-two-year-olds.

There is a final twist in Shannen's story. One elite American college chooses to release its admissions decisions a day later than its Ivy League peers: Stanford University. Shannen applied to Stanford, but almost as an afterthought. She didn't particularly want to go to school all the way across the country. And besides, Stanford was the longest of long shots, arguably the single hardest college in the country to get into. It accepts fewer than 5 percent of its applicants — and fewer than 4 percent of its regular-decision applicants, the pool in which Shannen had applied. No one is rejected by Penn and admitted to Stanford. It just doesn't happen.

Except sometimes it does.

The day after Shannen's Penn rejection was indeed pretty lousy, she told me later, though not quite as bad as she'd expected. Some of her classmates cried on her behalf, and some tried to comfort her, but mostly people assumed she didn't really want to talk about it, which was fine with Shannen. After school, she took the train home like she always did and sat down at the kitchen table and started doing homework, as usual. And then a little before 7:00 p.m., she remembered that Stanford's decisions were supposed to post soon. So she picked up her phone. This time, there was no frantic count-down, no trembling hands, no fumbled passwords — and when she saw the letter, there was no "sincerely regret." Instead, there was a "Congratulations!" And an "Everyone who reviewed your applica-tion was inspired." And a "You are, quite simply, a fantastic match with Stanford."

The room spun. Shannen screamed. Her mom came running. More screaming.

The whole evening was surreal, Shannen told me later, especially after the heartbreak and exhaustion of the day before. The main feel-ing she had was not joy but relief. She didn't necessarily prefer Stan-ford to Davidson — she'd never even visited Stanford's campus — but she knew it was more selective and more respected, and to Shannen and many others, that meant a lot.

But at the same time, getting into Stanford after being rejected by Penn made the whole application and admissions process, which Shannen had taken at face value for so long, seem suddenly random and capricious and even a little ridiculous. Was she really a fantas-tic match with Stanford and a terrible match with Penn? Maybe her friend Tess was right: It *was* just a crapshoot. It was all about luck.

And a system of economic mobility based on luck — whether it's the luck of which family and which neighborhood you're born into, or the luck of what a particular college-admissions officer happens to see in your application on a particular day — is a system that is hard to invest or believe in as deeply as Shannen had done. The next fall,

Shannen would go off to Stanford and study science and business and politics and take advantage of the many amazing opportunities that went along with the experience of being an undergraduate at an institution of unparalleled privilege and power. She might even get rich, like so many of her classmates. But she would never entirely get back the heartfelt, optimistic faith in the American system of higher education that had kept her working so hard for so long.

II

GETTING IN

---

1. Stress Test

The conversation usually begins when the kids are entering their junior year of high school, or sometimes even earlier. It starts in whispers, on the sidelines of the lacrosse game or at pickup after ballet practice or over cocktails at the school fundraising gala, one parent turning to another and saying, quietly, *So, what are you doing about test prep?* The question is always accompanied by a flurry of self-conscious disclaimers and ritual denunciations: *Isn't it ridiculous? Can you believe we're thinking about college so early! It gets crazier every year.* But there is no getting around the fact that Grace (or Josh or Sam or Chloe) just isn't the strongest test-taker. And with college-application season right around the corner, that fact is becoming a problem. If she's going to get in anywhere decent, she is going to need help with the SAT. So the question arrives: *Who do you know?*

And there is always someone. Whether that sideline conversation is taking place in Scarsdale or Winnetka or Mill Valley, there is inevitably, in an office park not too far away, a test-prep magician, a teen whisperer, a tutor with a reputation for raising scores on the SAT or the ACT by eye-popping margins. His rates are astronomical, of course, and his schedule is always full. But if you can get in, and if you can afford him, he's the guy you want.

In Washington, DC — or more precisely, in certain well-groomed and hypercompetitive suburbs just outside Washington, DC — the guy you want is Ned Johnson, the president and self-proclaimed "tutor-geek" of a company called PrepMatters. Ned founded PrepMatters in 1996 and built it into the largest test-prep company in the DC area. It now employs about fifty tutors at offices in Bethesda, Maryland; McLean, Virginia; and the Tenleytown neighborhood in northwest DC. Ned's rate as an SAT or ACT tutor is $400 an hour, and even at that elevated price he is very much in demand, booking more hours each year than any other tutor on his staff. The teenagers he works with attend the most exclusive private schools in Washington — Sidwell Friends, National Cathedral, Georgetown Day, Maret, St. Albans — and their parents work in the top levels of the White House and at the *Washington Post* and for lobbying firms you've never heard of. (Those are the ones with the real money.)

The ambitions and anxieties that draw parents into Ned's office are not altogether different from those that motivated the wealthy clients of William "Rick" Singer, the crooked college adviser who in the winter of 2019 was arrested and charged with orchestrating a massive criminal conspiracy to rig the college-admissions process for his clients' children. The pressure around elite college admissions that pervades many affluent communities these days can make almost every parent act a little crazy — even if only a small minority cross the line into the blatant test-cheating, credential-forging, and coach-bribing that Singer and his clients are accused of.

If you read through the wiretap transcripts prosecutors entered into evidence in the Singer case, though, what comes across is how pedestrian, even banal, Singer's mad schemes seem to have become to the accused parents — just one more bizarre box they had to check off in the delirium of the college-admissions process. Singer tells one father, a Yale-educated private-equity investor, that he needs an "action" photo of his son, so Singer can Photoshop the student's face onto that of a real football placekicker. The father laughs and says he'll look for one. "Pretty funny," he adds. "The way the world works these days is unbelievable."

The edge that parents are seeking when they bring their kids to PrepMatters is, by contrast, perfectly legal. Ned trains his students to master the SAT themselves; he doesn't hire a shady guy from Florida to take the test for them. But it's also true that when you show up at Ned's door as a parent, you know you're there to gain one more advantage in an unfair system. You're there because the way the world works these days is unbelievable.

In person, Ned is the furthest thing from shady you can imagine. He is a thin, cheerful white guy with fashionably nerdy glasses and a hairline that's beginning to recede; his sartorial choices tend toward the sweater vest and the corduroy jacket. He's in his late forties, a married homeowner and prosperous small-businessman, but he talks like a teenager who just consumed his first cup of coffee. Things are "freaking awesome" — unless they are "complete mayhem." He punctuates his stories with weird sound effects ("Neeeeep!") and silly voices. He is studiously polite; the closest he comes to swearing is when he says "Holy smokes!," which he does often. Though he is about the same age as the parents who hire him, he maintains a deferential distance, addressing them, courteously, not by their first names but as Mr. This or Mrs. That. With their teenage children, though, he seems much more himself, sharing corny jokes and laughing with them over tales of high school drama.

When I sat in on tutoring sessions in Ned's office, I was surprised by how little time he and his students spent talking about actual academic subjects. Sure, Ned would occasionally review some tricky concept in algebra or go over a principle of English grammar. But more often, he and his students talked about *life* — about the stress of attending a competitive high school and the pressures that often came with being a teenager in an ambitious and successful family in the upper reaches of the American upper middle class.

Ned is naturally empathetic, and he seems so at home with his students' references, so in tune with their concerns, that you might imagine he grew up like them, in an atmosphere of comfort and privilege. But in fact his own childhood was quite different. When Ned was young, his family lived in perpetual chaos, his father drinking heavily, his mother prone to flying into rages at unpredictable moments. Money was often in short supply, and the family moved from place to place until Ned and his twin brother were in middle school, when they landed in a small town in central Connecticut. There, the family's dysfunction tumbled into full-blown crisis. When Ned was in seventh grade, his mother made a serious attempt at suicide. Ned was the one who found her limp body, unconscious in the guest bedroom, and called 911. His father moved out not long after.

As teenagers, Ned and his brother both struggled to cope with the emotional fallout of their tumultuous upbringing: after his mother's suicide attempt, Ned retreated for a few months to a psychiatric hospital. But the boys excelled academically, finishing second and third in their high school class and winning admission together to Williams College, a prestigious private liberal arts institution in Massachusetts.

Of the two sons, Ned was the one who was closer to their mother, and in high school he assumed the role of peacemaker and therapist, trying to keep her calm and prevent her from sliding off the rails. He learned how to read her cues, avoid her triggers, soothe her fears. His efforts always proved futile in the end. Before long, her wild moods would once again slip loose, and Ned was often the target of her fury.

This unrelenting routine took its toll on Ned, but it was instructive, too — a kind of up-close master class in emotional instability. He developed, as a result, a keen sensitivity to anxiety and all its expressions, and he regularly puts this skill to work now in his tutoring practice. Sitting across his desk from his students, he watches and listens intently, focusing on their faces, paying close attention to their offhand remarks, looking carefully for clues to their fears and concerns. It can feel a little odd for him, to be re-creating in his working life those watchful, often painful moments from his childhood. But with his teenage students, the process feels far more hopeful. His efforts to allay their worries are not doomed to failure, as they were with his mom. They actually work.

The basic premise underlying Ned's tutoring strategy is that the kind of kids who are likely to make it into his office — surrounded by wealth, attending excellent schools, born to parents with multiple degrees — already possess the knowledge and academic skill they need to do well on the SAT or ACT. The obstacles holding them back from achieving top scores, Ned believes, are generally not intellectual in nature; they are at least as often emotional or psychological. Standardized college-admissions tests make kids anxious — it's almost as if they were designed that way — and one of Ned's chief tasks, as he sees it, is to reduce that anxiety.

So he spends a lot of time, in his tutoring sessions, talking about the importance of sleep and exercise and good diet and a balanced schedule. He explains to his students the essential facts of stress neurobiology, describing the competing roles of the amygdala and the prefrontal cortex, all in the service of helping them understand why, when they get stressed out, they perform less well on tests. And this approach is effective, Ned finds. When students take their own stress seriously, their stress levels usually go down and their scores usually go up.

A central part of Ned's strategy to reduce his students' anxiety is to get them to rethink their basic beliefs about the test itself. The College Board, which administers the SAT, and its rival, ACT Inc., insist in their public statements that their tests are objective, reliable measures of students' academic ability. And students internalize this idea. They walk into Ned's office convinced that their score on the test will reveal something significant about them: how smart they are or how likely they are to succeed — or even deeper truths, like their true position in their family's unspoken hierarchy or their inherent value as a person. Psychological research has demonstrated that students in the grip of this belief experience the tests as a threat to their very identity. And when your identity is threatened, your anxiety skyrockets, which means your concentration goes out the window, and it becomes much harder to perform well on complex mental tasks—like taking standardized tests.

So Ned makes the opposite argument from the one made by the College Board and ACT Inc. The SAT and the ACT are completely ridiculous, he tells students. Every reference he makes to the tests is dismissive—they're "stupid" or "silly" or "a bunch of malarkey." The tests are not in fact designed to measure how smart you are, he says. They are designed to assess how well you have mastered the tricks of taking standardized tests. Ned says this not only because he believes it—when you observe over and over, as Ned has, that tutoring can vastly improve kids' scores, it's hard to maintain the view that the tests are authentic measures of a student's academic ability—but also because dismissing the test, laughing at it, takes away the psychological power that it holds over many students. If you sit down to take the test believing it to be a true measure of your intelligence and ability, then a lot is at stake, and you're more susceptible to being derailed by anxiety. But if you sit down to the test thinking it is just a goofy little game, you're more likely to prevail.

So when Ned is not talking about the prefrontal cortex in tutoring sessions, he is usually teaching his students clever test-taking tricks. In multiple-choice algebra questions, for instance, he tells them they don't need to bother working through the actual math; instead, he says, they can try plugging a simple number like 2 or 10 into the equation in place of the variable; that often makes the answer obvious. On the reading-comprehension sections, Ned tells students to imagine that the questions were written by lawyers, not poets: if there's an answer that feels mostly right, look for tiny traps that might make it wrong. When there's a diagram in a geometry question, see if you can figure out the answer by just eyeballing the diagram, rather than doing the math. Whichever answer looks right usually is. These tips are often helpful in a practical way—they'll save you some time and might win you a few extra points on the test. But their real value, for Ned's students, is their psychological effect. Once you experience for yourself the fact that these dumb tricks actually work, the test becomes much less intimidating. It loses its magical power.

TECHNIQUES LIKE THESE are sufficient to help most of Ned's students improve their scores. But for others, the anxiety they feel about college in general, and standardized admission tests in particular, can be so overwhelming that Ned needs to go one or two steps further. One fall afternoon in Ned's Tenleytown office, I met a ruby-cheeked high school senior named Ariel. Her family was Modern Orthodox Jewish and highly educated, and her parents placed a premium on academic achievement; in her home, she said, college was "at the forefront of the brain, always." Her older brother had attended Cornell, and her older sister was at Penn, and Ariel had been talking with her parents since seventh grade about where she would go to college. At the end of her sophomore year in high school, she told me, her parents said to her, "OK, it's time to start studying," by which they meant time to start studying for the college admissions tests. By the time I met her, she had taken the ACT three times and the SAT four (in addition to taking dozens of practice tests). Ned was her third tutor; Ariel had liked the other two as people, but her scores with them had topped out at a fixed ceiling—about 26 (out of 36) on the ACT and 1250 (out of 1600) on the SAT.

Those numbers put her at about the eightieth percentile, nationally (meaning she was at the bottom of the top 20 percent of students nationwide), and she knew that wasn't high enough to get her into the elite colleges she aspired to attend, including the institution that had become her dream school: Washington University in St. Louis. By her calculations, in order to have a decent shot at WashU, she needed a 32 on the ACT, a score that would put her in the top 3 percent of American students. So Ned went to work. Throughout the summer of her senior year, he met with Ariel in his office every week, and together they would talk about sleep and the amygdala and the trick of using substitution on algebra problems. Gradually, Ariel's anxiety began to recede, and her confidence started to increase, and so did her scores. She broke through her previous ceiling, hitting first a 30 on the ACT, and then a 31. But then her progress stalled again, just short of her goal. She took one practice test after another but couldn't reach the 32 she felt she needed.

Then on Labor Day morning, Ariel got up early and went to a spin class at a local SoulCycle studio before coming into the PrepMatters office to meet Ned and take yet another practice ACT. That day, for the first time, she got a 32. Success, at last. Ariel immediately reached an unshakable conclusion: what had put her over the top wasn't her own ability, or Ned's tutoring, or how hard she had studied over the previous two years—it was SoulCycle.

Ariel became fixated on the idea of SoulCycle as test prep. As the date for the next ACT test approached, she convinced herself that if she was able to take a SoulCycle class that morning, right before the test, she would get a 32. No SoulCycle class that morning? She would fail. Ned tried to talk her out of this belief—"It's not about the bike," he took to saying, quoting Lance Armstrong—but Ariel was adamant.

And yet there was a significant obstacle standing in the way of her plan: SoulCycle studios didn't open early enough on Sunday morning for Ariel to get to a class before the test started at 8:00 a.m. She and Ned called every SoulCycle location in the DC area, but it was no use. Her anxiety began to rise again. She was "freaking out," she told me. She could feel Washington University slipping away.

And then, a few days before the test, Ned came up with a plan: if Ariel couldn't get to SoulCycle, he would bring SoulCycle to Ariel. On the morning of the test, at 6:00 a.m., he lugged two stationary bicycles to Ariel's family home. He and Ariel rode at full speed for twenty minutes, music blasting, candles burning, and then Ariel drove off to take the test. It might have been crazy, but it worked: Ariel got her 32 at last.

Ned still thinks it wasn't about the bike, not really. I mean, he does believe that vigorous exercise before a test often helps reduce a student's stress. But he thinks what really made a difference, in Ariel's case, was the validation she got from Ned's extravagant offer. He paid attention to her feelings, and in taking her anxiety seriously — in taking *her* seriously — he found a way to diminish its power.

The increase in Ariel's test scores during the time she worked with Ned had a huge impact on her college opportunities. Here's another way to look at those numbers: About 1.7 million seniors took the ACT in 2016, which means that in jumping from the eightieth percentile to the ninety-seventh percentile, Ariel went from lagging behind about 350,000 of her peers to being among the top 50,000 students nationwide. With Ned's help, she leapfrogged over more than 85 percent of the kids she was competing with for spots in the country's most selective universities. And it paid off. That December, she found out that she had been admitted, via early decision, to her first-choice school: Washington University.

A couple of weeks later, Ariel sent Ned a handwritten thank-you card. "You have given me my dream school," she wrote. "You taught me the importance of sleep and exercise, thinking of other options when something doesn't work out, staying calm, and being positive and optimistic. But most of all, you believed in me. You cared about my success as a student and a person. You have impacted my future in more ways than you will ever know."

YOU MIGHT WELL CONCLUDE, after reading Ariel's story, that she is completely nuts. Even *Ariel* thinks the whole episode was a bit unhinged. When she and I sat down together to talk in December of her senior year, she recounted her previous two years with the slightly bewildered air of someone coming down from a serious bender, a little uncertain what had happened or what, precisely, she had been thinking in the first place. I mean, would it really have made a huge difference in Ariel's life if she had ended up at the University of Maryland (like many of her peers from her private Jewish day school in suburban DC) instead of WashU?

In public, every authority figure in higher education will answer that question in the same reassuring way: *Of course it doesn't matter. What's important is finding the college that's the right fit for you as an individual. Future Nobel Prize winners and Fortune 500 CEOs graduate from Penn State as well as from Princeton. This generation of affluent high school students and their families are taking college admissions way too seriously, and they all need to just take a deep breath and relax.*

Among economists, though, this question has long been a matter of debate. Proponents of a more laid-back approach to college admissions base their argument largely on a 2002 paper, updated and extended in 2011, by Stacy Dale, a researcher, and the late economist Alan Krueger. Dale and Krueger analyzed records from twenty-seven selective colleges and universities, as well as a national database, and concluded that for well-off white and Asian students, there was no benefit at all, in terms of future earnings, to attending a more selective college. Yes, a graduate of Princeton will earn more than a graduate of Penn State, on average — but, the researchers said, that has everything to do with the talents and ambitions of the students whom Princeton admits and who choose to attend Princeton. If a particular student is admitted to both Princeton and Penn State, Dale and Krueger said, he will (on average) earn the same later on, whichever college he chooses. Dale and Krueger did determine that for certain cohorts of students who are typically less advantaged — like black or Latino students, or students whose parents had less education or earned less money — there *was* a real advantage to attending a more selective school. But not for the well-off children of well-educated white and Asian parents. For those students, they said, the economic benefit to attending Princeton or Harvard is exactly zero.

If the story Dale and Krueger tell is true, it comes as welcome news for many of us. Certainly it provides comfort to students who have just been rejected by Ivy League universities, as well as to their parents and others who care about them. Even beyond that cohort, though, the narrative their research supports is one that appeals to Americans in a deeper sense. If admission to elite universities is just another status symbol that the wealthy, in their madness, have chosen to fight over — the educational equivalent of a $5,000 designer handbag that is indistinguishable from its $80 knockoff — then the rest of us don't need to worry much about who gets in where and how many exercise bikes they ride to get there. But if an elite university education is genuinely valuable — if there really is a difference between Princeton and Penn State, or between Washington University and the University of Maryland — then the tale of Ned and Ariel's predawn ride takes on a different meaning.

So what is the real story? Are Ned's students just uptight maniacs (or the children of uptight maniacs)? Or do they know something the rest of us don't?

Caroline Hoxby believes she has an answer to this question. Hoxby is an economist at Stanford University; until Raj Chetty decamped for Harvard in 2018, the two of them worked a floor apart in the same building. Hoxby is more than a decade older than Chetty, but she has followed a similar path through the upper reaches of the academic economics establishment, studying and then teaching at Harvard before migrating to Stanford, with stops along the way, in Hoxby's case, at MIT and Oxford. Although their conclusions and methods sometimes differ, Hoxby and Chetty are both acclaimed and respected, in their field and beyond it; in fact, they are probably the two most influential researchers in the economics of higher education in the country today.

Hoxby has focused her research for more than a decade on the college-admissions process. But for many years, she avoided the debate over the relative value of attending a selective college. She was always somewhat skeptical of the methods that Dale and Krueger used, but she considered the available data too muddy either to confirm or rebut their conclusion. More recently, though, that muddy picture clarified for Hoxby, when she found a way to leverage many years of tax records — using the same IRS database that Chetty draws on for his research — to calculate "value-added" estimates for thousands of American colleges and universities.

Her method, briefly, involves combining the IRS data showing which college each student attends and their earnings a decade after graduating from high school with information from the College Board on where students apply, plus data from a national clearinghouse that reveals which college each student actually winds up attending. By merging these data points, and comparing them for millions of students who graduated from high school between 1999 and 2003, Hoxby was able to estimate, quite precisely, the causal effect of the college a student attends on his or her average lifetime earnings.

Her conclusion? Dale and Krueger were simply wrong. High-prestige colleges *do* pay off for the students who attend them, and in fact they pay off in a big way. According to Hoxby's data, if you attend a highly selective college where incoming freshmen have average SAT scores above about 1400 on a 1600-point scale (or about 30 on the ACT), your future lifetime earnings are likely to be more than $7 million—and that's about $2 million more than you'll earn if you take the identical skill set to a nonselective college. If you attend an even more elite college—one with average incoming SAT scores cresting 1500 (33 on the ACT)—the extra value that particular college will contribute to your lifetime earnings, on average, will be even higher, approaching a bonus of $3 million.

Two relevant pieces of data to consider: Washington University's average SAT score for incoming freshmen is above 1500. The University of Maryland's is below 1400. Which means maybe Ariel wasn't so crazy after all.

HOXBY'S DATA, of course, don't address the question of *why* attending a superselective college seems to pay off in future earnings. Do you actually learn more of value at those schools? Does attending those colleges make you more likely to choose a high-paying corporate career? Or is it about connections—are you just more likely to be assigned a freshman roommate who will go on to found the next Facebook? Hoxby's value-added research didn't answer that.

But in a separate study, Hoxby was able to demonstrate one clear difference between highly selective universities and their less selective peers: The more selective institutions spend a whole lot more money on their students' educations than less selective ones do. For a 2017 paper, Hoxby pored through the annual financial reports of thousands of colleges and universities, and she calculated how much each institution devoted each year to what she calls "core student resources," a figure that reflects how much a college spends strictly on its students' education — not counting professors' research budgets or the football coach's salary; just academic instruction, advising, facilities, and student support.

Hoxby found a strong and direct relationship between a college's median incoming SAT score and its core student spending: Low-selectivity colleges spend as little as $4,000 a year per student. Average-selectivity colleges spend between about $10,000 and $20,000 per student per year. The higher you climb on the rungs of the selectivity ladder, the faster institutional spending rises. Schools with a 1400 median incoming SAT score (like the University of Maryland) spend about $100,000 educating each student each year, and schools with a 1500 SAT score (like Washington University) spend about $150,000 — far more than they charge in tuition.

It is one of the most surprising facts to emerge from Hoxby's research: Despite all the headlines about skyrocketing tuitions at elite colleges, the most selective schools in the country are now actually *losing money* on each student they enroll. Lots of money. Yes, those colleges do bring in a lot of tuition from their students — but they spend considerably more on educating them. Even the wealthiest students at elite colleges receive a huge implicit subsidy from their institutions; on average, students at these colleges contribute just 20 percent of the total amount the institution spends on their education. Students at less selective institutions, meanwhile, receive much smaller subsidies.

To a certain extent, this spending gap has always existed. But over the last few decades, it has grown wider and wider. In 1967 the least selective colleges spent about $4,000 a year, per student, on their core education (in inflation-adjusted dollars), and the most selective spent about $17,000 a year. Today, the amount the least selective schools spend per student has barely budged—while the most selective schools spend a remarkable nine times as much as they did fifty years ago.

Hoxby points out that the decision by highly selective colleges to underwrite their students' education is rooted not in charity but in strategy. These high-prestige institutions are playing the long game—employing what Hoxby calls the "dynasty" model—betting that overspending today on their students will pay dividends in the future when those students become wealthy donors. So far, this gamble seems to be paying off. In recent years, charitable giving to higher education has skewed increasingly toward the richest and most selective schools. Charles T. Clotfelter, an economist at Duke University, has labeled this contribution advantage the "inequality dividend." As the wealthiest Americans have grown ever wealthier over the last three or four decades, they have spent some of that newfound wealth on cold-pressed olive oil and luxury SUVs and professional sports teams, but they have also donated a considerable chunk of it to universities, in tax-deductible contributions. And when they do give to universities, it is generally to the nation's most selective institutions—which are also, as Raj Chetty's data demonstrates, the institutions with the greatest concentrations of wealthy students. In 1990, Clotfelter calculated, the most selective American universities held an average endowment per student of $311,000. By 2013, that amount had tripled, growing to over $1 million per student—compared to less than $35,000 per student at a typical American college.

Among the donor class, there is no apparent desire to level this playing field by steering their donations away from wealthy institutions serving wealthy students and toward those with greater need; in fact, at elite institutions, contributions are pouring in at a faster rate than ever.

One recent example: In September 2013 Harvard University an-

nounced the biggest fundraising campaign in the history of higher
education. The stated goal was to raise $6.5 billion over five years. As
soon as Harvard's then-president, Drew Faust, announced the campaign, the cash flooded in, at rates that astonished even the university's own fundraisers. Steve Ballmer, the former CEO of Microsoft,
gave about $60 million to the computer science department. A hedge
fund manager named Kenneth Griffin gave $150 million, mostly to
fund scholarships, including two hundred to be named after him.
Gerald Chan, a Boston investor, gave $350 million to rename the
school of public health after his father, setting an all-time Harvard
fundraising record . . . which was broken nine months later when
John Paulson, another hedge fund manager, donated $400 million to
rename Harvard's engineering school after himself.

The campaign surpassed its five-year goal in two and a half years,
but even that didn't stop the money deluge. The school's take soon hit
$7 billion, and then $8 billion, and then $9 billion. Harvard's fund-
raisers were operating at this point a little like the cartoon character
Scrooge McDuck, searching desperately for a spare corner in the giant money bin in which to stash the latest billion. "We're running out
of professors to be endowed," one fundraiser told Harvard's student
newspaper, the *Crimson*. When the five-year campaign concluded in
the summer of 2018, the total haul was announced: $9.6 billion.

And as Harvard grew steadily richer, so did its freshman classes.
The *Crimson* surveys Harvard's incoming freshmen each year, and
its surveys from 2013 to 2017 showed that each new class was slightly
more affluent than the previous one. In 2013, 15 percent of Harvard's
incoming freshman class came from families with incomes under
$40,000, and 14 percent came from the families in the wealthiest cat-
egory, those with incomes over $500,000. Four years later, the pro-
portion of the incoming class from the under-$40,000 cohort had
fallen to 12 percent, while 17 percent of freshmen now came from
the ultra-affluent group. And it wasn't just Harvard. It has become
the persistent national pattern, in fact: increasingly wealthy donors
giving increasing amounts of money to increasingly wealthy institu-

tions, thus enabling them to spend increasingly large sums of money educating increasingly wealthy students. It is a phenomenon that seems unsustainable — and yet, at the same time, unstoppable.

2. Income-Typical Behavior

At the same time that Caroline Hoxby was tracing these growing gaps on the supply side of American higher education, she was uncovering and describing a generational shift that was taking place on the demand side: in the decisions that high school seniors were making about how and where to apply to college. In the 1960s, Hoxby found, most students chose the college they wanted to attend based on its proximity to home, on reports from friends and family members who had attended the school, and on a nebulous sense of "fit" — where they thought they would most likely belong and be happy. The result of this not-very-scientific-choice architecture was that the nation's highest-scoring high school seniors, as measured by standardized tests, wound up scattered in colleges all over the country. A top-ranked student in a small town in Michigan would be more likely to attend the University of Michigan or Michigan State than Stanford or Harvard or Yale. This meant that most colleges had a diverse mix of super-high-scoring and less-high-scoring students on their campuses. There was a range, of course: Students at the most selective schools, Hoxby found, had SAT scores that put them, on average, at the ninetieth percentile overall, and students at the least selective schools had test scores that put them at the fiftieth percentile. (Most students in the bottom half of the distribution didn't go to college.) But every college had its grinds and its jocks, its fair share of A and B and C students.

Over the decades, though, the college-selection process that high school students employed — and especially high-achieving, well-off students like the ones Ned Johnson was tutoring in DC — changed, and in a very specific way. Those students went from selecting their

target schools based on a variety of idiosyncratic personal preferences to making their decision based on just a single data point: the
incoming SAT and ACT scores of each school's freshman class. High-
scoring students wanted to go to college with other high-scoring students — and increasingly, that was all that mattered to them. That was
the new, mostly unspoken rule: you looked for the most selective
school that would admit you, and you went there.

Colleges responded by narrowing their selection process, as well.
If students were going to choose their colleges based almost entirely
on their fellow students' incoming test scores, admissions officers realized, it made sense for them to select the highest-scoring students
they could find. This evolving sorting system was both reflected in
and helped along by the increasing popularity of ranked lists of colleges, most notably those published, beginning in the early 1980s, by
U.S. News & World Report, which put a strong emphasis on incoming
standardized-test scores.

As this process unfolded over time, high-scoring students clustered together at a small number of highly selective colleges. The end
result of this evolution is that today, students at the most selective
schools have, on average, SAT and ACT scores that put them not at
the ninetieth percentile, as in 1962, but at the ninety-eighth percentile
overall. Almost every student at the most selective colleges is now
very high scoring, in other words, and those colleges are now the
only institutions that most very-high-scoring students will attend.

For students like Ned's, this leads to a confusing situation in junior
and senior year of high school. The official line is that we are still living in 1962: *Don't go crazy trying to get into a super-elite college! Just
choose the school that makes you happy, where you're going to find your
true identity and become your authentic self. You'll get a good education wherever you go.* But all around, there are signs that this official
line is just that, a line, and the real message is: *Get your scores as high
as you can, and then do exactly what all the other high-scoring students
are doing. Go to the most selective school that will admit you, period.*

For some students, this cognitive dissonance is more distressing than for others. One fall afternoon in the Bethesda office of Prep-Matters, I met a junior named Clara from an affluent Maryland high school. She was consumed by college anxiety — or more precisely, she was consumed by the college-related anxieties of those around her, most centrally her parents, who had graduated from Carnegie Mellon (her dad) and Yale (her mom). She described for me her hectic schedule, her sleepless nights, and her worries about letting everyone down.

The previous summer, her grandfather had given her one of those giant paperback guides to colleges, and she'd thumbed through it, picking out schools that seemed to her like a good fit, often places where she had friends or acquaintances who were happy. She came up with an eclectic list: William and Mary, Elon University in North Carolina, the University of Virginia — excellent, competitive schools, but not in the very top tier of selectivity. And that not-quite-top echelon was, to Clara, exactly where she belonged. She had taken a practice ACT test with Ned and scored a 27, which put her at about the eighty-fifth percentile of students, nationally. Her grades were quite good — As and A minuses — but they didn't put her at the tip-top of her class, and she told me she had had to work very hard to get them.

But when she showed her parents the list of colleges she aspired to, her father told her she could do better. He went online and found a list of the one hundred most selective American colleges. He scrolled down until he got to number 30, drew a line, and told Clara that she shouldn't apply to anything below that line. He and Clara and her mother whittled the list of thirty down to fifteen, and then Clara's father turned the list of fifteen schools into a spreadsheet to guide the college visits the family was planning for that winter and spring.

Clara's mom was especially focused on one particular institution for Clara: Yale, which was not only her alma mater, but also the school where Clara's older sister was a junior. "She's always talking about Yale," Clara told me. "She's like, 'You could get in, Clara. You could do it.' I always tell her, 'I don't want to get into a place where it's just because my mom knows somebody.' Or my dad with his spreadsheet. He put an asterisk next to places where he knows people. I'm like, 'I don't want to go to those schools. I don't want to get into this school because your business partner is on the admissions board and he can slip my name over here. That's taking away a spot from somebody who actually deserves to be there.'"

In the winter of her junior year of high school, Clara and her mother went to visit all the colleges on the spreadsheet, and a few more besides. After disappointing trips to Dartmouth ("a weird vibe," according to Clara) and Williams ("didn't feel comfortable"), Clara found a college she loved: Middlebury, a small liberal arts school in Vermont that is highly selective but didn't fall into that tiny ultraselective sliver that made up her dad's list. Incoming students at Middlebury have an average SAT score of 1375 (out of 1600), which is very high, but not as high as incoming students at Yale (1505). But what drew Clara was not Middlebury's numbers. It was the feel of the place. It was cold and snowy when she visited the campus, and students were outside making snowmen and building igloos. Exams were approaching, but no one seemed too stressed or competitive. At one point, Clara wandered into a study hall, a huge, beautiful room with long wooden tables and a fire burning in the fireplace at one end. Big windows looked out on the falling snow. "There were like ten kids clumped at a table, and they were all studying together," Clara told me. "They were serious, but they were also laughing and smiling, and they all had hot chocolate, and they were all bundled up near the fire. And it just looked like this was the best possible way to learn."

Clara and her mother visited Yale on that trip, too. Clara wanted to hate it, so that she would have a reason not to apply, and thus could avoid being rejected and feeling like a loser and embarrassing her mom. But she had to admit, she had a good time. Still, she couldn't help feeling that she would never be able to keep up with Yale's superachievers. "It was like, This kid built a rocket ship when he was sixteen," she said. "And I have done nothing special."

Back home, that spring, she worked harder in school (and slept less) than she ever had before. Her grades went up—and so, most notably, did her ACT scores. She and Ned met for weekly discussions of anxiety and algebra, and her score rose, steadily, from 28 to 31 to 32 to 33 and, finally, in June of her junior year, to 35 — one point away from a perfect score.

In the fall of her senior year, Clara's parents persuaded her to apply early-action to Yale, which meant she would get the decision in December. She was tempted not to include in her application the fact that her mother had attended Yale, but in the end, her mom convinced her to mention it. Clara applied to Middlebury, too, and that fall it remained her first choice. What she liked best about it, she said (along with the hot chocolate and the fire), was that she had no particular family pull or connections there. There was no asterisk next to Middlebury on her father's spreadsheet. If she got in, she would really have earned it, all on her own.

Then she got her acceptance letter from Yale, and there was much rejoicing — among Clara's parents, at least. Her mom bought her a stuffed Yale bulldog and a Yale banner and started looking through the course catalog, suggesting classes Clara could take the next year. But the celebration was interrupted when Clara told her parents that she was still considering Middlebury, if she got in. "I loved their support," Clara told me, "but I told them, 'I don't like it when you assume I'm going to Yale.' My dad would get mad and say, 'Are you just going through a phase? Do you just want to be different?' He was like, 'You don't take silver when you get gold.'"

And then Clara *did* get into Middlebury, and things at home grew very quiet indeed. "I opened the envelope, and I was so happy," Clara said. "My parents just kind of stared at me while I was crying. They were like, 'So, what are you going to do?'"

It was a tense couple of weeks. Yale kept sending letters and emails, encouraging her to say yes to their offer. They seemed to really want her. And she knew what her parents wanted her to do. Still, her heart was set on Middlebury. It was a difficult decision, and Clara wavered right up till the last day. But in the end, she made precisely the choice that Caroline Hoxby would have predicted: she picked Yale. You don't take silver when you get gold.

AS CAROLINE HOXBY pored through her data on college applications, she noticed something curious. The very predictable decision algorithm that she had discovered among high-scoring students (*Always go to the most selective school that will admit you*) actually only held true, reliably, for one particular group of high-scoring students: affluent ones. Admittedly, this was quite a large group. For reasons that come into clearer focus once you've spent a little time at Ned Johnson's tutoring centers, most high-scoring students *are* affluent, or at least well-off. But not all of them, by any means. And what Hoxby discovered is that most high-scoring high school seniors whose families had *low* incomes were behaving very differently from their wealthier peers when it came time to apply to college.

Hoxby's long path to this discovery started back in 2004, when she was a professor in the Harvard economics department. That year, Lawrence Summers, then Harvard's president, announced, to much fanfare in the press, a program that he called the Harvard Financial Aid Initiative. Henceforth, Summers declared, any Harvard undergraduate whose family's income was less than $40,000 a year would attend Harvard absolutely free.

Curious about the impact Summers's plan would have, Hoxby and a Harvard colleague named Christopher Avery proposed to Harvard's administrators that they study the plan's effect. Over the next two years, they examined data from the admissions office and found that, despite the headlines Summers's announcement produced, nothing much really changed. The Summers plan was supposed to unleash a flood of new applications from smart poor and working-class kids across the country, but the number of low-income students in Harvard's sixteen-hundred-student freshman class only went up by a grand total of about fifteen — and most of those, it seemed, were kids who probably would have gone to Yale or Princeton otherwise.

Hoxby was surprised—but when she revealed her results to Harvard's admissions directors, she found that *they* weren't particularly surprised. They had been skeptical of Summers's plan all along. They believed that the national pool of low-income students who had the academic qualifications to win admission to Harvard was vanishingly small, and that by senior year of high school, Harvard (and every other elite college) had intensely recruited every single one of them.

Hoxby and Avery went back to their data to see if they could understand what was going on. They expanded their database, adding data from ACT Inc. and further honing their geographical algorithms. And they soon concluded that the folks in the Harvard admissions office were simply wrong. The pool wasn't tapped out at all. There were plenty of high-achieving low-income students out there. In fact, Hoxby and Avery calculated that in each national high school graduating cohort there were about thirty thousand students with excellent academic records—a GPA of A minus and above, plus ACT or SAT scores that placed them in the top 10 percent of test-takers, meaning 29 and above on the ACT or 1300 and above on the SAT —whose family income fell in the bottom income quartile, meaning their parents earned less than about $42,000.

The problem wasn't that Harvard wasn't admitting these students; it was that Harvard didn't seem to know they existed. Hoxby and Avery concluded that had something to do with where Harvard was looking for potential students—and a lot to do with decisions those students were making about where and how to apply to college. When Hoxby and Avery looked more closely at this new pool of high-achieving low-income students, they discovered there was a small fraction—only about 8 percent of them—who behaved just like wealthy kids with similar scores, essentially following the advice that students at private high schools had been hearing for years from their college counselors: they applied to a range of colleges, including some highly selective ones, and went on to enroll at the most selective institution that admitted them. Those low-income students, whom Hoxby and Avery labeled "achievement typical," tended to live in big cities. Many attended private schools (on scholarship, presumably) or elite magnet high schools that historically sent plenty of students to the Ivy League.

In contrast to that small, ambitious group, the majority of high-scoring low-income students had aspirations that seemed much more constrained. They followed the same pattern as lower-scoring low-income students, applying to only one or two institutions, often including a local community college or a nearby nonselective public university. Most didn't apply to a single selective college. Hoxby and Avery referred to members of this cohort as "income-typical" students, their college decisions defined by their socioeconomic status and not by their academic ability. Compared to their achievement-typical peers, these students were more likely to live in small towns or rural areas in the middle of the country and to attend schools where they would be one of only a few high-achieving students. They were also significantly more likely to be white: 80 percent of them, in fact, were white, compared to just 45 percent of the achievement-typical low-income students.

Hoxby's theory was that the main obstacle standing in the way of those income-typical high achievers was an information deficit: they simply didn't know much about elite colleges and how to apply to them. They didn't know, for example, that they were eligible for fee waivers that would allow them to apply to college free of charge. They didn't know that with test scores as high as theirs, they would likely be admitted to selective colleges. They didn't know that if admitted, they would likely get lots of financial aid — so much aid, in fact, that it might actually be cheaper for them to attend an excellent private college halfway across the country than to go to the decent public university nearby. And they didn't know these significant facts, Hoxby hypothesized, because there was no one around to tell them. No one from their family or their high school — or maybe even their entire town — had ever attended a selective out-of-state college.

And institutions like Harvard weren't telling them this story either, at least not in an up-close and personal way. Elite colleges almost never sent recruiters to the high schools attended by these income-typical students, in part because the schools were usually in the middle of nowhere.

BY 2009 HOXBY and Avery had completed their research and were ready to publish it. But Hoxby persuaded Avery that they should delay publication of their results — not for a few months, but for a few years. It was an unusual move, especially since the data was so powerful and unexpected. But Hoxby had a notion that she could do more than just diagnose this problem. Teaming up with another economist, Sarah Turner, a professor at the University of Virginia who also specialized in the economics of higher education, she set about finding a solution. Together, they decided, they would try to create an intervention that would help deliver this largely invisible, unrecruited pool of high-scoring low-income students to the Harvard admissions office and to the admissions offices of other elite institutions.

Hoxby and Turner devised a strategy. Using data from the College Board and ACT Inc., they would identify thousands of these students. They would create a simple information packet, customized for each student and mailed to his or her home address. It would include all the information about college that the students didn't seem to know, plus a handful of simple fee-waiver forms to make it easier for them to apply to selective institutions. The two economists then would closely follow what happened to the students after they received their packets — and specifically how their behavior compared to that of a randomly selected control group of similar students who wouldn't receive a packet.

In the fall of 2010, the Expanding College Opportunities Project, as Hoxby and Turner named their collaboration, sent mailings to ten thousand randomly selected low-income high-scoring high school seniors. Each packet included a handsome red-and-blue accordion-style folder marked with colorful labeled dividers and stuffed with lots of useful and appealing information: a personalized letter, a booklet covering how and where and when to apply, a customized handout with information about college costs and financial aid, and eight fee-waiver coupons. There was even a refrigerator magnet with reminders of crucial dates. And then, using both individual surveys of students and administrative data from institutions, Hoxby and Turner tracked exactly what happened to each student — where they applied, where they were accepted, where they enrolled. In the fall of 2011 they sent out another fifteen thousand packets, and they tracked those students as well.

The results were impressive. Students who were assigned to the intervention group applied to more and better colleges than students in the control group, and the colleges they were admitted to had higher graduation rates, higher incoming freshman SAT scores, and higher instructional-spending budgets. And the effects weren't small. Students who received the packets were 31 percent more likely than control-group students to be admitted to what Hoxby and Turner called a "peer college" (meaning a school where the student's high SAT score matched those of typical freshmen) and were 19 percent more likely to enroll. All because of an intervention that cost, according to Hoxby and Turner, just six dollars per student.

By early 2013, Hoxby was ready to unveil the results of the experiment — and to release, at last, the study she had completed with Christopher Avery four years earlier. The rollout was executed carefully, with an eye toward maximum impact. In March, Hoxby and Avery presented their paper, titled "The Missing 'One-Offs': The Hidden Supply of High-Achieving, Low Income Students," at a prestigious biannual economics conference at the Brookings Institution in Washington, DC. The *New York Times* reported their findings on page 1. Two weeks later, Hoxby and Turner published their Expanding College Opportunities research, prompting a second big story in the *Times,* plus a tide of increasingly rapturous reporting. The *Chron-*

icle of Higher Education published an article about the research under the headline "The $6 Solution." *Smithsonian* magazine, in a profile of Hoxby, referred to her experimental mailing as a "magic packet," calling it "the crowning achievement" of her career, and concluded, "In a world where poverty and inequality seem intractable, this may be one problem on the way to being solved."

When I met with Hoxby in Washington that spring, she was pleased by the attention the work was getting and looking forward to what came next. "We're going to figure out a way to make all of this information out there actually useful to people," she said. What she and Turner had created, she said, was "an incredibly powerful tool for turning lots of data from the back room into something that you and I can use. I feel like we're on the verge of that." Her countenance was usually sober and serious, but now she broke out in a grin. "We're so excited," she said.

HOXBY'S TWO STUDIES garnered an unusual amount of attention in the press, but their larger impact, arguably, was on a collection of powerful people who read them — or read about them — and decided to take action. Michael Bloomberg, the recently departed mayor of New York City, pledged to devote significant funds from his personal foundation to try to expand on Hoxby's experiment. Gene Sperling, the director of President Obama's National Economic Council, was inspired by Hoxby's results to convene a White House summit of more than one hundred college presidents — featuring enthusiastic speeches by the president and First Lady — to discuss how to enroll more low-income students at selective institutions. But of all the public figures who were affected by Hoxby's work, perhaps none was in a better position to make lasting change than David Coleman.

A few months before Hoxby published her papers, Coleman had become the ninth president of the College Board, the organization that oversees the SAT and other standardized tests as well as high school Advanced Placement exams in subjects ranging from macroeconomics to music theory. I first met Coleman in the fall of 2013, about a year after he assumed the presidency of the College Board. Hoxby's research had only recently been made public, and as he and I sat across a polished wooden table in his family's apartment overlooking Union Square, it was clear her discoveries had affected him. "Frankly, I was shocked by her findings," he told me. "I was shocked that poor kids disproportionately do not take advantage of the opportunities they've earned. Even these kids who have done the hard work, who have done all this practice — they betray themselves at the moment of college selection." He shook his head. "I'm confused by their behavior on such a mass scale. You've got kids who make quite irrational choices."

Coleman, who was born in 1969, grew up in a home in downtown Manhattan where art and literature and ideas were discussed and debated every night over dinner. He rose through the meritocratic system of selective advancement that the College Board and the SAT had helped to forge. His score on New York City's Specialized High School Admissions Test won him admission to Stuyvesant, the most selective public high school in the city. His SAT score then helped get him into Yale, and from there he applied to and won the Rhodes Scholarship to Oxford University. In the world in which Coleman was raised, Hoxby's dictum — *Seek out the most selective school that will admit you, and go there* — was part of the daily catechism. It was in the water you drank.

So the choices made by the "income-typical" high-achieving students Hoxby had identified — like opting to attend their local community college instead of Yale — felt deeply misguided to Coleman. And the fact that he might now be able, as the president of the College Board, to do something to influence those students' choices struck him as a rare and important opportunity. From the institutional perspective of the College Board, Hoxby's experiment was appealing for a separate reason: it suggested there was a way to level the college playing field without challenging the position of standardized tests in the admissions process. This was a new idea. For decades, reformers who wanted to make higher education more equitable had proposed to do away with the SAT, or at least seriously downgrade its importance. By contrast, Hoxby's research, which used standardized-test scores to determine which students were worthy of special attention, reinforced the position of the SAT and proposed to make it still more powerful.

In their paper, Hoxby and Turner had explicitly invited the College Board and ACT to adopt and expand their project to send out targeted packets to low-income high achievers. Coleman now embraced Hoxby's challenge and committed the College Board to replicating her mailings on a huge scale.

"In the wake of Hoxby's results, we said, 'We're all in. Let's go,'" Coleman explained to me that fall. "We've decided that these kids are *within our care*. What that phrase means for us is: We care if they go off track, if they betray themselves, if they don't apply as broadly as they could. The information packet we're sending out now is just one component — and an extremely promising one — of everything we're going to do to make sure these kids go on. The idea, simply considered, is that kids who have earned these opportunities *must* take them."

3. Taylorsville

Coleman and Hoxby are both Ivy League graduates, both former Rhodes scholars, voracious readers, lovers of fine art. Coleman has graduate degrees in classical philosophy and English literature; Hoxby is a devotee of opera and ballet and a skilled French chef. In the ecosystem of high culture and advanced education where they spend their days, what Coleman was expressing is an accepted fact: if your academic achievements qualify you to attend one of the country's most prestigious universities, you simply must do so. To choose otherwise is, as Coleman often put it, a betrayal.

But in other parts of the country and on other rungs of the American class hierarchy, the issue of whether and where to go to college can feel much more complicated: emotionally charged and financially perilous, weighed down by tangled questions of family and identity and history and home. Those complications became especially clear to me whenever I visited Taylorsville, North Carolina.

Taylorsville is a small town in the remote western reaches of the state, where the Appalachian foothills start to rise toward Tennessee. There's a Walmart and an AutoZone and a Chinese restaurant and not much else; to get to a Starbucks or a movie theater — or just a town with more than five thousand people — it's at least a half-hour drive. Taylorsville is one of those American places, as Caroline Hoxby found in her research, where high-achieving low-income kids are often overlooked by selective colleges: it is sparsely populated, almost everyone is white, and only one in seven adults has a BA. Until recently, the economy in Taylorsville was sustained by a robust regional furniture industry, but over the last couple of decades, many of the good-paying local production jobs have been automated or lost to foreign competition. In the 2016 presidential election, three-quarters of the county voted Republican.

There is one high school that serves the whole county: Alexander Central, a sprawling redbrick building on the west side of Taylorsville surrounded by sports fields and pine trees. It was there, in the fall of 2015, that I first met Kim Henning, an athletic young woman with cool blue eyes and a swoop of brown hair who was just starting her senior year. She was exactly the kind of high achiever Hoxby and Coleman were targeting with their information packets: she had a GPA of 4.5, with a full slate of AP classes, and she was captain of the drum line in marching band. She had taken the ACT the previous spring and scored a 27. Her mind was focused on college, but the path to get there seemed uncertain and unclear.

Kim's mother had never attended college, and neither had the three men Kim's mother had married over the years: not the young Marine who got her pregnant while she was still a teenager and fathered her first two children, Kim's older brothers, Trevor and Orry;

not Kim's dad, also a Marine, who served two tours in Iraq and was now fixing cars in Florida; and not Kim's stepdad, Billy, who worked in a steel-fabrication plant and lived with Kim and her mother and her brothers in a small rented house in Taylorsville. Kim's mother was supportive of Kim's college plans, in a general way, and she would occasionally make vaguely encouraging comments, but she didn't know much about the application process, and it was hard for Kim to get her mom to focus on the practical tasks Kim needed her help with, like financial-aid paperwork.

On the whole, Kim felt as though her family was trying to hold her back from college rather than help guide her there. "They are really stereotypical," she told me. "They think I should just get married and have kids like they did. And that's one hundred percent not what I want to do. I'm not ready for kids at all. I really just want to go to college. It's something I've always wanted to do. I want to get out of Taylorsville."

Her dream school, when I met her that fall, was Cornell University, in Ithaca, New York, where she wanted to study environmental sustainability. "It's a reach," she told me, "but I really, really want to go there. If I could get into Cornell, that would be everything."

For all her devotion to the school, the way she had settled on Cornell as her first-choice college was a little random. Over the summer, her older brother, Trevor, had been planning a road trip to upstate New York. Kim looked at a map and saw there was an Ivy League college — Cornell — near where Trevor was headed, so she asked to tag along. She didn't know much about Cornell, but she knew that Ivy League colleges had a first-class reputation. So off they went.

It was a long drive to Ithaca: fourteen hours in Trevor's ten-year-old Suzuki hatchback with her best friend Ally, Trevor and two of his band mates, and a cat named Lint Trap. They ate takeout food from a Sheetz gas station in Pennsylvania and spent the night in the car in a Home Depot parking lot before waking up early for the campus tour. Kim loved Cornell. Ithaca had a familiar, comfortable small-town vibe — but at the same time, it felt different from Taylorsville: filled with bookstores and coffee shops and ideas and opportunities. She could picture herself there, reading and studying and making new friends.

When Kim and I spoke a few months later, though, her enthusiasm about Cornell had faded. "I did love it there," she told me, "but I wasn't thinking about how hard it would be. I'm going to be surrounded by people who were the valedictorians of their high schools and they've been, like, killing themselves to get to Cornell." She said she already felt burned out by the pressure of senior year, all the tests and applications and fees, and she wanted to find a college where she could actually enjoy herself. "I want to have fun in college," she said. "I don't want to just keep my nose in a book, which is what I would basically be doing at Cornell. Because that's what every kid there has been doing their whole lives."

But Kim also confessed her great fear about going to an elite college like Cornell: that she might fail. She didn't want to drop out and have to return home to Taylorsville. "That scares me a lot," she told me. "I'm horrified at the fact that I might end up back here. I've seen a lot of people do it. They'll be like, 'I'm going to college!' And they'll go, and then they drop out and come right back home." Coming home from Cornell in shame would be far worse than never going at all.

The two schools that had replaced Cornell at the top of Kim's list were Clemson, a large public university in South Carolina, which she'd visited several times for marching-band competitions and football games, and the University of Oregon, which her English teacher had mentioned to her one day in the hallway. Kim didn't seem to be getting much hands-on advice or direction from the counselors at her high school; she found Oregon appealing, she told me, "mainly because it is so far away." With her grades, she was arguably overqualified for either school, but that wasn't bothering her. It was nice to think about going to a college where she would be one of the highest-achieving kids on campus, instead of feeling constantly behind. "I could really thrive at Clemson or Oregon," she told me. "That caliber of college is something I can handle, no problem. I would be more in my zone."

She drove down to Clemson for a tour, walking around the campus and visiting the libraries and the dorms and the Carillon Garden and the reflection pond. It felt right. "I just, like, *knew*," Kim told me. "I felt like I was already home." Clemson even *looked* like home — just 160 miles southwest of Taylorsville along the Appalachian range, the same rolling foothills, the same pine trees, the same Chick-fil-A restaurants and Publix supermarkets. In the end, Kim didn't even apply to Cornell. She chose Clemson. She made the "income-typical" decision, to use Hoxby's term, rather than the "achievement-typical" one. She did exactly what Caroline Hoxby's packets were designed to prevent.

So was it a mistake? Had she betrayed herself?

WHENEVER KIM AND I discussed college — and we spoke often over the next couple of years — we somehow always ended up talking about family. From our first conversation, she was open about the fact that her home life was often messy. Her stepdad drank too much, and he and Kim's mom fought a lot. Things never got truly violent, but there were a lot of dramatic scenes: screaming matches, restraining orders, favorite items of clothing cut up with scissors, possessions dumped in a heap in the front yard.

Kim's happiest memories, growing up, were from a brief period when she was five. Her father was posted to Fort Irwin, California, halfway between Los Angeles and Las Vegas, and they all lived there together in the middle of the scorching Mojave Desert, Kim and her two parents and three older brothers, a real family for a while. But then the marriage began to deteriorate, and the family retreated to Taylorsville, where much of Kim's mother's extended family lived. Soon after they arrived, Kim's father left the country for Iraq, and though Kim didn't quite understand it at the time, he was also leaving his marriage and his family, for good. Kim was seven, and she didn't see her dad again till she was twelve.

In Taylorsville, "family" meant something different than it did in

Fort Irwin: not an isolated nuclear unit but a sprawling, scrapping jumble of grandparents and great-grandparents and second cousins and step-cousins and half cousins, all in and out of each other's lives and homes and business. Kim's family moved in with her grand-parents, and after Kim's mom's cousin was evicted from a rental down the street, she and her kids moved in as well, for a total of twelve fam-ily members crammed together in one small rundown house. School, in those days, was an afterthought for Kim. She liked to read and had an affinity for math, but she acted up in class and was constantly get-ting in trouble with her teachers. In sixth grade, she skipped so many days of school that the principal threatened to call the police on her mother.

Trevor, meanwhile, was in high school, and to everyone's surprise, he was suddenly doing well: good grades, AP classes, a positive at-titude. No one in the extended family had ever attended college, but Trevor decided he would be the first. He applied to Appalachian State, a four-year public college an hour away in Boone, North Carolina, and got in. Everyone was excited. Kim's mom was proud. She took out loans and stretched her budget, and the family had a big party to send Trevor off, carrying all their hopes with him.

And it was a disaster.

One November evening, I spent a few hours standing around the kitchen island in Kim's family's home in Taylorsville with Kim and Trevor and their brother Orry, while Trevor, who is now in his mid-twenties, told us the story of his misbegotten months at App State. It was late in the evening when I arrived at the house, but Trevor looked as though he had just woken up, bleary-eyed in a faded green T-shirt and sweatpants, gripping a mug of coffee and shuffling around the kitchen in flip-flops. He's a guy who wouldn't look out of place work-ing behind the counter at a record store in a southern college town: short and scruffy with a soft face, thoughtful eyes, a tuft of beard, and a few small tattoos on his forearms.

"College was very overwhelming," Trevor explained in his laconic Carolina drawl. "When I got to Boone, everyone else seemed to have their stuff together better than I did. I didn't really know what to do with myself." It was his first time away from home and family, and he didn't feel equipped for the basic life responsibilities that went along with being a college freshman, like filling out forms and paying bills and doing laundry. The academic load was daunting, too. "I realized I couldn't breeze through the work like in high school," Trevor said. "And the minute I started falling behind in classes, I just started drinking heavily and partying with everyone." As his beer consumption went up, his grades went down. His GPA, that first semester, was a 0.8, which led to a new nickname for Trevor in the dorm: Decimalé Ocho.

He withdrew from classes midway through his second semester, fell back to Taylorsville for the spring and summer, then returned to Appalachian State in the fall for a second try at college. He was no longer eligible for a dorm room, so he and a few friends moved into an off-campus apartment. It didn't take long for the party to start up again: Pabst Blue Ribbon and Vladimir vodka every night, a tab or two of LSD on special occasions. No one went to class much, which meant there was always someone to drink with. Trevor was aware that it was all highly irresponsible, but it also felt oddly vital, something he already knew he would look back on as a defining time in his life. There can be something tragically romantic about failing to live up to your promise — especially when you're experiencing that failure alongside a bunch of southern small-town misfits a whole lot like you who are all doing exactly the same thing.

Still, it went without saying that it couldn't last, and a few months later Trevor dropped out of college for good. "I got my one shot," he told me, "and I blew it." He spent the next few years wandering, in debt, hitchhiking around the country with friends, taking jobs here and there, occasionally getting into mild trouble with the law. It was not a happy time. Now Trevor was living back in his mother's home in Taylorsville, working at an AT&T call center, making a little more than minimum wage. Down in the basement, he and his brother Orry, who was studying welding at the community college thirty minutes away in Hickory, had rigged up a video game sanctuary, unpainted plywood countertops supporting an arsenal of consoles and monitors and headsets and controllers. The two brothers spent hour after hour sitting down there in the dark, playing Skyrim and Fallout 4.

TREVOR'S FLAMEOUT IN COLLEGE scarred not just him but the entire family. His acceptance to Appalachian State had felt like a good omen, a symbol of something positive and hopeful. If Trevor was able to succeed at college, that might mean a different future for all of them.

"Trevor was supposed to be the one who made it," Kim explained to me one afternoon. "When he didn't, it brought my whole family out of the spotlight. I think they were angry about it. They had invested money in him. They really thought it was going to go somewhere. And now that it's my turn, everybody is like, *We already went through this once.* Because they believed so much in Trevor, now they're afraid to believe even a little bit in me." To Kim, this felt deeply unfair. "I've never thought of myself as being like my family," she said. "I always felt like the bridge to a more successful future. But everyone sees me as just another Trevor. That's how I've been branded: as Trevor's remake."

Trevor, for his part, kind of liked the fact that he and his sister had things in common. Kim didn't see it that way. She'd been in middle school when Trevor was messing up at college, and watching his struggles scared her straight, inspiring her to turn things around for herself academically. Now that she was close to college, she was terrified by the thought that she might follow in his footsteps. So she kept looking for signs that she and Trevor were nothing alike. He took two AP courses? She took six. He never bothered to get a job in high school, while she worked at KFC after band practice and on weekends, saving money for college. If Trevor was going to be aimless and nonchalant, Kim would be ambitious and driven, signing up for clubs and after-school activities and summer enrichment programs all through high school—anything to propel herself forward.

In senior year, when Kim talked to family members about her college plans, she didn't get the kind of encouragement that Trevor had received six years earlier. Her stepdad told her he wouldn't contribute anything to her tuition and warned her that she probably wouldn't get in anyway. At the family Christmas party, her Uncle Larry, a truck driver, let her know that a college degree was a waste of time and money. He told her she should enlist in the Army, instead.

Among Kim and her mother and brothers, the tensions over college were subtler. They were encouraging of her plans, but Kim felt that it wasn't the sort of full-throated support that Trevor got. Maybe it was the fact that she was a girl. Maybe it was lingering fallout from Trevor's App State debacle. But her mother and brothers also seemed a little wounded by Kim's urgent need to distance herself from them. They took her ambition personally. And the more she talked about her accomplishments and her plans and how far away from Taylorsville they were going to take her, the more they seemed to retreat from her.

In Kim's family, what was valued most highly was not personal achievement; it was family loyalty. Kim's mom treated her wayward boys like prodigal sons, welcoming Trevor home after his misadventures, inviting Orry to move back in after his marriage failed, along with his new girlfriend, her two children, and his own two kids. She didn't care if her boys had screwed up here and there. She loved them, and she liked having a home that was packed to the rafters with family.

In the parable of the prodigal son, of course, the character who is aggrieved and resentful is the sibling who *didn't* screw up, who did everything right. That was Kim. "It drives me so crazy," she told me, "because no one in my family has a plan but me. But *I'm* the bad guy for having a plan and not wanting to be in Taylorsville. They think I'm antifamily. They give me such crap. They say, 'You don't even want to be here.' But that's not my goal. My goal is to go to college. And college just so happens not to be here."

RIGHT AFTER GRADUATION, Kim went down to Clemson for a three-week orientation program for first-generation freshmen, and she loved it. It was just what she had thought college would be like: challenging work, plenty of fun times, fascinating people. There were more students of color than white kids at the orientation, and Kim, who is white, fell in with a crowd of African American girls. She grew especially close to a girl named Shiayra, or Shi, who was from a small town in eastern South Carolina, not far from the Atlantic coast, and Kim and Shi made plans to room together in the fall.

After Kim got back from the orientation program, she and a few high school friends took a road trip out to California, camping and staying in cheap motels, a last fling before college. When she got back to Taylorsville in late July, Kim turned her attention to the last few pieces of paperwork Clemson needed her to submit. But a problem soon became apparent: her tuition bill.

Clemson had offered her a decent amount of financial aid, but there was still a sizable chunk that Kim and her family needed to come up with. Kim knew that her mother had no savings to put toward college, but she had assumed that they could cover most or all of what she needed with something called a parent PLUS loan, a relatively high-interest student loan, underwritten by the federal government, intended for families with lower credit ratings. But in July, Kim got the news that her mom's credit was too precarious even to get a PLUS loan—her mom had had trouble in the past with credit card debt, and she'd had cars repossessed. So as July turned to August, Kim spent her days searching for alternatives, making phone calls to relatives, asking if anyone would be willing to cosign a loan, calling Clemson's financial-aid office every day to see if they had other suggestions. No family members responded to Kim's pleas, and the people in Clemson's aid office, according to Kim, mostly just scolded her, telling her she should have worked out a strategy to pay her tuition long ago.

On August 10, a week before classes were scheduled to begin, Kim walked into the kitchen of the family home in Taylorsville, clutching a handful of financial-aid forms, and asked her mom to sit down with her and try to figure out a new plan. Her mother, no doubt feeling anxious and defensive and maybe a little guilty, did just what the people in the Clemson aid office had been doing to Kim: She launched into an I-told-you-so routine, telling Kim she should have thought to apply for more scholarships back in the spring. It was Kim's fault, she said, for not planning ahead.

Kim, of course, had done nothing *but* plan ahead for four straight years of high school. And now here was her mom, who hadn't thought to save a penny for her daughter's college education, acting like it was Kim who had screwed up. That did it: Kim broke down. She crumpled, sliding down the kitchen wall till she was sitting on the floor, her arms wrapped around her knees, tears flowing down her cheeks.

Trevor was in the kitchen, too. He didn't say much, but it was clear to Kim that he was on their mom's side. Kim looked up at them both, her face awash in rage and disappointment. "This is the only thing I have ever wanted," she said through her tears. "I want to go to college. I want a degree."

"Well, that's what life is," Trevor said. "You don't get everything you want."

"But everything that I have ever wanted, you got and you threw it away," Kim said. "Don't tell me this is just life, because you got exactly what I wanted, and you threw it away."

Kim's mom was crying now, too, and they all went back and forth a few times, blaming and comforting and commiserating. The fight ended, like most fights at Kim's house, with everyone retreating in silence to his or her own space: Trevor down to the video game room and Kim's mom to her bedroom. Kim felt suddenly exhausted, and she staggered to the living room and collapsed on the big black leather sectional couch.

She stayed there for two weeks.

ON THE FIRST MORNING of her two weeks on the couch, Kim called Clemson and officially withdrew from the university. After that, she couldn't think of a single thing to do. So she just lay there, day after day. She texted a bit with Shiayra and her other friends from the summer program, but it was too depressing to hear about them starting classes without her. She slept twelve hours a night. She watched ten straight seasons of *Grey's Anatomy* on Netflix.

Late every night, her stepdad would come home from work at the steel plant, see her still on the couch, and ask, "What season are you on?"

"Two."

The next day: "Four."

The next day: "Seven."

It was Kim's own prodigal-daughter moment, her turn to collapse in disgrace back into the waiting arms of her family. And true to form, they let her in. No one scolded her; no one tried to oust her from the couch. Her mom made her food. Orry kept his kids quiet when she was sleeping. Trevor would occasionally join her for three or four *Grey's Anatomy* episodes.

And then, after fourteen straight days on the couch, Kim decided it was time to get up. She was not ready to abandon her dream of college. She told herself she needed a plan to get to Clemson, even if she would have to start a semester or two late. The first step, she realized, was to make some money. She spent a couple of days looking online for a job and found a position an hour away in Charlotte at Lucky Dog Bark & Brew, a combination sports bar and dog park, that paid ten dollars an hour.

Kim learned that if she moved to South Carolina and took a full-time job there, she could establish residency and pay in-state tuition at Clemson, which would save her $20,000 a year. On Craigslist, she found a woman with a room to rent in a small town just outside Clemson, and once she had saved up enough for a few months' rent, she drove down, moved in, got a job at a dog kennel, and became an official South Carolina resident.

By January, she was enrolled full-time at Clemson, taking calculus and comparative politics and an introduction to engineering. The work was hard, but she wasn't freaked out by it. She didn't follow Trevor's path into dissolution and debauchery, like so many people in her family had predicted. Instead, she spent a lot of time in the library. She joined the women's rugby team and started traveling to games around the Southeast, getting muddy and bruised. Shiayra remained her best friend.

What was most amazing about spending time with Shi, for Kim, was watching the relationship Shi had with her parents, especially when it came to college. Shi's family was like Kim's in some superficial ways: her parents didn't make much money, they lived in a small town, they didn't have college degrees. But Kim couldn't get over how supportive and enthusiastic they were about Shiayra and her studies. Back when Shi had been applying to college, she told Kim, her parents were with her every step of the way, scouring websites and filling out forms and talking things through with Shi. Now Shiayra was pursuing a degree in world cinema, which was not exactly a guaranteed ticket to future riches, but her parents told her she was right to follow her passion. They called all the time, sent her little presents and warm texts. I asked Kim if she envied Shi that parental involvement, and she said no, she was just happy for her.

Meanwhile, Kim's ties to her own family seemed to be fraying. After rising from the couch, she had focused all her energy on getting herself out of the house and over the state line. And just like in high school, the more she pulled away from home, the more her family retreated as well. Phone calls were rare. She missed home, missed being a part of the family dramas—Billy's next court date, the latest squabble with an aunt or second cousin. "I would like to feel like I'm still part of the family," she told me, "but I definitely don't." She had stayed down in Clemson for Christmas, her first holiday away from home. She drove up to Taylorsville in January for her nineteenth birthday, but no one seemed to care much—there was no cake and no party—so after one night at home, she got in her car and drove back to Clemson.

I OFTEN THOUGHT about Caroline Hoxby's packets when I spoke with Kim. Kim's story certainly didn't refute the premise of Hoxby's experiment, but it complicated it. As a high school senior in a remote small town, Kim really did need more information and better advice about college than she was able to get from school or from home. But it was also true that the help Kim needed most urgently would not fit in a nine-by-twelve-inch mailer. What she needed was a combination of practical financial assistance—not advice on filling out federal student aid forms, but an actual student loan—and the kind of bountiful emotional support that Shiayra received from her parents.

As I wrote above, Hoxby's data did reveal a clear and important fact about how American higher education functions in the twenty-first century: These days, more than ever, a college's selectivity, as measured by its students' incoming SAT and ACT scores, directly predicts the amount of money the college spends on its students' educations. A purely rational calculation, therefore, would dictate that students should always go to the most selective institution they can get into. That's the best value, the greatest return on your investment. And for many students, that calculation seems to make sense.

But for others, like Kim, judgments about college are not always the result of a simple cost-benefit analysis. When I last spoke to her, she was halfway through her junior year at Clemson. She seemed fully at home, happy with her choice, majoring in geology, traveling with the rugby team, planning for graduate school. The real value she found at Clemson wasn't something she would express only, or even mostly, in terms of her future earnings. To her, what mattered was her friends and her rugby team and the science she had learned and the way it all made her feel about herself and her place in the world.

My conversations with Kim about college often reminded me of my conversations with Clara. There were, despite their obvious differences, some parallels between the two women's stories: They had both started out with a 27 on the ACT, although Clara, with Ned's help, had been able to raise her score by eight points, greatly expanding her options, while Kim never took the test again. And they both had wrestled with their college decisions. When Kim first told me she had decided to pursue Clemson instead of Cornell, it made me think about Clara's choice between Middlebury and Yale. Each young woman was choosing between a school where she felt more personally comfortable (Clemson, Middlebury) and one that was more prestigious (Cornell, Yale). And my first impression was that Kim had made the opposite decision from Clara's: Kim picked the comfortable college, and Clara chose the prestigious one.

But looked at from a different angle, I eventually realized, their situations were more like mirror images of each other. For Clara, Yale was certainly the more selective college, but it was also the easier choice. Picking Yale was a decision to weave herself more tightly into the tapestry of her family. She was honoring her parents' wishes, following in the footsteps of her mother and sister, writing the next chapter in a long and proud family legacy. For Kim, going to Cornell would have meant defying her family's traditions, ripping herself out of its fabric, moving to a part of the country where she had no ties and no cultural touchstones. Even going away to Clemson — a public university less than two hundred miles from home — had created divisions and rifts in her family that had not yet entirely healed.

But while I can't argue that Kim, as an individual, would have been happier if she had chosen a more achievement-typical college like Cornell, it is also true that a scenario in which students like Clara always wind up at colleges like Yale and students like Kim always wind up at colleges like Clemson seems far from ideal, and likely only to perpetuate the pervasive inequalities of American higher education.

Yale really does provide advantages to its students that Clemson does not. It really is a problem that (as Raj Chetty's analysis showed) only about 2 percent of Yale's students come from economic backgrounds like Kim's. But is that Kim's problem to solve? Or Yale's?

THE TIME I spent in Taylorsville caused me to temper some of my initial optimism about Hoxby's approach. But the premise behind her packets — that all it would take to change the trajectories of thousands of low-income high school seniors each year is some basic information and a gentle push — remained a dominant one in the national conversation about college admissions and student success. It was an appealing idea: that the inequities in higher education could be solved with a simple bureaucratic tweak. And it was appealing, too, for a certain audience, to think that the ultimate responsibility for the imbalances lay not with the universities, or with the higher-education system at large, but with the students, who were simply uninformed and misguided about where their most promising opportunities lay.

There were two large-scale attempts underway during those years to replicate and expand on Hoxby and Turner's work. One was the massive packet-sending effort run by the College Board under David Coleman. (I'll say more about that one in the next chapter.) The second, even more ambitious, was a $25 million five-year project funded by Michael Bloomberg.

In the fall of 2014, Bloomberg announced that his foundation, Bloomberg Philanthropies, was launching a national program called CollegePoint that would offer free advice and counseling on college admissions to tens of thousands of high-achieving high school seniors like the ones Hoxby targeted, students like Kim with high test scores and low or moderate family incomes. CollegePoint advisers, most of them recent college graduates themselves, would connect with these students not in person, and not through the mail (as in Hoxby's experiment), but through texts, emails, and video-chat services like Skype. The College Board and ACT Inc. agreed to provide lists of target students, and Bloomberg's foundation enlisted four nonprofit student-counseling organizations to do the advising, each one managing its own team of "virtual advisers," sometimes called e-advisers.

The largest of those four nonprofits was called College Advising Corps, and in the spring of 2017 I spent two days at CAC's headquarters in a suburban office park in Chapel Hill, North Carolina, watching several CollegePoint e-advisers as they worked. For thirty or forty minutes at a time, these young advisers spoke by video chat with high school seniors around the country, offering advice and support on which college to select and how to negotiate the blizzard of financial-aid forms and other documents that the students were facing.

The Bloomberg-funded virtual project is just a small part of the advising work that College Advising Corps does. Each year, CAC hires hundreds of recent college graduates — most of whom were first-generation college students themselves — and sends them into high schools in low-income communities and neighborhoods around the nation to serve for two years as college advisers to students there. The work of the organization's seven hundred in-school advisers is quite different from the work being done by its thirty-six e-advisers in Chapel Hill — and not only because one version involves face-to-face interactions while the other is mediated by screens.

Following Hoxby's model, the Bloomberg virtual initiative is targeted only at top-scoring students, and its e-advisers are supposed to steer those students to institutions on a specific list of highly selective American colleges. CAC's in-school advisers have a much broader mission, for the simple reason that very few students in high-poverty schools score high enough on the SAT to make the Hoxby cutoff. I have visited CAC advisers at more than a dozen schools around the country, from Wilkes-Barre, Pennsylvania, to Brownsville, Texas, to Detroit, and when I sat in on in-school advising sessions, the choices students were weighing were rarely between two selective colleges; those students were more often deciding between a community college close to home and a four-year state college a hundred miles away. Some of them were trying to figure out whether to attend college at all.

During my visit to Chapel Hill, the virtual advisers, in between their Skype sessions, talked with me about their work. While they valued the connections they had formed with students halfway across the country, many of them said they were concerned that the structure of the CollegePoint program was making it hard for them to give good advice to the students who needed it the most. The first problem was that even among the exclusive, high-scoring group that the project was targeting, the advisers were able to reach only a small fraction of the students. In the fall, each adviser was given a slate of about 250 names, selected using College Board or ACT data and a variation on the Hoxby algorithm. The adviser was then required to text each student on his or her list, inviting them to take part in the video-advising program. Most students didn't respond. Some replied to a text or two. Only a few took part in multiple advising conversations; most advisers told me that there were just 10 or 20 students from their original list of 250 with whom they were able to engage in a concerted way.

What's more, there were indications that the students who did take full advantage of the program were a self-selecting group made up mostly of individuals who were already ambitious and inclined to advocate for themselves and seek out opportunities. I observed four virtual advising sessions on my first day in Chapel Hill, and as it happened, all four high school students were immigrants to the United States: two were born in Brazil, one in Italy, and one in Nepal. They were wonderful kids, filled with drive and passion for a college education, but they did not fit the typical Hoxby demographic, which was disproportionately white and rural, and it was easy to imagine that these students would have found their way to an excellent college with or without the help of a virtual adviser.

There was another problem that concerned the advisers I met. CollegePoint's rules required them to encourage students to choose a college from a prepared list of 270 schools, compiled by the Aspen

Institute, where at least 70 percent of students were able to graduate with a BA in at least six years. (Advisers referred to this list as the Aspen 270.) CollegePoint counted an advising relationship as a success only if the student ended up enrolling in an Aspen 270 college. But the advisers I spoke to found the Aspen list to be rigid and arbitrary; in the real world of high school students, they believed, sometimes a school that wasn't on the list was a better choice than a school that was. For instance, the only historically black college on the Aspen 270 list was Spelman, a women's college. For certain young black men, the advisers believed, a historically black college like Howard or Morehouse might be a better choice than a majority-white college with a higher graduation rate. But if a student told his adviser he was considering one of those schools, the adviser's official mandate was to steer that student to a college on the list. (The advisers told me they generally ignored the mandate and just gave students the advice they believed to be most helpful.)

One of the virtual advisers I spoke with was a young black woman with tortoiseshell glasses named Jhenielle Reynolds, a recent graduate of the University of North Carolina at Chapel Hill. She explained that when you're a low-income student choosing a college, there are factors in your decision that the binary nature of the Aspen list didn't adequately reflect. "We know that Aspen schools are highly resourced in terms of their per-student expenditure," Reynolds said. "But are students going to feel comfortable and welcomed on campus? A college might be an excellent *academic* fit for the student, but that student won't perform well academically if they don't feel like they belong there." She told me she drew on her own experiences at UNC, which were not altogether positive, when she advised her students. "On paper, all of the Aspen schools will help you to succeed," she said. "But I've lived the experience of being an underrepresented minority at an Aspen 270 school, and I understand that there are nuances."

Reynolds said she also tries to ask the students she advises about their family situation. Are they a primary caregiver for their family?

Do they help translate English-language documents and phone calls into their family's native language? Those factors complicate decisions as well, Reynolds explained: "What are the implications of that student moving halfway across the country to an Aspen 270 school, versus maybe going to the flagship public college in their home state that might not be on the Aspen 270 list, but they got a full ride there?"

When Michael Bloomberg announced the CollegePoint initiative in the fall of 2014, he and his representatives told reporters that within five years, they hoped their virtual advisers would be persuading more than ten thousand students each year to switch from a low-graduation-rate college to an Aspen 270 school. But in the winter of 2019, when CollegePoint's evaluation team released its first data, it became apparent that the actual impact of the virtual college-advising project was much smaller — too small, in fact, even to register as statistically significant. The reason for the disappointing results remained somewhat mysterious. But the results themselves were clear: despite the $25 million Bloomberg had invested in the program, CollegePoint seemed to be changing the college-going patterns not of several thousand students each year, but of only a few dozen.

The CollegePoint results, though discouraging on their face, may provide the field with an opportunity to rethink not just the particular tools and tactics that CollegePoint employed, but also some of the basic premises of this body of research. Even if interventions like the College Board's packets and the CollegePoint advisers' video chats could be made effective at scale, would they be the right place to put our attention and resources? Are the demographic disparities evident on the nation's college campuses primarily the result of decisions made by students? Or do they have more to do with decisions made by the colleges themselves? And if we do want to level the college-going playing field for the country as a whole, is the best approach really to focus so much money and effort on getting a few more high-performing students to attend a small number of elite institutions?

While I was in Chapel Hill, I had a long conversation with Nicole Hurd, the CEO of College Advising Corps. She is a former religious

studies professor and college administrator who founded the organization in 2005, when she was working as a dean at the University of
Virginia. That year, she placed just a dozen new UVA grads as college
advisers in rural high schools around Virginia; now there are CAC
advisers in sixteen states, and together they serve more than two
hundred thousand students each year. Hurd is a thoughtful, reflective person, and when I spoke with her, she had been looking back
at the initial burst of media coverage of Caroline Hoxby's papers. She
reminded me about that "$6 Solution" headline that accompanied a
2014 article about Hoxby in the *Chronicle of Higher Education.*

"There *are* no six-dollar solutions," Hurd said firmly. "There just
aren't any silver bullets in this space. It was such a great story: the
young person who against all odds has succeeded and persevered
and is now off to a highly selective school. Who doesn't want to tell
that story? It's the American dream story. It's absolutely seductive.
So yes, we wanted to be a part of that story. We wanted to help those
kids. But that's not most of our kids."

Hurd explained the math behind her thinking: The total population targeted each year by CollegePoint was 75,000 high school seniors. Hurd cared about those students, and she wanted to do her
best to help them succeed. But each year there were 1.3 *million* low-
income high school seniors in the United States whose test scores
weren't high enough to earn them a text message from CollegePoint.
Those were the students Hurd's in-school advisers worked with every
day, and she was at least as worried about them. Their options were
far fewer, and much less appealing, than the options open to students
in the small group of high achievers targeted by CollegePoint.

"If we're trying to protect our democracy and create a robust economy," Hurd said, "we need to help more than seventy-five thousand
kids a year. We need to think about where those other kids are going, too. And are they graduating? And if they're not, what does that
mean for our country?"

III

FIXING THE TEST

———

1. Reputation Management

The College Board's effort to replicate Caroline Hoxby's packet experiment was in part an attempt by the organization to correct some of the inequities and imbalances in higher education. But the project seems to have had a second purpose as well, arguably just as important, if less high-minded: it appears to have been part of a large-scale exercise in corporate rebranding. The College Board, which was founded in 1900 by a group of elite eastern prep schools and colleges, is an unusual organization. Though it is technically a nonprofit, it doesn't really operate like one. Its top executives earn hundreds of thousands of dollars a year, and its headquarters occupies three floors of a gleaming tower in Lower Manhattan whose other tenants are mostly banks and hedge funds. (In the mall downstairs, lunchtime shopping options include Gucci, Hermès, and Louis Vuitton stores.) Annual revenues at the College Board are more than a billion dollars, most of which comes from student fees for the SAT and for AP exams.

When the trustees of the College Board went looking for a new president in 2011, there was a looming crisis imperiling this healthy cash flow. The ACT, which had always trailed far behind the SAT in popularity, was rapidly gaining market share, and the number of high school students taking the ACT was threatening to surpass the number taking the SAT.

On the surface, the competition between the ACT and the SAT was a simple business rivalry, no deeper than Coke versus Pepsi, and to many students and universities, the tests themselves seemed essentially interchangeable. But beneath the corporate battle lay a profound debate over the meaning and purpose of college-admissions tests, one whose history stretched back decades.

As the journalist Nicholas Lemann recounts in his book *The Big Test,* the SAT was created and cultivated, in the 1920s and 1930s, in the confines of the Ivy League, championed by the president of Harvard and administered by a team at Princeton. Its inventors had no interest in expanding the college-going population nationally; instead, their goal was to identify and locate a small number of especially bright middle-class students around the country who might be added to the existing student bodies at Ivy League universities, which at the time were populated mostly by wealthy young prep-school grads who cared more about attending debutante balls than university classes. When it was first developed, "SAT" stood for Scholastic Aptitude Test, and the exam was, for many years, presented and marketed to the public as a test of *aptitude,* an inherent intellectual ability that was independent of the work students did in school. There was no point in studying for the SAT, according to the College Board: you either were born with this magical thing called aptitude or you weren't.

In 1959 E. F. Lindquist, an education professor with populist leanings who worked at the University of Iowa, established his own testing organization, called American College Testing, or ACT. Lindquist had become well known, in testing circles, for developing a series of assessments that measured, in a standardized way, what students were learning in public schools. Now Lindquist turned his attention to developing an alternative to the SAT, which he marketed not to the Ivy League but to big public universities, mostly in the Midwest. The ACT was intended as a contrast to the SAT in almost every way. It was headquartered in Iowa City, far from the coastal elites. Its questions were more straightforward and more aligned with what public school students were studying, with none of the obscure vocabulary words and cognitive traps that for many students made the SAT an ordeal. Unlike on the SAT, if you guessed wrong on a question on the ACT, you didn't lose points.

These practical differences in the test reflected a different philosophy of testing. Lindquist believed that what was most relevant in judging a student's academic potential was not his or her intrinsic IQ (or "aptitude") but his academic achievement in high school — the kind of subject mastery that a typical Iowa farm boy might achieve in the classroom with sufficient effort. The purpose of the ACT was to identify these industrious youngsters, in large numbers, and convey them to the public university where they would be most likely to succeed.

As the ACT grew in popularity, especially in the Midwest and South, the College Board and the SAT experienced a series of identity crises. The original notion at the heart of the SAT was that it would overthrow the country's existing inherited aristocracy and replace it with a more democratic meritocracy; the test would locate genius wherever in American society it was concealed and help raise those intellectual standouts to positions of privilege and power. But as the SAT expanded, evidence mounted that the students who tended to excel on the test looked a lot like the scions of that old aristocracy. Rich kids reliably did better than poor kids; whites did better than blacks.

That wasn't particularly controversial early in the century, when Americans were more willing to accept the idea that higher education was naturally the province of wealthy white boys. But as a more egalitarian image of the country began to take hold in the 1960s and 1970s, the social and racial imbalances apparent in SAT scores became a growing public relations problem for the College Board. What had been intended as a tool to disrupt the reigning American class hierarchy was increasingly perceived as an instrument that perpetuated it. Crusading journalists, African American psychologists, even the reform activist Ralph Nader: all lined up to take a whack at the SAT, deriding it in articles and reports as a tool of discrimination and oppression.

In response, the College Board's leaders began to change the way they talked in public about the SAT. The first step was removing the word "aptitude" from its title. In 1990 the College Board declared that "SAT" no longer stood for Scholastic Aptitude Test; it now stood for Scholastic Assessment Test. (A few years later, "assessment" was abandoned, too, and now, officially, SAT stands for nothing at all.) As the name changed, so did the SAT itself, in small ways and large — and each revision took it a step closer to Lindquist's ideal: a test that reflected what students had learned in high school rather than a measure of their inherent intellectual ability.

But this emerging new identity for the SAT never sat entirely eas- ily with the College Board, either. If the SAT reflected what students learned in high school, then that logically meant they could study for it. Which meant that test-prep coaches could help them study for it. And the College Board had long insisted that test prep sim- ply didn't work. This article of faith had been under siege for quite a while — ever since 1946, in fact, when a recent graduate of New York's City College named Stanley Kaplan, the son of a Brooklyn plumber, began offering SAT-prep classes in the basement of his parents' home in Flatbush. Before long, every striving kid from Williamsburg to Co- ney Island was making the pilgrimage to Stanley's basement to learn how to beat the SAT.

The College Board tried at various points to ignore Kaplan, to dis- credit him, and to run him out of business. Nothing worked, and Kaplan built his basement SAT classes into a $50 million company. In 1981 Kaplan was joined in the test-prep business by his first seri- ous rival: a cocky Princeton sophomore named John Katzman, who started a company called Princeton Review out of his dorm room. Katzman was a child of the Manhattan prep-school elite, and stu- dents from those affluent precincts now flocked to Princeton Review classes the way working-class Brooklyn kids had flocked to Kaplan's basement. Katzman's success—and the improved test scores that his rich students started boasting about—reinforced the growing public perception that a student's performance on the SAT was primarily a reflection not of his aptitude or his achievement, but of his parents' financial resources.

Somehow, the ACT's reputation managed to survive—and even to thrive—while the SAT's took one hit after another. Though Kaplan and Princeton Review and Ned Johnson were demonstrating every day that expensive test prep could raise a student's ACT score just as effectively as it could raise his SAT score, the ACT was still perceived by the public to be more democratic, fairer, purer, more . . . corn-fed and midwestern, somehow, than the SAT was. And ACT Inc. managed to leverage that perception into a dominant advantage in an important new test market—one that ACT essentially invented.

Beginning in 2001, ACT's sales reps began trekking from Iowa City to various state capitals, far from the coasts—Springfield, Illinois; Frankfort, Kentucky; Lansing, Michigan; Cheyenne, Wyoming—and making a bold pitch to state education officials: sign a contract with us to make the ACT your official statewide high school exit exam. Instead of having students in your state pay us one by one to take the ACT on weekends, just pay us a lump sum, and we'll administer the test to every single high school junior in your state, during the school day.

State officials were receptive to ACT's proposal. This was the era of No Child Left Behind, when state education departments were feeling pressure from the federal government to ramp up statewide testing. If they signed a deal with ACT, they wouldn't need to invent a high school test of their own. State education commissioners were also able to present these contracts to voters as a step in the direction of equality and progress: no longer would college entrance tests be reserved for the high scorers or the high spenders; now every student in the state would have the same advantage in the quest for college.

It went without saying, in these discussions, that the ACT was more naturally suited to the role of a high school exit exam than was the SAT. The ACT was founded on the notion that it was aligned with what students were learning in high school, and the SAT was founded on the principle that it was entirely separate from what was going on in high school. True, the SAT had changed. But its reputation hadn't. And it wasn't hard for ACT's sales reps in these meetings in Frankfort and Lansing (and Bismarck and Baton Rouge) to persuade state officials that a company based in Iowa City might understand their students better than one in an office tower in Manhattan.

Before the College Board quite realized what was happening, education officials in a dozen states had signed contracts with ACT allowing every high school junior to take the ACT during the school day, with the bill for these hundreds of thousands of tests paid not by the students, but by the states. As the contracts piled up, the SAT's market-share advantage over the ACT, which had for decades seemed insurmountable, eroded further and further, year after year — until it disappeared altogether, just as David Coleman was hired to lead the College Board. In 2012, for the first time, more high school students took the ACT than the SAT. Iowa City had overtaken New York City at last.

IF COLEMAN WAS GOING to return the SAT to its former position at the top of the American test ziggurat, he needed first to repair its battered reputation. He began this rehabilitation campaign by doing something unprecedented in the history of the College Board: he admitted that the SAT's critics were right. "Unequal test-prep access is a problem," he told a reporter for the *New York Times Magazine*. "It is a problem that it's opaque to students what's on the exam." Costly test preparation had "corrupted" the SAT, Coleman said in a speech to college counselors. The test had "become captive to the advantages of wealth . . . certifying privilege rather than merit."

Rather than dispute or dismiss the correlations between income and SAT scores, as the College Board had done in the past, Coleman now highlighted those correlations and declared that they needed to change. The College Board released data showing that in 2013, students' SAT scores tracked their family income in a direct and linear fashion, starting at an average score of 1326 (out of 2400) among students whose families earned less than $20,000, and rising step by step to an average score of 1714 among students whose families earned more than $200,000. Back in the days when the College Board seemed to keep reworking its SAT acronym every few years, there was an old joke that the three letters should really stand for Student Affluence Test. Now Coleman was acknowledging that there was some truth in that joke — or at least that there *had* been, in the past, before his time.

Coleman announced three major initiatives designed to disrupt the correlations between family income and student test scores and to offer more opportunity to low-income students. First, he said, the College Board would overhaul the SAT itself, abandoning entirely its heritage as a test of aptitude and aligning it much more closely with what students were learning in high school. There would be no more tricks; no more obscure "SAT words." Second, he would undercut and undermine Ned Johnson and Princeton Review and every other test-prep provider by partnering with Khan Academy, an online learning system, to offer free College Board–approved SAT test prep to every student in the country. And finally, and most immediately, Coleman was going to take Caroline Hoxby's packet experiment and expand it into a much larger and more ambitious national project.

In the fall of 2013, the College Board mailed more than 30,000 packets to high-scoring low-income students across the country, each packet closely modeled on the ones Hoxby and Turner had sent out in their original experiment, each one including either four or eight fee-waiver coupons that allowed recipients to apply to top colleges for free. Coleman and his advisers expected the program to have a big impact. Earlier that year, when Hoxby and Turner publicly invited the College Board and ACT to replicate their experiment, they had made a bold and confident prediction: If the organizations took them up on this invitation, not only would they match the power-ful results Hoxby and Turner had achieved in their pilot experiment; they would far surpass them.

Here's why: A few months after they sent out their original pack-ets, Hoxby and Turner surveyed students in the treatment group and asked them if they remembered receiving the mailing. Sixty percent of them said no, they'd never seen it. Who knows why: Maybe it went to the wrong address; maybe their parents threw the envelope out without opening it; maybe they did read the packet but somehow for-got in the bedlam of senior year. But whatever the reason, Hoxby and Turner contended in their paper that if reputable organizations like the College Board and ACT took up the baton of the experiment and sent future packets out themselves, with respected institutional logos printed on the front of the envelopes, students would be much more likely to open the packets and take them seriously, and the effect of the treatment would be much larger. Target students, they calculated, might potentially enroll in peer institutions at a rate as much as 46 percent higher than without the intervention.

When Coleman was profiled by the *New York Times Magazine* in March 2014, he told the reporter that his researchers were at that very moment compiling data on the effects of the College Board's replica-tion of Hoxby's experiment. Their study, the article said, would be re-leased the following month. But April came and went with no public release of the results of the experiment. So did May and June and July. In November 2014 I asked the director of the College Board's com-munications office if the Hoxby replication research was ready for publication; he told me no, but he promised they would have findings to discuss in the spring of 2015. The spring of 2015 passed, as did the summer and fall, and still, no results were made public. Life went on. The sun rose and set. Babies were born, old people died.

In September 2016 I visited the College Board's glimmering tower in Lower Manhattan for my first interview with Coleman since our initial conversation in 2013. There were many things I wanted to ask him about, but at the top of my list was the elusive data from the College Board's Hoxby replication. When I arrived in Coleman's corner office, he handed me a five-page summary of recent innovations from the College Board, and at the top, it had some information about the effect of the mailings, which the College Board had renamed the Realize Your College Potential packets, or RYCP. I was in luck, I thought: solid results at last. Then I looked more closely at the summary.

The key finding, which Coleman read aloud to me, was this: "3.5 —4% of high school graduates in the classes of 2014 and 2015 who received the treatment and eight RYCP college application fee waivers were more likely to enroll in an RYCP college or university than identical control group students who did not receive the intervention materials."

As any high school senior who scores high on the SAT could tell you, this sentence doesn't make sense, either grammatically or mathematically. Four percent of treatment students were *more likely* to enroll in a selective college? How much more likely? Did this 4 percent *actually* enroll in a selective college, or were they just more likely to? Coleman stumbled over this sentence as he read it to me. He paused and looked at the paper again.

"'More likely' is interesting," he said, furrowing his brow. "The use of 'more likely'—I actually don't understand it myself."

I didn't want to hold up our interview over one awkward sentence. But the question this particular statement was purporting to address was a crucial one whose answer was long overdue: How effective were these packets at changing students' behavior at scale? Three and a half years after making the front page of the *New York Times*, did this famous experiment actually work? Was it really the "$6 solution"? Coleman promised to find clear answers from his researchers and get them to me as soon as possible.

This episode marked the beginning of a strange pattern in my dealings with the College Board that persisted over the next two years. Back in 2013 and 2014, the College Board had launched an array of equity-promoting interventions that Coleman had been eager to discuss with me and other reporters. But back then, those interventions were still mostly unproven and hypothetical—wishful thinking, at best. Now, in 2016, those interventions were finally producing concrete results, actual experimental data that could potentially prove valuable to the field. And yet the College Board seemed increasingly reluctant to share that data with the public.

And so my long wait for the Hoxby results continued. In September 2016, folks in the College Board's communications office told me they would send me the data in October. In October, they said they were compiling the results into a research paper that would be published in December. Early in the new year, they said that plans had changed again because of an internal debate over whether it was a good idea to release a detailed public report after all. As one communications official put it to me in an email, there were "concerns about how a formal research paper might be received externally."

Finally, in January 2017, the College Board sent me at least part of what I'd been asking for: a twenty-page "intraoffice memorandum," written nine months earlier by its policy research team, documenting the effect of the tens of thousands of packets that the College Board had sent out to high-scoring low-income students across the country in the high school graduating classes of 2014 and 2015. As soon as I read it, I understood why the College Board had been so reluctant to give it to me.

Caroline Hoxby and Sarah Turner, remember, had predicted confidently that the College Board's replication of their experiment would not only reproduce their impressive original results; it would produce much *greater* effects—boosting the number of targeted students enrolling in selective institutions by as much as 46 percent. Those were the bold predictions that had made headlines back in 2013. But that's not what happened when the College Board conducted its replication. Not even close.

The College Board sent out more than thirty thousand packets to students in the class of 2014 and a similar number to the class of 2015, more or less exact replicas of Hoxby's packets, all targeted at students who scored in the top 10 percent on the SAT and whose parental income fell in the bottom quartile nationally. There was also a control group of similar students who were eligible to receive the packets; the College Board didn't send them anything. The key research question was to compare the behavior of the treatment group, which did get the packets, with that of the control group, which didn't, and see how their paths toward college differed.

The answer, according to the College Board's internal memo, was that the two groups didn't differ much at all. For the high school graduating class of 2014, 37.2 percent of students in the control group enrolled the next fall in at least a "peer" institution (meaning a college where the average SAT score among incoming freshmen was similar to their own), compared to 39 percent of students who received the packet. That's a difference of less than two percentage points. For the class of 2015, 34.1 percent of the control group attended at least a peer institution, and 34.6 percent of the treatment group did the same. That is not an effect size of 46 percent; it is an effect size of one half of one percentage point. It implies that if 30,000 students across the country in the class of 2015 received packets, about 150 of them enrolled in a peer institution who wouldn't have otherwise. That might be good news for those 150 students, but it's not the kind of number you would expect from one of the most influential pieces of social science research of the last decade.

I wanted to ask Caroline Hoxby about the College Board's findings, but after our conversation in 2013, she stopped responding to my calls and emails. Likewise, Sarah Turner, after a brief email exchange, didn't respond to multiple requests for an interview. The researchers' official Expanding College Opportunities Project website, expand ingcollegeopps.org, was apparently abandoned at some point; the last time I checked, that URL hosted a collection of Indonesian-language articles about online poker. In 2018 the College Board quietly ended its practice of sending packets to high-scoring low-income students. And five years after the College Board told the *New York Times Mag-*

azine that the release of its replication results was just weeks away, the organization still had not published anything informing the public that its results had diverged so sharply from Hoxby and Turner's original findings.

2. Test Prep

In March 2014, David Coleman, wearing a slate-gray suit over an open-necked pale blue dress shirt, hosted an event at the South by Southwest education conference in Austin, Texas. He was at SXSW to announce two things: the coming overhaul of the SAT and the College Board's plan to offer free test prep for the SAT through Khan Academy. In press interviews that winter, Coleman had charged that paid tutors like Ned Johnson who helped students prepare for the SAT were "predators" who were taking advantage of teenagers and their families. Khan Academy and the new SAT, Coleman had said, would get rid of their kind at last. "This is a bad day for them," he told the *New York Times.*

Coleman's explanation of *why* these changes were such bad news for Ned and his peers involved a bit of a rhetorical flourish. The College Board had spent decades insisting that test prep like the tutoring Ned provided to his affluent students didn't improve their scores much at all. If that was true, though, it was impossible to argue that expensive test prep was unfair or corrupting; it was just a bunch of foolish rich kids wasting their time and money. Coleman couldn't quite come out after all these years and simply reverse the College Board's official line. So he focused instead on the *perception* of unfairness that Ned and his peers had created.

"We must confront the inequalities that now surround assessment, such as costly test preparation," Coleman asserted from the stage in Austin. "It is time for the College Board to say in a clear voice that the culture and practice of test preparation that now surrounds admissions exams drives the perception of inequality and injustice in our country." Expensive test prep hadn't produced *actual* inequality and injustice in America, just the *perception* of it — but that was bad enough. Or so the argument went.

Regardless of the questionable rhetoric, the College Board's plan to deliver free test prep via Khan Academy struck me as both intriguing and potentially important. So in the fall of 2016, a couple of weeks after my interview with Coleman in his office in New York, I traveled to Mountain View, California, in the heart of Silicon Valley, to meet with Sal Khan in the offices of Khan Academy.

Khan, then in his early forties, was raised in Metairie, Louisiana, just outside New Orleans, by a single mother who had emigrated from the West Bengal region of India. He attended a working-class public high school in Metairie, and the prodigious math ability he displayed there won him admission to MIT, where he studied math, electrical engineering, and computer science. He went on to get an MBA from Harvard and then settled down in Boston to work as a financial analyst for a hedge fund. Teaching, at that point, was the furthest thing from his mind.

In 2004, when Khan was still in his late twenties, the trajectory of his life took an unexpected turn. He learned that his twelve-year-old cousin Nadia, back in Louisiana, was struggling in math, and he offered to help. He began tutoring her over the phone; as they talked, they would link their computers using a rudimentary online drawing program called Yahoo Doodle so that Khan could show Nadia how to work out problems. When he and Nadia began to have trouble coordinating their schedules, Khan started creating short videos of his math lessons and posting them on YouTube, then a brand-new service, so that she could watch them at any time. The videos were intended for Nadia's eyes only, but their audience soon grew — first to Nadia's siblings and other young relatives in Louisiana, then to their friends, then to thousands of people around the world who needed math help and found Khan's simple, low-tech videos especially clear and useful.

Khan's face never appeared in his videos. There were no cartoon animals or complicated visual effects to keep students' attention. Instead, Khan's viewers would hear his patient and encouraging voice while on the screen they saw the digital equivalent of a blackboard: a black screen on which Khan wrote in various colors, drawing diagrams and solving problems. For five years, Khan kept making his videos in his spare time from a makeshift studio in his home in Boston, and his audience continued to multiply. Students from around the world posted grateful comments on YouTube and emailed him to say how much his videos had helped them. Being thanked and praised for contributing to society was an unusual experience for a financial analyst, and in 2009 Khan decided that his destiny was not to work at a hedge fund after all. He quit his job, withdrew his life savings, and moved with his wife and infant son to California to establish Khan Academy as a nonprofit organization.

Before long he had attracted a few powerful admirers in the tech world, starting with Ann Doerr, the wife of John Doerr, the prominent venture capitalist. Then in 2010, Bill Gates, in a discussion onstage at the Aspen Ideas Festival, mentioned to the audience that he and his eleven-year-old son, Rory, had been watching Sal Khan's videos together. Khan had had no idea. A week later, he was summoned to Seattle for an audience with Gates, and a few days after that, the Gates Foundation invested $1.5 million in Khan Academy. Google soon donated another $2 million, and Khan was able to move his operations out of the converted closet he was using as an office. Khan Academy now occupies the second floor of a Spanish colonial revival building less than two miles from Google's headquarters. The office has all the distinguishing marks of a Silicon Valley startup: an open-plan work space, wall-size dry-erase boards, exposed ceiling beams, brushed concrete floors, and dozens of young employees typing away at their standing desks.

A couple of years before Coleman's tenure began, Khan had approached the College Board with a proposal to offer SAT test prep through Khan Academy, but the officials he met with weren't interested. Coleman, however, saw great potential in a collaboration with

Khan, and in 2014, in Austin, Khan and Coleman announced the product of that collaboration: Official SAT Practice on Khan Academy. In many ways, Official SAT Practice is like every other part of the Khan Academy site: it combines clear, straightforward video lessons with hundreds of practice questions that are calibrated to a student's ability using adaptive software. Get a lot of questions right, and they get harder; get a bunch wrong, and they get easier.

Students who use Official SAT Practice are encouraged to link their free Khan Academy account with their free College Board account. If they do, the results of their PSAT — the precursor to the SAT that students usually take in their sophomore or junior year of high school — are shared with Khan Academy, which then uses each student's particular matrix of right and wrong answers to create a personalized learning plan to prepare the student for the SAT.

I was eager to meet Sal Khan, and not just for journalistic reasons. A couple of years earlier, I had started watching his math videos with my son Ellington, then in kindergarten, and Ellington was now working his way through the early stages of the Khan elementary school math curriculum. (Remarkably, Sal Khan is able to sound just as enthusiastic and engaged in his videos when he's explaining basic subtraction as he does when he is decoding complex algebra.) Ellington found Khan's videos easy to follow, and he loved the way Khan Academy turned learning math into a game: he earned "energy points" for answering questions and badges for completing different levels, and he enjoyed clicking through the various charts on the Khan site that showed his progress. So I arrived at the offices of Khan Academy as a big fan.

But I did have one lingering concern about the College Board collaboration, which I raised with Khan when we sat down together in his office. The site seemed perfect for an advantaged kid like Ellington, who had an interest in math, a relatively long attention span, and, perhaps most important, a parent with the time and inclination to sit beside him for twenty or thirty minutes a night, offering help and encouragement, as he listened to Sal Khan explain the intricacies of long division. But the premise behind Official SAT Practice was that it would help level the playing field that Ned Johnson and his peers had knocked off kilter. And in order for that to happen, students with fewer resources, in places like Taylorsville and Detroit and Brownsville, would need to be the ones taking greatest advantage of the tool, rather than kids like Ellington Tough or Rory Gates.

Khan said he and his colleagues had been worried about the same thing. "There are a lot of students, especially the students we want to reach, who don't have access to a computer at home or at school, or it's not as accessible as it might be in a rich suburban school," Khan said. "You or I as parents are much more in the loop, we know all the tools, we know, 'Hey, this Khan Academy thing, let's get our kids in front of it.' Whereas a mom who has two jobs or who doesn't speak English — is she going to be aware of it?"

Khan acknowledged that this concern was valid, but he said there were early indications from the College Board's internal data that suggested that my fears — and his — were unwarranted. The full data on who was using Official SAT Practice and how they were using it weren't public yet, Khan said, but he had seen one reassuring preliminary result: it seemed that black students were using Official SAT Practice more than white students. That struck me as a promising sign.

ON MAY 8, 2017, the College Board released its analysis of the first two years of data from Official SAT Practice. It was, David Coleman said in a conference call that afternoon with reporters, "our most significant announcement since we announced the launch of the new SAT" three years earlier. The news, according to the College Board, was all positive: millions of students were using Official SAT Practice; they were gaining significant points on the SAT as a result; and students from different races and classes and genders were all gaining equally.

There were four headline data points that Coleman and the College Board emphasized on the conference call and in press releases and videos that went out that day.

First, students who practiced for the SAT on Khan for twenty hours gained, on average, 115 points between their PSAT and their SAT. (Students who didn't practice at all on Khan Academy gained about 60 points, just by being a year or so older, so those twenty-hour studiers were gaining an additional 55 points over that baseline.)

Second, there were sixteen thousand superachieving students who increased their scores by a huge amount: 200 points or more.

Third, a great many students were practicing for the SAT on Khan Academy. Forty percent of all students who took the SAT said they had prepared using Khan Academy.

Finally, and most important: students from every demographic group benefited equally from Official SAT Practice. In the conference call, Coleman said that College Board researchers had "confirmed that practice advanced students regardless of gender, race, income, or high school GPA. It is good news that practice is an equal opportunity employer."

Sal Khan underscored this last point in a promotional video released that same day. "What's especially heartening is that we're seeing that gain be consistent across gender, race, and socioeconomic groups," he said. "And so this makes us feel really good not just from the Khan Academy's point of view or the College Board's point of view, but just in the overall theme of being able to help level the playing field."

The College Board's announcement got a ton of press: articles in the *Wall Street Journal*, the *Washington Post*, *Education Week*, and newspapers around the country through the Associated Press. Thomas L. Friedman, the best-selling author and *New York Times* columnist, devoted a column to the results. The articles all emphasized those same four points: there were a lot of students using Official SAT Practice; they were spending a lot of time studying; they were gaining a lot of points; and those gains were equally distributed by race, class, and parental education. Official SAT Practice was leveling the playing field at last.

But the press releases and early media coverage seemed to gloss over some important details, namely the demographic breakdown of student gains. How much, exactly, were students from different racial and income groups studying, and how much were they gaining? But the College Board wasn't saying much publicly beyond its one broad claim: that students from every group were gaining the same amount. When one or two reporters asked for more details, the College Board replied that it would not be publicly releasing score gains among specific demographic groups.

There was one particular fact they *were* willing to share: that "underrepresented minorities" were spending more time practicing than their white peers. It was precisely the point that Sal Khan had alluded to in Mountain View the previous fall: black students were practicing more than white ones. I heard David Coleman say the same thing in a speech the previous December in Washington, DC. The implication was clear, even if the details were still fuzzy: students from every group were using Official SAT Practice more or less equally, but traditionally disadvantaged groups were using it more than traditionally advantaged groups.

BUT INSIDE the College Board's offices in Lower Manhattan in the spring of 2017, the organization's data analysts had been looking at numbers that told a very different story than the one the public had been given. And those analysts were concerned.

It was true that studying for twenty hours on Official SAT Practice was associated with an average score gain of 115 points. But what the College Board didn't tell the public was that very few students had studied that many hours. The College Board sent invitations to 1,075,000 students in the high school class of 2017, encouraging them to link their College Board account to a free account on Khan Academy. Fewer than a quarter of those students — 250,000 — actually linked their accounts. Most of those 250,000 students studied for just a few hours, or not at all. Only 8,000 students across the country did at least twenty hours of practice and achieved that average gain of 115 points. So while the headline number in the College Board's media releases was technically accurate — twenty hours of practice did lead students to sizable gains — it left out the fact that fewer than 1 percent of the students who were invited to link their accounts actually studied that much. (The claim that 40 percent of students who took the SAT had used Khan Academy was based on a phone survey that the College Board later acknowledged to me was less reliable than the actual user data from Khan Academy, which suggested much lower usage rates.)

This is where dealing with the College Board grew especially frustrating — and my faith in the organization's good intentions began to wear thin. If only a tiny percentage of students studied for twenty hours, why lead your public presentation with that group's results? When I spoke later that summer with Aaron Lemon-Strauss, the College Board executive who led the collaboration with Khan Academy, he explained that the decision had been driven by a desire for positive media coverage. There was an original draft of the press release, Lemon-Strauss explained, that featured a chart comparing the effect of zero hours of Khan study (an average gain of sixty points over students' PSAT scores), with the effect of five hours (an average gain of eighty-four points) and ten hours (an average gain of ninety-seven points). That chart would have indicated much smaller gains than the numbers the College Board eventually released, but they would have been much more representative of what typical students actually achieved using Official SAT Practice.

Lemon-Strauss told me he liked that version, but he explained frankly that it was rejected by the College Board's communications team. "The pushback was, 'Well, we should be aspirational,'" Lemon-

Strauss said. Even if only a small number of students achieved those big point gains, their stories "were aspirational and inspirational and, to be honest, those stories get more press attention."

Then there was the question of the superachievers: the students who gained 200 points or more. What the College Board had found in the data, but didn't reveal to the public, was the odd fact that those students were not particularly big users of Official SAT Practice on Khan Academy. They studied for an average of less than seven hours on the site, less than half as long as the twenty-hour students who gained 115 points. Either the 200-point students were statistical outliers, able to achieve big gains with relatively little practice, or, more likely, they were doing lots of additional test prep somewhere else.

What really alarmed people inside the College Board's offices was the demographic data. For more than two years, they had been leading the public to believe that Official SAT Practice was closing or reversing historical gaps between the advantaged and the disadvantaged. In a 2016 presentation at South by Southwest about the Khan Academy collaboration, Coleman made this claim in a particularly dramatic way: "Never in my career have I seen a launch of technology at this scale that has broken down the racial divisions that so haunt this nation — never."

But the actual data were telling a different story.

A few times during the year leading up to the announcement of the results, data scientists from Khan Academy and the College Board got together in person for events they called hackathons. Because student data was too sensitive to send over the internet, the data scientists would carry their physical hard drives with them across the country to these hackathons. They would set up shop for a couple of days in a conference room in Washington or Silicon Valley, laptops and cans of Diet Coke scattered everywhere, and together they would try to make sense of the vast amounts of data they were collecting from the hundreds of thousands of students who were using Khan Academy and taking the SAT.

In March 2017, at the final hackathon before the May media release, the data scientists analyzed students' score gains according to a number of different demographic divisions. They found some good news, and they found some bad news. The good news — which was later released to the media — was that an hour of practice on Khan Academy seemed to increase students' test scores by a roughly equal amount no matter who you were. Twenty hours of practice raised wealthy students' scores by an average of 109 points; twenty hours of practice raised low-income students' scores by an average of 113 points.

The bad news — which was not released to the media — was that students in different demographic groups were not practicing for equivalent lengths of time. One PowerPoint slide that came out of the hackathon summed up the problem quite succinctly: "There *is* variation in Khan usage across different demographic groups. Among students who spent any time practicing on Khan, those who are Asian, male, and with more educated and higher income parents spent more time on Khan."

It was true, as Coleman and Khan had claimed, that black students, on average, spent a bit more time using Official SAT Practice than white students did. But the advantage that black students had over white students in study time was the *only* instance of a traditionally disadvantaged group using the site more than a traditionally advantaged group did. In every other case, the more advantaged students were the ones who used the site more. Asian students spent almost twice as long on the site as either black or Latino students did. Students in the top income quartile used the site for more time than students in the bottom income quartile. Boys used it longer than girls. Whites used it longer than Latinos.

The sharpest divides were by parental education: students whose parents had only a high school degree spent a little more than three hours on Official SAT Practice, on average, while students whose parents had attended graduate school spent almost five hours.

And because the effect of an hour of study on a student's score gain was consistent among all these groups, the extra hours of study that the more privileged students took advantage of meant that their scores increased more, as well. On the whole, according to the data from the hackathon, Official SAT Practice on Khan Academy had *increased* the existing gaps between students in groups that tended to score higher on the SAT and students in groups that tended to score lower.

The data analysts detected the same rich-get-richer effect when they divided students by their PSAT scores. Official SAT Practice wasn't helping struggling students catch up — it was allowing students who were already testing well to increase their advantage over the rest of the pack. Only about 10 percent of students with PSAT scores below 610 (quite low) spent any time on Khan Academy, and those who did log on spent less than two hours studying. By contrast, almost 30 percent of students with PSAT scores above 1220 (quite high) logged into Official SAT Practice, and those who did spent an average of five hours on the site.

The full picture painted by the data was, in other words, exactly the scenario that Sal Khan and I had each been worried about when we spoke the previous fall. Apart from that one anomalous result — the welcome finding that black students were, on average, studying a few minutes more than white students — Official SAT Practice was consistently reinforcing the privilege of precisely those students who already enjoyed lots of advantages in applying to college. Despite the best intentions of Coleman and Khan, their collaboration was not leveling the college-access playing field at all. It had made it more uneven than ever.

BACK IN 2016, when Aaron Lemon-Strauss and his team at the College Board were getting the first batches of data from the hackathons, they began to notice the pattern: plenty of students were creating Khan Academy accounts, but very few of them were sticking around to do much SAT practice. "We realized we had a bit of a hollow story," Lemon-Strauss told me. "We could declare partial victory in terms of all the students that were checking it out, but it wasn't much of a victory if they weren't spending very much time. We're not doing a lot for the world if we get a kid to go do half an hour's worth of practice on Khan Academy."

Clearly, this wasn't the story that the College Board chose to share with the world a year later. But internally, it was a big question: How do you make kids study harder? This question began to drive the work Lemon-Strauss and his team were doing. But he realized early on that they didn't have any particular expertise in inspiring students to stay motivated and keep working. So Lemon-Strauss and his team went looking for help.

As it happened, two prominent social scientists at the University of Pennsylvania — Angela Duckworth, a psychology professor, and Katherine Milkman, a professor with joint appointments at Penn's business school and medical school — had recently undertaken a vast interdisciplinary project they were calling Behavior Change for Good. Their highly ambitious goal was to improve human motivation in a variety of ways: to help people study harder, save more money for retirement, and go to the gym more often. Coleman and Lemon-Strauss asked Duckworth and Milkman if they could help motivate students to spend more time on Official SAT Practice, and the professors offered to try. They just needed funding.

During this same period in late 2016, Coleman had been having regular conversations with Jim Shelton, the former deputy secretary of education under President Obama. Shelton had just been hired by Mark Zuckerberg, the CEO of Facebook, and his wife, Priscilla Chan, to oversee education giving for the Chan Zuckerberg Initiative, or CZI, the philanthropic organization the couple had founded a year earlier as a vehicle to give away, in a strategic fashion, the bulk of their $60 billion fortune. Zuckerberg and Chan are proponents of what they call personalized learning — using adaptive technologies to create tailored educational pathways for individual students. Official

SAT Practice was a particularly ambitious example of personalized learning. So in May 2017 CZI gave the College Board a multimillion-dollar grant, with about a million dollars earmarked specifically for Duckworth and Milkman's project to increase motivation among students doing SAT practice on Khan Academy.

That same month, Duckworth and Milkman brought together in Philadelphia a remarkable assembly of two dozen or so of the most prestigious academics who studied behavior change, including economists like David Laibson, the chair of the Harvard economics department, and psychologists like Adam Grant, the best-selling author of *Originals* and other books. Daniel Kahneman, the Nobel Prize–winning author of *Thinking, Fast and Slow*, gave a keynote speech to the assembled experts, and over two days, they brainstormed strategies and offered advice on how to influence, in a lasting way, people's behavior — including students using Official SAT Practice.

Over the next six months, Duckworth and Lemon-Strauss and other researchers worked together to try to create an experimental intervention that would help to even out some of the demographic discrepancies that were appearing in the Khan Academy data. The original plan was to test out a variety of interventions on students who had signed up for Official SAT Practice. Some would get financial incentives to study more. Others would get regular text messages that would nudge them to sit down and study. Another group would see testimonials from older students that would encourage them to associate studying on Khan Academy with the kind of grown-up time-management behaviors they would need to employ in college. The plan was to time the interventions to the SAT exam that millions of American students would take in October 2017. The researchers could compare the average scores of each experimental group and determine which intervention had been most effective.

But as the October test date approached, it gradually became apparent that Khan Academy's data scientists would not be able to give the researchers the data they wanted in a fine-grained enough way to be useful. At almost the last minute, the research team switched gears rather radically. They dropped the Khan Academy experiment altogether and decided instead to study the effect of these interventions on students who used an older, more rudimentary SAT study tool: a "Question of the Day" smartphone app the College Board had created a few years earlier. Unfortunately, there weren't enough potential students to test out each intervention, so they pared the experiment back to just a single condition: a campaign to send students regular motivational text-message reminders. The researchers sent thousands of texts to students before each of the three SAT exams scheduled in the fall of 2017. Then they waited for the results. Had students who received the texts studied more?

We will never know, unfortunately. As Christmas approached, the College Board's analysts explained to the researchers that they were having trouble merging the data from the app with the data from the SAT exam itself, and by January 2018, when the College Board finally sent the merged data over to the researchers, it contained information on only 178 students, out of more than a million who had taken the exams. It was impossible to draw any conclusions from such a small sample.

This was the pattern with the College Board during the early years of David Coleman's presidency: one grand, well-publicized attempt after another to make the SAT more equitable and more fair, ending either in quiet failure or in a noisy claim of success that fell apart under more careful scrutiny.

By other measures, though, the early Coleman era was an extraordinarily successful one for the College Board. Back in 2012, remember, the organization was in an existential crisis. The number of students who took the SAT had for the first time fallen behind the number of students who took the ACT. As of 2014, there were thirteen states that had contracts with ACT to administer the test statewide; only two states had signed comparable contracts with the College Board.

But under Coleman's leadership, the College Board launched a campaign to stop and then reverse the slow drift of students and states to the ACT. The first step came in 2015, when Coleman persuaded Michigan's education department to abandon the state's long-standing partnership with ACT and sign a multimillion-dollar contract with the College Board to offer the SAT to every high school junior in the state. The next dominoes to fall were Illinois and Colorado, two more longtime ACT states that signed new contracts with the College Board. By 2017, there were contracts for the SAT with Connecticut and New Hampshire and New York City. The tide had turned.

When the new SAT debuted in 2016, David Coleman was profiled by Nick Anderson, a reporter for the *Washington Post*. Anderson pressed him about the finances of the College Board. Was the new SAT really about creating a more equitable college-access landscape? Or was it a product launch designed to compete with the ACT? Coleman seemed bothered by the idea that he might be motivated by something other than the interests of low-income students. He stood up during the interview and paced around his office. "I can do things, I really can, because they are good and just," he told Anderson.

Coleman cited Official SAT Practice as a prime example of his willingness to sacrifice revenue in order to further the cause of social justice: "You could have thought that test prep is *our* natural business," he said to Anderson. "If I was a pure businessman, why not expand into it? The facts of the case are, I destroyed several sources of revenue at one stroke—all that test prep we could have charged for." Coleman said similar things to me in our interviews: partnering with Khan Academy and sending out the Hoxby packets would inevitably put a dent in the College Board's finances, he told me, but it was worth it to level the playing field and boost the college prospects of less privileged students.

I do believe that Coleman cared, on a personal level, about the inequities in higher education and that the measures put in place by him may well have been a genuine attempt to address those inequities. But the financial argument he made to me and to Anderson ignored a basic fact of the testing marketplace. There was an obvious reason that a "pure businessman" would embark on a series of high-profile equity-promoting initiatives: to improve the SAT's dismal public reputation. In the era of state contracts, millions of dollars in testing fees can flow to either ACT Inc. or the College Board based on the decisions of a small number of education officials and politicians in state capitals. Those leaders don't want to sign contracts with institutions their constituents might consider to be discriminatory and unfair. That's how the College Board was perceived in 2012, when Coleman became president.

By 2017, the SAT and the College Board had been successfully rebranded in the public's mind as allies of the downtrodden and dispossessed. Well-publicized initiatives like the Hoxby packets and the Khan Academy collaboration hadn't had much if any positive effect on student outcomes. But the public didn't necessarily know that. Meanwhile, the overall distribution of SAT scores by family income was as unbalanced as ever. If anything, the gaps between the scores of affluent students and poor ones seemed to have grown even wider. For the thousands of low-income students who did well in their high school classes but struggled to earn high scores on the SAT, the test remained what it had always been for students like them: not an invitation to opportunity, but a barrier to it.

Armed with its new collection of state contracts, the College Board in 2018 reclaimed from ACT the lead in their decades-long competition for test supremacy. Iowa City fell to New York City once again. A record 2.1 million students took the SAT that year — nearly a million of them during the school day. The financial health of the College Board had recovered and was in fact stronger than ever. In its 2017 financial declaration, the College Board reported gross receipts for the year of more than $1.3 billion and total net assets — money in the bank — of $1.1 billion, another record. Coleman's personal compensation had grown along with the College Board's fortunes. He earned $750,000 a year when he was hired in 2012. Five years later, the College Board's grateful trustees had doubled his salary, and he was taking home more than $1.5 million a year.

3. Blessed

Back in his office in Washington, DC, Ned Johnson did not pretend that he was leveling the college playing field. He loved his tutoring work; he enjoyed the feeling of helping stressed-out teenagers learn to overcome their anxieties and believe in themselves. He liked the fact that as a result of his help, his students' scores usually went up and they often got into excellent colleges. But he had no illusions that the national college-admissions system was fair, and he was fully aware that the work he did every day to boost the scores of his affluent students made that system less equitable, not more so.

Sometimes, though, Ned would decide to use his powers for good, taking on a student pro bono from the kind of family that wouldn't be able to afford his services otherwise.

Ben Dormus was one of those students. The path that led Ben to Ned's office was highly unusual. Ben was the son of a black Haitian father and a white Canadian mother, both of whom had had long careers as social workers. For most of his life, his mother and father had worked as "house parents" in residential schools, living alongside young people from difficult backgrounds, often with serious behavioral problems, and providing them with counseling, support, and companionship. Ben and his family moved around a lot when he was young — from Miami to North Carolina to Calgary to Hershey, Pennsylvania. And then in the summer of 2015, when Ben was about to start his junior year in high school, the family moved to Washington, DC, when Ben's parents were hired as the directors of student life at Monument Academy, a free charter boarding school for students who had spent time in the foster care system.

House parenting is not a lucrative profession, and Ben's parents never had much money. They had both overcome challenges of their own when they were younger: Ben's dad emigrated from Haiti to Brooklyn as a teenager not speaking a word of English; Ben's mom grew up in a dysfunctional home in small-town Ontario. Things had not always been easy in Ben's family, especially early on in his parents' marriage, and Ben's older siblings had struggled as well. But by the time Ben came along, his parents were older and more established, and his upbringing, though never lavish, was full of books and public radio and conversations about politics. They were Seventh-day Adventists, and they took their faith seriously, living simply, trying to dedicate themselves to serving the common good. Ben was nine when Barack Obama was elected president, and even at that young age, he noticed some appealing similarities between himself and the president: both biracial, both the children of immigrant fathers, both from families without a lot of money. They even looked a little alike; people remarked on it. Obama's example gave Ben a sense of possibility and fired up his interest in politics and social policy.

When Ben and his family arrived in DC, they needed to figure out quickly where he would attend his last two years of high school. The default option was a large, low-performing neighborhood public school, but the founder of Monument Academy, his parents' boss, a woman named Emily Bloomfield, steered Ben instead toward a small magnet public school called School Without Walls that emphasized internships and experiential learning. Ben loved it, and as his junior year got underway, Bloomfield continued to talk with him about his education and particularly about his college prospects. She saw great potential in Ben, and when she introduced him to her husband, Byron Auguste, Auguste began to take an interest in Ben's future as well.

Auguste, it seemed, knew everybody. He was a Yale graduate with a PhD in economics from Oxford. He had worked for twenty years at McKinsey & Company, the consulting firm, rising to become its first African American senior partner. In 2013 he was named deputy director of President Obama's National Economic Council, and he was now running his own workforce-development nonprofit. Auguste and Ben began having long conversations about Ben's college plans. Auguste encouraged Ben to set his sights on Ivy League colleges, something Ben had never considered. In the spring of his junior year, Auguste arranged a weekend visit for Ben to Yale, where Auguste was a trustee, and where his and Bloomfield's own son was an undergraduate. Ben loved Yale. It was like nothing he had ever seen. It immediately became his dream school.

The only thing standing in Ben's way was the SAT.

Ben had taken the PSAT back in the fall of his junior year. He did very well on the verbal side — 720 out of 800, putting him in the top few percent nationally — but his math score was less impressive: a 580, which put him only in the top third of all students. Not exactly Yale material. Like millions of other students who had taken the PSAT that year, Ben got an email from the College Board inviting him to study for the SAT using Official SAT Practice on Khan Academy. Ben linked his accounts and dove in, spending many Saturday nights watching Sal Khan's videos and doing one practice question after another. In March of his junior year, Ben took the SAT for the first time. Despite all that practice, his scores didn't improve — in fact, his math score went *down* twenty points from where he had scored on the PSAT.

"That was a real shock," Ben told me. "It was very disheartening. I had all these notions of where I might go to college, what I might want to study. And you start to doubt yourself. When I talked to Byron, he said everything else was strong — I had a strong GPA, such a strong extracurricular involvement, got this great reading score, great scores on AP exams. But I literally felt like my math score on the SAT was bringing down everything about me."

It was at this point that Byron Auguste kicked Project Ben into high gear. He contacted Barbara Bergman, a private college coach who had spent sixteen years as the head of college counseling at the prestigious Georgetown Day School, and she agreed to take on Ben as a pro bono client. She, in turn, emailed Ned Johnson and asked if he would help Ben with test prep, and he said yes as well. As his senior year began, Ben, who in every other way was a fairly typical working-class or middle-class kid, suddenly found himself with a powerful mentor in his corner as well as free help from perhaps the best college-admissions coach and the best test-prep tutor in the DC area.

I first met Ben in Ned's Tenleytown office in October of Ben's senior year, the day after he had taken the SAT for the second time. Though he didn't yet know his score, he was feeling much better about his college prospects than he had the previous spring, and he attributed his new confidence to Ned's tutoring. What he was learning from Ned, he said, was different from what he had learned on Khan Academy. With Khan's lessons, the message was that there was just one way to do the math. "Sal is just very dry and cold-cut," Ben explained. "You can't say, 'Can you show me another way?' or 'Can you slow it down?'" With Ned, there was more face-to-face interaction, obviously, more back-and-forth. But Ned's tutoring also carried with it his underlying, and somewhat subversive, psychological message: that the SAT is not designed to measure your math ability. It is designed to measure your ability to take the SAT.

Ben was a convert. "Ned teaches you how to do the math," he said, "but he also teaches you the tricks and the strategies. His philosophy is: It doesn't matter if you're doing the math or not. It's about getting the answer right. If you can find a shortcut, even if it's not the most elegant math, then you should use it. All those tips and tricks and tools make you feel better, because now you know you have multiple ways to attack a problem."

"Did you have any opportunities to plug in numbers on the test yesterday?" Ned asked Ben.

"Oh yeah, for sure," Ben replied.

They were talking about a classic Ned technique: solving algebra problems by plugging simple numbers into the equation in place of variables. When it works, it magically turns a complicated algebra problem into a simple arithmetic one. Often you can find the answer without really solving the equation at all. Ben found that Ned's shortcut had helped him speed up on the test—but even more than that, it gave him back the confidence that his previous SAT score had shattered.

"I felt way more confident," Ben said. "Once you realize that there are loopholes and backdoors to the test, it loses its value. If you can skirt around what they want you to do and still get the right answer, you realize at that point that they're not really testing skills."

David Coleman's message to the media was that the new SAT and the Khan Academy collaboration were a knife to the heart of businesses like Ned's. The announcement of their introduction, remember, was supposed to be a "bad day" for test prep. But as Ned sat in his office, laughing and joking with Ben, he did not seem to be having a bad day. Business was as strong as ever. There was yet another $400-an-hour student sitting out front in the reception area, waiting his turn with Ned.

When we talked about the College Board's ongoing PR campaign, though, Ned started to get riled up. He was particularly teed off about Coleman's claim that the College Board was now "daring to take seriously the corruptions that have arisen around the exam process" because of "costly test prep" — a line that Ned could recite verbatim from a YouTube video Coleman and Khan had made three years earlier. Ned agreed with Coleman that there was something corrupt about the business they had both chosen. But to Ned, those corruptions were not something that he and his tutoring peers — stretching all the way back to Stanley Kaplan — had introduced into the system. To Ned, the corruptions were inherent in the test itself.

"If the SAT and the ACT continue to have an outsize role in college admissions, then anybody with any drive, with any sense, with any money is going to say, 'Geez, can we do a little better on the test?'" Ned explained. "The fact that people like me exist is not Ben's fault. He didn't start the process."

It was the strangest fact about Ned. His professional livelihood depended on colleges continuing to take the SAT and the ACT very seriously. But whenever he got the opportunity, he tried to convince the world that colleges should do the opposite — that they should downplay standardized tests in favor of more nuanced evaluations of students' ability. Ned would prefer to live in a world in which a sub-par SAT score wouldn't keep Ben out of Yale — even if it meant that Ned and test-prep professionals like him would have to find another way to make a living.

A few weeks later, Ben Dormus received his new SAT scores from the College Board. His math score — which went *down*, remember, when he studied with Khan Academy — had, with Ned's help, gone up by 110 points, from 560 (out of 800) to 670. That catapulted Ben from about the sixty-fifth percentile nationally to the ninetieth per-centile. And that did the trick. The following month, Yale admitted Ben to its undergraduate class of 2021. He would be attending his dream school. His life had changed.

Ben's unusual experience in the world of college admissions had given him a unique perspective on the intersections between social class and higher education in the United States. Because a few in-fluential and well-connected people decided they liked and believed in him and took him under their collective wing, he was able to get a rare glimpse into what applying to college is like when you have money and power. And to be honest, he told me later, he wasn't quite sure what to think about it. He felt lucky and grateful — "tremen-dously blessed," as he put it. "But at the same time," he added, "who am I leaving behind? Who am I betraying? The playing field has been leveled for *me* — but why should it be leveled for me alone? That has been tough for me to reconcile. Why is it that *I* deserve these things over anybody else? Why is it that *anybody* deserves these things over anybody else?"

IV

FITTING IN

---

1. The Outsider

On the first day of the first precept of her freshman Humanities Sequence at Princeton, KiKi Gilbert was the first student to arrive in class. Her precept—that's the Princeton word for a discussion section —was scheduled to meet each Tuesday and Thursday afternoon in a large room on the main floor of Joseph Henry House, a 179-year-old yellow brick mansion at the north end of campus. KiKi's first thought when she walked in was that she must have come to the wrong place. The room felt more like a formal Victorian drawing room than a classroom, something airlifted out of another century and dropped here in southern New Jersey. There was a fireplace along one wall with birch logs stacked in front of it. Brass chandeliers hung from the ceiling. In the corner stood an upright piano. The heavy dark wooden table in the center of the room was polished so intently that KiKi could see her reflection.

She sat down in one of the leather-backed chairs that surrounded the table and watched as her classmates arrived, in twos and threes, laughing and chattering and clutching their highlighted and underlined copies of *The Odyssey* and *The Iliad,* ready to talk about big ideas. The Humanities Sequence was a Princeton institution, a no-toriously rigorous full-year course for a few dozen freshmen taught collaboratively by six professors. You had to apply to get in. Over the course of the year, students read and discussed sixty classic works of literature and philosophy, from Homer to Virginia Woolf, with stops along the way for Plato, Dante, and Nietzsche. Lectures were held twice a week, but the heart of the course was the precept, these eighty-minute-long Socratic seminars in which fifteen or so intel-lectually ambitious teenagers gathered around a table and traded thoughts on the foundational texts of Western civilization.

There was a part of KiKi that had always believed she would end up in a room like this one, discussing books like these, however un-likely that outcome might sometimes have seemed. In third grade, she and her family were living in a rundown neighborhood in Eliza-beth, New Jersey, a fading industrial port city that was, as it hap-pened, less than an hour up the turnpike from Princeton. Her teacher that year, a black woman named Ms. Denise, was the first person who had ever called attention to KiKi's precocious intelligence. She told KiKi she was something special, the smartest student she had ever encountered. She gave her advanced work and introduced her to Harry Potter and told her that if she worked hard, her brain could take her anywhere she wanted to go.

KiKi had spent the last decade trying to live up to Ms. Denise's faith in her, and she had made it to Princeton despite enormous obstacles. Most of the time now she felt pretty sure of herself, confident in her intelligence and her ability. But today, her heart was pounding in her chest, and she couldn't get it to stop. She was anxious, consumed by doubt. It wasn't that she doubted *herself*, exactly. It was that she felt certain that everyone *else* doubted her, that all the other students tak-ing their seats around the table didn't believe she belonged in this room with them. KiKi could feel them looking at her as they filed in, and in everyone's eyes, she could see the same question: What is *she* doing here?

KiKi stood out in the room in one obvious way: she was black, the only dark-skinned African American student in her precept and one of maybe two or three in the whole Humanities Sequence. And at Princeton, her race felt like an issue. A week earlier, KiKi had attended Princeton's Academic Expo, an annual ritual just before classes begin. Each academic department sets up a booth in the atrium of the chemistry building, and first-year students who are trying to decide on a major can ask questions of professors and graduate students. KiKi already knew what she wanted to study at Princeton: philosophy. She had taken two years of introductory philosophy in high school, and she genuinely loved it. But she had a second defining interest, both personally and intellectually, and that was race: the complicated and thorny question of what it meant to be black in America.

So at the expo, she headed straight to the philosophy table and told the professor sitting there — who was white, like every other philosophy professor at Princeton — that she wanted to major in philosophy and study the intersections of philosophy and race. Hmm, he replied. We don't really do that kind of thing in our department. If that's what you want to pursue, you would probably do better to major in African American studies. To KiKi, already on high alert for signals of rejection and exclusion, it felt like a slap: We don't want you here.

And as her fellow students continued to file into the precept room, KiKi was aware of another important difference between them and her. She was poor, and most of them were rich. They had spent their young lives in an expansive world of boarding schools and tennis camps and vacation homes, while KiKi's childhood had been circumscribed by food stamps and subsidized housing and late car payments. That difference was perhaps less immediately evident than her race, but it still felt radiantly clear to KiKi. And whether it was her class or her race, her skin or her clothes, KiKi felt entirely out of place in Joseph Henry House.

KiKi tried her best to calm her racing heart, tried to convince herself that it was all in her head, that she did belong here, that her classmates weren't really judging her. These were liberal arts college students, after all, at the height of the "stay woke" era. But as they all opened their copies of *The Odyssey* and the discussion began, KiKi couldn't help but notice that every single seat at the table was now filled — except the two chairs on either side of her. She was isolated and alone in more ways than one.

THE RECENT HISTORY of American higher education is in part a story of stratification. Caroline Hoxby, in her research, described the way students with especially high test scores have over the last few decades converged on the nation's most selective colleges and universities, making those institutions less and less accessible to everyone else. Raj Chetty's research revealed that in parallel with this concentration of *high-scoring* students has come a concentration of *wealthy* students on highly selective campuses — and an almost complete exclusion, on those campuses, of students from the lowest income tiers. The boom in Ned Johnson's business, meanwhile, gives us a glimpse into *why* those two trends might be running in parallel: high-priced expertise like his helps affluent students acquire the ultrahigh test scores that those selective institutions demand. (The College Board's public relations machinations seem mostly to have been an attempt to distract attention from the fact that the SAT and the ACT were the instruments that helped to enable this concentration of privilege.)

Still, while it is true that only a small number of students from poor families are admitted these days to the most prestigious American universities, that number is not zero. There are some, like KiKi, who find a way to make it through the gates. But even then, they are not immune from the economic divides that define so much of higher education today.

While my reporting for this book took me to a broad spectrum of American higher education institutions, I visited a number of superselective colleges in my travels, and whenever I did, I would try to meet and speak with low-income and first-generation students enrolled there. (By "first-generation," I mean students whose parents didn't graduate from college.) Those students were all unique individuals, of course, each situation different. But in our conversations, I would notice certain repeated refrains: The students were grateful for the opportunities they had been given, and they recognized how lucky they were to be receiving a heavily subsidized, top-notch education. But on a day-to-day basis, they often found life at college to be emotionally exhausting. Being surrounded by so much concentrated wealth and privilege made them feel alienated and confused—and sometimes just plain mad.

Not long ago, a student in KiKi's position—a first-generation student from a low-income family attending a wealthy and highly selective college—might have felt entirely alone in her predicament. But in just the last few years, students like KiKi have begun speaking up and connecting with one another, across elite campuses and across the nation, gaining a sense of solidarity, and even identity, along the way. You can trace the beginnings of this new movement to 2013, when a new organization at Stanford called the First Generation and Low-Income Partnership organized a student workshop called "Class Confessions." Before the event, participating students, rich and poor, anonymously submitted stories about moments on campus when they had deliberately concealed their class background. The organizers printed those stories on brightly colored pieces of paper and posted them on bulletin boards that lined the walls of the room where they met. Over pizza, about fifty students read and discussed each other's confessions, many sharing for the first time these personal and sometimes awkward memories.

That workshop inspired low-income students at the University of Chicago to start a Class Confessions Facebook page, where students could anonymously post their stories of class anxiety at college. Similar anonymous Facebook and Tumblr pages soon emerged at Northwestern and Columbia and Brown, and by the end of that year hundreds of students had revealed their previously hidden secrets: going hungry during spring break, while the dining hall was closed; sending scholarship money home to broke relatives; feeling intimidated by the spending habits and vacation stories of wealthier classmates.

As time went on, the groups and events became less about rich and poor students communicating across class lines and more about low-income students talking among themselves, building a community. In 2014 students at Brown started a national organization, called 1vyG, to bring together first-generation students attending Ivy League and other highly selective colleges, and in the winter of 2015, 250 first-generation students from around the Ivy League and beyond gathered at Brown for the inaugural 1vyG conference. It is now an annual event.

ANTHONY ABRAHAM JACK, a young sociologist at Harvard, has spent much of the past decade compiling a detailed ethnographic study of the lives of first-generation students at elite universities. Not too long ago, Jack was one of those students himself; he was raised in the working-class, mostly black Miami neighborhood of West Grove by his single mother, who worked as a middle school security guard and never earned more than about $30,000 a year. When he was growing up, West Grove was pretty dicey, with incidents of gang violence and criminal drug activity, but Jack was a diligent student from an early age — a "pudgy nerd," as he described his younger self to me — and his mother helped guide him from Head Start to a gifted program in elementary school to a magnet middle school and then to an International Baccalaureate diploma program at Coral Gables Senior High. Jack is a big guy, tall and broad, and when he got to high school, he was persuaded to play football. He never saw the sport as anything more than a hobby, but he had the ideal physique for a tackle, and he excelled at protecting the quarterback.

At the end of his junior year of high school, he won an academic scholarship that allowed him to transfer, for his senior year, to Gulliver Prep, an elite private school in the Miami area with a forty-acre campus. Looking back, Jack believes that that one year at Gulliver altered his path through life more than any other. The football coach at Amherst College, a small, highly selective private college in western Massachusetts, made it a habit, every year, of calling up the Gulliver coach to see if he had any standout players who could handle the academic demands of Amherst. Usually the answer was no. But in 2002, during Tony Jack's senior year, the Gulliver coach told the Amherst coach that he might want to take a look at Jack's stats: six foot five, 1200 on the SAT, and a stellar GPA. The coach was impressed, and Tony Jack was awarded a full scholarship to Amherst, where he played varsity tackle for a year and then quit football to concentrate on his studies.

When Jack arrived at Amherst in 2003, the institution had just hired a new president, Anthony Marx, who had declared that it would be his mission to increase the number of low-income students on the Amherst campus; over the course of Marx's eight-year tenure, he would go on to boost the percentage of students eligible for a federal Pell grant from 13 percent to 22 percent. (The Pell grant is awarded based on financial need; about a third of American undergraduates have family incomes low enough to qualify.) As an undergraduate, Jack became something of an ally for Marx, offering Marx a student's perspective on his diversity strategy, encouraging him to consider not just the *number* of low-income students on the Amherst campus but also the *quality* of their collegiate experience.

Jack is a born noticer, a man with an eye for subtle status clues, and he became, at Amherst, an especially astute observer of the fine distinctions that existed between different categories of first-generation students on campus. He realized that the year he had spent at Gulliver, embedded in an environment of affluence, had helped prepare him, somewhat, for the culture shock that arriving at Amherst inevitably produced in low-income students. Poor kids who came to Amherst having never been around wealth were often totally freaked out, Jack noticed, by the riches they saw around them, while the cohort of low-income students who had attended elite boarding schools on scholarship before arriving on campus as freshmen seemed much more comfortable, or at least inured to the shock. Understanding the contours — and the implications — of those different reactions became Tony Jack's mission as an academic. After leaving Amherst, he enrolled in a doctoral program in sociology at Harvard, where he set about using the tools of that field to investigate the experiences of first-generation and low-income students at elite colleges.

Jack spent two years doing intensive fieldwork at an elite American college, conducting in-depth interviews with low-income students, and those interviews became the basis for his PhD dissertation and also for his first book, *The Privileged Poor,* which was published in the spring of 2019. Following the traditional practice of sociologists, he uses pseudonyms in the dissertation and the book for the students he interviewed, and he also uses a pseudonym — Renowned University — for the institution where he did his fieldwork. Since I'm not a sociologist, I'm not obliged to follow the conventions of sociology, so I can tell you that I suspect the university where he did his fieldwork was Harvard, since that's where he was working and studying during the years he was conducting his interviews. (I'll call the college "Renowned" here, as he does, but you should feel free to just replace that word with "Harvard" in your mind each time you see it.)

Jack interviewed more than a hundred undergraduates, inviting them one by one into his office to sit on his beat-up old couch and talk. About half of the students Jack interviewed were black, and because Jack shared so much of their background and so many of their past experiences, they often sensed in him a kindred spirit. The conversations would go on for hours, often requiring multiple sessions to complete. Jack supplemented his formal interviews with informal conversations with students in cafeterias and common rooms. For a time he convened regular Thursday-night watch parties for *Scandal,* the Kerry Washington ABC drama, that attracted dozens of students.

The project took over Jack's life. At one point he was scheduling four student interviews a day, at 9:00 a.m., noon, 3:00 p.m., and 6:00 p.m., subsisting on takeout meals scarfed down between interviews. The conversations with students were often funny and warm. But they could also be painful, interrupted by tears and full of long-buried anger. After a particularly intense series of interviews, Jack found himself waking up at 2:00 a.m. from vivid nightmares in which he was reliving some of the traumatic events his student subjects had described.

For many of the low-income students Jack interviewed, life at Renowned was confusing and difficult. Jose, a Latino from Los Angeles, said that college had come to feel like a toxic environment. He was a senior, and he explained that the four years had beaten him down, made him quieter and more self-conscious. "We come here, we're so alive and full of hope," Jose told Jack. "This place puts you in a depression." It was isolating, he said. "You feel like you don't fit in. You feel like you're alone, like there's no one that can relate."

William, a white student from a small farming town, said he felt shocked when he saw other students going out and buying lobsters to cook for dinner while there was free food in the dining hall. Ryan, a white student from an Appalachian mining town, told Jack about going with affluent friends to an exclusive eating club and almost committing a major faux pas by drinking from the finger bowl. Valeria, a Latina, said she was tired of explaining to wealthier students why she couldn't afford the ten-dollar cover charge at a campus dance. "It's nice to not have to explain yourself all the time," she said. "Here, less people get me."

COMING TO PRINCETON was not the first time KiKi Gilbert felt like an outsider. Her family moved frequently when she was growing up, and so she was constantly having to start over at new schools. Occasionally she would get a teacher like Ms. Denise, who immediately saw her academic ability. But more often, teachers and administrators would take one look at the new arrival, a small-framed, dark-skinned girl from a family in turmoil, and assume she fit a certain profile: another low-achieving student with limited ambitions.

At the end of KiKi's third-grade year — the Ms. Denise year — KiKi's mother moved the family from Elizabeth, New Jersey, to Indianapolis. The first place they stayed was hit by bullets one night in a drive-by shooting, so they relocated to a slightly nicer neighborhood in the city's northeastern suburbs, which landed KiKi, a few weeks into fourth grade, at a school called Brook Park Elementary.

Academically, Brook Park wasn't much better than KiKi's previous school, but there was one notable difference: Unlike the school in New Jersey, Brook Park had a sizable number of white kids — not the majority of students, by any means, but a considerable fraction. And these weren't just any white kids — they were well-off white kids, from a relatively affluent corner of the school district.

When KiKi first arrived, she was assigned to a classroom full of students who looked a lot like she did. That didn't seem out of the ordinary to KiKi — she had always been in classrooms full of kids who looked like her — until she noticed that there was a fourth-grade classroom right next door where the kids looked different. They were all white. Their classroom was nicer, too — better equipped and better organized. She asked one of her new classmates what was going on, and she was told that at Brook Park, students were grouped by ability. The classroom next door was a "stretch" classroom. Those kids were the smart kids.

If it hadn't been for Ms. Denise the year before, KiKi might not have had the thought that came into her mind next, or at least she might not have expressed it out loud: "But *I'm* one of the smart kids." But because Ms. Denise had helped convince her to be confident in her intelligence, KiKi did say it, and she kept saying it: *I belong next door.*

She talked to her teacher, and then she talked to the principal, and then she persuaded her mom to come in and raise a fuss on her behalf. Though they were resistant at first, the school's administrators finally agreed to let her take a placement test. KiKi aced it, and the next day she was moved to the stretch classroom.

It was not lost on KiKi, even at age nine, that in order to receive the education she needed and deserved, she had to demand to be separated from her fellow black students and placed among the white ones. She had never given much thought, before Brook Park, to her race, but she quickly came to understand that her family's background and the color of her skin were essential to how people saw her. She was black. She was poor. She was being raised by a single parent. And when people she did not know encountered those three facts, they made assumptions about her academic potential — assumptions that KiKi knew to be entirely wrong. It was painful. "My little fourth-grade mind was just racked with fury," she told me.

The chief lesson she learned at Brook Park Elementary, she says, was that if she wanted people to take her seriously as a student, she needed to convey a version of herself that would puncture the assumptions they made about her. She began to speak precisely and properly, jamming as many big words as she could into every sentence. She went to the library once or twice a week, checking out and churning through the thickest books she could find.

As a fourth grader, KiKi read *Little Women* and *David Copperfield*, then moved on to the rest of Dickens. She loved the stories those classic novels told, tales of deprivation and loss and absent fathers, but she mostly used the books as totems to ward off disrespect. She preferred hardcovers, because they were bigger and heavier, and she carried them with her wherever she went, reading in the grocery store, in the doctor's office, in the hallway at school, wielding these big fat books as a kind of intellectual armor, a sign to the world that she belonged in the stretch classroom and was entitled to all the privileges that went along with it.

Fourth grade was the beginning of KiKi's long and challenging fight to be respected for her intelligence. But it was also the beginning of something even more difficult: her search for a place to belong. Back in her school in New Jersey, she had got along with everybody. Even though Ms. Denise had singled her out as the smart girl, she fit in fine in the third-grade classroom. At Brook Park, things were different. She didn't have anything in common with the affluent white kids in her classroom. And all the kids who looked like her and lived like her were next door, doing less challenging work and reading much thinner books. KiKi felt stuck in the middle, at home nowhere.

She had the same dissonant experience in tenth grade, when her family moved to Charlotte, North Carolina, and she transferred to Myers Park High School, one of the most academically prestigious public schools in the city. Just like at Brook Park Elementary, there was a racial divide at Myers Park High, though now the rich kids (almost all of whom were white) were in the majority, and only about a quarter of the students were, like KiKi, black and low-income.

Just like at Brook Park, almost all of the black students at Myers Park were placed in "standard" classes, while most of the white students were in "honors." The most academically ambitious students were enrolled in the school's International Baccalaureate diploma program. KiKi had never heard of IB before arriving at Myers Park, but she quickly came to understand that the IB classrooms were where the smartest kids in the school could be found, and so IB was where she knew she needed to be. Almost all the other students in her IB classes were white or Asian American, with a few students from well-off black families mixed in. And then there was KiKi: the only poor black kid once again.

At Myers Park, the nameless fury that KiKi had felt as a fourth-grade student was focused and honed into an intensely felt racial awareness. KiKi was still reading the biggest, fattest white-establishment novels she could carry: *The Satanic Verses, Gravity's Rainbow, Sense and Sensibility.* But she also started reading Angela Davis and Eldridge Cleaver. She studied the Black Panthers and MOVE, the radical black group whose headquarters were fire-bombed by the Philadelphia police in 1985. She started a pro-black group at Myers Park called PRIDE, and she organized a race symposium to discuss the racial disparities in the makeup of the school's standard and honors and IB classes.

But despite KiKi's full embrace of her black identity, she still felt stuck in the middle. The high-octane education she was receiving meant she spent her days physically separated from the black kids in the standard classrooms. "I don't have a connection to the black student body," she told me when I visited Myers Park during her senior year. "Which is significant to me because that's who I'm fighting for.

But to be frank, I don't have much of a connection with anyone at my school." Her best friend that year was an affluent Chinese American boy in her IB classes who shared her liberal politics and her love of philosophy but whose life beyond the Myers Park campus bore little resemblance to hers.

The one time during high school when KiKi did get to experience a real sense of community was the summer before her senior year, when she was selected to attend the summer institute of Leadership Enterprise for a Diverse America, the same highly demanding college-prep program on Princeton's campus where I met Shannen Torres, the Stanford-bound student from the Bronx I wrote about in chapter 1.

LEDA scholars, who each year included some of the most academically driven and talented low-income high school students in the country, seemed to fall into two broad categories. There were the ones like Shannen: the one academic superstar at a low-performing high school where the majority of students were poor and almost no one went on to an elite college. And then there were the ones like KiKi: the lone low-income student of color on the top academic track at an affluent, mostly white public school where lots of students went on to elite colleges. (There were always a few white low-income students at LEDA's summer institute, but the large majority were black or Latino.)

For students in both categories — the ones like Shannen and the ones like KiKi — high school could feel lonely and isolating. LEDA scholars were, almost by definition, one of a kind at their schools, and it was often hard for them to find anyone to connect with on a deep level. And then suddenly they arrived on Princeton's campus for the summer program and found ninety-nine kids more or less just like them, all longing in the same way for community and connection. It was bliss.

When KiKi was preparing to come back to Princeton as an undergraduate, a year later, she knew it wouldn't be quite the same. She knew she was destined to be in a minority, both racially and economically. But still, she hoped that within that minority at Princeton, she would find her crowd, her family: kids like her who had fought through poverty and racial injustice and, despite the odds, reached the most exclusive level of American higher education.

2. Roots

In October 2017, a couple of months into KiKi's freshman year at Princeton, an article appeared in the *Washington Post* under the headline "How an Ivy Got Less Preppy: Princeton Draws Surge of Students from Modest Means." The article described a campaign by Princeton's leadership, underway for more than a decade, to "shed, once and for all, the reputation of a tradition-steeped university that caters mainly to the preppy and the privileged." Princeton had been making a concerted effort in recent years to enroll more low-income students, the *Post* reported, and the result was "a demographic revolution, with unprecedented numbers of students from modest circumstances becoming Princetonians." According to the article, the share of Princeton freshmen eligible for Pell grants had more than tripled in thirteen years, rising from 7 percent in 2004 to 15 percent in 2013 to 22 percent in KiKi's incoming class.

The *Post* article wasn't the only media attention that Princeton attracted with this new public commitment to admitting low-income students. There was also a *60 Minutes* piece, and the *New York Times* ran a column. The coverage was focused on what Christopher Eisgruber, the president of Princeton, told *60 Minutes* was Princeton's pledge "to be a real leader on socioeconomic diversity."

But the Princeton described in the *Post* and on *60 Minutes* didn't match up with the Princeton that KiKi was experiencing as a freshman. She didn't feel like she was on a campus in the midst of a demographic revolution. Not at all. As far as she could tell, Princeton was just as preppy and privileged as ever. When I spoke to her that fall, she told me she was having a remarkably difficult time finding *anyone* on campus who had traveled the path that she had: a black kid growing up in poverty and making it to this pinnacle of the academic elite.

Over the summer, KiKi had been invited to take part in Princeton's Freshman Scholars Institute, or FSI, a free seven-week orientation program for first-generation and low-income students. She had fun, and she met some people she liked, but there were only a few black kids in the group, and in general the students she met at FSI seemed more working-class or lower-middle-class than genuinely poor. Their experiences growing up were nothing like KiKi's. "My definition of low income is a lot different than Princeton's definition of low income," KiKi explained with a laugh when we spoke on the phone that summer. When the rest of the freshman class arrived in September, the income divide on campus only grew sharper. Everyone around KiKi seemed downright wealthy.

So what was the deal? Demographic revolution, or all-pervading affluence? What was the *Washington Post* seeing on the Princeton campus that KiKi was not—and vice versa?

The answer to that question begins with an understanding of the way Princeton and other institutions calculate the economic diversity of their campuses. The statistic that the *Post* cited is the statistic that pretty much everyone uses: the percentage of the student body, or of the freshman class, that is eligible for a federal Pell grant. "Pell percentage," as it is sometimes called, is a useful marker in many ways, and it is a figure that the federal government collects and reports for each college. But it is also something of a moving target. The federal education department has a complex formula that it uses to determine a family's eligibility for Pell. It depends on parental income, but also on the number of dependent children and the number of children currently in college. Some families making more than $80,000 receive Pell grants, and some earning less than $30,000 do not.

It has also become a lot easier for families to qualify for a Pell grant over the last decade or so. This is partly due to actions the Obama administration took to expand Pell eligibility during the Great Recession and partly due to the decline in real incomes among nonrich American households. The numbers are striking: Consider a family making $50,000 — pretty close to the middle of the middle class, just $10,000 below the national median. In 2000, fewer than one in five students from families earning $50,000 were eligible for a Pell grant. In 2011 more than three in five of those families were eligible.

So it is possible that Princeton and Amherst and other elite colleges that improved their Pell rates during those years did so not by admitting many more genuinely poor students, but by targeting Pell-eligible students close to the cutoff — the $80,000 Pell students rather than the $30,000 Pell students. And in fact, new research published in early 2019 by Caroline Hoxby and Sarah Turner, the economists known best for their targeted mailings to high-achieving low-income high school seniors, showed that certain selective colleges had been doing exactly that.

For their analysis, Hoxby and Turner chose two colleges that had won national recognition for making significant improvements to their Pell percentage. (They didn't identify the colleges publicly.) Using IRS data, they calculated the distribution of family incomes for students enrolled in those colleges and found that the schools were admitting only a few students with truly low incomes. The bulk of Pell students had incomes that were just below the federal cutoff. This "distorted behavior," as Hoxby put it, was made more glaring by the fact that the colleges admitted very few students whose incomes were just *above* the Pell cutoff. The colleges were gaming their numbers, deliberately selecting the highest-income students they could find whose admission would still allow them to claim an impressive Pell percentage. On average, an applicant just below the Pell cutoff was *ten times* more likely to be admitted and enrolled at these celebrated colleges than a student just above the line.

Princeton doesn't release any numbers that would let us determine if it is one of the colleges using the Pell-maximizing admissions practices that Hoxby and Turner uncovered. But there *is* some solid data that came out just before KiKi got to Princeton: the massive analysis of IRS tax records done by the economists Raj Chetty and John Friedman and their colleagues. According to Chetty's data, Princeton was nowhere near being a leader on socioeconomic diversity during those years. In fact, it was one of the least economically diverse institutions in the database of 2,395 American colleges that Chetty compiled.

Chetty's data (as I mentioned in chapter 1) showed that only 2.2 percent of Princeton's students, as of 2013, came from the bottom economic quintile, with family incomes below about $21,000 — the quintile that KiKi's family occupied. Princeton's was the second-lowest rate in the Ivy League, and one of the lowest figures of any college in the country.

Meanwhile, 17 percent of Princeton students came from families in the top 1 percent of the income distribution, and 72 percent came from families in the top fifth of the income distribution, the highest rate in the Ivy League. That means that only a little more than a quarter of Princeton students in 2013 came from the bottom *four* quintiles — basically, from every group but the rich — a figure that put Princeton behind 99 percent of all American colleges in the relative number of nonrich students it enrolled. That's not much of a revolution.

Chetty's data are a couple of years old, and so it is possible that President Eisgruber's latest diversity push will show up in later analyses. But look at the ten years that Chetty analyzed, from 2004 to 2013. During those years, according to Eisgruber and the *Post* article, Princeton more than doubled its Pell percentage, from 7 percent to 15 percent. But in Chetty's more precise data for those same years, the share of Princeton students who came from families in the bottom 40 percent, ranked by income, increased only a tiny amount, from 6.2 percent in 2004 to 7 percent in 2013. Although Princeton had managed to double its Pell percentage, it had only barely increased the number of actual low-income students on its campus.

KIKI'S EXPERIENCE of Princeton's economic diversity was shaped in part by the fact that her social circle, during her freshman year, was populated almost entirely by black Princeton students. And what she discovered, that first semester, was that although those students shared her skin color, they didn't, for the most part, share her economic background.

"Most of the black kids here aren't poor," she told me, her voice conveying a certain astonishment, when we spoke that fall. It had taken her a while to catch on to that fact, and it was taking her even longer to get used to it. When she was growing up, almost every black person KiKi encountered was from a family that struggled with money. That was simply the black America that she knew. But at Princeton, she was able to identify only about a dozen low-income black students in her fourteen-hundred-student freshman class. When she did encounter working-class or low-income students at Princeton, like in the FSI summer program, they were more likely to be white or Hispanic. She found the same thing when she got involved in Princeton's First-Generation Low-Income Council, which helps organize the IvyG conference. There were plenty of low-income white and Latino students who came to the meetings, but KiKi was surprised to find that she was one of the only African Americans.

The black students she met at Princeton were, in general, the children of well-educated professionals and entrepreneurs and corporate executives. They had grown up, mostly, in two-parent families, with family money, going to private schools. Those differences in their experiences created barriers that KiKi sometimes found hard to cross.

There was one other thing KiKi noticed about Princeton's black freshmen: many of them were the children of immigrants or immigrants themselves, their parents having moved to the United States from Africa or the Caribbean, often for work or graduate school.

That was something KiKi hadn't expected. Though she had grown up in mostly black communities, she hadn't met many kids from Africa. At Princeton, though, KiKi came to recognize, kids with recent African or Caribbean roots were everywhere. They seemed to make up the majority of the black student body.

It turns out that this phenomenon exists not only at Princeton but at most Ivy League–level institutions. It just doesn't get talked about all that much. The first people to bring it to public attention, more than fifteen years ago, were two of the nation's most prominent black intellectuals, Lani Guinier and Henry Louis Gates Jr. At a reunion of black alumni of Harvard in the fall of 2003, Gates and Guinier pointed out that most of the alumni in the room were first- or second-generation immigrants from the Caribbean or Africa or the children of mixed-race couples. And that same racial breakdown, they said, was evident at Harvard as a whole. As the *New York Times* reported the following June, Gates and Guinier said that "only about a third" of Harvard's black students "were from families in which all four grandparents were born in this country, descendants of slaves."

Gates and Guinier were basing this conclusion on some rather loose calculations from a variety of sources, none of them fully authoritative. (Harvard has made a point of not releasing official data on demographic variations among its black students.) But in the wake of the article in the *Times,* researchers began to search out better and clearer numbers. A 2007 paper by Douglas Massey, a Princeton sociologist, and colleagues was the first to produce some solid data.

Massey's paper showed that Gates and Guinier were right: first- and second-generation immigrants were vastly overrepresented among black students at highly selective American universities. And the more selective the university was, the higher its ratio of immigrant blacks to native-born blacks. Nationally, somewhere between 9 and 13 percent of the total population of black American eighteen- and nineteen-year-olds are immigrants or the children of immigrants. But at the highly selective colleges that Massey surveyed, 27 percent of black students were immigrants or the children of immigrants. At Ivy League colleges, the figure was 41 percent.

A separate, long-term study looked at the broad combined category that Gates and Guinier had identified: students from black immigrant families plus students with one black and one nonblack parent. The study, called the National Study of College Experience, found that this category had been growing steadily at highly selective private colleges, rising from about 40 percent of black students in the 1980s to about 50 percent in the mid-1990s to about 60 percent in the late 1990s.

Meanwhile, the total black population at elite colleges, which rose in the 1960s and 1970s, has stayed remarkably stable for decades. In a keynote speech at the 2017 conference of the National Association for College Admission Counseling, Shaun Harper, executive director of the Race and Equity Center at the University of Southern California, made a rather dramatic charge. He suggested that Ivy League colleges were essentially colluding with one another to keep their black student populations at exactly the same level.

"It's just too much of a coincidence," Harper said in his NACAC speech. "You mean to tell me that the *exact same* number of black folks applied to Dartmouth and to Stanford and to MIT and to Yale and to Princeton, and they all landed at the *same* place in terms of their enrollment? It just seems to me that there has been some determination about how many black students are worthy of admission to these institutions. It's just too similar."

At this litigious moment in the history of affirmative action, admissions officers at those colleges would be anxious to assure you that they do not collude, especially on matters of admissions and race. But when you look at the data, you can see the point Harper is making. The numbers really are startlingly consistent. About 15 percent of American high school graduates are black, according to the federal education department. But Princeton's student body is 8 percent black. Cornell's is 8 percent black. Brown's is 8 percent black. Yale's is 8 percent black. Harvard's is 8 percent black. The pattern is hard to miss.

And if you go back in time, you see the same thing. That 2004 article in the *Times* about Gates and Guinier reported that Harvard's student body at the time was . . . 8 percent black. The sociologist Jerome Karabel, in his book *The Chosen,* reported that way back in 1984, Harvard's freshman class was . . . 8 percent black. More recently, Princeton's undergraduate student population has been precisely 8 percent black every year since 2008 — except for 2011 and 2012, when it briefly dipped to 7 percent.

Whatever the reason may be for those numbers remaining stable, they are a clear sign that it is unlikely that Princeton (or Harvard or Yale or their peers) will increase the number of black students they admit anytime soon. Which means that for now, at least, every new son or daughter of black immigrants from Nigeria or Barbados those colleges choose to admit represents one fewer son or daughter of black parents living in generational poverty in Detroit or Chicago or — as in KiKi's case — Charlotte, North Carolina.

That simple math creates tensions on elite campuses, and every once in a while, those tensions bubble to the surface. During KiKi's first semester at Princeton, a public dispute broke out among black students at Cornell University. A group called Black Students United, or BSU, had organized a series of demonstrations that fall to protest racist incidents on campus and to press for a more diverse and inclusive campus. One particular demand stood out: "We demand that Cornell admissions come up with a plan to actively increase the presence of underrepresented Black students on this campus," the BSU said in its statement. "We define underrepresented Black students as Black Americans who have several generations (more than two) in this country. The Black student population at Cornell disproportionately represents international or first-generation African or Caribbean students. While these students have a right to flourish at Cornell, there is a lack of investment in Black students whose families were affected directly by the African Holocaust in America."

A black student named Marquan Jones wrote a column for the

Cornell Daily Sun to explain the context behind the BSU's demand. At Cornell, he asserted, "the voices of African American Black students are stifled. We are labeled as 'Just Black' on campus, and our Blackness is constantly called into question. There is a clear divide in the Pan-African Black community, and no one wants to talk about it. The fact is, African American students are the minority of the minority community."

This public airing of the debate is decidedly rare on American college campuses today. In contrast to the strong emotions at Cornell, most black Ivy League students I've asked about this topic say they don't feel the immigrant/native divide is a big issue. They do notice the phenomenon — it's hard to miss it — but they say it is more a matter of curiosity than of concern.

Like Harvard, Princeton doesn't publicly release data on the immigration history of its black students. So there is no way to know for sure what fraction of Princeton's black student body has roots in recent immigration and what fraction has roots in slavery. I can tell you that KiKi's impression, halfway through her first semester, was that the former category made up a clear majority on campus.

Why might Princeton's admissions office be inclined to favor black students with immigrant roots over black students with roots like KiKi's? That 2007 paper by Douglas Massey contains a clue. Massey found that at highly selective universities, students descended from voluntary immigrants from Africa or the Caribbean are more likely to have attended private school than students descended from Africans brought to the United States in slavery. They are more likely to come from intact two-parent households. Their fathers are much more likely to have graduated from college and to hold an advanced degree. And their SAT scores are, on average, more than fifty points higher. Admitting those students, instead of students like KiKi, would solve two problems at once for Princeton's admissions department. Princeton could hit its 8 percent black-student target (if, indeed, it does have a target), while still admitting students who, in every way but their race, have backgrounds a lot like the rest of Princeton's student body.

While such a strategy might make life easier for admissions departments, the fact that so few students had backgrounds like KiKi's was one more factor that made her feel different, like an outsider. Still, she gradually got used to the fact that almost all of the black students she encountered on campus were affluent, or the children of immigrants, or both. Her best friend at Princeton was a middle-class black student from Florida named Angelika; her father was from Jamaica. There was a boy from Oakland who KiKi took up with that fall (they weren't officially dating, she explained to me, but they were "non-platonically involved"); his father was from Ghana.

But being surrounded by so many black students with colorful tales of family in Africa and the Caribbean sometimes made KiKi feel inadequate. Being "just black," as she put it, made her feel like she was lacking interesting and identifiable roots, as though she were the only person in her social circle without a good story about her family's history.

"People are like, 'Where are your people from?'" KiKi said. "And you have to explain, like, 'My people aren't from anywhere.'"

KiKi was a student of black history, so she recognized, on an intellectual level at least, that she was indeed from somewhere. She was part of African American culture, the culture that had risen up from slavery—the culture of Frederick Douglass and Martin Luther King Jr. and Toni Morrison and Beyoncé. KiKi knew all that. And yet, in the context of Princeton, being a black woman with long and deep and sometimes painful roots in the black American experience made her feel, somehow, rootless. After Brook Park and Myers Park, KiKi was used to feeling like an outsider. But she had let herself believe that at Princeton, things would be different. "I thought I would come here and I would finally find this black circle," KiKi told me at the end of her freshman year. "And I did not. It was something that I wanted so badly—to be surrounded by black peers and to have that really loving black community."

KiKi was grateful for the mostly black world she was able to inhabit at Princeton. Compared to her divided life in high school, it was like paradise. But she still found it hard to feel at home. "It's so easy here to feel that you belong one minute," she said. "And then the next minute, you're all alone in the world."

WHEN TONY JACK arrived at Amherst as a freshman in 2003, he found himself surrounded by rich white kids. That part wasn't a shock; the same thing had been true at Gulliver, the private Miami-area high school where he'd spent his senior year. He'd been expecting them. What surprised him was the presence of rich *black* kids. Like KiKi, he'd never really encountered African Americans before who were able to talk casually about ski vacations in Colorado and studying abroad in France. In his neighborhood in Miami, kids like that just didn't exist.

But as his conversations with his new classmates continued and the talk got a little deeper, Jack discovered that their stories were more complicated than he had originally assumed. Yes, a significant percentage of the African American students at Amherst were truly affluent. But a good number of the black kids who had seemed so at ease chatting about Aspen and Provence also had stories to tell about high-crime neighborhoods, single mothers, incarcerated relatives, and groceries bought with food stamps. They had grown up poor, or in a struggling working-class home like his. When it came time for high school, though, these black students had managed to find their way to an elite American prep school, either through an established scholarship program or a random stroke of good fortune. And that had changed their lives.

It was a little like what Jack himself had experienced during his senior year at Gulliver Prep — although instead of just one year at a private school, these low-income black students had spent their entire high school careers in that world, many of them at prestigious boarding schools on generous financial aid. And those four years had been long enough for them to make friends whose families had ski chalets and beach houses, long enough to take part in the subsidized study-abroad programs that many exclusive private schools offer their students, long enough to infiltrate the culture of the American elite.

A few years later, when Jack, as a graduate student in sociology, began his fieldwork at Harvard — I'm sorry, at Renowned University — he encountered dozens of black and Latino undergraduates with a similar story: growing up poor, getting to private school on scholarship through some divine intervention, and from there winning admission to an elite university. This cohort of students became the focus of his research.

After almost ten years of study and analysis, Jack's conclusion is that at elite American universities today, there are two distinct categories of low-income students of color. One group spent their high school years at private boarding or day schools. Jack has labeled them the Privileged Poor. The ones who did not — who instead came to university straight from a regular public high school — Jack has labeled the Doubly Disadvantaged.

Jack's research has led him to two overarching conclusions about these groups. The first is that the Privileged Poor are vastly overrepresented at Ivy League and similarly selective colleges. Just a tiny fraction of the total population of low-income black American teenagers attend exclusive private schools, mostly by way of a handful of scholarship programs, including Prep for Prep and the TEAK Fellowship, that recruit and select low-income public school students in fifth or sixth grade, provide them with intensive training through middle school, and then shepherd them to a full scholarship at Brearley or Exeter or Milton Academy. Those programs are small — Prep for Prep sends about 120 students a year to private schools; the TEAK Fellowship sends about 25. But that little sliver of the black population, Jack discovered, produces about half of the low-income black students at Ivy League colleges.

In the same way that admissions officials at those colleges might find it easier to admit middle-class Pell grant recipients rather than poor ones, or the black children of immigrants instead of the black descendants of American slaves, Jack believes that they favor students from the Privileged Poor over the Doubly Disadvantaged as a way to "hedge their bets on diversity." Graduates of Choate or Andover are a known quantity in Ivy League admissions offices. Graduates of the large, mostly low-performing public high schools where the vast majority of low-income black American students spend their days are not. If you can fulfill your college's aspiration to achieve a certain amount of visible diversity without having to depart from your usual schedule of prep-school visits, that makes your job easier and more predictable.

The second big conclusion Tony Jack reached in his research was that Doubly Disadvantaged students had a much rockier experience once they got to college than Privileged Poor students did. And the most stressful part of the transition wasn't the academic work (though that was often stressful as well). It was their daily interactions with their fellow students.

"Engaging with their peers made them feel like strangers in a place they could not fully call home," Jack wrote in *The Privileged Poor.* "These encounters, which many of the Doubly Disadvantaged saw as assaults on their way of life, left them feeling socially isolated, emotionally drained, and, sometimes, angry. Their social and emotional well-being suffered. They encountered tacit social codes that they had never learned and that they struggled to decipher."

Privileged Poor students, by contrast, were quite familiar with those tacit social codes. They had been marinating in them for four years of high school. For them, the transition to the Ivy League was often actually straightforward, even easy. "Their high schools were a preview," Jack wrote, "a four-year trailer to the main feature."

One black Privileged Poor student, a girl called Stephanie, told Jack that coming to Renowned from boarding school was "literally déjà vu." Despite the fact that she had spent her early years in a crime-filled housing project, the immersive cultural education she had received at boarding school rendered everything she encountered when she arrived at college entirely familiar. Too familiar, in fact. When her fellow students let on that they were impressed or intimidated by the

mysteries of coed dorm life or ivy-covered Gothic buildings or inti-
mate Socratic seminars, Stephanie just rolled her eyes. "The things
that are exciting for people coming to college were very banal to me,"
she explained to Jack. "I wish I were excited. This experience is kind
of blah, 'cause I was used to it."

Despite Stephanie's world-weariness as a college freshman, the
reality is that class mobility is always jarring; no one who experiences it is immune from its disruptive force. The chief advantage the
Privileged Poor had was that they got the disruption over with early.
"For the Privileged Poor, it is not a matter of whether they experience
culture shock, but when," Jack wrote. "Culture shock occurs when
they enter their private school, usually as high school freshmen, not
when they enter Renowned as first-year undergraduates. Feelings of
isolation and difference hit them when they leave their distressed,
often segregated public middle school for a posh, white private high
school."

But that difference in timing was no small thing. It is far easier
to endure cultural reeducation as a fourteen-year-old, starting high
school, than it is as an eighteen-year-old, starting college. The iden-
tities of fourteen-year-olds are simply more malleable. And at college, the institutional ethos is for administrators to stand back and
respect students' differences. At prep school, the expected practice is
for schools to try to efface those differences, to teach students exactly
how to eat and dress and write and socialize and think. Indoctrina-
tion into cultural norms is part of the accepted curriculum in private
school. It's part of what parents are paying for.

As his research continued, Jack came to believe that one of the
most significant behavioral differences between his two groups had
to do with their relationship with their professors. "Academic life at
Renowned, as at every university, is inherently social," Jack wrote.
Privileged Poor students intuitively understood that fact, because the
same principle had been true in private school. Professors were authority figures, yes, but they were to be engaged with, not deferred
to. You flattered them, you joked with them, you went out for coffee

with them, you talked with them about movies and books — and then you asked them for help, not only with papers and problem sets, but with recommendation letters, internships, and advice on negotiating the mechanics of elite college life.

The Doubly Disadvantaged students Jack interviewed recoiled from this whole idea. For them, Jack wrote, "college is supposed to be about attending lectures, completing assignments, and studying for tests" — what they collectively called "the work." "Trying to figure out when, how, and even why personal connections are needed can paralyze them."

It wasn't just that these students didn't know how to fraternize with professors. It was that they found the practice distasteful, bordering on immoral. That was true of Valeria, the Doubly Disadvantaged Latina student. "I don't like talking to professors one on one," she told Jack. "My dad would always teach me, 'You don't want to get where you are based on kissing ass, right? You want it based on hard work. It'll take longer, but there's more value to it. You'll feel more proud.'"

Daniel, a Doubly Disadvantaged Latino, used some of the same language as Valeria. "These kids who go to professors after class and just talk to them," he said to Jack. "I have no idea what they're talking about. I don't have any questions beyond what they're teaching. They're kiss-asses! These people want recommendations, a spot in this guy's research team. I never wanted to grovel."

In the moral universe of the Doubly Disadvantaged, what matters is the work you do — the essays you write, the tests you take, the labs you complete. But the universities where they were enrolled operated on a different moral code. "The Doubly Disadvantaged express strong faith in the idea of meritocracy — believing that focusing on 'the work' is enough for success — but they actually stand to lose the most for believing so," Jack wrote. "Good work may bring recognition, and hard work may be rewarded, but academic performance alone is not always how you get ahead or get what you need in college."

KIKI SURVIVED the anxiety of her first Humanities Sequence precept, and as the fall term wore on, she and her classmates worked
their way through the pre-Socratics and Aeschylus and Sophocles.
She prepared for each class like she was girding for battle, making
careful notes and practicing her arguments. When I visited Princeton
that fall, she told me that the heart-pounding anxiety she felt the first
day of precept had disappeared. She was earning As on all of her essays, and she loved the books they were reading, and her confidence
had fully returned. But still, she said, each precept discussion felt to
her like a struggle for status and power and respect. A dominant "alpha group" had emerged in the classroom discussions, she explained,
led by one young white man, a loud talker who had no qualms about
"weaponizing his intelligence," as she put it — steering the conversation, stealing focus. KiKi was holding her own in the discussions, but
she said she would never be considered part of the alpha group.

"There's a way that an intellectual here is supposed to act," she explained. "There's a perception. You're either an intellectual or you're
not. There's a look." It wasn't just the color of her skin that made her an
outsider, KiKi said. It was the fact that she wore crop tops and Air Jor-
dans and box braids. She didn't fit the profile, and everyone knew it.

"Poor people don't become philosophers," she explained. "Or at
least they don't become philosophy majors at Princeton."

I sat in on one of KiKi's precepts, on a day when she and her classmates were discussing the work of two Roman writers, Cicero and
Plautus. I hadn't read the books, so I couldn't really follow the sub-
stance of the discussion. But observing the dynamics of the group,
the back-and-forth among fifteen young people auditioning for the
role of Ivy League intellectual, I saw some of the same currents that
KiKi did; there really was an alpha male who monopolized the discussion. But my main impression wasn't that KiKi was winning or
losing the war for status dominance. It was that she was fighting a
different battle altogether.

KiKi was intense and serious in precept, tightly wound, sitting up
straight, focused and alert. She didn't smile. When she spoke, her

voice was quiet and uninflected, and her sentences came out quickly, perfectly formed, in a rush of thought. I could picture the fourth-grade KiKi making sure her grammar was immaculate, wielding *David Copperfield* like a shield.

The other students were prepared and informed as well. But when they contributed their thoughts, they often gave the impression of doing so ironically, of being somehow above it all. They cracked knowing jokes and leaned back in their chairs with a studied nonchalance. The alpha dude took great pleasure, at one point, in comparing the character of Dionysus in Euripides's *Bacchae* to Walter White, the meth-dealing antihero of *Breaking Bad.* The agreed-upon posture in precept, for everyone but KiKi, was to be ostentatiously laid back — amused, but not aroused. Pop culture, high culture: same trope, different day.

In the game KiKi was playing, you scored points by being the smartest and the most well-read. In the game everyone else around the precept table was playing, you scored points by being the cleverest and most at ease. KiKi and her fellow students seemed to exist in two different universes, with very few points of overlap. The room that to her seemed like a foreign battlefield felt to the other students like home. The idea that they might not belong around this table in Joseph Henry House seemed never to have crossed their minds.

As the semester went on, KiKi noticed that students in her precept were forming friendships and study groups, chatting with each other before and after class. But outside of the debates around the precept table, KiKi never spoke to any of them, and none of them spoke to KiKi.

3. Pedigree

What KiKi was experiencing, and what Tony Jack was studying, was the way that social and economic divides *before* college reproduce themselves *in* college. Lauren Rivera, a professor of sociology and management at Northwestern University, has taken that analysis a step further to explore how those divisions persist *after* college, in the workplace. Her 2015 book *Pedigree: How Elite Students Get Elite Jobs* investigates the role, in college and beyond, of "cultural capital," a phrase coined by the late French sociologist Pierre Bourdieu to describe the knowledge and manners and taste that established families and institutions quietly pass on to their children to enable them to remain in the upper classes as adults.

Sociologists, as a practice, try to fit individuals into categories. But when Rivera, who is now in her early forties, tries to perform that analysis on her own upbringing, she gets a bit stuck. In some ways, she grew up fairly poor — lower class or working poor, she guesses, or maybe lower middle class. When Lauren was still a baby, her father, a small-time criminal from Puerto Rico, went to prison. Her parents divorced, and her mother, a Jewish immigrant from eastern Europe, raised her and her older brother alone, in Los Angeles, on a series of minimum wage jobs and temp gigs.

The class complication was that her mother's meager income was supplemented by sporadic financial support from Lauren's temperamental, eccentric grandfather, who fled Austria to escape Nazi persecution and had worked ever since as a small-time smuggler, shuttling various goods across international borders, often one step ahead of the law or the immigration officials. His unorthodox career, plus Lauren's mother's own spotty work history, meant that money was uneven and unpredictable when Lauren was growing up. And her family's spending was in general more aspirational than it was practical. There wasn't always enough to eat for dinner, but for years Lauren's grandfather paid to send her to expensive ballet lessons.

When Lauren's mother was younger, she hadn't been much of a student herself. She got mediocre grades in high school and transferred out of two colleges before finally earning a degree from a third. But she believed strongly in the importance of education for her children. She helped Lauren's older brother land a basketball scholarship at the Brentwood School, an exclusive private school in Los Angeles that educates the children of Hollywood royalty—as well as, occasionally, the children of actual royalty. Lauren's mother wanted to get Lauren into Brentwood as well, but Lauren wasn't an athlete, and they definitely couldn't afford the tuition.

Still, her mother was determined, and so one afternoon when Lauren was in sixth grade, she and her mother went to the Brentwood School for an official admission interview. It didn't get off to a very promising start. The administrators liked Lauren well enough, but they didn't seem inclined to hand her a full scholarship. But then, in the middle of the interview, there was a commotion in the office. The woman who ran the school bookstore walked in out of the blue and abruptly quit. Lauren's mom saw her opportunity. On the spot, she announced that she could do the job, and she could start immediately. She had never worked in a bookstore, let alone managed one. But she was sure she could figure it out, and she knew that children of staff members at the Brentwood School paid no tuition. She got the job, and Lauren got the scholarship—and with it, entrée to a strange new world.

Lauren had been around affluence before, but nothing like what she saw at the Brentwood School. The student parking lot was full of Porsches and Mercedeses. Her fellow students didn't live in houses, they lived in compounds. It was a blizzard of conspicuous consumption, California-style, designer labels and expensive handbags and private flights, and Lauren, shy and overweight and dressed in factory seconds, didn't even try to keep up. She wasn't bullied by the rich, popular kids, she says, just ignored. She hung out mostly alone or with the other scholarship students, and when things got too weird or too lonely, she'd go visit her mom in the school bookstore and recuperate.

Rivera considers that she received two educations at the Brentwood School. One, her formal education, was rigorously academic, and that won her admission to Yale. The other was her informal training as a student of status, carefully watching those around her. It was that second education that led her, eventually, to become a sociologist. She found the kids at Brentwood consistently bewildering, but also endlessly fascinating. It wasn't just that she couldn't afford what they had, it was also that she often didn't understand what they were talking about. "There were these rules of being that everyone seemed to know," she said. "Everyone except for me."

As high school ended, Rivera was still an outsider, but she felt, at last, that she had begun to grasp the nuances of the Brentwood ecosystem. Then she got to Yale. She didn't think there could be a place more privileged and exclusive than the Brentwood School, but there was, she says, and she was in it. She felt lost and disoriented all over again. The status cues she'd finally learned at Brentwood didn't apply at Yale. This was a world of old money, rather than new money, Tafts and Bushes and Vanderbilts. Everyone wore black; California pastels were frowned on. People read *The New Yorker*. Rivera had never heard of *The New Yorker*.

But after her years of social exclusion at the Brentwood School, Rivera yearned to be on the inside for once. She rushed an exclusive sorority, which brought her an instant social circle, and a very wealthy one. Fitting in was exhausting. At Brentwood, people knew she was a scholarship kid. There had been no point in pretending otherwise; her mother worked in the building.

But at Yale, Rivera worked hard to conceal her class, and for a while she was able to pass as a rich eastern sorority girl. She didn't talk much about her family, didn't tell anyone about her work-study job. She had to apply for a scholarship to pay her sorority dues, but she did her best to keep that a secret. When her sorority sisters would go out to eat at fancy restaurants, she'd make an excuse to skip out, or she would go but pretend she wasn't hungry and drink nothing but water. "I just wanted to be like everybody else," she told me. "It was my chance to finally be cool."

Yale was another valuable laboratory for Rivera's ongoing education in American class and status. But it wasn't much fun. "I often wish I could redo those years," she said. "In the past few years there has been a lot written about socioeconomic diversity at elite colleges, and how even if you're coming from a solid middle-class background, it can be a very alienating experience." But as a Yale undergraduate in the 1990s, she didn't have that context. So she assumed the alienation she was experiencing was unique to her. "I attributed a lot of what happened in college, the feeling of a lack of belonging, to something about *me*," she said, "rather than thinking: This is systemic. These are wealthy institutions filled predominantly with extraordinarily wealthy people, and there is no escape."

When Rivera graduated from Yale in the spring of 2000, she followed a postcollege path common to many Ivy League grads: She got a job in management consulting, spending two years working for the Monitor Group, based in London. It was a pleasant life, for a while, and a well-compensated one, but it didn't feel like a calling. Back at Yale, she had read Pierre Bourdieu's writing about cultural capital in a class on contemporary social theory, and now she couldn't get it out of her head. It seemed to explain so much of what she had seen at the Brentwood School and in college and even in the management consulting world she now inhabited in London. She was, deep down, still trying to understand how elites operated, still trying to make sense of what she had seen and experienced in high school and college.

So she applied to graduate school and (as Tony Jack would do a few years later) entered the PhD program in sociology at Harvard. For a while, she considered conducting, for her dissertation, an ethnographic study of bouncers—how they evaluated subtle status cues when deciding whom to admit to a nightclub. But she eventually chose a different cultural gatekeeper to study, a subject closer to home: the corporate recruiters who visit Ivy League campuses and hire recent grads for top-tier investment banks, law firms, and management consulting companies.

Rivera still had connections in the consulting world, and she used those to get herself hired as an unpaid recruiting intern. She stayed for nine months, helping to organize events and set up interviews. Her real job, of course, was as an ethnographer, observing and taking notes as she shadowed recruiters. Rivera felt once again like an outsider, surrounded by privilege, out of her element, trying to pass as someone she was not. In her book, *Pedigree,* she describes one moment in a training session for on-campus interviewers when she looked out from the back row at a sea of crisply pressed shirt collars. She looked down at her own sad, limp collar and wrote herself a note in the margin of her yellow legal pad: "*Iron.*"

Her colleagues at the firm had all been informed that she was a sociologist doing research for a book, and yet the fact that she had Harvard and Yale and the Monitor Group on her résumé meant that they saw her as an insider — even when she was sneaking off to the bathroom to scribble her research notes on cocktail napkins. To them, she was part of the club, someone with whom they could safely share the secrets of their profession. "You get it," they would say. "You're one of us."

IF YOU ARE looking for reassurance that the American meritocracy is fair and democratic and open to all, *Pedigree* is not the book for you. Backed up by her meticulous research, Rivera manages, in 350 pages, to undercut and overturn many of the stories we like to tell ourselves about who succeeds in the United States and why. It turns out it really *does* matter where you go to college — at least if you want to work in certain high-paying professions. Lacrosse bros really *do* run the world. It really *is* who you know, not what you know. An investment banker really *did* tell Rivera that it was "difficult" for women to be hired by his bank if they weren't "pretty." ("I mean, you don't have to be *hot,*" he clarified. "But you do need to be reasonably attractive.") By the time you reach the last page of *Pedigree,* you either want to go firebomb a bank or enroll your kid in squash lessons or both.

Rivera's central finding was that top law firms and management consulting companies and investment banks — known collectively as "elite professional service" or EPS firms — based their entry-level hiring decisions not on what candidates had achieved in college, but on who they were when they arrived at college years earlier. The hiring process was designed to create an *illusion* of fairness, a Potemkin meritocracy. Its true effect was what sociologists called "social closure," the opposite of social mobility: a system in which old elites maintained their positions of power and privilege and erected invisible barriers—or at least opaque ones—to keep out everyone else. At each stage of the process, Rivera wrote, the employers she studied used criteria to sort and evaluate candidates "that are highly correlated with parental income and education. Taken together, these seemingly economically neutral decisions result in a hiring process that filters students based on their parents' socioeconomic status."

Rivera explains that people in charge of hiring fresh college graduates for these companies are faced with an immensely challenging task. New hires at EPS firms, even successful ones, tend to stay in the job for only two or three years, which means the firms need to hire hundreds of new employees each year. The jobs they are filling are lucrative, paying as much as $165,000 a year straight out of college. And they don't require much specialized knowledge, or even complex skill, beyond the ability to dress nicely, follow instructions, and work very long hours. As a result, the recruiters regularly receive fifty or more applications for each position and have no reliable way to discern which applicants will perform best in the job.

In the face of this information deficit, Rivera found, the recruiters rely heavily on one particular credential: where each applicant went to college. Small distinctions matter; even being in the Ivy League is not elite enough. Recruiters highly favor graduates of just four "superelite" institutions: Harvard, Princeton, Yale, and Stanford. If you graduate from one of those colleges, rather than a "second-tier" Ivy League college like Brown or Cornell or Dartmouth, "it's light-years different whether or not we are going to consider your résumé," one consultant told Rivera.

If you have the misfortune to attend a college below the second tier, your application is more or less doomed. "I'm just being really honest, it pretty much goes into a black hole," a female recruiter explained to Rivera. "Unfortunately, it's just not a great situation. There's not an easy way to get into the firm if you're not at a target school."

The philosophy behind this sorting system is that the admissions offices at elite colleges know what they're doing. If you graduate from a top-tier university, that means you were admitted to a top-tier university. And according to the recruiters Rivera interviewed, that admission offer, even though it came when you were just a teenager, signaled a lot: that you're smart, that you learn quickly, that you can handle hard work. How well you did at college and what you learned there is largely irrelevant, the recruiters explained. What matters is that you got in. "Number one people go to number one schools," one lawyer told Rivera.

As Rivera points out, and as Raj Chetty's data underscores, when employers use the admissions offices of elite universities to do their screening for them, they inevitably replicate the inequities of that admissions system. Nonaffluent students are rare in those colleges, which means that it is rare for the résumé of a nonaffluent job applicant to wind up anywhere but in the black hole.

An applicant's alma mater is the first and most important screen that recruiters use. But even after recruiters eliminate candidates from colleges that aren't on their "target list," they still have far more applicants than positions. Which means they need a secondary screen. The criterion they chose for this second screen was surprising to Rivera. It wasn't college GPA. It wasn't relevant work experience. It was the extracurricular activities, especially athletics, that candidates pursued in high school and in college. Students who merely studied hard and learned a lot—like the Doubly Disadvantaged students who told Tony Jack that the responsible thing to do in college was focus on "the work"—were seen by recruiters as "bookworms" or "nerds" and frequently passed over.

As one consultant explained to Rivera, "We like to interview at schools like Harvard and Yale, but people who have, like, 4.0s and are in the engineering department but, you know, don't have any friends, have huge glasses, read their textbooks all day, those people have no chance here."

Students who devoted significant amounts of time to an extracurricular activity — varsity athletes and nationally ranked competitors — were seen by recruiters as having "drive" and "initiative" and "passion." They were believed to be good multitaskers, skilled at time management. Perhaps most important, they were also judged to be fun. And in professions where employees work long hours together and travel together, Rivera found, being perceived as a potentially fun friend greatly increased your chance of being hired.

"We look for someone who's got a personality, has something to bring to the table," a banking recruiter told Rivera. "You know, for lack of a better term, someone you can shoot the shit with." Typically, the recruiter explained, these expert shit-shooters "were in sports, they were involved in different activities on campus. The more well-rounded individual versus the candidate who has the 4.0, who's got all the honors and all the different Econ classes."

To be hired by one of these elite firms, Rivera was told, it was not enough just to have played a sport. It also mattered *which* sport you played. Recruiters were mostly unimpressed by students who took part, even at a high level, in easily accessible sports like wrestling or basketball or soccer. Instead, they preferred candidates who played sports with a high barrier to entry, either because of specialized equipment or expensive club fees or both — sports like lacrosse, field hockey, tennis, squash, and rowing. Of course, these sports, as Rivera notes, are played almost exclusively by rich and upper-middle-class white kids. They generally require a serious commitment in time and money, not just from students but from parents as well, often beginning in middle school or even earlier.

This created a system that was apparently open and meritocratic but that actually strongly favored young people from high socioeconomic backgrounds and eliminated the rest from consideration. "If you're not playing the right sport when you're fourteen years old, it's going to be really, really hard to get a job at Goldman Sachs after college," Rivera explained. "And who is playing the right sports? People whose parents know that this stuff is not just fun and games, people who have the money to pay for the equipment, people who know that lacrosse is this important insider thing." People, in other words, with not just financial capital but also cultural capital, young people whose parents somehow intuited, in middle school, precisely which extracurricular activities their children's investment-banking recruiters were going to be looking for a decade later, and who signed their kids up and shuttled them to and from practice accordingly.

Meanwhile, low-income students at elite colleges mostly didn't understand the rules of the game; they didn't understand that in some cases, the starting whistle had sounded years earlier. "In contrast to students from upper-middle-class backgrounds," Rivera wrote, "less affluent students are more likely to enter campus with the belief that it is achievement in the classroom rather than on the field or in the concert hall that matters for future success, and they tend to focus their energies accordingly." They still believed in "the work," in other words, in the version of the American meritocracy they had been taught as children to respect and put their faith in. And their chances to land a lucrative job after college suffered as a result.

4. Thanksgiving

The first thing KiKi Gilbert ever told me about her mother was that she was "restless." That was the word she used. It was a warm afternoon in late June, just after the end of her junior year of high school, and KiKi was in Princeton for the first time, taking part in LEDA's summer institute. She and I were sitting in the first-floor common area of her dorm, and I was asking her to help me understand why, as a seventeen-year-old, she had already lived in seven states and spent time at ten different elementary schools. KiKi explained that her mom was an aspiring songwriter, and that her family moved a lot for her career. Then she said that sometimes they moved just to move, because her mom valued fresh starts. And then she told me that her mom once flipped a coin on the side of an interstate to determine whether she and KiKi and her siblings, packed into the family minivan with all their possessions, would move to Florida or to California.

What KiKi was doing with me that day was trying to figure out which version of her life story she should tell. I was a stranger, a white journalist she was meeting for the first time, and she wasn't sure how deep to go, how much to reveal, how best to describe all that she had experienced. It was a dilemma she was beginning to wrestle with more broadly that summer, as college-application season loomed before her. She had a personal statement she needed to write for the common application, plus supplemental questions for many of the dozen or so colleges she was thinking of applying to. And then there were all the scholarship applications, each of which required its own essay, its own confession, its own version of KiKi.

The story that kept going around in her head — though she didn't tell it to me that June day — was the story of tenth grade. That felt like the year that had shaped her more than any other, though she was still working out exactly how. It was the first year she spent at Myers Park High School, the first time she had been exposed to high-level academic work, the first time she really understood the effort and sacrifice it would take to get to a place like Princeton. But it was also the year that her family's fortunes reached their nadir, the year her mother's relentless wanderings brought them to the end of the road at last.

KiKi's mother had always been creative and mercurial, prone to mood swings and dark depressions, fragile interludes when she would cut herself off from the world almost entirely. KiKi, her oldest child, was often her chief source of stability and comfort, supporting her mother through her more perilous moments, running interference when she had to deal with complex bureaucracies or authority figures. As the years went by, KiKi's mother's anxiety and depression and social isolation grew steadily worse. Her decisions became more erratic, and the family's moves became more abrupt.

After KiKi's fourth-grade year in the stretch classroom at Brook Park Elementary, her mother moved the family to North Carolina, then back to Indianapolis, then to another part of town. Each move seemed to KiKi like a step down — each time a smaller apartment, a sketchier neighborhood, a lower-performing school. KiKi didn't have to fight to get into the stretch classroom at her new schools, because they didn't have stretch classrooms; the students were all failing together. KiKi kept reading her thick books, but it seemed increasingly difficult to imagine that they might lead her anywhere rewarding.

She started high school at a giant low-income public school on the northwest side of Indianapolis. But as she was getting ready to begin her sophomore year, her mother decided it was time for another move. The plan, this time, was to try their luck in Atlanta. KiKi had a stepfather now and three siblings, including a baby brother who was a handful. He would later be diagnosed with severe autism, but at that point he just seemed wild and difficult to reach, prone to wailing inconsolably and hitting himself in the head.

Late that summer, the six of them loaded all their possessions into the minivan and drove through the night to a motel in Stone Mountain, Georgia, where KiKi's mother announced they would stay until she could find something more permanent in Atlanta. After a week, though, it became clear that she had badly miscalculated — not enough money, no solid opportunities — and they pulled up stakes again and set out for Charlotte, where KiKi's stepfather had some family connections.

By the time they reached North Carolina, KiKi had missed the first two weeks of her sophomore year of high school, and their situation was looking dire. They didn't have enough money to pay the security deposit on an apartment. As new arrivals to the state, they weren't eligible for housing aid. They looked for space in a shelter, but they couldn't find one that could provide the services that KiKi's autistic brother would need. Their last resort was to try to find an inexpensive motel that would rent them a room for an extended stay.

KiKi's mother, feeling desperate, called around and made a list of all the cheap long-term motels in Charlotte, and then she drove downtown with KiKi to the student placement office for the public school system. They were directed to a cubicle where a placement officer would determine where KiKi would start her sophomore year.

Usually the process for new arrivals to Charlotte was straightforward. The parent would give the person behind the desk the family's new address, and the placement officer would tell the parent which high school served that particular address. In KiKi's case, though, things were a little more complicated, because her family didn't have an address. Instead, KiKi's mother pulled out her list of possible motels and laid it on the desk and asked the placement officer to tell her which motel she should choose if she wanted KiKi to attend the best possible high school.

This was not a question that the woman behind the desk felt particularly inclined—or even able—to help with. It was already very late in the year to be enrolling in school. Most of the city's decent high schools were at capacity. And the simple fact was that in Charlotte, as in every American city, the excellent high schools are not located in the same part of town as the cheap motels. The intake officer looked at KiKi's mother's handwritten list. Then she looked at KiKi's mother. And then she looked at KiKi, who had traveled downtown, as always, with a giant book in her hands. She sat next to her mother, head bowed, reading something weighty and dense.

There was something in KiKi's studious manner, or maybe her mother's worried expression, that led the woman to understand that this decision was going to make a difference. She thought for a while.

"Myers Park," she said, finally. "Your daughter belongs at Myers Park."

The school was located in one of the wealthiest neighborhoods in the city, also called Myers Park, at the end of a long, curving, tree-lined street. The school's "transportation zone"—where you had to live in order to enroll — was mostly limited to Myers Park itself, but it also included one small low-income minority neighborhood in the west of the city, called Brookhill Village. And on its way to Brookhill, the zone's boundary briefly detoured to include a dismal cloverleaf interchange that carried cars from Interstate 77 onto Billy Graham Parkway. Right next to that interchange, wedged between a machine supply shop and a Wendy's drive-through, was one of the motels on KiKi's mom's list: the Arlington Suites.

That night, KiKi's family moved into an extended-stay room at the Arlington Suites, and the next day, at 7:00 a.m., KiKi was standing at the edge of the motel's parking lot, waiting for the Myers Park school bus to arrive.

SOPHOMORE YEAR of high school felt to KiKi like she was living on two separate planets hurtling in opposite directions. At school, she was surrounded by ambition and privilege — not the careless, designer-handbag privilege that Lauren Rivera found at the Brentwood School, but the anxious privilege of the aspirational American upper middle class. Even in sophomore year, the lives of her International Baccalaureate classmates revolved around college. They talked endlessly about their college lists and their college tours and where their parents had gone. Everything counted: your grades and your test scores and the teams you played for and the clubs you joined and the test-prep classes you went to after school. It was a relentless achievement culture that was both baffling and inspiring to KiKi. She soaked it in every day at school, and then she left it all behind every afternoon when she boarded the bus to go back to the Arlington Suites.

The six members of her family stayed for the entire year in a single, small beat-up motel room. Her mother and stepfather and baby brother took the bed, and KiKi and her two middle siblings slept on air mattresses on the floor. The Arlington Suites was not a motel in the usual sense; it was a homeless shelter with an ice machine. No one came there on vacation. Everyone who checked in seemed to be at the tail end of some sad story. There were fights in the hallways and drugs in the parking lot and rumors of prostitution and rape. It wasn't safe for KiKi to leave the room, and her siblings couldn't sleep if there was a light on. So she'd do her homework, late at night, in the bathroom, sitting in the dry tub with her books spread around her, typing her assignments on a phone with a cracked screen.

As the year went on, and KiKi's two planets moved further and further apart, she could feel herself removing herself, mentally and emotionally, from life in the motel. She still spent every night there, and every night was still terrible. But she began to feel as though her existence in the Arlington Suites was not quite real, like she was meant to be somewhere else, somewhere better — and not in a motivational-poster way, but an ontological one. Looking back on it now, she thinks her mental detachment was a kind of defense mechanism, a subconscious coping strategy to help her survive the trauma she was facing every day.

"I think that was one of the ways that I was able to make it out of living in a motel room with six people," she told me. "Having this constant narration of: I know where I'm going. I know where I'm going to be, and it's not going to be here. It gave me a shield of sorts against some of the more awful things that were going on around me."

Her family did eventually make it out of the Arlington Suites. They got approved for a housing voucher at the end of the school year and moved into a rental home on Charlotte's north side. It wasn't great, but it was better. KiKi got her own bedroom for the first time in her life, and she turned it into a kind of fortress. She put a lock on the door, and she papered the walls with evidence of her accomplishments: scholarship letters, newspaper clippings, an award she won in fourth grade. The moment she got home every afternoon, she would head straight to her room and lock the door and pretty much stay there until morning. Her mother would sometimes complain that KiKi was distancing herself from the family, that she was embarrassed by them, but after a year with nothing resembling privacy—nowhere to retreat to but the bathtub—distance was exactly what KiKi needed. She felt greedy for personal space.

When KiKi started applying for college scholarships and summer programs, each application required a personal essay, and every essay prompt seemed to be asking the same thing: Tell us about a time in your life when you overcame adversity. Tell us the worst thing that ever happened to you. KiKi thought about tenth grade and the Arlington Suites. And it gradually dawned on her that what she thought of as a personal story of an awful year had a certain currency in this world.

The people who gave out competitive scholarships and read college applications were moved by the fact that she had experienced such pain and remained a straight-A student. It was a story they wanted to hear: the homeless teen who made good. So she told it, again and again. And telling it made her feel sad and sometimes proud, but eventually mostly angry and more than a little cynical. The whole process began to feel transactional, like she was trading her pain for college admission offers and scholarship dollars. The worst year of her life had become a commodity.

And then she got to Princeton, and the value of that commodity shifted. It suddenly felt like a liability, not an asset, like something someone might use against her. Princeton was not a place where you shared your pain. It was a place where you shared your achievements. So KiKi didn't tell anybody at Princeton about the Arlington Suites. Not the kids in precept. Not her new well-off black friends. Not even Anjelika or the boy from Oakland with whom she became non-platonically involved. If people asked about her past, she found ways to smooth over its rough edges, to present a version of her story that wasn't quite false but wasn't entirely true, either.

KIKI HAD HAD this secret fantasy that she and her mother would grow closer when she got to college, that without the claustrophobia of cohabitation they might achieve a new kind of mutual understanding and warmth. But it hadn't worked out that way. That freshman fall, they fell into long and wary radio silences, and by the beginning of November, KiKi only knew what was going on at home by looking at her mother's Facebook feed.

When KiKi was accepted to Princeton the previous spring, her mother had decided to relocate the family to New Jersey as well. She had a songwriting connection who lived just outside New York City, and she thought it might be a good place to start over. So in June, after KiKi's high school graduation, they packed up the house in Charlotte, piled once again into the minivan, and moved north. KiKi went straight to the Princeton campus for her Freshman Scholars Institute summer program, and the rest of the family found an apartment in North Jersey, in between Hackensack and Paterson. Then a few weeks later they moved again, and then again.

Their latest place was only an hour away from Princeton, but KiKi hadn't visited, and her mother had driven down to campus only once, when she needed to borrow some of KiKi's scholarship money. KiKi knew her mother thought that she should be doing more to help out at home. But KiKi found herself wanting more from her mother, too.

It was an unfamiliar feeling. Over the years, KiKi had grown used to the idea that her college path was something she was going to have to walk alone. And most of the time she was OK with that. But at the beginning of September, when the rest of the freshmen arrived and she saw the parade of parents helping their kids move in, lugging suitcases and boxes, wearing proud smiles and Princeton sweatshirts, her heart sank a little. She was surprised that it hurt, but it did.

There was a weeklong fall break at the end of October. KiKi thought about going home to see her family, but she chose to stay on campus. And then it was Thanksgiving, another weeklong break, and KiKi decided she would stay put again and wait until Christmas to visit. As the Thanksgiving break began, KiKi watched the campus slowly empty out, everyone scattering to homes and family vacations in every corner of the country. Then the day before Thanksgiving, her mom got in touch and asked if she was coming home for Thanksgiving dinner, and KiKi decided she would, just for one night. The next morning, her mom drove down to Princeton to pick her up.

KiKi felt fine on the drive north. But when her mother opened the door to the family's new home and they walked in, KiKi was seized with a dark and desperate feeling. When she tried to describe it to me later, she said the only word she could find was "panic." It caught her off guard. Her reaction didn't really make sense. The apartment wasn't *that* bad. It wasn't the worst place they had ever lived. But it was small and loud and disheveled, everyone crowded into two rooms, her sister sleeping on an air mattress on the living room floor. It was better than the Arlington Suites, but it was a definite step down from their house in Charlotte. There was a hole in the ceiling near her mother's bed, dripping brown water into a bucket. Her little brother — now five — didn't have a dedicated place to play, like he did in Charlotte, and his screams echoed off the bare walls.

KiKi went through the motions that afternoon of a daughter coming home from college for Thanksgiving. She talked to her siblings and balanced her dinner plate on her lap on the couch and ate mac and cheese and collard greens. But inside, the panicky feeling never really receded.

She thought about the year in the motel and the mental trick she had perfected back then: persuading herself that she didn't really belong there, that the KiKi who was living in the Arlington Suites wasn't the real KiKi. That trick had allowed her to survive the motel, and it had carried her all the way to Princeton. True, she didn't always feel welcome on campus. She hadn't yet found the community and the loving black family that she yearned for. But she had grown confident that she belonged at Princeton — more than she'd ever belonged anywhere, in fact.

Which is maybe what made Thanksgiving so scary. In the months she had spent in the comfort and quiet of Princeton, she had let down her guard, dismantled the elaborate mental barricades she had constructed back in sophomore year, the ones that let her come back every night from Myers Park to the Arlington Suites and tell herself:

You are not really here. This is not really you. When she walked into the apartment in Paterson, and she saw the hole in the ceiling and heard her little brother's screams, she had no defenses to ward off the message that was suddenly, clearly true: This *is* you. This is your family. This is what you come from.

"I had put so much thought into escaping, into finding my rightful place," KiKi explained, "that I never really put much energy or thought into going back again, even if it was just for one night. I think that's where the panic and the discomfort came from. I felt like I was stuck in this place that I had tried for so long to escape."

It was hard, as well, to see her family in a situation that was so depressingly familiar. "It felt very cyclical," KiKi said. "Growing up as a kid, we would *always* do this. We would take all our stuff, and we would move somewhere new with all these dreams and hopes of something better, and the new place always ended up being somewhat worse. I just felt this deep sadness that this is the umpteenth time that my family has found itself in this position."

KiKi didn't blame her mother, she told me. She understood that the personal cycles her mother seemed compelled to keep repeating were etched within deeper cycles of poverty and racism and abuse and oppression that stretched back for generations, even centuries. Her mother and siblings seemed trapped in a system that kept them cut off from opportunity and left them with no room for error.

"Even though *I* had escaped," KiKi said, "when I went home I still had a front-row seat to all these terrible things. I could see very clearly how the world was stacked against my family." The worst part, she told me, was that she couldn't figure out how to change the situation. "I'm a philosophy major, so I spend all my time thinking through things," she explained. "But when I went home, I realized my family's problems were something I just could not think through. I could not find a solution."

KiKi spent Thanksgiving night on the couch, surrounded by her family. The next morning her mom drove her down the turnpike to Princeton. KiKi was relieved to be back in her dorm room, but still she felt empty and alone, and sad in a way that she hadn't for a long time.

A week later, she called her mom and explained that she wasn't coming home for Christmas. Her mom seemed disheartened, but she said she understood. KiKi went to Tampa Bay with Anjelika and spent Christmas in her family's condo on the beach. She never saw that apartment in Paterson again. That spring, her family packed up the minivan and moved back to Indianapolis to start over once more.

V

LETTING IN

―――――――――

1. The Admissions-Industrial Complex

I was sitting with Jon Boeckenstedt at a round folding table across from the BlueFuego booth, about to bite into my third lobster slider, when the snare drums erupted. I looked up, startled, and saw a dozen grown men dressed as Revolutionary War soldiers marching toward us down the carpeted aisle of the Boston Convention Center. They wore knee breeches and waistcoats and black tricorn hats, and the rat-a-tat-tat of their drums echoed off the high steel ceiling of the exhibit hall. The two men leading the formation were carrying a bright orange banner advertising the services of a customer-relations management firm. They marched past the ZeeMee booth, past CampusCast and College Raptor and then away down the aisle, still drumming, their promotional banner rippling proudly in the air-conditioned breeze.

Boeckenstedt and I turned back to our sliders. We were hungry. It had been a long day.

When you look at the business of college admissions solely from the perspective of the applicants — students like Shannen and Clara and KiKi and Ben and millions of others — the people who work in admissions offices can sometimes seem like powerful demigods, cruel and whimsical masterminds who grant the wishes of certain mortals and crush the hopes of thousands more, then sit back and wait for the giant tuition checks to roll in. But that is not, in fact, what it feels like to work in college admissions these days. Far from it. Life in admissions in the 2010s is a constant balancing act, precarious and stressful.

If you want to understand the pressures that the modern college-admissions professional faces, a good place to start is the exhibit hall at the annual conference of the National Association for College Admission Counseling, or NACAC, where members of this anxious tribe gather each year by the thousands. And there is arguably no better person to serve as your guide than Boeckenstedt, who oversees undergraduate admissions at DePaul University in Chicago and maintains, on the side, two frank and opinionated blogs about the business of enrolling college students.

Once upon a time, working in admissions was a sedate, gentlemanly affair organized around an orderly schedule of hosting booths at college fairs and paying visits to high schools to meet with prospective students. Each season was carefully orchestrated: mailing out brochures followed by sorting through applications followed by sending out acceptance letters. But changes in the economy, in technology, in demography, and in students' habits and preferences have combined to transform the admissions game into a fickle and unpredictable contest with increasingly high stakes. The applicant pool is going down, tuition discounts are going up, and small colleges are going bankrupt. And so the mood in the exhibit hall in Boston that fall afternoon was jittery and anxious, even before the guys with the muskets and snare drums showed up. The hundreds of vendors working the booths that surrounded us, handing out branded stress balls and fidget spinners and fluffernutter pudding shots, were all really selling the same thing: peace of mind.

"People in my job get fired all the time," Boeckenstedt explained. If next year's class is too big or too small, or if the incoming students' test scores are too low or they don't bring in enough revenue, it is the admissions director who takes the heat — and sometimes the fall. "Everybody on campus thinks they know how to do our job," Boeckenstedt said. "They think what we do is actually pretty simple. They have no idea how complex and how tangled it really is."

Boeckenstedt is a big, beefy white guy from Dubuque, born in 1958 into a family that has farmed the same stretch of eastern Iowa for generations, ever since his ancestors emigrated from Germany in the middle of the nineteenth century. His father drove bulldozers and graders for the Dubuque Dock Commission, and his mother kept the house and raised the kids. Neither of them attended high school, let alone college. Boeckenstedt paid his own tuition at the local Catholic high school, working twenty-five hours a week behind the counter at a pizza restaurant. He was a lackluster student, but he was always good with numbers, and after he scored surprisingly high on the ACT, one of his teachers told him he should consider college. He asked his best friend Tom where he was applying, and Tom said Iowa State, so Boeckenstedt sent an application there and nowhere else. He got in, and in the fall of 1977 he headed off to the campus two hundred miles away in Ames.

Boeckenstedt didn't really know what he was doing in college, and after a year at Iowa State, his money ran out. He went back to Dubuque and got a job in a factory that made weather shelters for loading docks. It seemed like his destiny: working with his hands as the men in his family had always done. But a year and a half of cutting foam and gluing it to lumber convinced him that he didn't want to spend the rest of his life doing factory work, so he took the money that he'd saved from his job, plus a small loan, and finished his BA at a tiny Catholic college in Dubuque, reading John Donne's poems and Shakespeare's sonnets by the banks of the Upper Mississippi River.

Boeckenstedt's first job in admissions was as an entry-level recruiter at Mount Mercy College, another tiny Catholic institution in Iowa, this time in Cedar Rapids. He took the position, hoping he could help young people make better decisions about college than he had been able to make as a high school senior. But for a long time, he felt like a bad fit for the job. Boeckenstedt is shy and introverted, not particularly fond of human interaction, and yet there he was, driving from one small midwestern town to another, doing his best to chat up high school students, trying to get them excited about Mount Mercy. The people who flourished in admissions, he noticed, were highly social pep-rally types — bubbly and warm and outgoing. Boeckenstedt's favorite part of the job was the long hours he spent alone in the car.

But he persisted in admissions nonetheless. He gradually realized that while he might never become entirely comfortable with people, he did have another skill that could prove useful: he knew how to work with data. He invented his own hand-drawn system to sort and analyze all the students he was meeting, using index cards and a pocket calculator and wide, green-lined computer paper. As he filled the long sheets with pencil notations, creating a kind of protospreadsheet, he began to detect patterns in the students' behavior — what sort of student, when recruited, would actually apply, and what sort, when admitted, would actually enroll. Understanding those patterns helped him do his job better. He moved on to a position at the University of Dallas and then returned to Iowa to work at Grinnell College. And as the years passed, something unexpected happened: the admissions profession changed, and it changed in his favor. The era of the cheerleaders began to give way to the age of the nerds.

In 1976 the dean of admissions at Boston College, a man named Jack Maguire, published an article in the college's alumni magazine describing a new way of thinking about college admissions that he had recently put into practice there. He called his system enrollment management, and it included some ideas that at the time were downright revolutionary. Maguire looked at admissions not as an art but a science, employing mathematical models and following the principles of modern business management. He used market research to find new and better-qualified applicants. He analyzed data, loading thousands of student records onto the giant mainframe computers of the day, tracing patterns of application and enrollment. And he deployed financial aid not just as an individual response to a student's unique need, but strategically, as a way to attract and retain the students who would best serve his institution's long-term goals. Maguire's new approach brought in thousands more applications and helped pull Boston College out of a financial crisis.

It took a few years for Maguire's methods to catch on and spread beyond Boston College. But by the late 1980s, when Jon Boeckenstedt was finding his way in the profession, they had begun to take hold at institutions across the country. And while Boeckenstedt might not have been a good fit with traditional admissions work, he had the perfect personality for enrollment management. He was analytical and methodical and precise. He thought strategically. He found great satisfaction in identifying patterns within unruly collections of data. As the field evolved, Boeckenstedt began to rise professionally, winning one promotion after another. He is now responsible at DePaul for recruiting, admitting, and enrolling twenty-five hundred freshmen each year.

Jack Maguire's once-radical approach has become the industry standard. Forty years ago, not a single institution of higher learning had a department of enrollment management; now, almost every American college and university has one, usually overseeing admissions, financial aid, and, at some colleges, student support. The men and women who work in those offices are called upon not only to curate one highly qualified freshman class after another; they are also responsible these days, as much as anyone on campus, for ensuring the financial health — and even the long-term survival — of the institutions where they work.

There is a tiny minority of American colleges where tuition revenue doesn't matter a whole lot to the institution's financial health. Harvard and Princeton and Stanford have such enormous endowments and such dependable alumni donors that they are able to spend lavishly to educate their students with only a small percentage of the funding coming from the students themselves. But the anxious masses swarming through the exhibit hall in Boston, stuffing giveaway branded sweat socks into their giveaway branded tote bags, worked mostly for colleges that operated on a different, more straightforward, financial model, one that depended almost entirely on tuition.

That model has recently come under considerable strain. According to Moody's Investors Service, a quarter of private American colleges in 2018 were operating in the red, spending more than they were taking in, and there were hundreds more that were barely getting by. So if you're in a job like Boeckenstedt's, sitting in the admissions office, sorting through applications from prospective freshmen, you don't have the luxury, these days, of making your decisions based solely on abstract notions of merit and excellence and fairness and equity. What you're looking for — to put it bluntly — is customers, ideally ones who will pay large amounts of money for the service you are offering.

Upstairs, in the convention-center meeting rooms, the NACAC conference featured a variety of high-minded and informative presentations about serving undocumented students and creating STEM pipelines and streamlining the community college transfer process. But down here in the exhibit hall, in the heart of what Boeckenstedt called "the admissions-industrial complex," even the Revolutionary War soldiers were hustling product. It was *Glengarry Glen Ross,* the campus version, and the fluffernutter pudding shots were for closers only.

COLLEGE ADMISSIONS MAY BE a business, but it is a strange and complex one, far more convoluted than selling real estate or used cars. That is mostly because of the obvious but still odd fact that colleges choose their customers at the same time their customers choose colleges. At all but the least selective institutions, a significant number of potential customers are simply turned away — told they cannot purchase, at any price, the service the college is selling. And the decisions that enrollment managers make about which students to accept and which ones to reject have implications that go well beyond the composition of next fall's freshman class. Which students you accept and which ones you reject *this year* will help to determine who will apply to your college *next year.*

That phenomenon is due, in large part, to the power of the "America's Best Colleges" list produced each year by the editors of *U.S. News & World Report.* The list rewards colleges for admitting students with high SAT scores, and it also rewards them for having a low "acceptance rate" — the percentage of the applicant pool that is admitted. The more high-scoring students you admit, and the more students of any kind that you reject, the better *U.S. News* likes you. DePaul, where Boeckenstedt works, accepts about 70 percent of the students who apply, and the students who enroll have an average SAT score of about 1200; *U.S. News* ranks it 119th on its list of national universities.

The *U.S. News* list is openly loathed by admissions folks; in a 2010 poll, only 3 percent of NACAC members said they thought the "America's Best Colleges" list accurately reflected the actual best colleges in America, and 87 percent said the list forced universities to take steps that were "counterproductive" to their educational mission in order to improve their ranking. But this widely shared distaste for the list doesn't mean people in admissions ignore it. Quite the opposite. They know that American high school students and their families take the *U.S. News* rankings very seriously. Remember Clara's father in suburban DC, refusing to consider any college that wasn't one of the thirty highest-ranked institutions in the country? He is not alone, not by a long shot. Researchers have demonstrated, using data analysis, what enrollment managers know in their bones: If you rise even one place on the *U.S. News* list, you will receive more and better applications from next year's crop of high school seniors. And if you fall even one place on the list . . . well, God help you.

So if you're an enrollment manager, you have an incentive to admit a lot of rich kids, because they can pay the tuition, and you have an incentive to admit a lot of high-scoring kids, because they will bolster your *U.S. News* ranking, and you also have an incentive to reject a lot of students of any kind, because that, too, will help your ranking. All three of these goals can be served, to a certain extent, with a single strategy: getting lots and lots of high school seniors, ideally wealthy and high-scoring ones, to apply to your college.

But that's not as easy as it might appear. Sure, *you're* aware of the unique charms of your particular college, but most high school students have never heard of it, and they have thousands of alternatives from which to choose. So you need to market your college to them. One of Jack Maguire's insights, decades ago, was that colleges should target their marketing directly to the students they most want to reach and tailor their pitch to make it especially appealing to precisely those students. In 1976 that meant glossy four-color brochures and direct-mail campaigns. Today, though, enrollment managers have access to digital and database technologies that Maguire could not have dreamed of, and those tools allow colleges to aim customized marketing campaigns at increasingly narrow segments of the American high school student population, inundating them with texts, calls, email messages, and thoughtful gifts until they finally give in and apply.

Even then, your problems as an enrollment manager are not solved. The reality is that you don't just need a lot of applications. You don't even just need a lot of high-quality applications. You also need to be able to predict, with high confidence, exactly how those students will respond if you admit them. Which means you need to use predictive analytics: a relatively new and powerful tool, increasingly popular in the business world, that employs large databases and self-adjusting algorithms to predict consumers' future behavior based on their personal history and on the patterns followed in the past by consumers like them.

This is where enrollment management, to me at least, begins to resemble quantum physics. To explain what I mean, I first need to define one more admissions-business term: "yield." When colleges send out acceptance notices to students, they expect that a significant number of those students will turn down the offer and enroll somewhere else. The percentage of accepted students who wind up actually enrolling is a college's yield rate, and that figure has been falling steadily at American colleges for decades. The average yield rate among four-year, not-for-profit colleges now stands at 27 percent, nationwide. Which means that if you're a college-admissions director, and you have eight hundred seats in your freshman class, you will need to admit, on average, about three thousand students in order to fill them — and then hope that you've guessed exactly right about how many idiosyncratic and emotional seventeen-year-olds will say yes to your offer.

And it's not enough just to get the *number* right. You also need to make sure the eight hundred students who say yes include enough high-income and high-scoring students to pay your bills and keep your *U.S. News* ranking high. And as any teenager who's had his heart broken can tell you, the high school students you want the most are often the ones who want you the least. Because most high school seniors employ the Hoxby principle when they're making their college decisions (*Choose the most selective school that will admit you*), you're inevitably going to lose a lot of the most appealing students you admit.

This is where financial aid enters the picture. In the days before Jack Maguire, financial aid was an entirely separate department from admissions. First, a college's admissions staff would choose its incoming class, and then its financial-aid department — usually located in a different building — would dole out grants to the students who needed them. One of Maguire's key insights was that strategically targeted offers of financial aid could help you lure in exactly the freshmen you wanted. It was a new idea — giving aid to students who didn't need it — and it didn't seem, at first, to make sense. But in the 1980s, the first private colleges began experimenting with this new strategy, giving these grants the euphemistic name "merit aid," and they found it worked remarkably well. It turned out that giving grants — even relatively small ones — to students with high family incomes made it significantly more likely that those students would enroll in your college. (If you called the grant a "scholarship," it worked even better.) And if a high-scoring student was willing to pay, say, $30,000 of your $40,000 tuition, that was still a pretty good deal for your college.

Over the last thirty years, this strategy has spread to almost every private college in the nation, and most public ones, as well. As time has gone on, however, enrollment managers have found that while the approach worked quite well when only a few colleges were doing it, it works much less well now that everyone is. Beginning in the early 2000s, the practice of giving out merit aid evolved first into an arms race among colleges and then, more recently, into what is beginning to look like a death spiral. At private, nonprofit four-year colleges, 89 percent of students now receive some form of financial aid, meaning that almost no one is paying full price. And that aid goes increasingly to well-off students; American colleges collectively now give more institutional aid to each student with a family income over $100,000, on average, than they do to each student with a family income under $20,000.

Colleges still publish official tuition rates, just like they used to, and those published rates are often astoundingly high. But the official numbers have become almost entirely divorced from reality. Each year, colleges offer larger and larger "tuition discounts"—another euphemism for merit aid—in order to attract the students they want. In 2018 the average tuition discount rate for freshmen at private, nonprofit universities hit 50 percent for the first time, meaning that colleges were charging students, on average, less than half of their posted tuition rates. Rising tuition rates may still dominate the headlines, but the truth is that discount rates are rising just as quickly, which means that the actual revenue colleges take in each year stays more or less flat. And as any used-car salesman can tell you, a permanent half-off sale is not a great long-term business model.

If colleges were simply giving every student the same 50 percent discount, that would be challenging enough for enrollment managers. But in fact, the discounts they offer vary widely from student to student. In fact, if you pick any two freshmen at the same college, they are likely to be paying completely different tuition rates. Those rates are based not on the true value of the service the college is offering or even on the ability of the student's family to pay; instead, they are based on a complex calculation of what the student is worth to the college and what the college is worth to the student.

The consultants many colleges hire to perform those calculations — known in the trade as "financial-aid optimization" — are the hidden geniuses of enrollment management, the quants with advanced math degrees who take predictive analytics to an even more esoteric level. They spend long hours behind closed doors, parsing student decision-making patterns, carefully adjusting their econometric models, calculating precisely how many dollars it will take to get Chloe or Josh to choose your college.

In the exhibit hall in Boston, the companies that employ these backroom prodigies had some of the biggest and most well-appointed booths on the floor. These firms aren't the ones with the cute dot-com names; their corporate titles sound venerable and refined, as though they belong on tins of biscuits being sold in posh London department stores: Hobsons; Royall; Kennedy & Company. Outside the ranks of enrollment management, the work these companies do is almost entirely unknown. Their names never appear on the marketing emails they send to students on behalf of colleges, or on the financial-aid award packages they assemble and present to them. But collectively, they play as big a role as anyone in shaping where American high school seniors, in the millions, go to college.

IN 2006, DANIEL GOLDEN, a Pulitzer Prize–winning *Wall Street Journal* reporter, published a book about the admissions process at elite American colleges titled *The Price of Admission*. In the course of reporting the book, Golden went looking for stories of prestigious universities that had given preference in admissions to the children of big-money donors, and he found, hidden away in secret files at

Harvard University, an eerily prescient example: the case of Jared Kushner. At the time the book was published, Kushner was little known outside of the Park Avenue charity-ball circuit, but a decade later he became a household name when his father-in-law, President Donald Trump, made him a senior White House adviser.

Golden revealed that in 1998, Kushner's father, Charles, donated $2.5 million to Harvard, just as Jared was beginning his senior year at the Frisch School, a private school in New Jersey. Administrators at Frisch told Golden that no one at the school believed Kushner could possibly get into Harvard on his merits. He was not a particularly good student, they said, and his test scores were below Ivy League standards. "Jared was certainly not anywhere near the top of his class," Margot Krebs, the head of Frisch's college-prep program, told Golden. But after Charles Kushner met personally with Harvard's president, the admissions office decided to overlook Jared's academic shortcomings, and he was invited to join the class of 2003.

"It was an unusual choice for Harvard to make," Krebs concluded.

Or perhaps not. Golden also reported on the consistent advantage that elite colleges gave to "legacies," the children of alumni, and that practice has only accelerated in the years since his book was published. More than a third of legacy applicants are admitted to Harvard today, compared to fewer than 5 percent of applicants overall, and many of those legacies apparently take a shortcut to get there. In 2018 a lawsuit against Harvard by a group claiming discrimination against Asian American applicants compelled the university to produce documents confirming the existence of a long-rumored last-minute backdoor admissions process called the "Z-list." Harvard seems to use the Z-list—which comes with a requirement that admitted students take a gap year before enrolling—as a quiet way to admit legacies and children of wealthy donors with lower grades and test scores. The documents showed that almost half of Z-list students in recent years were legacies, the vast majority were white, and their high school records were, according to the *Harvard Crimson*, "more comparable to rejected students than to those of other admitted students."

Harvard, like most Ivy League colleges, doesn't have a department of enrollment management. It's partly a prestige thing, according to Boeckenstedt: enrollment management is seen by elite colleges as too down-market for their taste, too crass and mercantile. Of course, Harvard's lack of an enrollment-management department doesn't mean their admissions process is immune to market forces. It just means that those market forces tend to exert themselves personally, one at a time, usually in quiet conversations or discreet emails among fundraisers and administrators and donors like Charles Kushner.

Backdoor stories like Jared Kushner's can be appealing to read in part because they seem to confirm our suspicion that the elite admissions game is rigged in favor of plutocrats. But from the perspective of the exhibit hall at the NACAC conference, Kushner's story is just one particularly vivid example of the demands that market incentives impose on admissions directors at every college, up and down the selectivity scale. At Harvard, those demands may come in the form of a phone call from the president or the development director. At most other universities, it comes when you receive your financial-aid-optimization report from Hobsons or Royall or Kennedy & Company.

The rise of predictive analytics in aid and admissions has had the effect of automating and turbocharging the financial pressures that enrollment managers have always felt. The composition of a college's predictive model and the specific nature of its inputs may differ somewhat from one institution to another, but the output is always the same: *Admit more rich kids.* It's true everywhere: Wealthy freshmen help with your budget. They help with your donors. And they help with your *U.S. News* ranking, which will then help you to attract more and higher-scoring rich kids to your applicant pool next year.

In an ideal world — or if you're an institution at the top of the selectivity pyramid — the wealthy students who apply to your college will all be academic superstars. But the reality is that there is a limited supply of high-scoring, well-off seventeen-year-olds, and those students are very much in demand in college admissions. As a result, colleges that aren't in the very top tier of selectivity often feel compelled to admit their own Jared Kushners: wealthy students with less than sterling academic records.

"Few enrollment management people will admit this publicly, but we're all sort of in the same boat," Boeckenstedt told me. "Admissions for us is not a matter of turning down students we'd like to admit. It's a matter of admitting students we'd like to turn down."

There is a popular and persistent image of college admissions in which diversity-obsessed universities are using affirmative action to deny spaces to academically talented affluent kids while they admit low-income students with lower ability in their place. Boeckenstedt says the opposite is closer to the truth. The easiest category of students for most enrollment managers to admit, he explains, are below-average students from high-income families. Because their parents can afford tutoring, they are likely to have decent test scores, which means they won't hurt your *U.S. News* ranking. They probably won't distinguish themselves academically at your college, but they can pay full tuition. And perhaps most important, they don't have a lot of other options, so they're likely to say yes to your offer of admission.

"These are the kids who will gladly pay more to move up the food chain," Boeckenstedt explained. "I call them the CFO Specials, because they appeal to the college's chief financial officer. They are challenging for the faculty, but they bring in a lot of revenue."

In recent decades, CFO Specials have become the biggest and most attractive growth market for colleges across the United States. According to a 2007 study by the economists Lance Lochner and Philippe Belley, students with below-average test scores and above-average family incomes increased their college attendance rates between the early 1980s and the early 2000s by more than 85 percent, a faster growth rate than any other cohort. If you're applying to college, this is an excellent time to be a CFO Special. And if you're running an admissions office, your mandate, like it or not, is to find as many CFO Specials as you can.

2. Going Test-Optional

Over the last decade, two distinct conversations about college admissions and class have been taking place in the United States. The first one has been conducted in public, at College Board summits and White House conferences and meetings of philanthropists and nonprofit leaders. It is the conversation that informs some of the interventions I wrote about in chapters 2 and 3, from Caroline Hoxby's packets to Khan Academy's SAT prep to CollegePoint's video counseling. The premise of this conversation is that the problem of inequity in higher education is mostly a demand-side problem: Poor kids are making regrettable miscalculations as they apply to college. They are "betraying themselves." Selective colleges would love to admit more low-income students — if only they could find enough highly qualified ones who could meet their academic standards.

The second conversation is the one going on in the exhibit hall at the NACAC conference, among the enrollment professionals who labor behind the scenes in the admissions-industrial complex. This conversation, held more often in private, starts from the premise that the biggest barriers to opportunity for low-income students in higher education are on the supply side — in the universities themselves, and specifically in the admissions office. Enrollment managers know there is no great shortage of deserving low-income students applying to good colleges; they know this because they regularly reject them — not because they don't want to admit these students, but because they can't afford to. Admissions professionals are well aware that they spend much of their time and energy looking not for more high-achieving low-income students but for more low-achieving high-income students — more CFO Specials. That's how they make their budget. That's how their institutions stay afloat.

It is entirely possible, in fact, that *this* is the reason that the thirty thousand packets the College Board mailed out each year to high-achieving low-income students didn't make much of an impact on the kind of colleges those students attended. Maybe it wasn't so much that the students who received the packets were reluctant to apply to prestigious colleges. Maybe those colleges were reluctant to *admit* them — and when they did admit those students, maybe they didn't give them enough financial aid to make it feasible for them to attend.

In public, university leaders like to advertise the diversity of their freshman classes and their institutions' generosity with financial aid. In private, they feel immense pressure to maintain tuition revenue and perpetuate the sort of institutional prestige that is reflected on the *U.S. News* list. That public priority and that private one are inevitably in conflict, and the place on each campus where that conflict plays out is the admissions office.

Michael Bastedo, an education researcher at the University of Michigan who studies enrollment management, wrote about this divide in a recent paper. "College presidents can publicly claim that they want more racially and economically diverse incoming classes, while privately demanding that their chief enrollment officer increase revenues and prestige," Bastedo explained. "Enrollment managers become the faceless, pragmatic technocrats of the institution, while everyone else gets to pretend that all enrollment goals can be pursued simultaneously."

Most of the time, Jon Boeckenstedt is quite content to be DePaul University's designated faceless, pragmatic technocrat, sitting alone in his office with a can of diet ginger ale and a few Excel spreadsheets, predicting yields and calculating aid packages. But in recent years another, more public side to Boeckenstedt has begun to emerge through his blogs and on Twitter. That side wants to expose some of the hidden truths of enrollment management, to bring these internal institutional conflicts out into the light of day.

Though Boeckenstedt can be sardonic, even a little dour, he is not, in his heart, cynical about admissions. He chose to work at DePaul,

he told me, in part because of its institutional mission. With an undergraduate population of more than fourteen thousand students, it
is the largest Catholic college in the United States, founded in 1898 by
followers of St. Vincent de Paul to serve the children of German and
Irish Catholic immigrants in turn-of-the-century Chicago. Today,
DePaul enrolls a relatively large number of less privileged students:
a third of the students in each freshman class are first-generation,
meaning neither of their parents went to college, and 36 percent
of the most recent incoming class were eligible for Pell grants. For
Boeckenstedt, the son of a manual laborer father who never earned
more than $17,000 a year, those statistics are meaningful.

"I wasn't just a first-generation college student," he reminded me.
"I was a first-generation *high school* student. I couldn't have imagined, when I was a kid, living this life that I'm living. I want to make
that possible for other people."

Boeckenstedt's preferred medium of expression these days is the
infographic. Over the last few years, he has taught himself to use
sophisticated data-visualization tools, and he regularly posts the results on one of his blogs, *Higher Ed Data Stories*. For one recent post,
Boeckenstedt created a detailed, multicolored chart that compared
admissions data from more than a thousand colleges and sorted
those colleges according to three variables: their mean freshman SAT
score, the percentage of their freshmen who receive Pell grants, and
the percentage of their students who are black or Latino.

Boeckenstedt's graph demonstrates, in a particularly vivid way,
what might be called the iron law of college admissions: The colleges
with high average SAT scores — which are also the highest-ranked
colleges and the ones with the lowest acceptance rates and the largest endowments — admit very few low-income students and very few
black and Latino students. Boeckenstedt's chart shows an almost perfect correlation between institutional selectivity and students' family
income, a steady, unwavering diagonal line slicing through the graph.
With only a few exceptions, every American college follows the same
pattern.

Boeckenstedt argues that there is an invisible incentive structure guiding the process of admissions that so far has made it impossible for any college to deviate significantly from the iron rule. "In general, the higher your freshman class SAT, the lower the percentage of freshmen on Pell, and the less diverse you are," he wrote. "Thus, when we ask universities to be 'excellent' and we define 'excellence' by input variables like SAT or ACT scores and selectivity, this is what we're left with: Colleges who want to do the right thing have to act counter to their own interests."

The incentive structure that Boeckenstedt observes has two main features that stand in the way of enrollment managers who want to "do the right thing," as Boeckenstedt puts it, and admit more low-income students. The first is the simple need for tuition revenue. Unless colleges can reduce their costs — which means reducing the amount they spend on their students — it is going to be difficult for them to resist the lure of wealthy students who can pay full price. And there are several perverse incentives in the marketplace that make it hard for colleges to cut spending. The most basic one is the fact that the all-powerful *U.S. News* algorithm rewards them for spending a lot of money: higher faculty salaries and more spending on students lead directly to better rankings. If you reduce your costs, your ranking will fall, which means that next year your applicant pool will shrink. So instead you keep your costs high, which means you need a lot of tuition revenue, which means you need to keep admitting lots of rich kids.

Among the wealthiest colleges, the incentives preventing admissions directors from bringing in more low-income students are more nuanced, but no less powerful. Boeckenstedt points out a fact that is somehow simultaneously totally obvious and yet still kind of dumbfounding: the colleges that can most easily afford to admit low-income students are the ones that admit the fewest. DePaul has a much smaller endowment than, say, Harvard or Princeton. And yet somehow its leadership finds the money to admit and give aid to more than twice as many low-income students, proportionally, as those elite colleges do.

Remember: the two dozen or so richest and most selective colleges in the country don't rely on tuition revenue. They could easily admit freshman classes made up entirely of academically excellent Pell-eligible students and charge them nothing, and the cost in lost tuition would amount to a rounding error in their annual budgets. But not only do elite colleges not take that step; they do the opposite, year after year. They admit *fewer* Pell-eligible students than almost any other institution. They have the most resources to spend on educating low-income students, and they do the least.

Why don't they do more? The answer, in Boeckenstedt's opinion, is that staying "elite" depends not just on admitting a lot of high-scoring students. It also depends on admitting a lot of rich ones. Researchers have shown that when colleges take steps to become more racially or socioeconomically diverse, applications tend to go down in future years. "Maybe — just maybe — the term 'elite' means 'uncluttered by poor people,'" Boeckenstedt wrote. "And maybe that's the problem."

Finances aside, there is a second big structural problem standing in the way of colleges that want to "do the right thing": the extraordinary power of standardized admission tests, and the apparently unbreakable relationship between family income and SAT or ACT scores. Here's one example: In 2017, according to College Board data, if you were a student who took the SAT and your parents earned more than $200,000 a year, there was about a one in five chance that you scored above a 1400 (out of 1600). If your parents earned less than $20,000 a year, there was a one in *fifty* chance that you scored over 1400. The correlation between family income and SAT scores is not just a slope — it's a cliff. (And remember: that 2017 data was collected *after* the full rollout of the College Board's Coleman-era interventions, including the overhaul of the SAT and the introduction of Khan Academy's Official SAT Practice.)

So what do you do if you're an enrollment manager interested in doing the right thing? Boeckenstedt has an answer: quit paying so much attention to the SAT and ACT. "If colleges and universities are serious about enrolling more first-generation students, low-income students, or students of color," he wrote, "they need to take a serious look at the weight of tests in the admissions process."

In 2010 DePaul University's administrators, under Boeckenstedt's leadership, did just that: they took a serious look at their reliance on standardized tests in admissions. And what they decided, after much internal debate, was that they needed to make a change in the way they ran their admissions. Over the previous few decades, a growing number of American colleges and universities had become "test-optional," meaning they stopped requiring applicants to submit SAT or ACT scores. DePaul decided to join them. In February 2011 the university announced that beginning with the next year's admissions cycle, prospective students could choose whether or not they wanted DePaul to consider their test scores as part of their application. And with that, DePaul became the largest private nonprofit university in the country to offer test-optional admissions.

THERE IS A LONG-STANDING, ongoing, and often heated debate over the comparative value of standardized-test scores and high school grades in predicting a student's performance in college. But most people who have studied the data agree on three basic premises.

First, that the two measures track each other pretty well; most students who get good grades in high school also get good test scores.

Second, that high school grades alone are better than test scores alone at predicting a student's freshman GPA or likelihood to graduate from college on time.

Third, that adding a student's test scores to her high school grades produces, on average, a slightly more reliable prediction of her performance as a college freshman than her high school grades alone.

Beyond those three points, there's a lot of disagreement—not only over what the data say, but over what they mean. People who oppose the use of standardized tests in admissions tend to focus on the first two of those three premises. People who support their use tend to focus on the third.

The group that supports the use of the tests in admissions—which includes the many researchers employed by the College Board and ACT—often argues that more information is always good. Even if test scores offer up just a small amount of extra predictive power, they say, that's still valuable: every little bit helps. Standardized-test skeptics, including Jon Boeckenstedt, respond that the small statistical benefit gained by adding the SAT to a student's high school grades is outweighed by the fact that the tests consistently favor well-off students to such a strong degree.

Among the millions of students who take the SAT each year, about two-thirds receive scores that are in line with their high school grades. For those students, the SAT doesn't really matter at all—their test scores send exactly the same signal to college-admissions offices that their high school grades do. The students for whom test scores make a difference in admissions are the two groups who have what testing researchers call "discrepant" scores—meaning either that their SAT score is much higher than their high school grades would predict, or their high school grades are much higher than their SAT score would predict. Those two categories each make up about a sixth of each national cohort of high school seniors.

Students in the first discrepant group—let's call them the inflated-SAT group—get a big boost from the SAT. Maybe their high school grades are only average, but they do great on the SAT, way better than their grades would have predicted. For them, a college-admissions system that puts a lot of emphasis on test scores is a good thing.

For students in the second discrepant group—let's call them the deflated-SAT group—the SAT is a major obstacle. Maybe they have excellent high school grades, but their SAT scores are mediocre, much worse than their grades would have predicted. For them, a system that puts a lot of weight on test scores is a disaster. They would benefit instead from a test-optional system, like DePaul's, that allows colleges to ignore their scores and put more emphasis on their high school grades.

So if we're trying to determine the overall effect of standardized admission tests — and of test-optional policies — on American students, one big question is this: Who are the students in each of these two groups, the inflated-SAT students and the deflated-SAT students? How do they compare with each other — apart from the obvious fact that one group does better on standardized tests and the other does better in the classroom?

It turns out that the College Board has actually examined this question quite carefully. In 2010 three College Board researchers sat down and analyzed data from more than 150,000 students who took the SAT across the USA, and they found that the sociocultural demographics of the two "discrepant" groups differed substantially. The study these researchers produced remains the best and most complete analysis of discrepant scores that has been done to date.

Here's what the College Board found: The students with the inflated SAT scores were more likely to be white or Asian than the students in the deflated-SAT group, and they were much more likely to be male. Their families were much better off, too. Compared to the students with the deflated SAT scores, the inflated-SAT students were more than twice as likely to have parents who earned more than $100,000 a year and more than twice as likely to have parents with graduate degrees. These are the students — the only students — who get a big boost in admissions from the SAT.

Then there's the second group, the deflated-SAT group, the ones whose SAT scores were significantly lower than their high school grades would have predicted. According to the College Board's demographic analysis, those students were twice as likely as students in the inflated-SAT group to be female, twice as likely to be black, and almost three times as likely to be Hispanic. They were three times as likely as students in the inflated-SAT group to have parents who earned less than $30,000 a year, and they were almost three times as likely to have parents who didn't attend college.

According to the College Board's own research, then, for about two-thirds of high school seniors, the SAT doesn't matter much at all.

For about a sixth of them — a group that is disproportionately male, affluent, white or Asian, and with highly educated parents — the SAT improves their chances to get into selective colleges. And for another sixth — a group that is disproportionately female, black or Latino, low-income, and first-generation — the SAT is the factor that most significantly undermines their chances.

It was data like this that compelled Boeckenstedt and his colleagues at DePaul to change the university's admissions policy back in 2011. DePaul's requirement that applicants submit SAT scores was making it difficult for them to enroll students from that deflated-SAT group, and that was a problem for the institution and its mission. In many ways, the students in that cohort were a lot like the Irish and Polish and German boys who thronged to DePaul a century earlier. This new generation of low-income strivers was more likely to be female, and their skin was often several shades darker than their European predecessors, but beyond those differences, they were exactly the kind of students DePaul was founded to serve: Chicago kids from poor and working-class families, often immigrants or the children of immigrants, earning good grades in public school and eager for the opportunity to better themselves through higher education. Because their test scores were low, they often weren't even applying to DePaul; they assumed they wouldn't be admitted. But DePaul's internal research predicted that if they did make it to the university, they were likely to succeed.

About 10 percent of the students in each twenty-five-hundred-member freshman class at DePaul are now admitted without anyone at the university ever seeing their scores. Demographically, those students are quite different from the rest of DePaul's applicant pool: they are more likely to be low-income — 48 percent of them are eligible for Pell grants — and more than half are black or Latino.

After they are admitted, DePaul asks nonsubmitting students to submit their test scores anyway, for research purposes, and after several years of following their progress, here's what Boeckenstedt and his colleagues have found: Students who enroll at DePaul having chosen not to submit their scores do indeed have much lower ACT and SAT scores than students who choose to submit their scores. The average ACT scores of nonsubmitters are about five points lower than those of submitters, which is a substantial gap on the ACT's 36-point scale. But despite those low test scores, nonsubmitting students do just as well at DePaul as the submitters do. Their freshman GPAs are equivalent. They have exactly the same likelihood of returning to DePaul for their sophomore year. And the six-year graduation rate for nonsubmitters in the first class admitted under the test-optional policy was 69.4 percent, just two and a half percentage points below the 72 percent graduation rate for the class as a whole.

When Boeckenstedt looks at all that data, his conclusion is that the nonsubmitters' low test scores were essentially a false signal, predicting an academic disaster in college that never arrived. Allowing those students to apply without submitting their scores not only encouraged more of them to apply. It also made it easier for Boeckenstedt and his admissions staff not to get distracted or be misled by that false signal. It made it easier for them to do the right thing.

THE DATA from the first few years of test-optional admissions at DePaul University were welcome news for Jon Boeckenstedt and his colleagues. The change in policy hadn't transformed DePaul's admission patterns altogether, but it had enabled the university to achieve an important, if modest, goal: to enroll hundreds of high-performing low-income and first-generation students each year who might not have been admitted (or even applied) otherwise, and to do so without compromising the university's academic quality.

But for the College Board and ACT Inc., the results from DePaul — and the broader national movement toward test-optional admissions — represented a serious challenge to their corporate interests. The number of American colleges that offer test-optional admissions has been growing steadily since Bowdoin and Bates became the nation's first test-optional colleges in 1969 and 1984, respectively. Currently, about half of the top one hundred schools on the *U.S. News* list of the best liberal arts colleges in the nation are test-optional, as are a number of larger national universities, including Wake Forest, Brandeis, and George Washington. (Advocates take great pleasure in pointing out that in 2006 David Coleman's mother, Elizabeth Coleman, introduced test-optional admissions at Bennington College, where she was president.)

Test-optional admissions don't pose an immediate risk to the revenue streams that sustain the College Board and ACT Inc. Now that the testing institutions have signed contracts with so many states to provide statewide in-school testing, they won't be bothered much if the rise of test-optional admissions means a few thousand additional students each year decide not to submit their scores — or even not to take the tests at all.

The threat that the College Board and ACT Inc. face from test-optional admissions is more existential than economic. The SAT was designed, in part, to help colleges keep out exactly the kind of students that DePaul's test-optional policy is now allowing in: students with high grades and low test scores. If those students are now succeeding at DePaul and other test-optional colleges *despite* their low test scores, well, then, maybe the scores don't mean what they are supposed to mean.

In 2017 the College Board launched a public relations campaign to counteract and critique the movement toward test-optional admissions and to call into question the credibility of students' high school grades. The strategy the company's leaders chose was an audacious one. They decided to make the case that high school grades gave an unfair advantage to privileged students, while the SAT benefited less privileged students — despite the fact that their research had for years demonstrated the opposite.

The cornerstone of the College Board's strategy was a new academic paper by two in-house researchers, Michael Hurwitz and Jason Lee. The paper, titled "Grade Inflation and the Role of Standardized Testing," begins by observing a genuine phenomenon, which is that the high school grades that students report to the College Board when they take the SAT have been gradually increasing over the last couple of decades, rising from an average GPA of 3.27 in 1998 to an average GPA of 3.38 in 2016. Hurwitz and Lee analyzed this change in high school grades by the type of school that students attended, and they showed that the biggest increase in GPA during those years took place among students at private schools. They used that fact to argue that grade inflation was benefiting white and Asian students and wealthier students, at the expense of everyone else.

The problem with this argument is that the paper itself includes data that shows that grade inflation has actually been quite consistent across racial and socioeconomic groups. What has not been consistent, the data in the paper shows, is changes in *SAT scores* among these different groups.

Consider the data for black students and Asian students—the racial groups that typically score the lowest and the highest, respectively, on the SAT. Between 2001 and 2016, high school GPAs for Asian students did increase—they went up by 0.12 grade points. But GPAs went up for black students, too, by almost the same amount: 0.11 grade points. But while their GPAs were moving in parallel, the SAT scores that black and Asian students were receiving diverged quite sharply over the same period. Asian students' SAT scores went up by fifty-five points, on average, between 2001 and 2016, while black students' scores went *down* by sixteen points.

So the data in the paper show that Asian students did gain a significant advantage over black students in college admissions during those fifteen years—but the advantage was entirely due to the rise in their SAT scores, and not to the inflation of their high school grades.

You can see the same thing when you sort students by their parents' education level. Between 1998 and 2016, high school GPAs for students whose parents had a graduate degree improved by 0.15 grade points. GPAs for students whose parents had only an associate's degree rose by the exact same amount. Grade inflation provided no advantage for the more privileged students. But over those same eighteen years, the average SAT score for students whose parents had graduate degrees went up by five points, while the average SAT score for students whose parents had only an associate's degree went *down* by twenty-seven points. Again, the additional admissions advantage that the more privileged group gained was due entirely to the rise in their SAT scores and not to any change in their GPAs.

This data is sitting there in plain sight in the paper's tables and charts. (It's in Figure 3.9 and Figure 3.10, if you're interested.) But in the text of the paper, the authors reach a conclusion that is the opposite of what those data say. "The use of high school grades in admissions is fraught with equity issues," an introduction to the paper asserts. Grade inflation "is disproportionately impacting white and Asian students, as well as students from higher socioeconomic backgrounds," the authors write.

"If grade inflation continues," they warn, "admissions staff may need to rely more heavily on standardized tests like the SAT or ACT to differentiate students." As a result, "test-optional policies may become unsustainable."

In other news: Black is white. Up is down.

The College Board gave a prepublication copy of Hurwitz and Lee's grade-inflation paper to a number of education journalists in the summer of 2017, and it generated a lot of coverage: stories in *USA Today*, in the *Atlantic*, in *Education Week*, and in Breitbart News and a number of other online publications. None of the coverage pointed out the disjunction between the paper's data and its stated conclusions. The public relations campaign continued with an online "advertorial" in the *Atlantic* — an article, titled "When Grades Don't Show the Whole Picture," that resembled a regular *Atlantic* article but was, on closer inspection, flagged as "sponsor content" that was "posted by the College Board". The text of the advertorial reflected the message of Hurwitz and Lee's paper: "Gaps in high school GPA have widened over time, making it more difficult than ever for minority and lower-income students to distinguish themselves as academic contenders through their grades alone."

There was only one force that could level the playing field for these disadvantaged students, the advertorial suggested: the SAT. "While the title of valedictorian might not hold the same meaning it once did, the SAT does," the text concluded. "Submitting SAT scores as part of a college application can open doors to opportunity not just for a privileged few, but for all students."

But the College Board had clear evidence in its own research that undermined the notion that SAT scores helped low-income students while GPAs hurt them. Every few years, its research department publishes an authoritative analysis of students who take the SAT. It's called the National SAT Validity Study. And each iteration of the validity study shows the same thing: family income has a huge effect on students' SAT scores, and it has almost no effect on their high school grades.

The College Board's validity study published in 2018 showed that working- and middle-class high school students—students whose parents earn between $40,000 and $80,000—have an average GPA in high school of 3.63. Wealthy students—kids whose parents earn more than $200,000—have an average high school GPA of 3.66, almost exactly the same as the working-class kids. High school grades give no real advantage to wealthy students, according to the College Board's own data. They don't benefit "a privileged few." They are not "fraught with equity issues."

When you introduce the SAT into the equation, though, those equity issues quickly do start to get fraught. According to that same validity study, students in the $40,000-to-$80,000 family-income cohort have average SAT scores of 1624 (out of 2400), while students in the over-$200,000 cohort have average scores of 1793. That's a 169-point advantage for the well-off kids. You can find the same story in every SAT validity study, going back more than a decade: wealthy kids get no advantage from their high school grades, but they get a huge boost from their SAT scores. If colleges want to favor wealthy applicants, they should continue to emphasize SAT scores in their admissions decisions. If they want to level the playing field for non-wealthy kids, though, they need to focus on high school grades.

Despite its awkward presentation of the facts, the College Board's anti-test-optional public relations campaign was in many ways a success. The education press largely repeated the claim that grade inflation was benefiting the affluent. In early 2018 the Hurwitz and Lee paper was included in a book on test-optional admissions edited by three employees and former employees of the College Board and published by Johns Hopkins University Press — kind of a book-length advertorial. The book gave a scholarly imprimatur to the College Board's case against test-optional admissions. Like tobacco-industry research on lung cancer or oil-company research on climate change, its main effect was to muddy the waters, to give journalists and educators who weren't intimately familiar with the data the impression that the relationship between SAT scores and income was a complex matter of ongoing debate.

But the College Board's public relations victory was short-lived. In June 2018, a few months after the book was published, the University of Chicago announced that it would no longer require applicants to submit the SAT or ACT, becoming the most prestigious American university ever to go test-optional.

The announcement felt like a turning point in the history of test-optional admissions. The University of Chicago is one of the most selective institutions of higher education in the nation, currently tied with Yale for third place in the U.S. News ranking of national universities. It is one thing for DePaul University, a warm and welcoming school with a social mission rooted in Catholic ideas of justice and fairness, to eliminate the requirement for standardized tests. But the University of Chicago has a national reputation for being cold and conservative and cerebral. There is nothing softhearted about the place. And yet its admissions directors had reached the conclusion that the university could keep recruiting and admitting intellectually dominant freshman classes without relying on standardized tests.

The announcement raised a stark question, one that resounded from Iowa City to Lower Manhattan and through every office of enrollment management in between: If the University of Chicago doesn't need the SAT, who does?

3. Trinity's Problem

In the fall of 2014, Angel Pérez was hired to run the enrollment-management department at Trinity College, a small liberal arts school occupying a picturesque hundred-acre hilltop campus in Hartford, Connecticut. A few months earlier, Trinity's board of trustees had named a new president, Joanne Berger-Sweeney, a neuroscientist who was both the first woman and the first African American president in the college's history. Pérez was one of her first hires.

Trinity was in many ways a typical northeastern private college. It was founded by Episcopalians in the early nineteenth century, and ever since, its student body had been dominated by white, wealthy graduates of New England prep schools. Its architecture was Gothic, its squash team was nationally ranked, and despite its small size (about twenty-two hundred undergraduates) it managed to support five separate student a cappella groups. Two of Trinity's most famous graduates were George Will and Tucker Carlson, meaning that the college had pretty much cornered the market on conservative TV personalities known for wearing bow ties.

Pérez had grown up in very different circumstances. He was born in Puerto Rico in 1976 to a teenage mother and a father who delivered milk door-to-door. When Angel was five, the family moved to New York City to find better opportunities, but landed instead in a public housing development in the South Bronx during the worst years of the borough's crack-fueled descent into chaos. Angel's father worked in a factory that made elevator parts, which gave the family a bit more financial stability than many of their neighbors. But he drank too much and lost his temper and was sometimes violent with Angel's mother. Angel's memories of childhood are mostly of a pervasive fear, both at home and on the streets. He was a pale, nerdy kid who loved books, which made him easy prey for the gangs that controlled his neighborhood. Twice he was attacked on the street and beaten so badly that he ended up in the hospital.

Angel's first glimpse of college came through a TV screen, watching *A Different World,* a spinoff of *The Cosby Show* set at the fictional Hillman College. It gave him a vision of what life outside the Bronx might look like, and it let him imagine that he, too, might someday find himself in a peaceful, safe place where you were allowed to read books all day. In high school, he joined every club, did summer internships, ran for student government — anything to stay out of the apartment, anything to improve his chances for a better future. A guidance counselor at his high school persuaded him to apply to Skidmore College, a selective private institution in upstate New York that Angel had never heard of. He filled out his application using an electric typewriter in his high school's student government office. He took the SAT just once, and he scored poorly. But magically, miraculously, someone in Skidmore's admissions office decided to ignore his lousy test score and admit him anyway, with full financial aid. It was a decision that changed Angel's life.

Soon after his graduation from college, Pérez began his career in admissions, first at Skidmore, then at the Claremont Colleges in Southern California, rising into leadership positions and earning a master's degree and a PhD in higher education along the way. His underlying professional motivation now seems to be to do for young people what that guidance counselor and that admissions officer did for him: spot hidden potential in students with unconventional academic records and transform young lives through college admissions.

When Pérez arrived at Trinity in June 2015, the school had for several years been in the grip of a slow-moving but unrelenting crisis, and enrollment management was at the heart of the problem. The changing demographics of the Northeast were working against colleges like Trinity. As the population aged and young families moved south and west, the region's stock of high school graduates shrank every year. At the same time, the rise of merit aid and the competitive spiral of tuition discounting meant that prep-school kids who were able to pay full tuition now had colleges fighting over them, dangling merit aid as an incentive. At Trinity, tuition revenue had been falling steadily for several years, and the college's finances were looking increasingly dire.

I first visited Trinity in the winter of 2017, a year and a half after Pérez arrived. I sat with him in his office, which looked out on the campus's football field, and he described how the college's admissions strategy had functioned in the years before he was hired. "We were taking some students who probably should not have been admitted, but we were taking them because they could pay," Pérez explained. "They went to good high schools, but they were maybe at the bottom of their class. The motivation wasn't there. So the academic quality of our student body was dropping."

Remember those two "discrepant" groups that the College Board's researchers identified? The first group was the deflated-SAT students, kids like a young Angel Pérez whose high school grades were much better than their SAT scores would predict, and who were disproportionately low-income, first-generation students of color. That wasn't who Trinity was admitting. Instead, each year, Trinity was admitting more and more students from the second discrepant group, the inflated-SAT students, kids whose high school grades were noticeably worse than their SAT scores would predict — the cohort that the College Board's researchers had identified as being disproportionately wealthy, white, and male.

"OK, you're not motivated, you're doing the minimum at your high school," Pérez said, describing the students Trinity used to admit in droves. "You have not worked as hard as your peers. But you did the test prep, and you learned how to play the SAT game."

At Trinity, Pérez's predecessors in the admissions office had been able to capitalize on a truism of academic life in the United States: at expensive prep schools, even kids close to the bottom of the class usually have pretty good SAT scores, mostly because they and their families have access to costly test prep. For enrollment managers at a place like Trinity was before Pérez arrived, SAT scores can provide a convenient justification for admitting the kind of students you need to admit to make your budget. It's hard to feel good about choosing an academically undeserving rich kid over a striving and ambitious poor kid. But if the rich student you're admitting has a higher SAT score than the poor student you're rejecting, you can tell yourself that your decision was based on their relative "college readiness" rather than their relative ability to pay.

The problem is, rich kids who aren't motivated to work hard and get good grades in high school often *aren't* college-ready, however inflated their SAT scores may be. They generally don't suddenly change their academic behavior when they arrive at college. At Trinity, this meant there was a growing number of affluent students on campus who couldn't keep up in class and weren't particularly interested in trying. "It had a morale effect on our faculty," Pérez told me. "They were teaching a very divided campus. The majority of students were really smart and engaged and curious, and then you've got these other students" — the affluent inflated-SAT group — "who are wondering, How did I get into this school?"

A few weeks before my first visit to Trinity, Raj Chetty and his team of economists released their Mobility Report Cards for American colleges, making headlines across the country. Trinity College distinguished itself in the data as having one of the wealthiest student bodies in the nation; the median family income for students at the college (as of 2013) was $257,000, the fifth-highest figure in the country. The most striking statistic, though, was that 26 percent of Trinity's student body came from the very wealthiest cohort of American families, those with incomes in the top 1 percent. That was the highest concentration of ultrarich students to be found at any college among the 2,395 institutions that Chetty and his researchers had examined.

Trinity had become like a grand experiment to see what happens when a college keeps admitting more and more CFO Specials.

The experiment was not going well. In the short term, the strategy succeeded in propping up tuition revenue, and SAT scores weren't declining much. But the climate on campus was in free fall. "We were admitting some students who had serious behavioral issues," Pérez explained. "Their guidance counselors told us that things had already gone south in high school, but we felt the pressure to take them because they could pay. When you do that, you deteriorate not only the quality of the academic experience but also the quality of the social experience." Trinity had a growing reputation as a party school, and problems related to student alcohol abuse were rampant. One frat party left a student paralyzed from the chest down. After another incident, a student was hospitalized with brain and spinal injuries.

Hidden away among the growing army of CFO Specials on the Trinity campus was a small cohort of low-income students. When Pérez arrived, about 10 percent of the student body was eligible for a Pell grant, and many of them were students of color. There were two things that were true about Trinity's low-income students. First, they were doing very well academically. In fact, they were significantly outperforming the rich kids on campus. The six-year graduation rate for Pell-eligible students at Trinity was 92 percent, compared to 76 percent for the rest of the student body. The second fact was that these low-income students — at least the ones I spoke to — were mostly miserable at Trinity, trying and often failing to find their place on a campus where the dominant student culture was overwhelmingly privileged and white.

Soon after he arrived, Pérez concluded that Trinity's existing enrollment-management strategy was unsustainable — financially, academically, and morally. He recommended to the president and the board of trustees that Trinity abandon its previous approach to admissions and move in more or less the opposite direction. If the tools of enrollment management had got Trinity into this mess, Pérez reasoned, maybe the same tools could now get it out. He proposed that Trinity switch to test-optional admissions, giving primary consideration to students' high school records and personal statements instead of their SAT and ACT scores. He proposed to recruit and admit more low-income students and first-generation students. And he proposed that Trinity take steps to make those less privileged students feel more welcome and valued on campus.

President Berger-Sweeney and the Trinity trustees agreed, and in October 2015, just four months after Pérez's arrival on campus, Trinity announced to the world that it was going test-optional, beginning with the class of 2020, whose applications were already beginning to trickle in that fall. Word spread quickly, and by the application deadline in early January, 40 percent of applicants had opted not to submit their scores. The class that Pérez and his team selected in the spring of 2016 wasn't much different demographically from Trinity's previous freshman classes. It was still pretty white and wealthy. But by Trinity's new measures of academic quality (which emphasized high school grades and a rigorous curriculum over test scores), it was the most highly qualified class in years.

When the *U.S. News & World Report* list came out the next fall, though, Trinity had fallen six spots on the ranking of the nation's top liberal arts colleges, from No. 38 to No. 44. The *U.S. News* algorithm generally penalizes colleges for offering test-optional admissions, and it doesn't give them points for increasing their percentage of low-income or first-generation students. Trinity's student body was becoming more diverse and more academically accomplished — but by *U.S. News*'s standards, the college was heading in exactly the wrong direction.

Soon after the *U.S. News* ranking came out, seventeen members of Trinity's English department, representing almost all of the department's faculty, sent a letter to the college's board of trustees acknowledging that Trinity's slide in the rankings might "spark some misgivings among Trustees about admissions policies enacted by Angel Pérez." But the professors urged the trustees to ignore the rankings, stay the course, and continue the new direction in admissions. The students that Pérez was admitting, they explained, were qualitatively different than those in earlier classes. They were more rewarding to teach. They were just plain better students.

"We perceive in many of these students a refreshing array of qualities that were all too rare in prior years: intellectual curiosity, openness of mind and spirit, and genuine will to engage with their peers," the professors wrote. If Pérez's new admissions policies were "having inadvertent, temporary effects on USNWR's dubious 'selectivity' measure," they concluded, "we think this is a small price to pay for one of the most exciting transformations Trinity has witnessed in many years."

THERE ARE A FEW weeks each year, beginning in late February and extending through March, when Pérez's idealistic vision of Trinity College as a place newly committed to inclusion and excellence meets up most bluntly with the practical demands of twenty-first-century enrollment management. The long journey to choose Trinity's freshman class begins much earlier in the academic year, with digital recruitment campaigns and high school visits throughout the summer and fall. Then Pérez and his team of a dozen admissions officers spend the early winter months in careful, individual consideration of each of the six thousand applications submitted by students from across the country and around the world.

Pérez calls this the "read your conscience" phase of the admissions process. He instructs his staff not to think about financial pressures during those initial reads, he told me, not to calculate who can pay and how much. Instead, they simply consider each student as an individual and ask themselves: Does this person belong at Trinity? Can they do the work? Will they add to our community? Do they deserve to be here?

By the end of February, those questions have resulted in a "tentative admit" list of about thirty-two hundred prospective students. This is way too many. Trinity's freshman class each year is made up of about six hundred students. But half of them are selected in the early-decision round in the fall. Early-decision admissions became popular among American colleges, especially selective liberal arts colleges like Trinity, in the 1980s and 1990s. Students are allowed to apply early-decision to just one college, and if they're admitted, they make a binding commitment to enroll in that college. The benefit, for students, is that their chances of admission at any college are generally higher when they apply early-decision. Researchers have found that for a variety of reasons, early admissions benefits affluent students more than middle-class or poor ones, and that's certainly true at Trinity, where the three hundred or so students admitted early are quite a bit wealthier, on average, than the rest of the freshman class.

About half of the early admits are athletes. Trinity is a Division III college, the largest and least elite division of the National Collegiate Athletic Association, and according to NCAA rules, Division III schools are not allowed to offer athletic scholarships. But coaches do recruit athletes, and colleges are allowed to offer those athletes preferential admission. Beginning early in the fall, Trinity's coaches and athletic director bring Pérez their wish lists of prospects, and while Pérez is, strictly speaking, under no obligation to admit students from their lists, he feels pressure to admit a lot of them, and he mostly admits them early. Though the stereotype of college athletes is that they are more likely to be African American and lower-income, most of Trinity's recruited athletes play sports that are popular in prep schools and rare in urban public schools: field hockey, lacrosse, golf, rowing, and, especially, squash. The result is that at Trinity, as at many other Division III schools in the Northeast, the recruited athletes are actually more white and more wealthy, on average, than the rest of the freshman class.

For Pérez, as for many enrollment managers, the benefit of early admissions is mostly about eliminating uncertainty. In an era of falling yields, it is reassuring to know in January that you have at least half your class in place and committed to your college. But the flip side of that commitment, of course, is that when Pérez and his admissions team begin to debate their regular-decision admits at the beginning of March, they have just three hundred remaining slots they can fill. Trinity's yield in recent years has been about 30 percent, but that includes the three hundred early admits, who have basically a 100 percent yield rate. Among the students Trinity admits via regular decision, it has less than a 20 percent yield rate, meaning that Pérez needs to offer admission to about seventeen hundred regular-decision students in order to yield three hundred freshmen who will matriculate the following fall. Once Pérez and his team are finished reading their consciences, they still need to cut about half the names from their list of thirty-two hundred tentative admits to hit that number.

In the winter of 2017, when I was spending time at Trinity, the first five hundred cuts were relatively easy. Pérez divided his admissions counselors into teams of two or three depending on which region of the country they were responsible for, and each team set up shop in a different office or conference room around the admissions building. The teams considered the tentative admits from each high school in their region, debated their comparative merits, and rejected the least qualified. That reduced the tentative admit pool from thirty-two hundred students to twenty-seven hundred — which meant there were still about a thousand students to cut.

It was at that stage, on March 6, that Pérez called in the quants. Like most enrollment managers, Pérez contracts with an outside financial-aid-optimization company to perform econometric modeling on his applicant pool. The company he worked with was called Hardwick Day, a Bloomington, Minnesota, firm that, after a recent round of consolidation in the industry, is now a division of a giant higher-education consulting company called EAB. Pérez was in constant contact with Hardwick Day in March as the winnowing continued, looking to their algorithms to bring a small measure of clarity to what often felt like an ambiguous and imprecise process.

There were two numbers that Pérez knew he needed to hit on May 1, the last day that admitted students could accept or reject Trinity's offer of a spot in the freshman class. The first number was the total size of the class, which had to be as close as possible to six hundred students. The second number, even more pressing, was the combined tuition revenue those six hundred students needed to bring in.

Back in February, Trinity's board of trustees had decided on the tuition target for the class of 2021: $19 million. At Trinity, tuition provides about two-thirds of each year's operating budget, and the college needs that money to pay faculty salaries and utility bills and maintenance costs. In recent years, the revenue from tuition had been declining at Trinity, mostly because of tuition discounts, with worrying results for the overall budget. The college had refinanced its debt and renegotiated contracts with vendors, but it was still running an annual operating loss of $8 million, and that figure was growing each year. So it was crucial that tuition revenue not fall short of the goal.

The $19 million Pérez needed to generate represented about $32,000, on average, from each enrolled student. Trinity's official, list-price tuition that year had risen to $54,000, before room and board, which meant that Pérez was aiming for a 42 percent discount rate, overall. But even with that sizable discount in place, crafting a class that could produce that much revenue was going to be a challenge. There were plenty of highly qualified applicants who needed full financial aid, or close to it, and Pérez wanted to admit as many of them as he could; he was trying, after all, to make the college more diverse. But he knew he would need to balance each full-need student he admitted with enough full-paying students to hit his revenue target.

This was the math problem that Pérez presented to Hardwick Day on March 6: Help me find the right seventeen hundred students to produce a class of six hundred freshmen who will be willing to pay, together, $19 million — and tell me how much of a tuition discount I need to offer to each one. (Hardwick Day's predictive models allow analysts to identify, based on the behavior of past students, precisely what tuition each student would likely be willing to pay. A white student from Danbury with a 3.1 GPA and a 1200 SAT? Hardwick Day's models might predict that if Trinity offered him a $15,000 discount, he would say yes, but if it offered him a $5,000 discount, he would go to the University of Connecticut, instead.)

Over the next two weeks, data flew back and forth between Hartford and Bloomington as Pérez and his team gradually whittled down their pile of tentative admits to twenty-five hundred, and then twenty-three hundred, and then twenty-one hundred, trying to balance the students they wanted with the ones they needed. Each morning, Pérez would give his team a new set of instructions, based on the previous day's analysis from Hardwick Day. One day, the tentative admit pile had too many men from the Northeast who needed financial aid, so they spent the day slicing away at that demographic. The next day they needed to cut women from the Northeast. And on it went. After each round of cuts, Pérez and his team would send their new, whittled-down collection of proposed admits to Hardwick Day, and an hour or two later, a Financial Aid Monitoring Report, in the form of a PDF file, would show up in Pérez's email in-box.

Each report included a precise prediction of the overall class size and tuition revenue that Pérez's latest set of theoretical admits would produce, and each time, the big picture was the same: the class size was too large, and the tuition revenue was too small. There were too many full-need students on Pérez's wish list, and not enough full-pay ones.

The reports from Hardwick Day went deeper into the data, too: the firm provided a specific predicted yield rate, tuition-revenue total, and academic profile for each demographic slice of the pool of tentative admits: students from California; women; students who could pay full price; international students; Latino students. Pérez would use those predictions to try again, each day paring a few more students here and there, trying to get closer and closer to his two targets: six hundred students, $19 million.

The math was cold and hard, but in the admissions building, the process was growing more emotional. By this point, Pérez's admissions counselors felt personally attached to many of the tentative admits. Each morning, they would gather in a conference room down the hall from Pérez's office. One by one, Pérez would project the application profile for each student whose fate was still uncertain onto a large monitor on the wall, and together he and his staff would discuss and debate and horse-trade over each one. Counselors often made passionate defenses for certain students — only to learn, a few hours later, that the latest report from Hardwick Day had ruled them out.

By March 17, a week before Trinity's admission offers were due to go out to the class of 2021, Pérez and his team were still twenty-five students over their target class size and several hundred thousand dollars short of the tuition target. Staff morale was low. Pérez decided it was time for him and Anthony Berry, the director of admissions, to make the final cuts. So they sent the rest of the admissions staff home, and over the weekend, the two men sat in Pérez's office and removed students one by one. Early in the process, they had done what they could to protect highly qualified low-income and first-generation students. But at this point, with the tuition revenue estimates still shy of Pérez's $19 million target, every student they were cutting was a full-need, low-income student.

Test-optional admissions can make it easier, on one level, for enrollment managers to admit high school seniors like a young Angel Pérez — low-income students of great promise with lousy test scores. But going test-optional doesn't relieve the immense financial pressures weighing on enrollment managers at most American colleges today. Some colleges that have gone test-optional have been able to use the policy to significantly increase the number of low-income and first-generation students they admit. But on the whole, researchers have found, when colleges go test-optional it usually doesn't change the racial or economic diversity of their incoming class much at all. Pérez and his counselors were highly motivated to admit low-income students, but they were faced with enormous pressures in the opposite direction — from the athletics department, which wanted more squash champions; from the development and alumni offices, which wanted more legacy admits; but mostly from the CFO, who needed that $19 million in tuition revenue to keep the college in operation.

In the end, Pérez mostly hit his targets. He enrolled 580 students in the class of 2021, and they brought in just slightly more than $19 million. Fifteen percent were first-generation, 14 percent were eligible for Pell grants, and 16 percent were black or Latino. All those numbers were a bit higher than when Pérez arrived, but only a bit — and they were all still short of the goals that Pérez aspired to.

WHEN ANGEL PÉREZ first read through Matthew Rivera's application to Trinity College, back in the winter of 2016, it felt a little like he was looking into a mirror. Matthew was a Latino kid from the Bronx with a complicated home life and a drive to succeed, just like Pérez had been two decades earlier. Both Angel and Matthew were born to teenage mothers. Both grew up in public housing. Both attended public high school in Manhattan and worked in fast-food jobs after school to help out with bills at home. (Angel had been a cashier at the Wendy's in Times Square; Matthew folded burritos at a Chipotle in Riverdale.) Each was the first in his family even to think about going to college.

Those biographical parallels caught Pérez's attention, but that wasn't why he wanted to admit Matthew to Trinity College. He wanted to admit Matthew because Matthew was an excellent student, with an academic average of 93 percent from a demanding high school. And he also wanted to admit him because Matthew was a first-generation, low-income student of color — exactly the type of student Pérez believed Trinity didn't have enough of, the kind of young man who would bring a new and different perspective to the campus, one Pérez thought it badly needed.

Matthew chose not to submit his standardized test scores with his application, which was probably wise. He had received a 21 (out of 36) on the ACT, well below the average for freshmen at Trinity, which is 29. It was a test score that carried with it a clear message: Matthew probably wouldn't be able to handle the academics at a selective college like Trinity. But Pérez, of course, never got that message, because he never saw Matthew's test scores. So he and his staff admitted Matthew to Trinity's class of 2020 — the first freshman class that Pérez and his new team selected.

When Matthew arrived on the Trinity campus that fall, it quickly became clear that his ACT score had not been an accurate predictor of his academic potential, and his high school grades had been. In his first semester, he got straight As, earning Faculty Honors, the highest level of academic achievement at Trinity.

But in every way other than academic, Matthew found Trinity exceedingly hard to take. It wasn't like he had been totally unaware of the existence of well-off white kids before he arrived at college. His high school had been majority-white (though only barely), and there were a handful of rich kids who went there. But the cultural divide at Trinity was on a whole different level. "Coming to Trinity is a little scary, because you actually see, like, really, really, *really* rich white kids," Matthew told me. "In high school, the rich white kids, they didn't carry themselves like they were better than everyone else. Everyone treated each other as equals. But at Trinity, the rich white kids, they treat themselves like, Oh, yeah, I'm *way* better than you."

Matthew gradually came to learn the signifiers of wealth at Trinity: the boat shoes and the Vineyard Vines shep shirts and the Mercedes G-Wagons in the student parking lot. Matthew didn't wear that stuff — he dressed like a regular kid from the Bronx, in jeans and T-shirts and hoodies — and he didn't have a car, let alone a Mercedes. He was working three student jobs, in addition to his studies, and sending the extra money home to his mom.

Economics wasn't the only division Matthew saw within the student body. There was also race. Matthew identified as both black and Latino (his dad was Dominican), and as far as he could see, white students at Trinity and black and Latino students at Trinity didn't go to parties together or sit together in the dining hall. The only students of color who seemed to bridge this divide were athletes. Matthew's theory was that white prep-school kids were comfortable hanging out with black athletes, but they reacted differently when they encountered a dark-skinned student like Matthew—a studious, tough-looking, urban public school kid. He did his best to start conversations and meet people, but it felt to him like no one from Trinity's white majority wanted to give him the time of day.

In his second semester, Matthew took a sociology class, and he loved it. Before long, he had decided to major in sociology. He read Émile Durkheim and Max Weber and Karl Marx and critical race theory, and it gave him an intellectual framework for what he was seeing on Trinity's campus, the conventions and rituals and divisions. In his sociology and political science classes, he was usually one of just a handful of students of color. And in class discussions, he had to contend with comments from white students that he found absurd: mass incarceration is black people's fault; undocumented immigrants never pay taxes; women in American society are more privileged than men.

"Every time a student says something like that, I feel the need to participate," Matthew told me. "If I don't say anything, these students would just be left with the false ideas that they have, because the professor never corrects them on it." It was good intellectual training: it taught him to speak up, to articulate his ideas clearly, to make succinct arguments. But it was exhausting, and it didn't seem to change anyone's mind. In every single class, it felt like he was being called upon to defend his people. His identity was constantly on the line.

There was one weekend in April of his freshman year when he made a real effort to cross Trinity's color lines. It was Spring Weekend, a big annual social extravaganza on the Trinity campus that involves a lot of DJs and frat parties and carnival games and public drinking. One of his close friends was a black athlete who spent a lot of time with white students, so Matthew tagged along with this friend that weekend to parties and concerts, trying to immerse himself in the full white Trinity social experience. He had a terrible time. Everyone was superdrunk or high on cocaine, he told me, and every encounter felt tense and weird, bordering on open aggression.

Later that week, Matthew and I hung out for a while in a basement coffee shop below Trinity's main dining hall. He seemed pretty down, still a little shell-shocked from Spring Weekend, and not quite sure what approach to try next. "This school is changing me for the worse," he said. "I'm not naturally an introvert, but it's turning me into one."

There were moments that spring when he thought about leaving, maybe transferring to the state university in Albany, where some friends from his neighborhood were enrolled. He knew it wasn't any-where near as selective a school as Trinity, and he probably wouldn't get as generous a financial-aid package as the one he had received at Trinity. But he still thought the trade-off might be worth it. "That's what I keep asking myself," he said. "Should I go there and be happy and not get as good an education? Or should I stay here and just be miserable?"

That summer, most of his classmates from Trinity went off to do prestigious internships and summer programs abroad, but Matthew didn't feel up to applying for that kind of thing. After the emotional stress of freshman year, he needed to retrench and recuperate and do something easy and familiar. He went back to the Bronx and lived with his family and saw friends and worked forty hours a week at the same Chipotle where he'd worked in high school. Trinity felt very far away.

But when he got back to campus for his sophomore year, he was tired of serving burritos and ready for a change. One of Matthew's closest friends at Trinity was the president of a student organization called the Men of Color Alliance, and in August he asked Matthew to be his copresident. Matthew said yes, and that led to an invitation from AJ Johnson, a local black pastor in Hartford, to represent Trin-ity at Calling All Brothers, an event marking the beginning of the school year at a downtown public elementary school. Leading men of color from the community dressed up in suits and at 7:30 a.m. greeted the young black students one by one as they arrived for the first day of school, applauding and high-fiving them and encourag-ing them to work hard in the coming academic year. Matthew stood alongside these men, shaking students' hands, surrounded by black-ness and positivity. It felt great.

Matthew hadn't experienced much of Hartford during his fresh-man year. Trinity, traditionally, is almost entirely cut off from the city where it makes its home. Demographically, Hartford is nothing like Trinity. In fact, it's a lot more like the Bronx: its population is just 16 percent white, and half of the city's children live in poverty. But despite its economic and social challenges, Hartford is a city with a vibrant social service sector of churches and nonprofits, and Call-ing All Brothers introduced Matthew to the men who helped run those organizations: a Baptist minister named Rev. Y. Trevor Beau-ford; a state representative named Brandon McGee; an entrepreneur named Abdul-Rahmaan I. Muhammad. Matthew found these men immensely inspiring: intelligent and committed and professional and ambitious, leaders of a black community dedicated to helping its young people escape poverty and get an education. It suddenly felt like exactly the work he wanted to do.

That fall, he found himself spending every free moment off cam-pus in Hartford, volunteering and organizing and helping out how-ever he could. Beauford and McGee and Muhammad and Johnson became his mentors, and working with them became the focus of his sophomore year. The next summer, he didn't go back to the Bronx or to Chipotle. Instead, he stayed in Hartford and took a job helping run camps and college-readiness workshops with Muhammad and Beauford, trying to uplift Hartford's young black men and women.

As his junior year at Trinity began, he was still getting good grades, earning Faculty Honors, completing his sociology requirements one by one. But his center of gravity had shifted from the Trinity campus to downtown Hartford. He had mostly given up on trying to connect with the white majority at his college. Trinity had become a place for him to gather tools and knowledge and credentials and then take them to do the work he felt called to do.

One fall afternoon, Matthew and I were strolling down the Long Walk, a bucolic trail of concrete paving stones that runs through the center of campus, lined on one side with alder and beech trees and on the other with old ivy-covered brownstone buildings. As we looked up at the stained-glass windows and tall Victorian arches above us, I asked Matthew: So, does this place feel like home?

He smiled a bit and shook his head. "No," he said. "It feels like a job."

Matthew had effectively solved his own problem at Trinity, but that hadn't really solved Trinity's problem. All of the energy and effort and new ideas that Pérez hoped Matthew would bring to the Trinity campus were being directed instead to downtown Hartford, where Matthew was welcomed and appreciated and his work was rewarded.

It is part of the paradox of the project that Angel Pérez has undertaken at Trinity — and the broader paradox of elite college admissions in the age of enrollment management. With each new freshman class, Pérez is demonstrating that test-optional admissions can help bring in highly qualified students from diverse and challenging backgrounds, and that they can succeed at Trinity, academically, despite test scores that would under different rules have kept them far from any selective college. But the financial pressure Pérez is working under makes it hard, or maybe impossible, for him to build up a critical mass of those students on campus. And meanwhile, the dominant culture of the institution Pérez is trying to transform is strong and deep-rooted and often resistant to change. Trinity these days sometimes feels like a host trying to reject the transplanted organ it needs to survive.

Pérez sees his new recruits as a vanguard of change at Trinity, the fruits of a different kind of enrollment management, the first settlers in this new and more equitable world. And that might turn out to be true. Maybe Matthew and students like him will change Trinity in the years ahead. Or maybe they won't. Maybe they'll punch the clock, do their work, get their degrees, and leave Trinity more or less as they found it, with a championship varsity squash team and five a cappella groups and a demographic clock ticking away toward a crisis they cannot solve.

VI

STAYING IN

---

1. The Graduation Gap

There are certain American universities where almost every student who enrolls as a freshman goes on to graduate — if not in precisely four years, then in five or six. At Princeton, for instance, the six-year graduation rate stands at almost 97 percent, meaning that only a few dozen students from each entering class fail to collect a Princeton diploma. But at most institutions, things don't work that way. Nationally, only about 60 percent of students who start a four-year degree manage to graduate in six. At two-year colleges, including community colleges, the dropout rates are much higher — only three in ten students earn a degree or certificate within three years.

Until recently, most administrators who led American colleges and universities didn't really see this as their problem to solve. Some students succeed; some students fail. That's the students' business. Sink or swim. In the last few years, though, things have begun to change, and many colleges are now trying to address what has turned out to be a surprisingly challenging question: If you want your students to graduate, what do you do?

In 2012 the University of Texas in Austin became one of the first large public institutions to make a serious effort to answer this question, appointing a chemistry professor named David Laude to be the school's first "graduation-rate champion." Laude, who was in his mid-fifties and had been teaching at UT for twenty-five years, was given a very specific mission along with his new title: to increase the university's four-year graduation rate to 70 percent. At the time, only a little more than half of UT's freshmen were graduating within the traditional four years.

When Laude took on this new role, the university was in turmoil. Texas's Republican governor, Rick Perry, had publicly supported a proposal from a conservative Texas policy institute to reorganize the state's public-university system to make it more efficient and businesslike, more accountable to both students and taxpayers. Under the new plan, faculty at UT and other Texas universities would be ranked by their scores on student evaluations, and they would be compensated according to the amount of tuition revenue they generated. Students would be treated like customers, engaged in an essentially commercial transaction: exchanging their tuition fees for future earning power.

Perry's proposals hit the UT campus in Austin like news of an approaching meteor. Many faculty, alumni, and administrators viewed them, with alarm, as an attack on the traditional role of the public research university. Bill Powers, UT's president, was technically a state employee, serving at the pleasure of a board of regents appointed by the governor. And yet he publicly rejected Perry's plan. His administration issued an official rebuttal to the institute's proposal, arguing that while students should indeed be treated with respect, "they are not customers in the traditional sense. The higher education experience is not akin to shopping on iTunes or visiting Banana Republic." *Texas Monthly* reported that the regents were considering firing Powers for insubordination.

Under pressure, Powers and his leadership team managed to identify one issue where they felt they might be able to accommodate the governor and his allies: improving the university's graduation rate. If you were going to make even a slight nod toward treating your students like customers, the fact that half of them weren't getting their degrees in four years seemed like a good place to start. And the four-year graduation rate at UT was something of an embarrassment to Powers and his fellow administrators; the flagship public universities that UT considered its academic peers — institutions like the University of Virginia and the University of North Carolina at Chapel Hill — had four-year graduation rates that were twenty or thirty percentage points higher than UT's.

Powers had formed a task force in 2011 to investigate UT's lagging grad rate, and the task force concluded in its report that it would indeed be possible to increase the four-year rate from 51 percent to 70 percent. But to do so, the report stated, there would need to be a single administrator — a graduation-rate champion — who would be responsible for the campus-wide effort. Laude took the job, and in the summer of 2012 he packed up his books and family photos and his wall chart of the periodic table of elements and moved from the natural sciences building into a sprawling office two floors below the president's in the UT Tower, the iconic three-hundred-foot-tall clock tower that looms over the campus.

For Laude, being so close to the center of power at the university was an odd feeling. He had always seen himself as an outsider in establishment academic circles. As a freshman in the 1970s at the University of the South, a small private college high up in the Tennessee mountains, Laude had felt bewildered and out of place, a working-class Italian Catholic kid from the Central Valley of California trying to find his way at a college steeped in privilege and tradition, where students from wealthy southern families joined secret societies and wore academic gowns to class. "It was a massive culture shock," Laude told me when we first met. "I was completely at a loss on how to fit in socially. And I was tremendously bad at studying. Everything was just overwhelming."

Laude drifted unhappily through that first semester in Tennessee, isolated and homesick, earning Cs in most of his classes, unable to catch up. By the time he slunk home for Christmas, he had made up his mind to drop out. But his father, a former Marine and college football star, would not tolerate a quitter. He ordered his son back to Tennessee, and back Laude went. Eventually, Laude figured out how to survive at college, and he went on to a successful academic career. But he never quite left behind the sense of himself that he developed in his freshman year: a poor kid from the sticks, an outcast from the intellectual elite.

The first challenge Laude faced as graduation-rate champion was that no one seemed to know what a graduation-rate champion actually was. The University of Texas had never had one before. As far as Laude could tell, no university had. He had been given a very precise mandate — to achieve the 70 percent on-time graduation rate in five years — along with about $30 million to spend during that time, but no clear road map on how he was supposed to accomplish this ambitious goal.

The task force that created Laude's job had painted in its report two somewhat contradictory portraits of the University of Texas. The first was of an institution that was functioning well, though with some small bureaucratic flaws. The report pointed out hopefully that although UT's four-year graduation rate stood at just 51 percent, about 75 percent of UT freshmen were graduating in five years. In fact, 64 percent of them were graduating in four and a half years, meaning there was a sizable proportion of each class that was just a few months behind schedule. According to this first, relatively benign portrait of the university, the most efficient way for Laude to reach the 70 percent goal was simply to target the low-hanging fruit. With a few administrative tweaks, the report suggested, Laude's mission would be complete.

But when Laude read the report, he saw in its pages a second, more complicated portrait of the university, one that showed the institution to be deeply out of balance. According to an appendix, there were significant gaps in retention and graduation rates between different demographic groups on the Austin campus. Fewer than 40 percent of black and Latino students were graduating in four years, while 57 percent of white students were doing so. First-generation students —those whose parents hadn't gone to college—had four-year graduation rates that were more than twenty percentage points lower than students whose parents had both graduated from college. The same patterns held true when Laude looked at Pell eligibility: the students whose families had higher incomes were mostly graduating on time, and the poorer kids mostly weren't.

It was certainly true that some of the students who weren't graduating in four years were going on to get a degree in five or six. But a lot of them, especially the ones from more disadvantaged backgrounds, were leaving the university altogether. Thirty percent of first-generation students at UT dropped out or were dismissed before they could complete their degree, compared to just 12 percent of students whose parents had both gone to college. At the University of Texas, Laude realized, how quickly you graduated—and whether you graduated at all—depended, more than anything, on who your parents were and how much money they earned.

So Laude decided to expand his mission. He wouldn't just tweak the bureaucracy to get a few more privileged students over the finish line on time. He would instead use the resources at his disposal to address the university's glaring graduation gaps head-on, to try to improve the UT experience, in a comprehensive way, for the thousands of students who weren't thriving in the present system.

It was partly a practical decision: Laude figured it would be hard to hit his 70 percent target without addressing the problems of the students whose graduation rates were the lowest. But his recalibration was also inspired by his memories from decades earlier in Tennessee: memories of being a confused, alienated college student, far from home, without money or connections or inside knowledge, on the verge of dropping out. Through a combination of parental pressure, timely help, and a few lucky breaks, Laude had metamorphosed from a near-dropout into an academic success story. How many of the students who were dropping out of the University of Texas each year had the same hidden potential to succeed?

WHEN YOU LOOK at the national statistics on college graduation rates, you can see, on a larger scale, the pattern that Laude observed in the University of Texas data. Well-off American college students are much more likely to complete a bachelor's degree than students from less affluent families. According to one study, only about a quarter of college students born into the bottom half of the income distribution will manage to collect a BA by age twenty-four, while almost 90 percent of freshmen born into families in the top income quartile will finish their degree by the same age.

Part of that gap in graduation rates is due to the fact that affluent young Americans attend, on average, very different institutions after high school than everyone else does. Wealthy students usually go to prestigious private four-year colleges with large operating budgets and generous endowments, and those colleges usually have high graduation rates. Low-income students are more likely to attend cash-strapped two- or four-year public or for-profit colleges, and those institutions often have quite low graduation rates.

Those correlations, of course, make it difficult to identify the root cause of these graduation gaps. Are low-income students dropping out because they are attending underresourced colleges? Or do less selective colleges have higher dropout rates because they enroll so many low-income students? Or to ask the same question in the opposite way: Does Princeton have a 97 percent six-year graduation rate because it surrounds its undergraduates with a protective army of tutors and therapists and "learning strategies consultants" whose services are available free to every student? Or because Princeton's admissions staff selects students who are highly likely to graduate, no matter which institution they attend or what obstacles are placed in their way?

Researchers have found that when students from different economic backgrounds do end up at the same college, their graduation rates are in fact usually quite similar. In a 2015 report, the Education Trust showed that at any given four-year institution in the United States, students who were eligible for Pell grants had six-year graduation rates that were only about five percentage points lower, on average, than non-Pell-eligible students at the same institution. So there *is* a graduation gap within most institutions, but it's a relatively small one. And that is true, in general, whether the institution in question has high or low graduation rates overall.

To take a couple of Texas examples: At Rice University, a prestigious private college in Houston, where about 90 percent of students graduate in six years, the graduation rate for Pell-eligible students is just 0.6 percentage points lower than the rate for non-Pell-eligible students. At the University of North Texas, a less selective public institution in Denton, only about 50 percent of students graduate in six years — but again, there is less than a two-percentage-point gap between the graduation rates for the university's Pell and non-Pell students. (There are a few institutions, nationally, where the Pell graduation rate is actually *higher* than the non-Pell graduation rate, and at the top of that list is Trinity College, where superachieving Pell-eligible students like Matthew Rivera graduate at rates as much as sixteen percentage points higher than the more affluent students who aren't eligible for Pell grants.)

But at the University of Texas at Austin, according to the task force report that led to Laude's appointment, the six-year graduation rate for Pell-eligible students was eleven percentage points lower than the six-year rate for non-Pell students. And UT's four-year graduation rates showed an advantage of *eighteen* percentage points for its non-Pell students over its Pell students. So what was going on? What was so different about UT?

Laude thought that at least part of the answer to that question lay in UT Austin's unique admission policy, which is the legacy of many years of legal and legislative battles over affirmative action. In 1996

UT's historical practice of considering race in admissions decisions was ruled unconstitutional by the Fifth Circuit Court of Appeals. In response, a bipartisan coalition of rural white and urban Hispanic members of the Texas Legislature came up with and passed into law an alternative strategy to maintain a diverse campus in Austin.

The law, commonly called the Top 10 Percent Rule, stipulates that graduating seniors in any high school in Texas whose GPA ranks in the top tenth of their class will be automatically admitted to the campus of their choice in Texas's public-university system. The legislature requires UT Austin to set aside about two-thirds of each freshman class for these automatic admits. As the Austin campus has grown more popular, the criterion for automatic admission has tightened; Texas high school seniors now have to be in the top 6 percent of their class to earn admission.

At high schools in the wealthier suburbs of Dallas or Houston, students in the top 6 percent of the class look a lot like the students anywhere who go on to attend elite colleges. They are mostly well-off and mostly white, and most of them rack up high SAT scores. What sets UT apart from other selective colleges is that the university also admits the top 6 percent of students from public high schools in Lubbock and Brownsville and Houston's Third Ward, who fit quite different demographic profiles and have, on average, much lower SAT scores.

Despite fears among some on the left that the Fifth Circuit's decision would put an end to diversity at UT Austin, the introduction of the Top 10 Percent Rule actually made the campus *more* diverse than it had been under race-based affirmative action. And the university's new diversity was not just racial. In the decade after the law went into effect, minority enrollment at UT did increase, but at the same time, so did enrollment from rural communities and from schools statewide with high-poverty populations. Meanwhile, enrollment went *down* among students from suburban schools and from "feeder" schools that had, in the past, sent a lot of students to UT Austin. In 1996, before the Top 10 Percent Rule, the university admitted students from fewer than seven hundred different Texas high schools; by 2007, UT was admitting students from more than nine hundred high schools across the state.

AS A RESULT of the law, the student body at the University of Texas now looks quite different, demographically, than the student bodies at other selective flagship campuses around the country. There is no strict definition of a "flagship" public university, but usually the term is used to refer to the biggest, best-funded, most selective public university in each state. And as it happens, state flagship institutions, as a group, have gone through their own transformation recently, in most cases moving in the opposite direction from the University of Texas. Their student bodies have become more white and Asian than before, more wealthy, and less reflective of the population of their states.

This nationwide transformation of state flagships started in the 1990s, but it accelerated in the period after the 2008 financial crisis, when many state governments, confronting sudden deep budget deficits, sharply reduced their funding for higher education. It has long been true that at public universities, out-of-state students pay higher tuition than in-state students. Faced with daunting new budget shortfalls, administrators at state flagships began to see those high-paying out-of-state students as an important potential revenue stream, and they recruited and admitted more and more of them. Though each state's public universities were established to serve the young people living in that state, many public flagships now admit thousands of students from out of state each year—in some cases, more than half of the student body. At the University of Oregon, 53 percent of freshmen come from out of state; at the University of Vermont, 77 percent do.

Once public flagships decided to compete for out-of-state students who could pay their elevated tuitions, they felt compelled to follow the same principles of enrollment management that selective private universities were employing—the tactics that Jack Maguire had introduced decades earlier. They targeted and recruited affluent students from around the country. They increased their rejection rate, and they used SAT scores as their primary admissions criterion, in a bid to improve their standing in the *U.S. News* college rankings. They used merit aid strategically to persuade admitted wealthy students to enroll.

After a few years of this process, the student bodies at many prestigious public flagships have come to look much like the student bodies at elite private institutions anywhere in the country: they enroll a lot of rich kids and very few poor kids. At the University of Virginia, only 13 percent of undergraduates are eligible for Pell grants — a lower rate than at Princeton University or Trinity College. At the University of Michigan, the figure is 16 percent. At the University of Alabama, the flagship public institution of one of the poorest states in the nation, the median family income for undergraduates is now higher than at Bryn Mawr College.

The University of Texas, by contrast, has been largely constrained from using the tools of enrollment management because of the Top 10 Percent Rule. Without exactly intending to, the state's legislators helped create at UT a different, more old-fashioned kind of flagship college than the model emerging at similarly prestigious flagships across the country. The University of Texas's student body is simultaneously more diverse and more cohesive than that at other flagships, made up, as it is, of high-achieving young Texans from a wide range of backgrounds. There are still more rich kids than poor kids at the university, but the Top 10 Percent Rule means that the economic gaps on campus are far less egregious than those at other elite flagships.

There is one other fact about UT's admissions policy that makes the university a particularly interesting test case — a sort of natural experiment allowing for a comparison between two different approaches to admissions. As I mentioned, the Top 10 Percent Rule applies to only two-thirds of each incoming class. The Texas legislature mostly allows UT to set its own policies for the remaining third of each freshman class. And when UT's admissions department is given the freedom to choose that part of the class, it follows exactly the same market-based dictates of enrollment management that every other selective university does.

In this third of each freshman class, UT pursues private school kids with high test scores but middling GPAs, out-of-state students who can pay full tuition, varsity athletes, and the children of potential donors. (In a disheartening Texas twist, the university has in the past also been known to use this third of the class to admit politically connected but academically unqualified applicants who came bearing letters of recommendation from the state legislators who control the university's budget.) Each year, then, two-thirds of UT's incoming class looks a lot like Texas, and the other third looks a lot like the freshman class at the University of Virginia or the University of Michigan: mostly wealthy and mostly white, packed with full-paying students with high SAT scores.

From David Laude's perspective, as he settled into his new job in the Tower, the most significant effect of the Top 10 Percent Rule was that it produced each year a freshman class that arrived on the Austin campus with a much wider range of academic preparation than the freshman classes in Ann Arbor or Chapel Hill or Berkeley. University of Texas freshmen are generally excellent and diligent students; by definition, every automatic admit at UT was near the top of his or her class in high school. But some of those automatic admits arrive in Austin having graduated from high schools with a full slate of AP classes and ample opportunities for after-school tutoring, and some come from high schools with no AP classes and very little in the way of a college-going culture.

The SAT scores of those two groups tend to reflect their different levels of preparation and family resources, and as a result, UT's incoming SAT scores are spread over a much broader spectrum than incoming SAT scores at typical elite state flagship or private institutions. To be more specific: Both the University of Texas and the University of Virginia have a large cohort of incoming freshmen with SAT scores above 1500. What UT has that the University of Virginia does not is another large cohort of students who have SAT scores below 1100.

As Laude tried to figure out just what he should be doing in his new job, he found that his thinking was beginning to coalesce around two complementary theories. The first was that the university's outsize graduation gap had a lot to do with those gaps in academic preparation. The automatic admits from Lubbock and Brownsville and the Third Ward were, in many cases, precisely the students who were most likely to graduate late or drop out altogether. Laude's second theory was that it didn't have to be this way. Those kids weren't dropping out because they didn't have the potential to succeed at the University of Texas. They were dropping out because the University of Texas was not prepared to help them succeed.

IN ADDITION TO his administrative duties, David Laude taught Chemistry 301, the department's big freshman survey course, a prerequisite for almost every student going into the natural sciences. Traditionally, introductory math and science courses like Chemistry 301 are seen by university professors and administrators as tools to separate the highly capable wheat from the academically hopeless chaff. The courses are rigorous and demanding, and many students fail, and even among those who pass, many do so poorly that they abandon the sciences altogether. This is seen by many in the field as a feature, not a bug. It's a *good* thing to cull the herd. There's a shtick that some professors like to do at the beginning of these courses, where they tell two or maybe three students to stand up, and announce that, statistically, one of them will not make it to the end of the course. When Laude started teaching Chemistry 301 back in the mid-1990s, he used to do this routine himself. It felt virtuous, like he was protecting the integrity of science.

But as time went on, Laude began to think differently about the students who were failing his course. It was partly that he himself had almost failed introductory chemistry as a student that first semester at the University of the South, and that near-failure almost deterred him from what became a very successful scientific career. But he also began to look more closely at the records of the students who were failing. And what he found was that the distribution of grades in Chemistry 301 didn't follow the nice sweeping bell curve he expected. Instead, they traced what he called a "bimodal distribution" — more like a lop-sided barbell than a church bell. In each class of five hundred students, there were four hundred or so who did quite well, clustered around the A and high-B range. Then there was a second cluster of perhaps a hundred students whose grades were way down at the bottom — Ds and Fs. For them, Chemistry 301 was the end of the road, the abrupt conclusion to their career in science or medicine or engineering.

To get a better sense of who these struggling students were, Laude started pulling records from the provost's office. It wasn't hard to discern a pattern. The students who were failing were mostly from low-income families. They had usually attended public high schools that offered few advanced classes. They were often first-generation college students. They were white kids from rural West Texas or Latinos from the Rio Grande Valley or African Americans from Dallas or Houston. And almost all of them had low SAT scores — low for UT, at least — often below 1000 on the 1600-point scale.

In 1999, just before the beginning of the fall semester, Laude looked through the records of every student who had signed up for freshman chemistry and identified about fifty who possessed at least two of the "adversity indicators" common among students who had failed the course in the past: low SAT scores, low family income, less-educated parents. He invited those fifty students to apply to a new program, which he called the Texas Interdisciplinary Plan, or TIP. Students in TIP, who had SAT scores, on average, about two hundred points lower than the rest of the class, were placed in their own, smaller section of Chemistry 301, also taught by Laude. Rather than dumb down the curriculum for them, Laude insisted that they master exactly the same challenging material as the students in his larger section. In fact, he scheduled his two sections back-to-back: identical material, identical lectures, identical tests. But for the smaller group, he did more, supplementing his standard lectures with extra instruction and dedicated peer mentors and faculty advisers.

And it worked. The TIP students, who had scored two hundred points lower on the SAT, concluded the course that fall with the same grades, on average, as the students in the larger section. They returned for their sophomore year at rates above the average for the university as a whole, and three years later they had graduation rates that were *higher,* on average, than the students in the larger section of Chemistry 301, the ones with SAT scores two hundred points above theirs.

That experience changed Laude's thinking about his job in the classroom and his role at the university. In the past, he'd always put the responsibility for students' failure in his class on someone else: on the students' subpar high schools or their disengaged families or on the students themselves. Now he decided the responsibility really lay with him. If his students failed, it was because he was letting them fail.

When Laude was named UT's graduation-rate champion in 2012, he brought the lessons of TIP with him to the Tower. The categories of students who had been failing Chemistry 301 before TIP were the same ones whose four-year graduation rates were now well below average in the university as a whole. If those chemistry students could succeed at such high levels with the help of TIP, Laude thought that a comparable array of supports and interventions might create a more level playing field for the university's student body as a whole.

First, though, Laude needed to figure out exactly which students needed help. It was one thing to identify the students who might struggle in a five-hundred-person chemistry class. Laude was now responsible for the entire freshman class — more than seven thousand students. He conscripted a team of data scientists in the university's office of institutional research who specialized in predictive analytics. By deconstructing the records of tens of thousands of recent UT students, they were able to develop a statistical model that combined fourteen separate variables, from family income to SAT score to high school class rank to parents' educational background, into a single algorithm that could reliably predict an incoming student's likelihood of on-time graduation. They called this new tool the Four-Year Graduation Rate Dashboard.

In the spring of 2013 Laude and his staff fed into the Dashboard the data for each of the high school seniors who had just been admitted to UT Austin's class of 2017, and the algorithm spat out, for each student, a precise prediction, to the second decimal place, of how likely he or she was to graduate in four years. For some students, it was all but certain. For others, on-time graduation seemed the longest of long shots. The Dashboard indicated that about one in six freshmen had worse than a 40 percent chance of graduating on time. That was twelve hundred students in total. That group became the focus of Laude's attention. He wasn't sure he could get all of them to succeed at the University of Texas. But he thought he could design a system that would help most of them get there. If he did, he calculated, he would hit his 70 percent target — and he might change the university in the process.

I MET DAVID LAUDE in the fall of 2013, when he was about a year into his job. When you first encounter him, Laude can seem like an unusual choice for a high-level position in university administration. He is tall and stiff, with a stern look and a loud, gravelly voice that calls to mind Sam the Eagle from *The Muppet Show.* He is friendly enough, but not especially diplomatic; his manner is blunt and plain, and he doesn't seem driven by a particular need to be well liked. Still, the more I got to know him, the more it became clear to me that his unique combination of skills and experiences had actually prepared him quite well for the unusual mission he had been given.

Laude is a scientist, with a deep faith in data, and he liked the stark clarity of his assignment: 70 percent or bust. He appreciated, as well, the way the impersonal calculations of the Dashboard allowed him and the university to direct resources to students objectively and dispassionately. It was true that those twelve hundred students in the class of 2017 that the Dashboard had identified as least likely to succeed were disproportionately poor and disproportionately students of color, but it was important to Laude that they were being targeted for extra support not because they were part of some particular demographic category, but because they had been selected by the Dashboard's algorithm. Which circumstance in their life had pushed them below a 40 percent likelihood of on-time graduation? Laude didn't care. The algorithm said they needed help, so they'd get help.

But while he was mathematically precise about *whom* to help, he was downright improvisational when it came to *how* to help them, relying more on instinct and emotion than on science. Laude knew rationally that certain interventions and programs must inevitably be more effective than others. But in 2012 the field of student success was relatively young, and there was little in the way of firm evidence for what worked and what didn't. Given his tight deadline, Laude didn't have the time to road test different approaches himself. So instead his strategy was to take the students with the lowest chance of graduating on time and surround them with an all-encompassing network of support. He called it the "kitchen sink" approach. "You throw a million different treatments out there," he told me, "knowing that every student is different, and you trust that students will find and exploit the thing that works for them."

The first step Laude took was to fund a portfolio of academic-success programs at colleges across the university—natural sciences, liberal arts, engineering, etc.—all of them following the same principles that helped define TIP: small classes, peer mentoring, extra tutoring help, and engaged faculty advisers. "There are always going to be both affluent kids and kids who have need who come into this university," Laude explained. "And it will always be the case that the kids who have need are going to have been denied a lot of the academic preparation and opportunities for identity formation that the affluent kids have been given. The question is, can we do something for those students in their first year in college that can accelerate them and get them up to the place where they can be competitive with the affluent, advantaged students?"

At the same time, though, Laude was convinced that it didn't make sense to address students' academic challenges in isolation from their nonacademic ones. What he experienced as a freshman at the University of the South was common, he suspected, among many students at the University of Texas, especially in their first year: academic pressures conflated with financial and psychological pressures, and they became impossible for students to disentangle. When you're socially isolated *and* worried about money *and* struggling in all your classes, it doesn't feel like three distinct problems. It feels like one big problem. So in addition to the academic supports, Laude introduced summer programs to help orient incoming freshmen, and he expanded the university's mental-health support network so that students could access counselors in every college on campus.

At the center of this part of Laude's strategy was a new program called the University Leadership Network, or ULN. "The success programs are about academics," Laude explained. "The ULN is about that other aspect of their development, about their personal development, about their maturation."

In order to be selected for ULN, incoming freshmen needed not only to fall below the 40 percent cutoff on the Dashboard; they also had to have what the financial-aid office called unmet financial need. Which meant, in practice, that the five hundred students chosen each year to be in ULN were among the lowest-income students in the freshman class. Because of their financial constraints, the Dashboard estimated that most of them had an even lower chance of on-time graduation than the other students Laude was targeting: 30 percent or 20 percent or lower.

In their freshman year, students in ULN met for weekly lectures on topics like time management and team building, as well as follow-up small-group discussion sessions with their fellow ULN members. In sophomore and junior and senior year they took part in professional and academic internships on campus that exposed them to opportunities and connections around the university, and they moved into leadership positions as mentors or residence-hall advisers. In exchange for all this, they received a $5,000 scholarship each year, paid in monthly increments.

Laude's theory was that the network of support and engagement his office was helping to create would function as a kind of campus-wide safety net, giving struggling students something to grab on to when they felt themselves slipping. "What I want to see in a few years is that those ULN students, who right now have maybe a 30 percent chance to graduate, are actually graduating at something like a 65 percent rate," he said. "That's our theory. If you do this right, then during that period of time between the ages of eighteen and twenty-two you can arrest the damage that eighteen years of mediocre academic preparation has done to a student. If you can put somebody in the right place, in the right environment, with the right support structures, you can do wonders."

2. Belonging

When Amy A. arrived at the University of Texas as a freshman in the fall of 2013, she was placed in the first-ever ULN cohort. Amy was an automatic admit to UT, ranked twelfth in her graduating class of 350 from a mostly low-income high school in a racially diverse suburb of Dallas. Amy's parents were immigrants from West Africa who spent decades sacrificing and saving in order to send Amy and her brothers to college. In high school, Amy was not only a good student, she was also outgoing and involved in everything. She loved public speaking and student leadership and organizing service projects. At the Pentecostal church in Dallas that her family attended, where the pews were filled with African immigrant families like hers, Amy was known as the A student, the future college graduate, a success story waiting to happen.

At her high school, though, Amy found it difficult to get her hands on clear and reliable information about college. Most of the school's graduates went to community college or straight into the workforce, but Amy aspired to a high-quality four-year college. She just wasn't sure where to go, or how to pay for it, or what steps to take to get there. During her senior year, she would often stop in to the school's guidance office, looking for help with scholarships or financial aid, but the counselors there would just shrug. They advised her to start at the local community college and maybe consider transferring to a four-year school later on. The whole process was enormously frustrating to Amy, and it sometimes brought her to tears. "It felt like they were trying to hide education from me," she told me. When her AP English teacher finally brought in someone to talk to the most academically minded seniors about college, it was a representative from Everest College, a for-profit trade school in Fort Worth whose parent company wound up filing for bankruptcy a few years later.

Without much help or guidance from her school or her parents, Amy applied to a handful of public and private colleges in Texas and Oklahoma. In the end, she chose UT Austin, in part because her acceptance letter came with an invitation to take part in the summer orientation program that David Laude's office had just introduced.

I first spoke with Amy a few months later, in January of her freshman year, in a coffee shop near campus. She told me it had been a hard year so far. She had enrolled at UT with a very specific career goal in mind: dentistry. It was a path she had chosen a year earlier, as a senior in high school, when she typed into Yahoo's search engine "top paying jobs in America" and "dentistry" popped up close to the top of the list. Amy had no particular interest in teeth, but to her, that wasn't the important consideration.

"Dentistry, that's a high-paying career," she told me firmly. "When you come to college, you have to focus on a major that can get you money. So I put away what I love doing, like public speaking and business and working with people — I put that away in order to seek a career that will give me money, instead of happiness."

This plan felt to Amy like the responsible and conscientious one, but in practice, it wasn't working out. She struggled in calculus in her first semester, finishing the course with a C minus. Her bigger problem was Chemistry 301, which like calculus was a prerequisite for any premed degree. "I tried and tried, but it wasn't working," she told me. "It wasn't clicking in my head." She went to her professor's office hours, and she visited the campus learning center for extra tutoring, but each time she sat down to take a test, everything she had learned seemed to fly out of her head. "It was very, very scary," she said.

In November, at the last minute, she "Q-dropped" chemistry. That meant the course wouldn't count as a failure on her transcript. But it still left a scar. "It was really depressing," she told me. "For me to drop a class, it felt like I didn't belong at UT. It felt like this was a school made for valedictorians, and I should have started at community college, like my advisers recommended." On Facebook, she would scroll through posts from high school friends who had chosen community college, and they all seemed to be having fun and getting As.

When she went home for Christmas, she wasn't sure if she was going to return to school after the holidays. "I felt like such a failure," she said. "I knew I couldn't drop out of college, because the little children in my church, they look up to me. They see me as the college girl. They see me as this smart, impressive young lady. But I felt like I'd failed them." When people at church asked her how school was going, she couldn't admit she was struggling. She didn't tell anyone back home that she'd dropped chemistry, not even her parents.

Amy finally did decide to return to Austin, but she didn't know how long she would stay. It was just a week later that she and I had our coffee-shop conversation, and when we parted, I felt genuinely uncertain what would happen to her. Amy seemed smart and resourceful, but she also seemed beaten down by freshman year. She had endured some serious setbacks, the kind that often cause students to spiral into academic failure.

Three years later, just before a return trip to Austin, I sent Amy an email, hoping her UT address was still functioning. It was. Not only had she not dropped out, she told me, but she was a few months away from graduation. In December 2016, halfway through her senior year, we sat down again, this time in the lobby of the student affairs building, and she caught me up on what had happened since our last meeting.

At the start of her second semester as a freshman, after that depressing Christmas back home, Amy met with her academic adviser and explained her situation. The adviser gently suggested that instead of making her college and career plans based only on which path would be the most financially lucrative, Amy might want to think about what she actually *enjoyed* doing, what she cared about in life. For Amy, the answer to that question was easy: She liked people. She was happiest when she was organizing groups and making lists and helping others.

Amy's adviser suggested that instead of majoring in the natural sciences, she might be happier taking courses in communications or business. So in the spring of her freshman year, she tried out some communications courses, and she found she liked them. At the end of freshman year, she applied to UT's college of communication. She was accepted. Her confidence began to return.

The University Leadership Network helped, too, she told me. She felt inspired by the lectures on leadership and professionalism that ULN students were required to attend each week in freshman year. "I learned so much from them!" she told me. "ULN by far is the main program that helped me to succeed in college."

In the spring of her sophomore year, Amy took a management course at the business school, and the professor devoted one lecture to explaining the field of human resource management. The students around her seemed bored and unimpressed by the minutiae of the HR profession. But to Amy, the lecture was a revelation. "That class period was just amazing to me," she told me. "The professor kept describing HR and what the department does, and I was like, 'That's exactly what I want to do!'"

Amy approached the professor after class and gushed, and the professor invited her to take a course she was scheduled to teach the following year, usually open only to business-school students, that focused entirely on human resource management. Amy told me it was the most exciting and rewarding class she took in her four years at college. Human resource management, she decided, was the career she had been destined for all along.

Amy had arrived at UT as a low-income first-generation automatic admit with a subpar SAT score. According to David Laude's Dashboard, her chance of success at the University of Texas was quite low. And she did struggle at UT. She seriously considered dropping out. But she persisted, and wound up loving her time in college. She found courses she enjoyed and a career she was excited by and a diverse and loyal group of friends. And much to David Laude's professional relief, Amy graduated with her BA in exactly four years.

WHY DID AMY SUCCEED? How was she able to bounce back from the trials of her freshman year? What made it possible for her to persist to graduation when so many other students, at the University of Texas and elsewhere, are fatally derailed by the kind of obstacles she managed to overcome?

Does David Laude get the credit? Does her adviser, the one who steered her toward a new major? Did the ULN seminars she attended make the difference? How about her summer orientation program? Did that help?

Or was Amy's ability to persist something she brought with her to Austin? Was she born with it? Was it somehow encoded in her mind through the messages she received from her parents or her church or her high school?

Amy was one of a handful of students from the class of 2017 at the University of Texas whom I met as freshmen in 2013 and 2014 and then reconnected with again three years later, in their senior year. In those later conversations, I learned that most of them had followed a path through college something like Amy's: they endured some rough patches in freshman year, with the hard times sometimes continuing into sophomore or even junior year, but eventually reached a moment when they were able to turn things around.

Jessica, from a border town on the Rio Grande called Eagle Pass, cried in freshman year as she told me about the sacrifices her Mexican immigrant parents had made to send her to Austin; when I met up with her again in senior year, she had studied abroad in China and delivered a research paper in Berkeley and was graduating with a degree in geology.

DeMarcus, from Houston, Q-dropped chemistry *and* calculus in his first semester at UT, and all through freshman year he experienced debilitating episodes of depression and insomnia and anxiety. It took him five years to graduate, but he eventually found friends, developed strategies to manage his anxiety, and earned his BA in psychology, with a minor in geology.

Micah, also from Houston, was almost kicked out of his computer science major because he couldn't seem to pass his operating systems class. After failing the first two tests, he spent a couple of days curled up in bed watching *Key & Peele* videos, convinced his coding career was over before it began. But then he finally got up, found a way to master operating systems, and managed to stay in computer science. He graduated on time and right away found a job as a full-stack developer with a real estate company in Austin.

Laude's kitchen-sink approach did make a difference for students at the University of Texas — and the evidence for its success comes not just in the stories of individual students. The data support it, too. Laude and his team fell a few percentage points short of their assigned goal for the class of 2017, Amy's cohort. In that class, 66 percent of students graduated in four years — up from 51 percent when Laude was hired. But a year later, the class of 2018 hit President Powers's 70 percent target.

Those campus-wide four-year graduation rates were the numbers that led the press releases and earned headlines at UT in 2017 and

2018. But what made David Laude proudest was the fact that the biggest gains in UT's four-year graduation rate came among the categories of students whose rates were the lowest when he was named graduation-rate champion. Pell-eligible students at UT improved their four-year graduation rate from 40 percent in 2012 to 61 percent in 2018. First-generation college students improved their four-year rates from 41 percent in 2012 to 62 percent in 2018. Students with SAT scores in the lowest quartile for UT improved from 39 percent to 63 percent. Black students improved from 37 percent to 58 percent; Hispanic students from 43 percent to 64 percent.

DESPITE THOSE GENUINE SUCCESSES, not everyone from the class of 2017 had such a happy story to tell. Another UT freshman I met in the fall of 2013 was a young woman named Victoria, who had graduated fourth in her class from a small public high school in San Antonio. She loved math and science, and like almost every science major at UT, she planned to take introductory calculus as a freshman. In order to get a leg up on her future classmates, Victoria audited an introductory calculus course at a community college in San Antonio the summer before she came to Austin, and she learned a lot.

But when she arrived at UT, she took the computerized math diagnostic exam that every freshman was required to complete, and she bombed. Her low score meant that she wasn't allowed even to enroll in introductory calculus at UT, despite having already completed a college calculus course. Victoria would have to retreat to precalculus and then work her way back up. Instead, she decided to abandon math and science altogether, and she signed up that first semester for a hodgepodge of humanities courses.

Victoria's confidence was shaken, just like Amy's was in her first semester. Like Amy, Victoria worried that her academic failures meant that she didn't belong at UT. But Victoria found it harder to recover from those anxieties than Amy did. The ULN seminars and discussion groups were a comfort to Amy, but not to Victoria. She felt intimidated by the fact that everyone else in ULN seemed to have such clear goals and plans. ULN just didn't feel like a community where an uncertain and indecisive person like Victoria could really fit in.

Meanwhile, Victoria said, things back at home in San Antonio were in constant disarray. She told me family stories of drinking and dysfunction, chronic illness and chronic money trouble, all of which weighed on her mind throughout her freshman year. She finished her first semester at UT with a GPA below 2.0, which meant she was placed on academic probation, with a warning that if she didn't get her GPA back up above 2.0 before the end of freshman year, the university would kick her out for a semester. She didn't, and it did.

She lived at home in San Antonio the next fall, working at Macy's. She was eager to return to UT Austin after Christmas, but her grandmother died just before it was time for Victoria to leave for school. The death hit Victoria hard, and she fell into a depression, which made it even more difficult for her to concentrate in class — or to function in general. Her fiancé, who shared an apartment with her off campus, couldn't deal with her sadness, so he moved out, which only made her sadder. Victoria kept dutifully attending all her classes, but she wasn't really taking in any information. At the end of the semester, her GPA was still below a 2.0, and UT dismissed her again. This time the university's rules stipulated that she couldn't return for three years.

When I next saw Victoria, in the middle of what would have been her senior year, she was halfway through her second suspension. She was working as a hostess at a fancy restaurant in downtown Austin and still planning to return to UT — unless she could land a high-paying bartending job. She still wasn't sure what she wanted to do with her life.

One of the most troubling categories of American dropout is made up of college students who arrive on campus with a profile more or less exactly like that of Amy and Victoria and Micah and everyone else in ULN: low-income students with good but not great SAT

scores. At the University of Texas, those students now mostly graduate on time. In the nation as a whole, they mostly do not.

One national study from 2010 specifically examined the trajectories of college freshmen with SAT scores between 1000 and 1200
(on a 1600-point scale) — not the very highest scoring students, but
certainly above average. If those high-scoring freshmen grew up in
a family in the top income quartile, this study found, two-thirds of
them would go on to graduate with a BA by age twenty-four. But if
those freshmen came from a family in the bottom income quartile,
only one student in six was able to complete a bachelor's degree before twenty-four. The vast majority dropped out, despite their college-ready SAT scores.

Which brings a certain urgency to the question I asked earlier:
What was it that kept Amy (and Jessica and Micah) in school and on
track? And why didn't it work for Victoria?

IN THE LATE 1970s, two psychology researchers at Duke University
conducted a small but influential experiment that attempted to identify some of the mysterious mental processes at work during those
tumultuous moments when college students are deciding whether to
stay in school or to drop out. The researchers, Timothy Wilson and
Patricia Linville, recruited forty Duke students, all at the beginning
of the second semester of their freshman year, all of whom reported
that they hadn't done as well as they wanted in their first semester
and all of whom said they were worried about their GPA.

The entire experiment lasted less than an hour. The freshmen were
divided into a treatment and a control group, and they were told they
were part of a survey about the college experience. Students in the
treatment group were shown some statistics that conveyed a simple
message: *Things get better.* Freshman grades were often lower than
students expected, these statistics showed, but GPA usually improves
after the first semester of freshman year. The treatment students
then watched videotapes of four Duke upperclassmen telling much

the same story, but from a personal perspective: *The first semester of freshman year was challenging for me, but after that one rough semester, my GPA rose.*

Wilson and Linville tracked the academic progress of these forty students for the next year and a half, and they found that the students in the treatment group did considerably better in their classes than the students in the control group, and fewer of them dropped out. It was a small sample, but the experiment raised an interesting question: What kind of messages might best soothe the troubled minds of anxious college freshmen?

More than twenty years after the Duke study, two young researchers at Yale University borrowed Wilson and Linville's method for their own experiment. The Yale researchers, Gregory Walton and Geoffrey Cohen, had both studied at Stanford University under Claude Steele, a social psychologist famous for his work on stereotype threat. Steele's theory holds that when people are in situations where they have reason to worry that they might be judged according to a stereotype — like African Americans at elite, majority-white colleges — their anxiety about that potential judgment can cause them to underperform.

Walton and Cohen suspected that underperformance by racial minorities on college campuses was not just a matter of anxiety about intelligence and ability. They thought there was likely a social aspect to it as well. The college years are a period of often intense anxiety about *belonging*: Do I fit in? Can people like me feel at home here? Think of Amy's fear, when she dropped chemistry, that she didn't belong in a university full of valedictorians. Or Victoria's anxiety, in those ULN meetings, that everyone else had their lives way more figured out than she did. To her, ULN wasn't a place where existentially uncertain people belonged.

Walton and Cohen hypothesized that black students at a highly selective university like Yale would be anxious not just about their academic performance, but also, more broadly, about fitting in — feeling that they belonged in the social milieu of their college. To test this, they designed an experiment that exposed college freshmen to the reassuring message (again, delivered by upperclassmen) that it was totally normal to worry in freshman year whether you really belonged in college — most people felt that way at first — but that those worries naturally dissipated over time.

Again, the sample size was small, so it was hard to draw any firm conclusions from the study. But the intervention — lasting no more than an hour — did seem to improve the GPAs of African American students in the treatment group, and that improvement persisted through senior year.

As Walton and Wilson and others have continued to conduct experiments in this realm, they have developed a theory for what might be producing these results. Their hypothesis is that there are certain moments in our lives, like having a first child or enrolling in college, that are so deeply disorienting that they scramble our personal narrative — the story we tell ourselves about who we are. That's not a comfortable situation: We humans get attached to our personal narratives, and we prefer them to be stable. In these periods of dramatic change, we get a lot of messages from the world that are ambiguous, that can be interpreted in different ways. Our inclination is to try to fit those messages into a coherent narrative. Which means we are much more open — for better or worse — to new stories about who we are. My baby won't stop crying. Is that just what babies do? Or am I a terrible parent? I failed my first chemistry test. Is that normal, or am I in the wrong major — or at the wrong university?

The uncertainty that comes along with these moments of transition, uncomfortable though it is, can be a good thing, psychologically: it leaves us open to positive messages and productive stories. That may be why that original Duke experiment had a beneficial effect on students' academic performance. They didn't know how to interpret the disorienting fact that after years of being an excellent high school student, they were suddenly getting bad grades. If at an unsettled moment like that someone provides students with a coherent narrative to hang on to — *This is totally normal; it's a temporary problem and it will go away* — they are likely to grab on to it with both hands.

Of course, students in that untethered state are also more likely to latch on to a less hopeful narrative. Victoria, a very good math student throughout high school, suddenly gets results from her diagnostic math test at UT that provide her with a completely different story of herself: she's actually a *lousy* math student, way out of her league at a competitive college. Victoria didn't try to argue against this new narrative; she just accepted it. Disoriented by the transition she was experiencing, she was ready to believe anything.

Compare her experience to Micah's. Those first two tests in his operating systems class were sending him a loud, clear, painful message: *You're no good at this. You don't belong in computer science.* For a while, Micah wasn't sure whether or not to believe this new narrative about himself — that was the week he lay in the fetal position watching *Key & Peele* — but then he decided: Nope, that story's not true. I *do* belong in computer science. And it turned out he was right.

When I spoke to Greg Walton one fall afternoon in his office at Stanford, he explained that freshman year of college, especially, is full of these ambiguous moments, and students generally don't have enough context to figure out on their own how to interpret them. The point of his experiment with Cohen, and others like it, is to steer students, in these moments of uncertainty, toward a story that is going to help them rather than hold them back.

"What we wanted this to do was to convey to students that when something bad happens on campus — when you feel excluded or you feel lonely or you feel rejected or you get criticized — you don't need to draw a global inference from that," Walton said. "It's still a bad experience if your professor criticized you, but it doesn't mean you don't belong in general. Your professor might just be a jerk."

Early in 2012, a young researcher named David Yeager was hired by the psychology department at the University of Texas as an assistant professor. Yeager had just earned his PhD from Stanford, where he had worked closely with Walton and Cohen, and he was steeped in this new body of research and this new approach to intervention. Up until that point, the experiments Yeager and Walton and Cohen had tried were all relatively small in scale. But soon after Yeager arrived at UT, he was approached by administrators who asked him if he might be able to create an intervention that could be given to all seven-thousand-plus members of the next incoming freshman class.

Yeager and Walton had never tested out their method on such a large scale, but they managed to design a workable intervention in just a few weeks. Beginning that May, every student in the class of 2016, which entered UT in the fall of 2012, was invited, as part of their online orientation, to read and respond to a series of personal reflections, ostensibly from UT upperclassmen, about freshman year. As with the earlier experiments, the message was that freshman year could be hard, but that the pain was only temporary. *Sometimes you'll feel like you can't keep up. Sometimes you'll feel like you don't belong. But that's normal, and you'll get over it. Things will get better.* The class was divided into a control group and three treatment groups. At the end of freshman year, Yeager and Walton looked through UT's official records to see how likely members of each group were to have stayed enrolled, through the end of freshman year, with a full-time schedule of classes.

For students whose parents had gone to college, the intervention didn't make any difference — perhaps because they didn't have as much belonging anxiety in the first place. But for first-generation and other disadvantaged students, there was a small but distinct impact of encountering the "it gets better" messages: 69 percent of students in the control group remained enrolled in a full course-load throughout freshman year, compared to 73 percent of students who had experienced any of the interventions. It was a modest effect — but it was also an inexpensive and minimally intrusive intervention, costing just a few dollars per participant and taking only about half an hour for students to complete.

When Yeager and Walton looked at graduation data for the class of 2016, though, six years after the students enrolled at UT, the effect

of the intervention had mostly faded out. Their menu of brief interventions seemed to make a real difference in the short and medium
term, improving students' academic behaviors and even boosting
their GPA. But so far, at least, those interventions didn't seem to be
powerful enough to change students' minds about this more momen-
tous decision: Should I hang in there till graduation? Or should I just
give up?

3. An Intrusive Culture

In the years since David Laude first moved into the Tower in Austin,
student success has evolved into a national movement, with conferences and research papers and significant investments by foundations
and philanthropists. There is still a lack of clarity in the field over how
to find the best strategies and programs and scale them effectively,
but certain practices do seem to be making a difference, and in my
travels, I visited a number of colleges that were experimenting with
some of these new methods to keep students enrolled and on track.

At the University of Central Arkansas, which is in a small town
a half hour north of Little Rock, I sat in on a college writing class
where administrators were testing out a relatively new and nationally well-regarded method for teaching remedial math and English.
At many colleges, large numbers of freshmen are required to pass
remedial (also known as developmental) classes in English and math
before they are allowed to enroll in regular college-level courses.
Those classes not only don't help students earn credit toward a degree
(though students pay the same tuition for them as they would for any
other course); they also often have high failure rates. When students
have trouble passing a developmental course, they often find themselves caught in a remedial trap, stuck for a year or longer in boring
and basic high school–level courses in algebra or English composition before they are allowed to advance to the real stuff. Some of
them never make it out.

The alternative method they were using at UCA was called the corequisite model, which aims to let students get the help they need catching up while at the same time earning college credit in more challenging and engaging courses. The class I sat in on, Writing 1310, was not remedial; it was the standard first-year writing class that every UCA freshman is required to take. The professor, Becky Bogoslavsky, taught a class of twenty students that met three times a week. (On the day I was there, the class was discussing strategies for revising essays.) Though she never mentioned this fact in class, ten of Bogoslavsky's twenty students had scored 18 or below on the writing section of the ACT, meaning they were required by UCA's rules to complete the university's remedial writing course, while the other ten had scored 19 or above. On Mondays, Wednesdays, and Fridays, Bogoslavsky taught both the high-scoring and low-scoring students together, in the same class, without distinguishing between them at all.

And then on Tuesday and Thursday mornings, Bogoslavsky would meet in a separate class called Transitional Writing with the ten students from her Writing 1310 course who had lower ACT scores. On those days, she would go over the same material the larger class was covering that week in Writing 1310, but she'd do so in more detail, proceeding more slowly and carefully, paying extra attention to whatever difficulties these less well-prepared students might be having. The idea was that when they got to the regular 1310 class the next day, they would be prepared and comfortable with the new material.

I spoke to a couple of Transitional Writing students after the class, and they said that this combination class gave them a sense of confidence. They didn't feel like they were behind and isolated, as they might have if they were taking only a remedial class; they knew they were keeping up with students whose test scores showed them to be more college-ready. But they also didn't feel lost and abandoned the way they might have if they were simply tossed into an advanced class with no additional help or support. So far, the effort seems to be working. Over the last few years, an average of 80 percent of students enrolled in the corequisite writing classes at UCA have passed both the transitional class and Writing 1310 — compared with just 25 percent who were passing both the remedial class and Writing 1310 before UCA adopted the corequisite model.

GEORGIA STATE UNIVERSITY, a large, minimally selective public institution in downtown Atlanta, has found a different tool to stop its students from dropping out: a student counseling service that uses sophisticated data analysis to track student progress and intervene early, before small problems turn into major crises. I spent a couple of mornings at Georgia State shadowing a student adviser named Emily Buis, who worked in a small office on the fifth floor of the university advisement center that looked out on the giant red neon Coca-Cola sign looming over downtown Atlanta. Buis was friendly and warm; she wore chunky glasses and a cardigan sweater and had a calendar on her wall with photos of cats doing yoga poses. Her approach to the students she was advising was empathetic and reassuring, but it was also highly informed by data.

Georgia State uses some of the same predictive analytic strategies that David Laude employed in creating the UT Dashboard. On Buis's desk sat two big computer screens, angled so that she and visiting students could both see them at the same time. When she met with students, she used the screens to call up students' digital academic records, which were clearly laid out and color-coded and filled with a ton of information: which courses the students had taken and how they had done in those courses and when they had met or talked with Buis previously and what problems they addressed when they spoke. There was a GPA calculator that she could summon onto her screen, as well as a degree planner and a course catalog: a whole suite of interwoven programs and applications that made getting to a BA at Georgia State seem as linear and straightforward as mastering the early levels of a video game.

One of the first students to arrive in Buis's office on a mild morning in March, just after spring break, was Nicolas, a thin, soft-spoken, sharply dressed freshman with a sweep of sandy blond hair. When Buis opened his file on her screen, a big red circle popped up that read "Predicted risk level: High!" Nicolas had done very poorly in his first semester at Georgia State. Remember Kim Henning's brother Trevor, who messed up so thoroughly in his first semester at Appalachian State that he earned a GPA of 0.8, a grade so low that his friends turned it into a new nickname for him? Well, Nicolas managed to complete his first semester at Georgia State with a GPA of 0.25. He got an F in every class except Survey of United States History, where he somehow eked out a D.

As Buis talked through Nicolas's situation with him, she was encouraging but clearly concerned. The university had placed Nicolas on academic probation, and in order to escape probation, he would need to raise his cumulative GPA above 2.0. Given his abysmal first semester, Buis told Nicolas, he would need to earn almost perfect grades in the second semester if he wanted to get back in good standing before summer. His low grades also meant that he had lost his HOPE Scholarship, which the state of Georgia grants to high-achieving high school graduates, and without it, Nicolas was having a hard time figuring out how to pay for college.

The good news, though, was that Nicolas was doing exceptionally well in his second-semester classes: all As except for political science, where he had a B plus. "I've never been this motivated before," Nicolas said to Buis. "I want to put this behind me as quickly as possible." He said he was planning to major in philosophy or literature or both, and he was aiming to go to graduate school: a master's degree, at least, maybe a PhD.

All of which made me wonder: What the heck happened that first semester? And what changed afterward?

A month later, when I was passing back through Atlanta, I emailed Nicolas to see if he would sit down and talk with me. We arranged to meet late on a Monday evening in April at a Waffle House in the middle of Georgia State's sprawling urban campus. Over eggs and hash browns and many cups of coffee, Nicolas filled me in.

Like so many of the students I had spoken to — like Kim and KiKi and Amy and many others — the story of Nicolas's time in college seemed inextricable from the story of his family. Technically, he is a first-generation college student: his mother spent a little time in community college, but never graduated, and his father dropped out of high school at fifteen. But one generation earlier, on his father's side, at least, everyone was getting degrees: Nicolas's grandmother has a master's degree in English; his grandfather has a master's in school administration; and his step-grandfather has a doctorate in mathematics.

Nicolas's father dropped out of high school in part to rebel against the academic expectations of his parents, and now Nicolas was trying to succeed academically in part to rebel against his father. His father, who ran his own debt-collection business in Savannah, Georgia, had told Nicolas that he would only contribute financially to Nicolas's college education if Nicolas studied business at the University of South Carolina — which is perhaps why he was studying literature and philosophy at Georgia State.

"We've got a pretty bright family," Nicolas told me. "We just have some problems with authority."

In high school, Nicolas was weighed down by a deep depression that filled his mind with suicidal thoughts. By senior year, he had taken to burning himself with cigarettes, and he was drinking so much that he regularly blacked out. Through it all, he was an accomplished student and a voracious reader, finishing high school with straight As. He took the SAT just once and got a perfect 800 on the Critical Reading section. But he arrived in college feeling unsteady and uncertain about who he was and what he was doing. "When you have all that stuff behind you," he explained, "a big transition gets even bigger."

Nicolas had hoped that college would feel like an intellectual adventure, full of new ideas and intense discussions about literature and politics, but in fact, it felt about the same as high school. His survey classes were boring. He hated the way professors tried to make you jump through hoops with extra-credit assignments and points for class participation. He wanted to write long essays or just have conversations with professors in which he could demonstrate his understanding of a book or an idea. Disillusioned and depressed, Nicolas started skipping classes. He found a group of friends who, like him, enjoyed drinking bourbon and smoking cigarettes and talking about art and ideas, and that became his life, whiskey sours and Camels and conversation every night until he passed out. At the end of the first semester, he didn't show up to any of his final exams.

The moment things changed, he said, was over Christmas break, when he was sitting in the living room at home with his mother. He pulled out his phone and looked up his first-semester grades, which had just been posted, and for the first time he came face-to-face with that 0.25.

"Well," his mom said. "What are you going to do?"

He thought about that for a while. What *was* he going to do? He decided right then that he didn't want to be a college dropout. He wanted to be an academic. He wanted to live in a world of ideas. And if it took some boring classes and silly extra-credit assignments to get there, he thought he could probably handle it.

He still drank a fair amount in spring semester, but only after his homework was done each night, and he managed to get up every morning and go to class. As Emily Buis had told him that March morning, he needed a 3.75 in his spring semester in order to escape probation. In the end, he earned a 3.93. A few months after receiving almost all Fs, Nicolas finished the spring semester on the dean's list.

He credited his adviser for a lot of his success. "I love Miss Buis," he told me. "If it weren't for her, I don't know what would have happened. She really cared."

I visited Nicolas once more in Atlanta, in the fall of his sophomore year, and he was still doing well. He seemed positive and upbeat. His family's drama was continuing to weigh on him, but school was getting more interesting: higher-level classes, the kind of deep discussions about big ideas that he had been looking for.

And then the following year, when I tried to reach him again, Nicolas had disappeared. He no longer responded to my emails and texts. He seemed to have withdrawn from Georgia State. Then I noticed he had deleted his Facebook page. He didn't just drop out of college. He dropped off the map.

I remember thinking, that night back in the Waffle House, as I talked with Nicolas over eggs and coffee, that the effort to help more college students graduate is always going to be something of an asymmetrical battle. Yes, on the one side you've got predictive algorithms and corequisite programs and experimentally designed belonging interventions. But on the other, there is the psychological minefield of being an American eighteen-year-old, and the particular strengths and burdens and complexities each one brings to campus. Any science that tries to steer college students in one direction or another is inevitably going to be an inexact one.

AT THE UNIVERSITY of Central Arkansas and Georgia State, as at UT, the interventions that seemed to work best combined the practical assistance students needed with psychologically astute messages of belonging, support, and connection. If you were a Georgia State student sitting across from Emily Buis, the implicit message you might hear buried underneath her advice and direction on how to negotiate the institution's bureaucracy was: Someone is looking out for me. Someone wants me to stick around.

In an office building in downtown Chicago, a relatively new college called Arrupe is trying to institutionalize that message of welcome and inclusion in a new way. It is a two-year college, and its graduation rate is only a little more than 50 percent. But nonetheless, I think it may be doing a more impressive job of keeping its students enrolled and on track for success than any other institution I visited.

Arrupe opened its doors in the fall of 2015 to 160 recent graduates of Chicago public and parochial and charter schools. The college is part of Loyola University, a large private Catholic institution in Chicago with a very good academic reputation. At Loyola, the average incoming ACT score is 27. Three-quarters of undergraduates are white or Asian, and about a quarter of students receive Pell grants. Annual tuition is $44,000; 77 percent of students graduate within six years.

Arrupe's students fit an entirely different profile. Their average ACT score is 17, and their average high school GPA was 2.85 (a B minus). Almost all of Arrupe's students are black or Latino, and three-quarters of them are eligible for Pell grants. (Most of the others are undocumented immigrants, making them ineligible for Pell grants and other government aid.) The admissions process at Arrupe is rigorous — a little less than half of applicants are admitted — but students are evaluated mostly not on their test scores but on the basis of a personal interview with Arrupe staff and faculty. Unlike almost every other college in the country, Arrupe *favors* students with greater financial need. If you apply to Arrupe and you're not either undocumented or eligible for a Pell grant, you are likely to be rejected or placed on the wait-list.

In Chicago — and really in the country as a whole — there are very few reliable postsecondary options for students who meet the profile of an Arrupe student. Chicago does have a large system of community colleges, but their graduation rates are generally below 20 percent, and very few students successfully transfer to a four-year institution. At Arrupe, the normative goal for students is a bachelor's degree, either at Loyola or another university.

Costs are kept relatively low; Arrupe spends about $20,000 a year on each student, which includes providing them with a laptop and offering them breakfast and lunch every day. Students are expected to come up with about $1,700 of that amount — almost every student has a part-time or full-time job, usually in retail sales or fast food — and the remaining $18,000 or so comes from Pell grants; from the

Illinois Pell equivalent, which is called a MAP grant; from financial aid from Loyola; and from private fundraising by Arrupe's founding dean, a Jesuit priest named Stephen Katsouros.

Katsouros, who is in his late fifties, was born in Queens, New York, where his family owned a diner; he jokes that the first English sentence he learned was "We are happy to serve you," the slogan on every diner coffee cup in the city in those days. After graduating from Fordham, a Catholic university in the Bronx, he spent his twenties living on the Lower East Side, working at the Nativity Mission Center School, a Catholic middle school just off Houston Street that educated boys who lived in the housing projects nearby. Gradually, Katsouros came to realize his heart was in service and the church, and in 1987 he began the process of joining the Jesuits. He spent most of the next two and a half decades teaching and ministering in New York. And then, in 2014, the president of Loyola University, seized with a desire to make a Loyola education less exclusive, invited Katsouros to come to Chicago as the founding dean of Arrupe.

Katsouros's goal for the college is to provide to students the same kind of life-changing, intensive education that the Nativity School did for its middle school boys. Katsouros says he wants Arrupe's students to "have the experience of a private liberal arts education in the Jesuit tradition"; they study Shakespeare and macroeconomics and philosophy, all in preparation to move directly on to a four-year degree.

Katsouros is convinced that the psychological research on belonging done by David Yeager and Greg Walton is highly relevant to the needs of his students in Chicago, who have often been made to feel unwelcome in academic environments. (He has brought Yeager to Arrupe three separate times to speak with his staff.) Katsouros believes that the belonging message, for students like those at Arrupe, needs to be expressed loudly and frequently. "Our success is based on the fact that we have a very intrusive culture here," Katsouros told me. "In the Jesuits we talk about *cura personalis*. It's Latin for 'care for the whole person.' We know a lot about our students. Not just academically, but their backgrounds, their interests, their aspirations. Their family dynamics. We spend a lot of time with them."

His students are almost all first-generation, and usually they have had very little exposure to college culture before arriving at Arrupe. Their lives are complex: some have babies; they often have struggles with housing; many have experienced violence. Simply getting to school every day can be a challenge. So Arrupe's students need far more personal connection and institutional flexibility than students do at other colleges, Katsouros believes. There are two full-time social workers on the staff, and any time a student misses two consecutive classes, they get a call from a social worker, checking in on them. But everyone on staff, including the professors, sees student outreach as part of his or her job. When Blanca, a second-year student, had a baby at the beginning of the fall semester, Katsouros called her in the hospital to congratulate her and make plans for the baptism — and then to urge her to hurry back to class.

"Our students know where the writing center is on Loyola's campus," Katsouros told me. "But they don't go there. What is more effective is a tutor standing at the door waiting for them as they're leaving a class, saying, 'Father Katsouros said that you might want to talk with me about your essay.' We are extremely in their faces."

The work I saw being done at Arrupe was hard, both for Father Katsouros and his staff and for the students, many of whom seemed to be experiencing near-constant crises — lost jobs, housing trouble, fights with family, money worries. Academics were challenging for many of them as well; college-level math or ethics is a big step up from the fare at most Chicago public schools. I visited philosophy classes and English classes and statistics classes at Arrupe, and I was always impressed by the level of focus and seriousness that the students brought to their studies. But still, Arrupe students frequently went off track. Even with all those in-your-face supports, almost half of them didn't make it to graduation.

And yet, 51 percent of the students in Arrupe's first two classes did graduate on time, most of them with no debt, and 88 percent of those graduates transferred directly to four-year universities, including Loyola and Georgetown and the University of Wisconsin in Madison. Next fall, another two hundred young Chicagoans will enroll at Arrupe as freshmen, and Father Katsouros and his staff—along with teachers and administrators at UT and Georgia State and colleges and universities across the country—will try once again to find the precise combination of common sense, innovation, and human kindness that will convince their students to stay.

VII

HANGING ON

---

1. Who Needs College?

Let me take you back for a moment to a scene I described in chapter 2 of this book: the evening I spent in Kim Henning's family's house in Taylorsville, in the Appalachian foothills of western North Carolina, with Kim, the A student who chose Clemson over Cornell, and her two older half-brothers. It was late on a Friday, and the coffeemaker was going, and the three of us stood for hours around the kitchen island, talking about money and family and college.

Trevor was there, the oldest sibling, aka Decimalé Ocho, the one who flamed out so spectacularly in his freshman year at Appalachian State. He and Kim, standing across the island from each other, represented, in some ways, the twin poles of our ongoing national debate about higher education and social mobility. Kim, who was then a few weeks away from her planned move to South Carolina and was still anxious about whether she would really be able to overcome the remaining obstacles standing between her and Clemson, saw a college education as her deliverance, the key that might unlock the financial and personal shackles that had been holding her and her family back for generations. Trevor, though, still shaken by his experience at App

State, was much more cynical about college and the possibilities it presented. He took responsibility for the mistakes he had made as a student, but he also felt like the system was rigged against people like him, designed to make opportunity inaccessible and expensive. He still owed thousands of dollars in student loans, but he had stopped paying them back, and now every year the state seized his income tax refund and put it toward his debt.

And then there was Orry, the third sibling, whose relationship to college was harder to fit into a neat category. While Kim and Trevor had both been standout students at Alexander Central High School in Taylorsville, taking AP courses and graduating with GPAs close to the top of their respective classes, Orry's journey through adolescence and high school was rockier. He had never known his father, who left the family before Orry was born, and the absence of a stable male role model in his life, he told me, had led him into some wild and self-destructive behavior, especially in his early teens. He had had to repeat his freshman year of high school, and he only barely passed his sophomore year. He finally made it through Alexander Central, but he graduated 388th in a class of 389.

Orry's original plan had been to join the Marines straight out of high school. A recruiter came to the house a few times during his senior year to go over paperwork, and everything seemed set. But then the Marines looked up Orry's police record, which included charges of underage drinking and possession of drug paraphernalia, and the recruiter told him they weren't interested anymore. Orry switched his plan to the Navy, and that seemed promising for a while—until he learned the Navy's rules about visible tattoos. Orry had a four-leaf clover inked on the back of his neck that would extend an inch or two over the collar of a Navy dress uniform, and that was all it took for him to wash out of the Navy, too.

So when he finished high school, Orry went to work. First he spent a year installing locks for a local company, and then another year doing oil changes at the Taylorsville Snappy Lube. Those jobs paid minimum wage or a little more, and the work wasn't steady or predictable. Nothing you could build a life on. At twenty-one, Orry got married, and he and his wife moved into a rented trailer in Taylorsville. His stepfather Billy helped him get his next job, drawing wire at the factory where Billy was already working. It was hard work, loud and dirty and repetitive, but it paid $13.90 an hour, a lot better than Snappy Lube. After a year and a half, Orry was fired for missing too many days of work, but he soon managed to land a job at another steel-wire factory, thirty minutes away, for $14.50 an hour. Then he got fired from that job, as well.

It was by that point the spring of 2016, and Orry was twenty-four, separated, and unemployed. He was raising two children with his ex-wife, Katie, and he was living with a new girlfriend named Crystal who had two kids of her own. Orry had been working hard for five years, and yet he was broke, with nothing saved. At every job he'd had, he'd been made to feel as though he was disposable, like he didn't really matter. He never had any control over his schedule or his work assignments, and his employers seemed both willing and able to fire him for the slightest mistake. (His jobs were all nonunion, like most manufacturing jobs in North Carolina.)

Crystal was also unemployed that spring, and she suggested they both think about going back to school. At first, college seemed like the last thing Orry might want to consider. He had always hated school. And Trevor's App State debacle still hung like a dark cloud over the whole family. But Crystal showed Orry the website for Catawba Valley Community College in nearby Hickory, and he saw that the school offered an associate's degree in welding. He had done a little welding in high school, and he had liked it. That made the notion of college a lot easier to imagine. "It dawned on me that by firing me, they had given me an opportunity," Orry told me, talking about his former employer. "I could go to college to better myself, and I could find a different job, something that was away from all this."

When I met Orry that first night with Kim and Trevor in Taylorsville, it was November 2016, and he was just a couple of months into his first semester at CVCC. So far, he said, he liked it. "When I first got there, I just had this sense of accomplishment," he told me. It was the opposite of how he used to feel every day in high school. "I was doing something that everyone told me I'd never be able to do," he explained. The welding was challenging, but he was already pretty good at it, and he could feel himself getting better.

On the surface, Orry seemed quite different from most of the other young high school and college students I'd been meeting, the ambitious and determined achievers like KiKi Gilbert or Ned Johnson's SAT students in suburban DC, or even Orry's sister, Kim. Orry had long metalhead hair, a scraggly beard, plentiful tattoos, and a horseshoe ring piercing his septum. He wore a lot of denim and leather and cultivated a dark, antiauthoritarian vibe; his favorite bands, he told me, were Axe Wound and Five Finger Death Punch. The evening I met him, he was swigging Mountain Dew straight out of a family-size bottle and vaping a custardy tobacco blend called Dr. Crimmy's Kitty Milk, punctuating his stories by expelling giant clouds of cheesecake-flavored vapor into the air above us.

But what was true for KiKi and Kim and Ariel and the others was true for Orry, as well: Somewhat to his surprise, he now saw college as his path to a better life, not just for himself but for his young family. "I want my kids to have stuff I didn't have growing up," he told me. "I don't want them to have to wonder where their next meal is coming from. I want them to have the chances I never had."

THE PARTICULAR DEGREE PATH that Orry had chosen to pursue was, at that moment in American political history, freighted with symbolic meaning. In April 2014 the *Wall Street Journal* published a column by Josh Mandel, the treasurer of Ohio, a Republican who, two years earlier, had run unsuccessfully against the Democrat Sherrod Brown for the US Senate. The column was titled "Welders Make $150,000? Bring Back Shop Class," and its premise was that in rural Ohio, there was such a shortage of skilled tradespeople that employers were regularly hiring welders at salaries of $150,000 a year and up.

Some Ohio welders, Mandel said, were earning more than $200,000. In the column, Mandel contrasted the bountiful opportunities available to blue-collar workers without college degrees with the dismal prospects he said many college graduates faced: "Too many young people have four-year liberal-arts degrees, are thousands of dollars in debt and find themselves serving coffee at Starbucks or working part-time at the mall."

Mandel's column was not the first to tap into the skepticism many Americans were feeling, in those postrecession days, about the value of a four-year college degree. But it helped direct the focus of that conversation toward one particular profession: welding. Three months later, the *Journal* upped the ante on Mandel's $150,000 welder by publishing an essay claiming that in Appalachia and Texas, welders were earning $7,000 a week, which is the equivalent of an annual salary of more than $350,000. In a Republican presidential debate the next year in Milwaukee, Senator Marco Rubio declared, "For the life of me, I don't know why we have stigmatized vocational education. Welders make more money than philosophers. We need more welders and less philosophers."

The rich-laborer meme wasn't restricted to welding. *Bloomberg Businessweek* published a story with the headline "Want a $1 Million Paycheck? Skip College and Go Work in a Lumberyard." But welding was the profession that mostly stayed front and center. At a summit meeting sponsored by the American Enterprise Institute a few weeks after the 2016 election, three separate speakers, including House Speaker Paul Ryan, extolled the benefits of a welding career. President Trump invited a welder from Dayton to be one of the guests of honor at his first State of the Union address. Secretary of Education Betsy DeVos, trailed by reporters, visited welding classes in Orlando, Fort Worth, suburban Chicago, and Far Rockaway, Queens. And the president's daughter Ivanka brought the media with her to a community college near St. Louis, where she pulled on a welding mask herself and tried her hand with a torch.

The case that was being made for welding during these public events was almost never simply a case for welding. It was also a case against college: America didn't just need more welders; it needed fewer philosophers, too. In frequent segments on Fox News and the Fox Business Network, the economic argument that there were untold riches to be made in the skilled trades fused with a cultural critique of anyone who chose to pursue a bachelor's degree instead. "I think there's an element of snobbery in America," proclaimed Stuart Varney, who hosts his own show on the Fox Business Network. "If you work with your hands, you're down *there,* and if you work with your brain, you're up *there.* And I bitterly resent that."

It was perhaps a sign of the times that this expression of class resentment against educated snobs was being rendered in a plummy English accent by a well-heeled graduate of the London School of Economics. But it wasn't only Varney: you could hear the same arguments, day after day, on *Fox & Friends* or *Tucker Carlson Tonight*: four-year colleges were offering America's youth nothing but safe spaces, emotional-support dogs, and towering mounds of student debt; meanwhile, high-paying welding jobs were sitting vacant because millennial snowflakes were afraid to get their hands dirty.

ONE OF THE MANY odd things about the rhetoric that posits welding as the antithesis of college is that in order to become a welder, you actually have to go to college. Welding is hard and complicated. You can learn the basics in a high school shop class, as Orry did, but to do it well, you not only have to master multiple precise manual skills, many of which take careful training and painstaking practice; you also need a pretty deep scientific understanding of the metal you're working with and the electrical and chemical processes you're using to manipulate that metal. To earn an associate's degree in welding technology at Catawba Valley Community College, Orry would have to pass thirteen separate welding courses, starting with basic metal cutting and moving up through stick welding, plate and pipe welding, and gas metal arc welding. He would also be required to pass basic classes in math and English, as well as more conceptual courses in welding metallurgy and the symbols and specifications used in blueprints.

Orry's first year at CVCC went well, mostly. It wasn't completely smooth—he failed his required English course, which was offered only online. But in his welding classes, he earned nothing but As and Bs. After that first year ended, he ran into some bureaucratic trouble with his financial aid, he told me, and he took both the summer and the fall of 2017 off from school. I was in occasional touch with him that year through Facebook, and for a while, I wondered whether he might just be finished with college. But then he started up again as a full-time student in January 2018, and the following month, I traveled to Hickory to visit him and get a tour of CVCC and the welding shop where he took most of his classes.

When we met up, Orry said he was glad to be back at school, but otherwise, he told me, life was not going well. He was broke, more broke than he had ever been. He and Crystal had just been evicted from their house in Hickory for chronic nonpayment of rent, and about the same time, their car was stolen. There was a moment, he told me, right after getting the final eviction notice, when he almost gave up on school and everything else. He spent three days on the couch playing Fortnite and Rocket League on his Xbox, too depressed to go to class or even get out of the house. He found himself daydreaming about just leaving town, ditching Crystal and the kids, hitching a ride to another state and starting over.

What finally spurred him back into action, he told me, was the sight of his children. They kept asking if he was all right, and he didn't want them to think that it was OK to give up when you hit a problem. So he roused himself from the couch and set about trying to get back to class. That was no easy task: without a car, he would need to take a city bus to school, but he was so broke he couldn't afford bus fare. He explained his situation to the administrators at CVCC, and they gave him a stack of bus tickets, which felt a little embarrassing, but also like a lifeline. By the time I arrived in February, he was back at school, taking more advanced welding courses, plus a drawing course, plus remedial math, plus that online English class again.

A few months later, when he got to the end of that semester, he told me he felt as though he had reached a crossroads, in more ways than one. His welding classes had gone well, he said, but he had had to drop the English class again — it was still offered only as an online course, and he didn't have internet access. He and Crystal had broken up, and he was back together with his ex-wife, Katie; Orry and Katie and their two kids had moved in with his mother.

There was a part of Orry that wanted to go right back to school in the fall and finish his degree, but he wasn't sure how to pull it off. He was still about sixteen credits shy of the sixty he needed to complete his associate's degree, and those included his required English and math classes, which he wasn't confident he could pass. That summer, he found a job in Wilkesboro, working in a factory that manufactured doors. It was a good position, operating a press, but the work was hot and exhausting and his schedule was brutal: twelve-hour night shifts seven days straight, from 6:00 p.m. to 6:00 a.m., followed by seven straight days off. There was no way he could manage school while working those shifts. He was earning $16.75 an hour, which he knew was a decent wage, but it was only a couple of dollars an hour more than he had been making before he started college. And he now had $19,000 in student loans that he would soon have to start paying back.

Orry was no longer feeling all that optimistic about the welding profession. Despite the sunny claims of the *Wall Street Journal* and Marco Rubio, the real-life welding jobs that Orry was able to find in western North Carolina were paying experienced welders between $12 and $15 an hour, which was less than he was making at the door factory. Orry knew that better-paying welding jobs existed, but they were all far away, in Colorado or Arizona or working on a pipeline in Alaska. Those jobs were generally short-term and physically arduous, and if Orry went out and chased one, he'd have to leave his kids behind. Now that he was back together with Katie, and they had what felt like a genuine family, he wanted to stay close to home and be a real father, the kind of steady male presence that he himself had never had growing up. Besides, even those well-paying welding jobs didn't pay *that* well — maybe $30 or $40 an hour, if he got lucky.

THIS WAS THE OTHER glaring flaw at the heart of the case for welding as the ideal alternative to college. The vast majority of American welders were not earning $150,000 a year. Not even close. According to the Bureau of Labor Statistics, the average annual salary for an experienced welder in 2014 was a little more than $36,000 a year — which was only about $12,000 above the poverty line for a family of four. That said, for someone Orry's age, just starting out, a $36,000-a-year salary would be pretty decent. It beats what you make at Snappy Lube, and it is comparable to starting salaries for many young people with bachelor's degrees. But $36,000 was the *median* salary for the entire welding profession, meaning there were as many welders making less than that figure as there were making more. And most welders whose earnings are represented in that figure are *not* just starting out. They're in their forties and fifties, often trying to support a whole family.

The good thing about welding as a profession is that it has a relatively high salary floor. You're almost always going to make more than minimum wage, even starting out. But the downside, economically, is that welding has a pretty low salary ceiling. Welders at the ninetieth percentile of income for the profession, according to the Bureau of Labor Statistics, earn $63,000 a year before taxes. Those are, statistically, the top earners. The salaries that make headlines in the *Wall Street Journal* are somewhere between rare and apocryphal.

Which leads to an intriguing question: Given the sobering reality that those unbiased statistics convey, why has the wealthy-welder myth become so widely accepted, at least in certain circles? Why does Marco Rubio believe — or claim to believe — that welders make more than philosophy majors? (They do not.)

Let me offer three possible reasons.

The first and most obvious one is that the people making the speeches and writing the newspaper columns and taking part in the cable-news segments don't know any actual welders. I have now spent several long evenings on YouTube, watching one video after another of these pro-blue-collar cable-news segments from the last few years, and I can report that the one consistent characteristic of these televised conversations about the folly of the four-year college degree is this: everyone on camera in these discussions has a four-year college degree. So that is potential reason number one: simple ignorance.

The second possible reason is wishful thinking, topped with a dollop of nostalgia. Money aside, welding is an impressive and admirable pursuit. When Orry showed me around the welding bays at CVCC, I quickly understood why he liked the work, and why he was proud of what he had learned. It is a burly, physical job, but there is delicate artistry in it as well, fine craftsmanship with a creative spirit. It would be so cool if you really could make $150,000 a year doing it. And an economy in which a manual laborer could reliably earn enough money to support a middle-class family — which is to say, an economy like the United States once had, decades ago — would indeed be more equitable, more socially stable, and more family-friendly than the actual economy we have today.

The third possible reason for the ubiquity of the wealthy-welder myth is less benign: If we are able to persuade ourselves that there are plenty of lucrative opportunities available for young people like Orry who didn't much like high school, it absolves us of our shared responsibility to address the reality of his limited economic prospects. If the only reason more young people aren't making $150,000 a year is that they are cosseted crybabies who can't handle the hard work of welding, well, then, that's on them. But if the real problem is what Orry has come to understand — that it is entirely possible to study welding for two years, go thousands of dollars into debt, and in the end be able to earn only $12 an hour — then there is a larger, societal problem we need to solve.

Meanwhile, if you are able to define welding training, in the public mind, as something *separate* from college, rather than what it actually is — a college major like any other — it allows for other rhetorical sleights of hand. It provides a way to distract public attention from policy shifts that have made it more difficult for young people like Orry to reach the middle class. The most obvious one being that over the past decade, as the make-believe story of the rich welder has grown and spread, public spending on the community colleges where actual young people are trying to learn actual welding has shrunk — in some states, quite drastically so.

In North Carolina, the amount the state government spends on each community college student declined, after adjusting for inflation, from $5,830 per student in 2007 to $4,891 per student in 2016, the year that Orry enrolled at CVCC. That's a cut of about 16 percent — and it took place during a period when state tax revenues in North Carolina actually went *up*. The state has the money, in other words, but state legislators are choosing not to spend it on institutions like Catawba Valley Community College. Which leads to the question: *Why?* Why don't North Carolina taxpayers insist that the government fund community colleges so that young people like Orry can learn the skills they need to earn a living? Perhaps because they have been told, over and over, that "college" is the *opposite* of what Orry is doing. It's the place where pampered whiners go to major in gender studies. What's the harm in cutting *that* budget?

What happened in North Carolina mirrors what happened in most other states: when the recession hit in 2008, tax revenues dropped sharply, and state governments cut their spending on higher education. Then the recovery arrived, and tax revenues went back up — but most state governments didn't replace the funding they had cut from the budgets of community colleges and other public colleges.

Those budget cuts in North Carolina had a direct impact on Orry's experience at CVCC. First, they added to his tuition costs, and thus to his debt: community college tuition in North Carolina has increased by 60 percent since 2007. (CVCC charges about $2,300 a year.) But this new revenue from North Carolina's community college students has not been enough to compensate for the cuts in state spending, which means that Catawba Valley Community College and schools like it across the state have had to find ways to cut budgets and cut corners. That is why, for instance, the English class that Orry needs to pass in order to get his degree is offered only online: because it's cheaper that way. There is no doubt that Orry would benefit from high-quality face-to-face instruction from a caring and conscientious English professor. But he is almost certainly not going to get it. And that is going to make it much harder for him to pass, and thus to graduate. Orry says he is still determined to finish his associate's degree, but if he doesn't manage to do so, he won't be alone. Right now, only 23 percent of students at CVCC are able to complete a two-year degree in three years.

2. Lower Ed

While Orry was in North Carolina, trying to figure out his path to a better life — and whether a college degree was going to be a part of that path — a young man named Taslim Mohammed was asking himself some of the same questions six hundred miles away in New York City. I met both Taslim and Orry in the fall of 2016, and though they were on the surface quite different, their situations, in my mind at least, seemed linked.

Taslim was a second-year computer science student at the City College of New York, a four-year public college in Upper Manhattan. Historically, there is probably no institution of higher education in the United States more closely associated with upward mobility than City College. It was the first free public college in the nation, and beginning in the late nineteenth century, it was a famously powerful springboard to the middle and professional classes for tens of thousands of economically disadvantaged young New Yorkers, especially Jewish immigrants from eastern Europe. Since the 1970s, public funding for City College — and the larger City University system it is now a part of — has been cut substantially; tuition has gone up (it is now almost $7,000 a year), while spending on instruction has gone down, and its reputation has suffered as a result. But when Raj Chetty's group handed out its Mobility Report Cards in 2017, City College was near the top of the list, lifting a greater proportion of its students each year from childhoods in the bottom economic quintile to adulthoods in the top economic quintile than almost any other institution in the country.

When I visited City College in 2016, I had a long conversation with Taslim in the cafeteria on the second floor of the college's main administration building. Like countless City College students before him, Taslim was an immigrant, a Muslim whose family had brought him to New York as a small boy from an impoverished village in Bangladesh. His parents, Taslim told me, were conservative and traditional — they had an arranged marriage, and his mother wore a hijab whenever she left their home in central Brooklyn. His father supported the family by driving a cab. Neither of his parents had much education, but in their Bengali immigrant community, their social status was very much tied up with their children's academic success. They were counting on Taslim to become a doctor or a lawyer or an engineer. Something respectable they could use to impress their friends.

At first glance, Taslim seemed to be an archetypal City College student: a public school graduate from a struggling immigrant family with a sharp brain and a knack for numbers. But Taslim differed from that ideal in one critical way: he didn't like college. His classes were boring, he told me, and his commute from home was long, and he found it hard to make friends. His disaffection had developed early on in his first semester, when he got bad grades on his first few tests. He slipped into a depression. He couldn't concentrate on his schoolwork. Between classes, he sat alone in the library and played video games on his laptop. In high school, he had aspired to be a programmer for Google. But by the end of his freshman year of college, he was questioning that goal — and then he began questioning whether he belonged in college at all.

"Maybe college isn't for everyone, however much your parents or your high school might hype it up to be," he told me. "I really only went to college because I had to. If I told my parents I didn't want to go, they'd probably disown me."

He still liked computers, he said. But he was thinking now that he didn't want to program them. He wanted to fix them. What he really wanted to be, he had decided, was an IT person, the guy you turn to in a big office when your computer freezes or your printer won't work. And to do that job, he believed, there was no need for a college degree at all.

He had recently found and applied to a program called Year Up, he told me, a national nonprofit that each year enrolls thousands of young people who are looking for an alternative to a college education. The yearlong program Taslim had applied to consisted of six months of training in the kind of computer knowledge and office etiquette you need to work in in-house information technology support, followed by a six-month hands-on corporate internship. Year Up students earn college credit, usually, as well as a small stipend and a lot of potentially useful work experience.

Taslim hadn't shared this new plan with his parents. He hadn't talked to them at all about his academic woes. When they accidentally caught a glimpse of his freshman transcript from City College, he made up a far-fetched story, telling them that it wasn't his *real* report card; it was just a sample transcript to show what it would look like, in theory, if he *had* done badly. Incredibly, they bought it. Taslim knew Year Up would not fly at home, and if he got in, he planned to spend the entire year pretending he was still enrolled in college. It might be hard to pull off, but if it meant a decent escape route from his current predicament, he said, it would be worth it.

"Year Up is my light at the end of the tunnel," Taslim told me. "Some people have the passion and motivation for college. Sadly, I did not. But if you have the right connections, you can make do in life without a college degree. College is not one-size-fits-all. For some people it works, and for some people it doesn't."

ONE OF THE CENTRAL questions that Taslim and Orry and many other high school seniors and college students have been asking in the last few years is this: *Is college worth it?* When you pose this question to economists, they usually give you either a quick answer or a slightly more deliberate one. The quick answer is: *Yes.* What economists call the college wage premium — the amount by which wages for college-educated adults exceed, on average, wages earned by those who don't have a degree — is about as high in the United States as it has ever been. Back in the 1970s, that gap was relatively modest; college graduates earned just 40 percent more, on average, than nongrads. Now they earn 84 percent more.

The college wage premium is a basic function of supply and demand: when there are more college graduates than the market can bear, the wage premium goes down. When the higher education system isn't producing as many graduates as the economy demands, the wage premium goes up. So this is an important starting point for any discussion of the value of a college degree. Despite the dominant political rhetoric suggesting that the United States has too *many* college graduates, the clear signal from the labor marketplace is that in fact we have too *few*.

The somewhat more nuanced answer economists give to the is-college-worth-it question is: *It depends.* It depends on who you are and where you go and what you take and how you do when you're there and how much debt you amass along the way. If you don't complete your degree, enrolling in college is most likely *not* worth it. College dropouts earn, on average, only about $3,000 a year more than adults who graduated from high school and never attempted college, and that small salary advantage is usually negated by the dropouts' larger student debt. If you do manage to graduate, the selectivity of the college you attended affects the value of your degree, as does the major you selected. (Engineers really do earn more than almost everyone else.) And because low-income students are less likely to attend the highly selective schools that have the greatest positive impact on a graduate's earning power, low-income college graduates, as a group, derive less financial benefit from their degrees than college graduates from high-income backgrounds derive from theirs. According to research by the economists Tim Bartik and Brad Hershbein, if you grow up in a lower-income family, your BA will add an average of $335,000 to your lifetime earnings. But if you grow up in a higher-income family, your BA will add an average of $901,000 to your lifetime earnings.

Though economists are still adamant that most of the time, for most young people, college is a valuable investment, there are indications in national polling data that the public is growing disillusioned with higher education. Some polls show public skepticism rising sharply in just the last few years. In a 2013 poll conducted by NBC News and the *Wall Street Journal,* for example, 40 percent of young adults between the ages of eighteen and thirty-four said that a four-year college degree wasn't worth the cost. When the same question was asked again four years later, that figure had jumped to 57 percent.

Some of this new skepticism may simply be an artifact of our current political discourse; when your media diet includes a large helping of negative stories about college, it is not altogether surprising if you develop a poor opinion of higher education. (The demographic group that currently harbors the most consistently negative feelings about college is old, wealthy Republicans.) But these growing doubts about college, especially among young people, may also reflect a more profound shift that is taking place in the American economy.

The MIT economist David Autor has dug deeply into the research on the college wage premium, and the data he has uncovered further complicates the overall positive message about the effect college degrees have on mobility. Autor's analysis indicates that, yes, Americans with college degrees do earn much more, on average, than those

without college degrees. But the growth of that wage premium in recent decades, Autor found, was driven mostly by college graduates
who didn't stop at a BA but went on to earn an advanced degree. As a
group, men with *only* a bachelor's degree have actually not increased
their income at all (adjusting for inflation) since the early 1970s.
(Earnings for women with just a BA have gone up a bit, but much
less than for women with advanced degrees.) The apparent growth
in the college wage premium has come about partly because of the
increased salaries of high earners with graduate and professional degrees, and partly because the average income of Americans without
a bachelor's degree has *fallen* since the early 1970s. College graduates
with just a BA only *seem* upwardly mobile when compared to the
declining prospects of those with less education.

This phenomenon is certainly significant in economic terms, but
its deeper and more lasting effect may be a psychological one. A generation ago, earning a four-year college degree was rightly seen as a
way for individuals to move up in the world. Today, for many young
Americans, a BA is simply an insurance policy against moving *down*.
That dark fact has changed the way many of us think about college.
It means that the pursuit of a BA has come to feel less aspirational
than it once did, and more anxious. It means that when young people
make their decisions today about college, they often are motivated
less by hope and more by fear.

WHEN ALICIA POLLARD graduated from high school in North Carolina in 2012, she opted out of college, just like Orry did, moving
instead first to Dallas and then, with a new friend named Danielle,
to Austin. They found an inexpensive apartment in a distant suburb,
and they both quickly landed minimum-wage fast-food jobs. When I
met Alicia in the fall of 2017, she was still working in fast food, but she
had advanced professionally: She was now the drive-through director at a Chick-fil-A franchise in a strip mall in northwest Austin. But
she had ambitions that went beyond the restaurant industry, she told

me, and she had come to the conclusion that she couldn't achieve her goals without a college degree.

I met Alicia because she had enrolled, earlier that year, in an unusual new program called PelotonU, a hybrid college model, run by a local nonprofit, that combined the online academic curriculum of a degree-granting public university in New Hampshire with a storefront study space in Austin where students had access to personal tutoring and support, a quiet place to work, and, if they wanted it, a sense of community and connection that usually eluded students who tried to complete a college degree online. Students could work at their own pace, and some of them progressed very quickly, completing an associate's degree in less than a year. Tuition was $2,750 a semester, about the same as nearby Austin Community College; if PelotonU students were Pell-eligible, as most were, their Pell grant would often cover their entire tuition bill.

Alicia was pursuing an associate's degree in general studies with a concentration in business. She worked hard on her assignments, and she took them seriously, but her approach to her studies was frankly utilitarian: what motivated her was not the content she was learning but the degree she was earning—and the difference she hoped that degree would make in her life. At twenty-three, she told me, she was feeling increasingly trapped economically. Her management job at Chick-fil-A paid her $17.50 an hour, with no health insurance or other benefits. She lived with her boyfriend and tried to keep her expenses low, but Austin was not cheap. She was in debt, with a car loan and a hefty credit card balance, and every month that debt grew.

Alicia's anxiety about her financial situation often got tangled up, in our conversations, with her regrets about her past. Early on in high school, she had been a basketball star, playing center at school and on a regional traveling team. In her freshman year, she started receiving letters of interest from colleges around the state. She was getting respectable grades, but most of her time and energy went into basketball. That seemed like the most reliable path to college, and though neither of her parents had gone, Alicia understood that college was, in some abstract way, the thing she was supposed to do.

Then in the summer after sophomore year, her family's foundation, already shaky, began to erode. Her parents divorced, and then her father was laid off from his job as a supervisor in a food-distribution warehouse. The family scattered: her mom, a postal worker, moved in with her own mom, and Alicia stayed with her dad. Alicia, feeling abandoned and confused, drifted away from basketball and found solace and a new kind of communion in her high school's party crowd. She drank beer and skipped class and neglected her homework and never even applied to college. Now, in Austin, she felt mad and regretful about the decisions she had made and the time she had wasted. "I didn't understand how you got from being a child to being an adult, or what you needed to be successful," Alicia told me. "Even graduating as a senior, I didn't have that knowledge. I just wasn't taught it."

Much of Alicia's new motivation for trying to change the path she was on had to do with her father. He was sixty-four and living alone in Dallas. He had worked his whole life in physical jobs, but his body could no longer handle that kind of labor, so he worked now as a driver, shuttling people to the airport and back, sometimes picking up shifts for Uber. He was able to support himself, barely, but he had no savings or pension or other retirement. No safety net at all. Alicia was devoted to her father — he was her best friend, she told me — but she looked at his life now both as a cautionary tale and a problem for her to solve: a cautionary tale because it represented how limited a person's options could be without a college education, and a problem to solve because she knew the only way he would ever be able to stop working was if she were able to support him.

Since arriving in Austin, Alicia had worked for Subway, then Dunkin' Donuts, then Chick-fil-A, moving up, as she went, from shift supervisor to assistant manager to general manager. Her attitude toward her work seemed oddly out of step with the abiding ethos of the modern low-wage service economy: she was loyal and conscientious in a profession where neither quality was particularly rewarded. The career dissatisfaction she was feeling wasn't just about money. She felt worn down by the lack of job security and her chaotic and unpredictable work schedule. At Chick-fil-A, she was required to maintain "open availability" from 5:30 a.m. to midnight, six days a week, which meant she could never really relax, never make plans with her boyfriend. The whole system seemed designed to undercut the stable, middle-class life that she aspired to. "It doesn't allow you the lifestyle to be an adult," she told me. "It doesn't allow you to raise a family."

Throughout her years working in food service in Austin, Alicia had kept an eye open for entry-level jobs as an office administrator. She had applied for a few positions, but never even got an interview; employers always wanted either a college degree or office experience, and Alicia had neither. But not long after our first conversation, she heard about an opportunity that sounded more promising. Her friend Danielle's mother worked at a real estate title-insurance company, and the company was hiring a new administrator. The job was the lowest position in the office, and it paid $35,000 a year, no more than her Chick-fil-A job, but they would train her and give her benefits, and there was a chance to advance. Alicia applied for the job, and the interview went well. They said they wanted to hire her. Excited, she tendered her letter of resignation at Chick-fil-A — an actual typed letter, which she left in the owner's in-box at work.

But then the day after her last shift at Chick-fil-A, the hiring manager at the title-insurance company informed her that she didn't have the job, after all; there had been a sudden hiring freeze. Alicia was devastated. She had felt so hopeful, certain that she was moving up at last. In a single phone call, she went from being a newly hired office administrator to an unemployed fast-food worker. There was something about the experience of having a professional job almost in her hands and then having it snatched away that was worse than never having seen it as an option at all.

"Not getting that job wasn't what depressed me," she told me a few weeks later. We were sitting in an airless conference room down the hall from the PelotonU office, and Alicia looked pale and drawn. "It wasn't losing this particular opportunity. What got me was the fear of not being able to get myself out of the food-service industry because I didn't have the right education. It's like a prison." She shook her head, her eyes watering. "And it's all because I didn't realize that I needed college to be able to get a good job. It's just crazy how talented people can be, and intelligent — but it's going to college that matters."

WHEN ALICIA WOULD try to analyze what it was that had brought her to such a financially precarious moment, her first instinct was to blame herself. Lying awake at night, she would trace how various mistakes and shortsighted decisions she had made at sixteen seemed to have led directly to her economic insecurity at twenty-three. But she wasn't quite ready to shoulder all the blame herself. She felt as though she had been blindsided by a set of larger forces shifting within the American economy and education system — forces that her parents and her teachers hadn't warned her about, or even grasped themselves.

In high school, she told me, teachers and counselors did say college was a good idea. But they always portrayed a degree as a nice extra, the thing you pursued after high school if you were feeling ambitious and wanted an especially lucrative career. "They made it seem like a degree is what you need to have a *great* life," Alicia said. "But I assumed that without a degree, things would still be OK, right? But that was wrong. And I was never aware of that. I've been learning that along the way."

After two harrowing weeks in a hiring freeze, Alicia successfully landed the job at the title-insurance company. It was a big improvement over Chick-fil-A. She liked her coworkers, and she learned a lot, and after a year, she got a promotion to escrow assistant. Even though she had finally secured an office job not because of an education credential but because of a personal connection, she kept up her studies at PelotonU, completing her associate's degree in two years and then starting right in on her bachelor's. She didn't quite trust that her office job would last; real estate was a fickle business. A BA, she thought, might not lead immediately to a promotion or a better position, but it would at least give her a little more protection and a few more options when the next downturn came.

Taslim, meanwhile, did get into Year Up after our conversation at City College, and he spent a year doing IT in a big Manhattan office, just like he wanted, and that led to more IT jobs, some paying as much as $25 an hour. But then he decided to go back to school, after all, enrolling in an associate's program at the Borough of Manhattan Community College. He still didn't like college much. But as was true for Alicia in fast food, the jobs Taslim was able to get without a degree were mostly unstable and unreliable — part-time, short-term, no benefits. The IT department for the company where he did his Year Up internship had been outsourced to an overseas contractor, meaning that he was sitting in a corporate office in Midtown, but technically he was working for a company in India. The last time I spoke with Taslim, he was taking classes part-time and working part-time in corporate IT and thinking about taking an online "boot camp" class that would teach him how to write code.

Alicia and Orry and Taslim each occupied a different sector of the labor economy, but their employment situations had a lot in common: erratic work schedules, a lack of job security, and employers who expected them to figure out for themselves how to get the training and education they needed to advance in their jobs. The economic system in which they functioned sent them the clear message that they needed credentials in order to achieve success — but it was left up to them to improvise how best to attain those credentials. What they wanted most from college was a small guarantee of security in an economy that seemed determined to provide them with as little security as possible.

In 2017 a sociologist at Virginia Commonwealth University named Tressie McMillan Cottom published a book titled *Lower Ed* that helps to illuminate the choices facing Orry and Taslim and Alicia and millions of others like them. The book's nominal subject is the business of for-profit colleges, a sector of the higher education economy that experienced an enormous boom in the first decade of this century, increasing in size from four hundred thousand students in 2000 to two million in 2010, during the same period that so many state governments were making drastic cuts to their higher education budgets. The sector includes everything from strip-mall cosmetology colleges to online PhD programs in business administration at the University of Phoenix, and its remarkable growth came about despite its notoriously poor outcomes for students: high tuition, low graduation rates, and high levels of student debt. In 2012 for-profit colleges were educating just 12 percent of the nation's college students, but those students accounted for 44 percent of the nation's student-loan defaults.

The question Cottom sets out to answer in her book is: *Why?* Why would such a manifestly lousy product sell so well? Her answer is that for-profit colleges, during their boom years, figured out how to exploit a new and pervasive gap in the relationship between the education system and the labor marketplace: a job market that demanded more skills, a public education system that didn't reliably deliver them to the nation's young people, and a higher education ecosystem that wasn't equipped or inclined to offer the education and training those young people were being told they needed. In order to make money amid those anxious circumstances, for-profit colleges didn't need to deliver an actual education; they needed only to deliver the promise of one. And during that period of rapid growth, for-profit colleges became very good at making beguiling promises; the industry spent more than twice as much on marketing and profit taking as it did on actual student instruction.

In her book, Cottom takes pains to consider the for-profit sector (which she refers to as Lower Ed) as part of a broader economic and educational landscape. "For-profit colleges are something more complicated than big, evil con artists," Cottom writes. "They are an indicator of social and economic inequalities and, at the same time, are perpetuators of those inequalities . . . The growth and stability of Lower Ed is an indication that the private sector has shifted the cost of job training to workers, and the public sector has not provided a social policy response."

At the opposite end of the prestige spectrum from Lower Ed is, of course, Higher Ed: selective institutions like Princeton University and Trinity College and the University of Texas. Our instinct, often, is to consider those elite institutions as part of an entirely separate sphere from the world of Lower Ed. Cottom encourages us to think of them as two sides of the same coin. "Lower Ed can exist precisely because elite Higher Ed does," she writes. "The latter legitimizes the education gospel while the former absorbs all manner of vulnerable groups who believe in it: single mothers, downsized workers, veterans, people of color, and people transitioning from welfare to work."

Stories of successful low-income students like Shannen Torres and KiKi Gilbert and Matthew Rivera are appealing in part because they validate our faith in the education gospel (as Cottom calls it), the American idea that even if you are born without wealth or privilege, you can still succeed in elite higher education. But Cottom would argue that Shannen's and KiKi's and Matthew's stories demonstrate only a very narrow case: that mobility through higher education is possible when you work extraordinarily hard in high school, graduate at the top of your class, and then get unusually lucky, both in the schools that choose to admit you and the professors and advisers and mentors you encounter once you enroll — and that even then, the path through college can often be difficult and lonely and strewn with unexpected obstacles. For more typical low-income students like Orry and Taslim and Alicia, who were only average performers in high school, the implicit deal offered by our patchwork system of higher education is a less inspiring one: unstable, low-wage service and manufacturing jobs, or a scramble for credentials that is expensive and confusing and not particularly fun.

In the first decade of the twenty-first century, for-profit colleges seemed to promise an alternative to that scramble, but that promise proved mostly illusory. Under President Obama, the federal education department, through a series of regulatory changes and court challenges, imposed some much-needed restraints on those for-profit providers, which led many of them to go out of business. (Education officials in the Trump administration are now doing their best to loosen those restraints.) But getting rid of those toxic colleges did nothing to address the anxiety and need in the higher education marketplace that they temporarily salved.

A handful of promising and responsible nonprofits have attempted to step into that void. PelotonU and Year Up are two of the best, and they have provided solid, low-cost opportunities to Alicia and Taslim and thousands of others. But they are still small and mostly unproved, and even at their most effective, they offer young people only a modicum of additional security in a chronically insecure education and employment landscape.

"Based on the education gospel," Cottom writes, "we increasingly demand more personal sacrifice from those who would pursue higher education: more loans, fewer grants; more choices, fewer practical options; more possibilities, more risk of failing to attain any of them." That uneasy bargain is a recipe for continual economic anxiety for young people charting their path through Lower Ed. It means that for now, at least, Alicia, Taslim, and Orry are destined to remain in a kind of educational twilight realm, where the right choices are rarely clear, and where mobility, when it comes, can feel halting, uncertain, and fragile.

VIII

GETTING AN A

---

1. Ancestors

Uri Treisman was sitting in his office on the tenth floor of the University of Texas mathematics building, his laptop open on the wooden desk in front of him, scrolling through a long list of names and photographs, like a student cramming for a final exam. It was nine o'clock on a hot Tuesday morning at the end of August, and in half an hour, six floors below, Professor Treisman was scheduled to deliver, to 110 UT freshmen, the opening lecture of Math 408C: Differential and Integral Calculus. Before he took the elevator downstairs to begin teaching, though, he had given himself a homework assignment: to memorize the name and face of every student in the class.

It was a challenging list this year. There were two Diegos, two Juans, and two Angels; a Sunny and a Sunbeam, an Oscar and an Oskar, and a Brett and a Rhett. Plus a Yuhang, a Xochitlinda, a Karishma, and an Amphone.

"Amphone," Treisman said thoughtfully. "That's a traditional Lao name. How do you say 'welcome' in Lao?"

Treisman knew it wasn't strictly necessary for him to memorize every single name before the first lecture, or to welcome each student in her mother tongue. He was well aware that this was not standard math-professor behavior. But he had been teaching calculus, in one form or another, for more than fifty years, and along the way, he had come to believe that taking a first-semester calculus course was for his students not just an intellectual trial; it was also, for better or worse, a kind of psychological journey, one that would help mold their identity as college students and as human beings. Over the decades, Treisman had developed a roster of techniques, some based in science and some in personal experience, that he deployed, strategically, to try to shape that journey for his students. Greeting them by name the first time he met them, he believed, was a good way to start.

Treisman's own first encounter with calculus came in 1960, when he was a ninth-grade student at Ditmas Junior High, a block from his family's apartment just off Ocean Parkway in the Flatbush section of Brooklyn. As a teenager, Treisman advertised himself in the neighborhood as a kind of universal tutor for hire. He could teach you any subject you wanted, he promised, satisfaction guaranteed or your money back. Most of his clients were Catholic schoolgirls who needed help with their Latin homework, but that year, Harriet Rockmaker, his upstairs neighbor, was struggling in her basic calculus course at Brooklyn College, and despite the fact that Treisman was four years younger than Harriet was, her mother hired him, at ten dollars a session, to help her pass. From the local public library, Treisman borrowed a copy of Schaum's Outline, a rudimentary calculus text, and he worked through the problems with Harriet, trying to keep one step ahead of her, figuring out the subject as he went along.

Harriet passed the course and moved on with her studies, but the experience had sparked Treisman's curiosity about calculus, and it soon grew beyond what Schaum's Outline could teach him. That summer, he found in the library two more textbooks that went a little deeper into the subject, and alone in his small bedroom at home, Treisman read and calculated and marveled.

One of the great oddities in the history of mathematics is the fact that calculus was invented more or less simultaneously in the late seventeenth century by two men in two countries, working independently: Isaac Newton, the English scientist, and Gottfried Wilhelm Leibniz, the German philosopher. The most pressing scientific questions of that era all had to do with motion and change—how the planets moved in the sky; how ships navigated across the ocean; how fluids and gases and heat could be manipulated to produce power. In each field, the central issue confounding scientists was the same: When you observe a body in motion at a particular point, what can you determine about where it has been and where it is going? It was a question that the existing tools of mathematics, in geometry and algebra and trigonometry, were unable to answer.

Newton and Leibniz both came to understand that the way to solve this problem was to consider the process of continuous change as the accretion of an infinite number of infinitesimally small moments. Their system of calculus was the scalpel that allowed scientists and mathematicians to carve time and space into those minute fractions and then to reassemble the parts into a new and more comprehensible whole. Calculus became the essential mathematical tool of the industrial revolution, its methods enabling engineers to harness steam power and astronomers to chart the orbits of the planets and economists to codify the laws of supply and demand that underlay mass production and global trade.

To Treisman, sitting alone with those library books in his bedroom in Flatbush almost three hundred years later, calculus seemed not just a powerful mechanical instrument but also a sublime intellectual creation. Underneath the prosaic rules and formulas that he had helped Harriet memorize, he saw a mathematical system of elegance and complexity, a new way of looking at the world up close. And for a long time, that's all calculus was to Treisman: a beautiful diversion. An art project, painted in numbers.

More than a decade later, though, when he was a graduate student in mathematics, teaching undergrads at Berkeley, Treisman discovered that in the context of American higher education, calculus had also become something rather sinister: a factory for academic failure.

Students, especially those from modest backgrounds, were arriving at Berkeley with plans for a career in math or science or engineering, only to be laid low, again and again, by freshman calculus. It wasn't happening only at Berkeley, either. Across the country, Treisman wrote at the time, freshman calculus had become "a burial ground for the aspirations of myriad students seeking better lives through higher education."

Much of his life since then had been dedicated to trying to solve that problem. He was the founder and executive director of the Charles A. Dana Center, located in Austin, which had grown to employ eighty people in a variety of projects and initiatives to improve math education nationally, from kindergarten through college. Treisman's efforts had brought him renown in the overlapping worlds of mathematics and education and public policy, and at seventy-one, Treisman had reached a point in his career where he spent much of the year on airplanes, serving on commissions and panels and advisory boards and providing counsel to wealthy foundations and state education officials around the country.

Each August, though, he would plant himself again in Austin for the fall to teach his assigned section of Math 408C. As is true at most institutions, teaching freshman calculus is not considered a high-status position at the University of Texas; senior math professors generally do whatever they can to avoid it. But Treisman loved it, and he was always trying to get better at it, even after all these years. He used his section of calculus as a kind of ongoing laboratory for his ideas, a place to ground his national ambitions for educational reform in the real-life challenge of teaching complex math to teenagers.

The clock on his office wall now read nine fifteen, and though Treisman still wasn't certain he would be able to tell Adrian Salinas from Adrian Rivera, he closed his laptop. It was time for class.

"All right, a new crop," he said, standing up. "I feel like an expectant father."

DOWNSTAIRS, THE NEW ARRIVALS were waiting for him, taking their seats in the John A. Wheeler Lecture Hall, the big window-less auditorium on the main floor where Treisman's section of Math 408C was scheduled to meet on Tuesday and Thursday mornings. His students were almost all freshmen, still moving into their dorm rooms and finding their way around campus. More than half of them were enrolled in UT's school of engineering, but there were also some math majors, a few budding neuroscientists, a handful of future doctors and teachers. With few exceptions, they wore the uniform of the modern American college student: T-shirts and jeans, baseball caps and running shoes.

In other important ways, though, Treisman's class looked different from the other sections of freshman calculus at UT — and, for that matter, different from almost every freshman calculus class in the country. While freshman calculus nationally is populated mostly by white and Asian students, mostly from well-off families, more than half of the students in Treisman's class were Hispanic, with plenty of African American and Middle Eastern and Bengali and Filipino students mixed in as well. White faces were in a distinct minority, making up maybe a fifth of the room.

"We have rituals in this class," Treisman announced, standing on the lip of the small raised stage at the front of the room, his hands clasped behind his back, looking out at his students. "And the first ritual is that our classes start with music." With the help of an assistant and a few dongles, he had attached his laptop to the auditorium's audiovisual system, and the screen behind him began to play, loudly, a YouTube performance of a song called "La Tienda de Sombreros" by Monsieur Periné, an energetic Colombian band — strings and drums and a flute, a singer in a colorful patchwork dress. As the song played, Treisman circulated, shaking hands with students, making jokes, introducing them to one another, startling some of them by greeting them by name.

"This class is an introduction to calculus," Treisman said when the song was over. "But it's not your standard introduction to calculus. It is designed to prepare you for advanced study, and it is designed to prepare you to be leaders in your fields. It's also an introduction to the University of Texas."

He held up his right hand with his pinky and index finger extended, the symbol of the University of Texas Longhorns.

"Doesn't this look geeky?" he asked. "Isn't it embarrassing to do this?"

The students laughed and nodded.

"Well, get over it," Treisman said. "This is us."

David Yeager, the psychologist, was a friend of Treisman's, and Treisman knew from Yeager's research with Gregory Walton that students who had just arrived at UT, especially those from families without a history of college-going, were in a moment of profound disequilibrium, trying to make sense of what they perceived to be conflicting messages about their ability to belong and to succeed at the university. So Treisman's first lecture was full of positive words about belonging: You're a Longhorn. You're a mathematician. You're a future leader. You're one of us. That was what the music was for, the hand signs, the nerdy jokes about Texas A&M, UT's cross-state rival.

But one of the central insights that Treisman had drawn from the time he spent teaching at Berkeley, decades earlier, was that simply *saying* a lot of warm and encouraging things to new students wasn't enough, on its own, to persuade them that they belonged and that they could succeed at advanced work. He had to *show* them it was true. And Treisman believed, perhaps paradoxically, that in order to do that, he first needed to get them off balance, to shake them up, to challenge them in ways they weren't used to. And the tool he chose to disrupt their sense of confidence was math itself.

"What is an even number?" Treisman asked.

"Two!" someone called out.

"Two is an *example* of an even number," Treisman replied. "What is the *definition* of an even number?"

That took a little more thinking. On the overhead, Treisman showed the students how to use advanced mathematical notation to precisely define the set of even numbers and then the set of odd numbers, and then how to use that formal language — full of Greek letters and strange backward *E*s and terms like "iff" and "QED" — to prove that the square of an even number was always even and that the square of an odd number was always odd. It was the kind of problem and the kind of notation that Treisman had limbered up with back in high school, but to the students in 408C — even the best-prepared ones — it was a foreign language. And that was the idea. If the students were confused together, the divisions between them would start to dissipate.

"Everybody in this class will struggle," Treisman announced. "No matter who you are, questions are going to be flying at you that you can't answer. And when that happens, you're going to experience stress. And if you don't understand that stress, you'll think it means, 'Oh, shit, I don't belong here. I belong at A&M.' But in fact, that stress is an indicator that your understanding is deepening. It's not a sign that you're *not* learning. It's a sign that you *are* learning."

ONE OF THE STRANGE facts about freshman calculus as it is taught at American universities today is that most of the students who enroll in the class have already *taken* calculus — the exact same introductory course — in high school. Not long ago, it was quite rare for American students to study calculus in high school; when Treisman enrolled in AP Calculus in his junior year at Erasmus Hall High School in Brooklyn, he was one of just 6,000 students taking the course in the entire United States. But today, about 650,000 American students take AP Calculus in high school each year, and another 150,000 take a non-AP high school calculus course. Together, that makes up about a fifth of the total population of high school seniors.

At first glance, the rapid growth of AP Calculus might seem like a really good thing: American high school students are suddenly, en masse, embracing and comprehending highly challenging mathematics! But in fact, AP Calculus as it is taught in many high schools today bears little resemblance to the deep conceptual calculus that Treisman and his classmates learned at Erasmus Hall. Instead, students are usually taught a thin, flattened-out version of the subject. To pass AP Calculus, educators have found, you don't need to understand the underlying principles of calculus. You just need to memorize a large number of rules, formulas, and techniques and then use them to churn through one question after another.

As pretty much every AP Calculus student or teacher today will tell you, the recent national enthusiasm for AP Calculus is not really about calculus. It's about college. Taking AP Calculus has become a general-purpose symbol of academic achievement, a signal to college-admissions officers of "eliteness," the way taking Latin was seen a generation or two ago. In one recent survey, 80 percent of college students who had completed AP Calculus said they took it because they thought it would look good on their college applications. And they were right: highly selective colleges are much more likely to admit students who have taken AP Calculus, even if those students have no plans to pursue math or science or engineering in college.

One particularly striking example: in 2017, 93 percent of freshmen admitted by Harvard University reported that they had taken calculus in high school. That's not 93 percent of the engineering students or the math majors — it's 93 percent of everyone in Harvard's freshman class, the French majors and the music majors and the historians and philosophers and poets. The message to ambitious high school students is clear: Whatever your interests, whatever you plan to study in college, if you want to get into a school like Harvard, you better first take AP Calculus.

And yet there are two big problems that go along with AP Calculus having become a de facto college entrance requirement. The first is that most high school students in the United States couldn't take calculus if they wanted to. Only 48 percent of high schools, nationally, offer a course in calculus; in Texas, only 43 percent do. And as you might predict, the schools that offer calculus are not randomly distributed in the population. Schools with a lot of white students are almost twice as likely to offer calculus as schools with a lot of black and Latino students. There is a divide by social class, as well. A third of students at private schools take calculus in high school, compared to about a sixth of students at public schools. And students whose families have incomes in the top quintile (meaning they earn more than about $125,000 a year) are four times as likely to take calculus in high school as students whose families have incomes in the bottom quintile (meaning they earn less than about $25,000).

The second problem doesn't have to do with fairness; it has to do with math. The fact that so many students now take calculus in high school has, according to many math educators, actually undermined the teaching of calculus in college. The fever to accelerate students into AP Calculus means that high schools often rush past the math skills that are truly valuable in college calculus, like a deep understanding of the principles of algebra and trigonometry. "Too many students are moving too fast through preliminary courses so that they can get calculus onto their high school transcripts," according to a 2017 report from the Mathematical Association of America and the National Council of Teachers of Mathematics. "The result is that even if they are able to pass high school calculus, they have established an inadequate foundation on which to build the mathematical knowledge required for a STEM career."

At the University of Texas, as at colleges and universities across the nation, freshman calculus has become a crucial proving ground, the class that determines, more than any other, whether students will succeed in college and beyond. Each fall, fifteen hundred UT students take Math 408C, the largest enrollment of any course at the university, and that is in large part because it is a prerequisite for nearly every science and engineering major. When students do well in freshman calculus, they are firmly established on a path that leads to a variety of appealing and lucrative professions. (The average annual salary for new engineering graduates from UT Austin is more than $70,000.) But if they do poorly, those ambitions can quickly founder.

And the reality, at UT and elsewhere, is that freshmen often do poorly in calculus. Because of the AP Calculus boom, students who arrive in freshman calculus *without* having taken the subject in high school — which was, remember, the norm not too long ago — now find themselves at a real disadvantage, surrounded by classmates who have already spent a year studying the material that the new calculus students are encountering for the first time. But even students who passed AP Calculus in high school often struggle in freshman calculus; about 40 percent of retakers, nationally, earn a C or below, even though they've already passed the course once before. And if you don't manage to get at least a B in freshman calculus, it becomes very difficult to continue successfully with a major in science, math, or engineering.

The students sitting in Treisman's class had arrived at UT with widely varying levels of math expertise. Most of them were automatic admits under the Top 10 Percent Rule, which meant that they had all been in the top echelon of their high school class — but in very different high schools, all over Texas. Many of them hadn't had the option of taking calculus in high school. And among those who *had* completed AP Calculus, many had studied with less experienced teachers in disorganized schools, and as a result, their understanding of calculus was sometimes shallow and frail. Treisman knew that those students, especially, were likely to be feeling anxious about their place in 408C, in the university, and in life.

As the end of the first lecture approached, Treisman projected onto the screen behind him a document titled "Your Mathematics Genealogy." It was a numbered list of mathematicians, going backward chronologically into history. Number one, at the top of the list, was "YOU — yes, YOU." Number two was Treisman.

"Here's the deal," Treisman said. "I am your teacher. And you get a lifetime deal. I am your teacher for life."

The third name on the list was Treisman's PhD supervisor at Berkeley, Leon Henkin.

"My teacher was Leon Henkin," Treisman continued. "So he's your grandfather. His teacher was Alonzo Church at Princeton, one of the great logicians and problem solvers of the twentieth century. He is your great-grandfather."

The list rolled on, from Church through Veblen and Moore to Poisson and back into the eighteenth century.

"Your ninth-generation ancestor is Joseph Lagrange," Treisman said. "Lagrange is the one who modernized the calculus. It's really his stuff that you're learning. He is your ninth generation back. Euler, one of the greatest mathematicians of all time, is your tenth generation."

Treisman kept going, through the Bernoulli brothers and Malebranche to Gottfried Wilhelm Leibniz himself, fourteen generations back, who along with Newton invented calculus.

"So this is your lineage," Treisman informed the students. "It's your family heritage." He walked again to the front of the raised stage. "The connection between you and me is a deep relationship that goes back in history. You have a direct line back to the founder of this subject. Calculus is in your blood."

IVONNE MARTINEZ WAS SITTING in the front row, wearing her brother's oversize flannel shirt with the sleeves rolled way up, squinting up at Treisman's list of scientists and mathematicians and trying to decide whether she should really believe there was a place for her in that history. She found Treisman's first lecture bewildering. Every time she thought she was beginning to grasp a concept, he moved on to another one, and by the end she felt completely lost. It was not a feeling she was used to. She had always been an academic overachiever, graduating near the top of her class at Memorial High in San Antonio. Everyone had warned her that college — especially freshman calculus — would be a lot harder, but she didn't expect to feel *this* out of place. She was planning on being a math major at UT, but here she was in her first math class, with no idea what was going on. That seemed like a bad sign.

Ivonne was born in Piedras Negras, a small Mexican city on the Rio Grande, just over the border from Texas. Her early memories were happy ones — the neighborhood kids played together outside every day, and her parents worked in office jobs that didn't seem too stressful. But when she was six, her father, going through old family paperwork, learned something his parents had never told him: that he'd been born not in Mexico but in Texas, which meant that the whole family could legally immigrate to the United States. Ivonne's father was perfectly content in Mexico, and he didn't particularly want to move, but her mother insisted, saying there would be more opportunities for the children — Ivonne and her older brother and sister — on the American side.

They moved to San Antonio, two and a half hours away, to a neighborhood on the city's west side that was, in many ways, much like Piedras Negras. Everyone spoke Spanish, even at school. Their neighbors ate *pozole* and *menudo*. But the streets in San Antonio were more dangerous, so the kids couldn't play outside anymore. And Ivonne's parents, both unilingual Spanish speakers, could no longer find white-collar work. Her father got a job moving boxes in a plumbing-supply warehouse. Her mother started cleaning other people's houses.

For the first few years, life in San Antonio was hard. Money was tight, and Ivonne's parents were always stressed about bills. The family couldn't afford real furniture — for a long time their fridge was just an ice chest in the kitchen — and they depended on donations of clothing and food from a local church. Ivonne and her brother and sister missed Piedras Negras. Some nights they would cry and say they wanted to go back. And for a while, Ivonne's parents were thinking pretty seriously about giving up and returning to Mexico.

But then, gradually, life improved. The kids all learned English. Ivonne's father was promoted at the warehouse. And her mother got a job as a custodian at the local elementary school. Ivonne was in middle school by then, and in the afternoons she would sometimes walk over to the elementary school and help her mother finish her cleaning so she could come home for dinner a little early. "Estudia mucho para que no trabajes como yo," her mother would tell Ivonne: *Study hard so you won't have to work like me.*

And Ivonne did. They all did. Ivonne's brother had the hardest transition to the United States; he was already in the eighth grade when they arrived, and he didn't speak any English. But he caught up quickly and graduated from high school and went on to community college and then to the San Antonio campus of the University of Texas, where he became the first in the family to earn a BA. Ivonne's sister, Ileana, came next, and she went a step further: In high school, she joined Upward Bound, a federally funded program for low-income and first-generation students with college aspirations. She finished seventh in her graduating class, and she was admitted to UT Austin under the Top 10 Percent Rule.

And then Ivonne did better still. She was accepted to Upward Bound in high school, just like her sister, plus she joined the robotics club and the debating team. She finished second in her class at Memorial, which meant she gave a speech at graduation, where she was able to acknowledge her parents publicly for the sacrifices they had made for her and her siblings. The school posted the whole ceremony on YouTube, and Ivonne's mother watched it over and over that summer, asking Ivonne to translate for her what she had said in English, onstage.

Ivonne's brother and sister had both struggled in college, especially at first, and they took a certain big-sibling pleasure, when Ivonne was still in high school, in telling her how shocked she was going to be when she got to freshman year. Memorial High, they told her, doesn't prepare you for the real world. Ivonne liked it at Memorial—she had warm feelings about the place and the people —but she knew she wasn't getting a first-rate education. Two hundred of the five hundred students who started with her in freshman year had dropped out by graduation. Her teachers kept leaving, too. Ivonne took the Memorial High version of AP Calculus as a senior, but there was a lot of turnover in the math department, and the class suffered as a result.

Like Ileana, Ivonne was admitted to UT automatically under the Top 10 Percent Rule. Ileana, an economics major, was about to start her senior year at UT, and the two sisters decided to share an apartment in Austin, a half-hour bus ride from campus.

Not being in a dorm made Ivonne feel a little cut off from the other freshmen, but she was friendly and outgoing, and she did a good job, early on, of making connections. Back in Upward Bound, the instructors had drilled into Ivonne and the other college-bound students the importance of finding, early on in freshman year, a group of students to study with — and the importance of making sure the students you were studying with were at your academic level or higher. *Don't be the smartest one in your study group:* that was the rule.

In the first meeting of her calculus discussion section, Ivonne, still feeling lost, heard a voice from the row behind her that sounded much more confident and knowledgeable than she was feeling. She turned around and saw a student named Marcos, and with a smile she asked him for help. They chatted a little after class and decided to start studying together. Over the next few days, Ivonne asked two female students, Malini and Cypress, to join their new study group as well, and the four of them began meeting up a couple of times a week in the library to go over calculus problems together.

Ivonne had, without quite knowing it, gathered around her a particularly high-powered study group. Marcos, whose parents were engineers from Argentina, had gone to a private international school in Houston. He took college-level calculus in his senior year and aced it, plus he was the valedictorian of his graduating class and a National Merit Finalist, meaning his standardized-test scores were in the top 1 percent nationally. He always seemed willing to answer Ivonne's questions, but her calculus knowledge was so far behind his that she felt embarrassed to keep asking him for help. Her Upward Bound instructors had warned about the dangers of being the smartest one in your study group. But they hadn't said anything about the perils of feeling like the dumbest.

One of the things that made freshman calculus so hard, especially the way Treisman taught it, was that in order to master the material, you had to get your brain working on two levels at once. The first was a basic mechanical level — memorizing formulas, applying rules and theorems correctly, plus getting all the lower-level math right: remembering how to factor a quadratic equation and what the cosine of pi is and how to reduce fractions and evaluate logarithms. Because calculus was built on a foundation of trigonometry, geometry, and algebra, you had to be able to correctly utilize, every day, pretty much all the math you'd learned since middle school. To Ivonne, it seemed that in every homework question there were a million little ways to go wrong.

And then floating somewhere above that mechanical level, there was a conceptual level. Calculus could seem almost philosophical at times: What *is* infinity, anyway? When a number gets infinitely close to zero, is there a point where it actually becomes zero? So at the same time that you were wallowing down in the muck of rules and formulas and algebra and trig, your mind also had to be soaring up in the stratosphere with Newton and Leibniz, looking down on the mortals below and comprehending the big picture, at one with the entire universe.

From the beginning of the course, Ivonne felt like she was falling behind on both levels at once: missing the forest *and* the trees. And it felt increasingly hard to keep asking Marcos for help. "I think it's just a confidence thing," she told me that fall. "I get intimidated. After he explains a problem, I feel obligated to say, 'Oh, yeah, I understand.' I can't just ask him multiple times to explain the same thing. I'd rather not put him through that."

Marcos was perfectly nice about the disparity in their knowledge. "He told me, 'If we didn't have such a strong math team in my school, I'd probably be struggling as much as you,'" Ivonne said. "I guess he tries to understand where I come from. But understanding is not the same thing as living through it."

As time went on, Ivonne came to notice that there were differences between her and her study-group friends that went beyond the mathematical — or maybe they went hand-in-hand with the mathematical. "We don't come from the same social status," she explained. "I get self-conscious about that, too."

Her new friends told stories about family vacations to Europe and South America. The only international trip Ivonne had ever taken was when the family drove back over the border to Piedras Negras. Malini's mom was an engineer; Ivonne's mom was a custodian. "In my community," Ivonne told me, "that was normal, for your parents to just work regular jobs. But here I sometimes feel ashamed." She paused. "I know I shouldn't. I know it makes my mom feel proud that she has three kids going off to college. But I still sometimes do."

Ivonne tried everything she could think of to catch up. But the material wasn't clicking, or at least it wasn't clicking fast enough. On the first test, in the middle of September, she got a 67. That was only a little lower than the median grade, but it still felt like a failure to Ivonne, especially after she saw that Marcos got a 100. The day Ivonne got the test back in class was her nineteenth birthday, which made it harder to accept the bad grade. "I just felt sad," she told me. "I missed home, and I was failing. I felt lonely and stressed." When she walked in the door of the apartment that afternoon, she collapsed on the couch in the living room and started crying.

Ileana was there, and she did her best to comfort her little sister. "It's OK," she told Ivonne. "This is just the way it is for poor Latinos. It's *normal* for us to be doing bad. We're not groomed for college math."

It was basically an anti–pep talk — *People like us never do well* — and Ivonne wasn't quite sure how it made her feel. It wasn't exactly reassuring. But to Ivonne, it seemed like the simple truth. Marcos was Marcos, and Ivonne was Ivonne. Graduates of Memorial High just didn't get 100s on freshman calculus tests. It was kind of a depressing way to look at things. But in the moment, with her sister's arm around her on the couch, it felt to Ivonne like a kind of relief.

2. What Is X?

Uri Treisman grew up, like Ivonne, in a financially strapped immigrant family that put a high value on hard work and education. And like her, in his youth he was often consumed with crushing self-doubt. Treisman was born into the working-class intellectual hothouse that was Jewish immigrant postwar Brooklyn. Life for him and his friends revolved around four holy institutions: socialist study groups, advanced mathematics, the Brooklyn Dodgers, and Hebrew school. Treisman's mother was a firm atheist, but her father, Isadore, an immigrant from Lithuania via Ellis Island, was an Orthodox mystic, an eccentric, shuffling figure who told fortunes in old-age homes for a living. He persuaded his daughter that Uri, his grandson, should attend Hebrew school. Even as a young boy, Uri loved studying Talmud, and he and his old-world grandfather would spend long afternoons together, debating the wisdom of the rabbis.

Intellectual discussions were everywhere in the neighborhood in those days. Louis, the local kosher butcher, hired Uri and a few other neighborhood boys, beginning in the third grade, to deliver parcels of meat door-to-door. In between deliveries, he would lecture them about the need for a socialist revolution, eventually persuading them to start attending meetings of the Workmen's Circle, a Jewish group that promoted socialist thought and Yiddish culture. Before he turned ten, Uri and his friends were reading Karl Marx's letters to Friedrich Engels and the psychoanalytic writings of Erich Fromm.

Though Treisman may have traveled in an intellectually precocious orbit, he was emotionally fragile as a boy. Life at home was uncertain and unsettling and sometimes downright scary. Not long after Uri was born, his father was diagnosed with schizophrenia, and after a frightening psychotic episode while Uri was still in kindergarten, he was committed to a state psychiatric hospital. He spent most of Uri's childhood in locked wards, visiting home for just a week or two each year, visits that Uri and his younger brothers both yearned for and dreaded. Uri's mother, forced to support the family alone, worked long hours taking care of terminally ill patients in their homes. Money was always scarce.

Treisman's elementary school, PS 179, was like a junior-division Mensa meeting. At least four kids in his class went on to earn PhDs in mathematics. Surrounded by giant brains, scarred by his father's mental illness, Treisman felt out of his league. It was an intellectually cutthroat environment, and the competition culminated with an IQ test that every student at PS 179 took at the end of sixth grade, just before moving on to junior high. The stakes for the test were high. If you scored 130 or over (which meant you had an IQ in the top 2 percent of the population), you were admitted to the "rapid advance" program, meaning you were sent to an accelerated track in junior high that would allow you to complete seventh, eighth, and ninth grades in just two years.

That week, Treisman's father was home from the hospital, and the night before his son's IQ test, he careened once again into full-blown madness, his worst episode ever, screaming and ranting on the street and physically attacking the superintendent of their apartment building. The police came and took him away. Uri watched the whole thing, helpless and terrified. When he took the test the next day, his mind was electric with images of his father's breakdown. And when the results came back, all of Treisman's friends—Lonny Solomon, Gerry Sussman, everyone—had scored over 130, and Uri had scored 128.

Jewish Brooklyn in the 1950s was perhaps the only time and place that a score of 128 on an IQ test would make an eleven-year-old boy feel like an outcast and an intellectual cripple, but that was the effect it had on Treisman. There was no talk of Uri retaking the test; in that era, the results of an IQ test were seen as a biological fact, like your blood type, not subject to change. A 128 Uri was, and a 128 he would always be. Lonny and Gerry and the other sixth-grade geniuses all moved on to rapid advance, and Uri went with the rest of the neighborhood's mental defectives to the regular track at Ditmas Junior High.

When Uri was in eighth grade, the rapid-advance boys in ninth grade began studying algebra. When they ran into Uri on the street, they would tease him.

"What is X, Uri?"

"Hey Uri, tell me something. What is X?"

Treisman had no idea what X was, and it killed him. He had to find out. One afternoon, he walked through Prospect Park to the main branch of the Brooklyn Public Library, on Grand Army Plaza, and told the librarian he wanted to borrow a book about algebra. He didn't know where to start, and neither did the librarian. She searched through the stacks and came back with a dusty old hardcover titled *Chrystal's Algebra*, a thick British textbook published in the Victorian era. Treisman took it home and over the next few months, in secret, he taught himself algebra.

For Treisman, there was nothing impressive about the fact that he was learning algebra on his own; instead, he felt ashamed that he hadn't learned it earlier. When he finished *Chrystal's*, he went back to the librarian and asked for more. "This book has words like 'whence-forth' and 'hitherto' in it," he explained. "Do you have anything more . . . modern?"

The librarian went once again to the stacks and came back with a book titled *A Survey of Modern Algebra*. What neither the librarian nor Treisman understood in that moment was that in the math world, "modern algebra" doesn't mean algebra presented without words like "hitherto" and "whenceforth." It is a highly advanced form of abstract algebra that covers specialized subjects like fields and group theory and Galois theory. It was way beyond what the rapid-advance kids were learning; most math students don't encounter modern algebra until their later undergraduate years or in graduate school. But, ignorant of that fact, eighth-grade Uri Treisman took the book home and quietly began to struggle through the problems. The next year, tutoring Harriet Rockmaker, he moved on to *Schaum's Outline* — but still in secret, still feeling inadequate and ashamed.

The disconnect between Treisman's perception of his math ability (woefully substandard) and his actual math ability (incredibly advanced) didn't become apparent to him or anyone else until tenth grade, when Treisman entered Erasmus Hall High School. Erasmus Hall was another landmark of overachieving postwar Jewish Brooklyn. It's where Bobby Fischer went to high school, and Barbra Streisand and Bernard Malamud. It wasn't a magnet school, and there was no special test to get in, but it was filled with intellectually ambitious immigrant kids.

Because of his sixth-grade IQ test, Treisman wasn't allowed into the honors track at Erasmus, and so on the first day of tenth grade, he was assigned to a standard geometry class. The teacher began lecturing in a slow, ponderous voice about the properties of triangles, and Treisman felt suddenly angry and humiliated. He had worked so hard to catch up with his peers, and yet here he was, still stuck in the slow class. Years of mathematical resentment boiled over. He stood up, in a rage, and called his teacher a "fucking moron." It was a memorable turn of phrase, one that quickly got him kicked out of class and sent down to the office of Irving Deutsch, the chair of the Erasmus Hall math department. Weeping, mortified, Treisman apologized to Deutsch and tried to explain that after wrestling with quintic equations and teaching himself field theory, he couldn't sit through a year of lectures on triangles.

To Treisman's surprise, Deutsch was sympathetic. He listened. He asked some questions about Treisman's secret math education, and then he sent him back to triangle class with instructions to apologize to his teacher. A week later, he called Treisman to his office and told him that he had found a different way for him to study math. Treisman would no longer have to go to basic geometry. Instead, every Monday, he would take the subway up to City College, where Deutsch had enrolled him in graduate-level math classes. In tenth grade, Treisman took real analysis at City College, a skinny teenager surrounded by college kids. In eleventh grade, he moved on to complex analysis.

In his senior year of high school, Treisman was elected president of the XYZ Club, the mathematics team of Erasmus Hall, two hundred students strong, which in math competitions regularly beat the teams from New York's selective public schools like Bronx Science and Stuyvesant. He had leapfrogged over the rapid-advance kids. Objectively, he was one of the top math students at one of the best math schools in New York City.

But the doubts that had descended on Treisman back in sixth grade still held him in a firm grip. Deep down, he could not shake the fear that just like his grandfather and his father, there was something inescapably deficient about his brain.

TREISMAN FOUND AN ESCAPE from the pressures of mathematics in an unlikely place for a Brooklyn kid: on a farm. His Talmud studies and Workmen's Circle classes had led him to discover the Labor Zionist youth movement known as Hashomer Hatzair. During high school, he started going to meetings up in the Bronx where passionate young men gave speeches about moving to Israel and working on a kibbutz, and beautiful, brilliant long-haired girls did Jewish folk dances and looked deep into his eyes while discussing class struggle. Treisman loved it. And after graduation, as the other members of the XYZ Club went off to City College or Brandeis or the Ivy League, Treisman turned his back on mathematics, and in fact on all of higher education, flew to Israel, and joined Kibbutz Dalia, a Hashomer Hatzair collective farm in northern Israel.

Treisman worked hard every day, cleaning out the chicken coop and planting and harvesting sugar beets. At night, he and the other young workers would sing folk songs and discuss poetry. He felt connected to the land and connected to his labor and connected to the people around him. Thousands of miles away from everything he had ever known, he finally felt at home. And then one hot afternoon, a little less than a year after his arrival, Treisman was working in the chicken coop in sandals, when he suddenly felt a sharp pain in the little toe of his left foot. He looked down and saw that he had been bitten by a pit viper, one of the deadliest snakes in the world. Medics at the kibbutz injected adrenaline into his heart and rushed him to the hospital in Haifa. He survived, but only barely, and Hashomer Hatzair flew him to Los Angeles to recuperate in a hospital there.

He had one friend in LA, a young woman whom he'd met through the kibbutz movement. When he got out of the hospital, he moved into a little cabin behind her family's house. Once he regained his strength, her father, a landscaper, gave him a job on his gardening crew. Another friend hired Treisman to help him remodel old Volvos. And for a couple of years in his early twenties, that was his life: yard work and auto repair and, in his spare time, volunteering for the kibbutz movement.

Then the landscaping company got a contract to keep up the grounds of the campus of Los Angeles City College, in East Hollywood. Treisman worked with the crew there, digging weeds and trimming hedges. It had been a few years since he had been in a classroom or picked up a math book, and he mostly felt certain that he had left academic life behind. But he got in the habit of taking his lunch break on a bench right outside the temporary trailer where the math classes were taught. He found it comforting, somehow, as he ate his sandwich each day, to listen to the sound of the professor's voice through the open window talking about variables and equations. One afternoon, the professor, a guy in his forties named Jack Stutesman, came out and noticed Treisman listening in, and they started to chat.

"Are you interested in math?" Stutesman asked.

It was a good question. *Was* he interested in math? Treisman didn't think so. He hadn't thought much about math since his XYZ Club days. But clearly there was some reason that he was eating his lunch outside the math trailer every day. Stutesman invited him to join the class, and Treisman started eating his lunch inside the trailer instead of outside. When Treisman told Stutesman about the math he'd done in middle school and high school, about Galois theory and complex analysis, Stutesman gave him some of his advanced textbooks and offered him personal instruction in higher math.

When Treisman talks now about his reentry into the world of

mathematics, his stories have a slightly dreamy quality, like he's still mystified by how it happened. There was, it seems, not a lot of intention involved—at least not on Treisman's part. "I was not thinking of being a mathematician," Treisman says. "It was just something I was doing recreationally." But a series of mentors saw his ability and guided his path back into the heart of the discipline. He completed two semesters of math at LA City College, then transferred to San Fernando Valley State College, and then a year after that, he was steered over to UCLA, where the math department was operating on a much higher level.

"I was working with real mathematicians again," says Treisman. "It was heaven. They latched on to me and brought me into the fold." He took only graduate-level courses, concentrating on classical Italian algebraic geometry, and at the end of three semesters, UCLA granted him a BA and awarded him the Sherwood Prize, which went each year to the top-performing math student in the university.

"I loved it," Treisman says. "But I still did not see mathematics as a career."

To most of us, Treisman's path back to the world of mathematics would seem to be entirely predestined. The president of the XYZ Club at Erasmus Hall wins the Sherwood Prize for top math student at UCLA. Makes perfect sense. Sure, he took a brief detour through farming and landscaping and community college, but *of course* Treisman returned to high-level math. And of course he would go on to get a PhD. And of course he would spend the rest of his life as a math professor.

But to Treisman, in his midtwenties, in the late 1960s, that path didn't seem straightforward at all—or even particularly appealing. Most of the time, he felt that his true self was still sitting outside that trailer on the campus of LA City College, eating his sandwich and listening to the sounds of simple algebra through the open window and getting ready to go back and mow the lawn. "I didn't want a life that was just the mind," he told me. "I came from a working-class family. Not doing physical labor felt like a betrayal."

When Treisman tells the story of his time in Los Angeles, it is clear that there was another factor at work as well, a gnawing fear that stretched back to that IQ test in PS 179: the fear that he just wasn't smart enough. Even after he was awarded the prize as the best math student at UCLA—even after he was admitted to graduate school at Berkeley—Treisman still doubted his own ability. "I had terrible bouts of insecurity," he said. "I didn't truly believe that I was smart. There was this deep reservoir of internal fear that I would be revealed, that I was not as good as people thought I was. And it was a paralyzing fear."

That fear—what psychologists sometimes call impostor syndrome—is not unusual among college students and graduate students, especially first-generation college students like Treisman was. He sees it all the time today among his Math 408C students. Even when he was a student, he was able to recognize, on one level, that his doubts about his ability were irrational. But identifying a problem and naming it doesn't make it go away. "These were forces that were dark and amorphous," he explains. "They are not amenable to rational counterargument. They permeate you like a fog, like a mist of self-doubt."

In every way that the outside world could perceive, Treisman's first few years at Berkeley were a success. He passed his qualifying exams. He served as a teaching assistant for advanced courses. He helped other students with their dissertations. But all the while, he felt profoundly stuck, like he wasn't in the place he belonged, like he wasn't doing the work he was supposed to be doing.

"At Berkeley, you were supposed to be great," Treisman says. "And I felt certain that I would never be great."

BACK IN 408C, Treisman devoted much of September to something called epsilon-delta proofs—a tool that allows mathematicians to determine and demonstrate whether a function (like $y = x^2$) is continuous at a certain point. Epsilon-delta proofs used to be an essential part of the standard AP Calculus curriculum, but they were dropped, as AP Calculus expanded, because they were just too difficult. They scared off too many students. Epsilon-delta proofs had become rare even at the college level; none of the instructors teaching other sections of 408C at UT ever mentioned them to their students. But Treisman spent weeks on them.

There were two reasons for this. The first was that Treisman thought it would benefit his students later on if they learned now how to dig into calculus in a deep and fundamental way, just like he and his friends in the XYZ Club at Erasmus Hall had done decades earlier. "I want to give them a competitive advantage," Treisman told me that fall. "I'm trying to help them break into the inner circle of mathematics." Epsilon-delta proofs weren't particularly helpful if your goal was just to solve one formulaic calculus problem after another, but they were instrumental, Treisman believed, in understanding what calculus *was* — how the arcane rules and theorems students were memorizing reflected the real world of movement and change.

The second reason Treisman taught epsilon-delta proofs was the very fact of their difficulty. He understood that doing complex proofs was stressful and disorienting, especially for underprepared students like Ivonne. But to Treisman, that disruption was important. "Almost every student in calculus gets their self-confidence destroyed at some point," he explained. "I want to be there when they have the crisis."

The challenge that Treisman faced — and it was one he struggled with all through the semester — was how to properly calibrate that loss of self-confidence in his students. Yes, in theory, it would work perfectly: student confronts epsilon-delta proofs; student loses confidence; Treisman helps student rebuild confidence; student masters calculus and gets an A. But what if the student loses her confidence — and then just never gets it back?

This was what seemed to be happening to Ivonne Martinez. On the first midterm, halfway through October, she got a 59, eight points worse than her score on the September test. To Ivonne, it felt like a rerun — another bad calculus grade, another bus ride home, another cry on the couch, and more words from her sister telling her that her situation was inevitable, given where she came from.

The question that kept running through Ivonne's mind that fall was simple: *Why am I failing?* In her darker moments, it came out as a wail of despair. But there were other moments when Ivonne asked that same question more calmly and analytically: Seriously, why *am* I failing? Is it possible for me to succeed in this class? And if so, what do I have to do to make it happen?

Part of what Ivonne was confronting in those moments was two intertwined stories of mobility. One was the American story of social mobility—and particularly, the story of social mobility through higher education. It doesn't matter where you come from, that story goes; a college education will set you on a path to success. The other was the story of math mobility: math skill, according to this story, is not innate; with hard work and good instruction, almost anyone can master even a complex subject like calculus.

Treisman's 408C class was designed to reinforce both of those messages of mobility, every day, in countless ways. But the reality was that persuading students of these ideas was sometimes an uphill battle. Deep down, most Americans don't entirely believe either one of those stories. We don't really believe that most people can succeed in higher math, and we don't really believe that a college education erases social disparities. Even those of us who *are* inclined to believe still have our moments of doubt.

In Treisman's calculus lectures, Ivonne was hearing optimistic messages of mobility: She could succeed; she could get a PhD; she could be a high-level scientist. And she wanted to believe them; she knew how far she and her siblings had already come. Why *couldn't* she just keep ascending? But when she studied with Marcos and Malini, they seemed to be on a different plane of existence than she was. It felt like they knew calculus in their bones, and their math advantage seemed to Ivonne to be inextricable from their social advantages: their educated parents, their excellent high schools, the places they had traveled and the things they had seen. She liked them both, and they tried to be helpful when she was confused, which was pretty much always, but every time she finished a study session with them, she felt a little worse about herself, and her failure in 408C seemed a little more inevitable.

Her talks with Ileana reinforced that sense of inevitability. Ileana saw math and wealth as totally intertwined: to her, Ivonne's struggles in calculus — which mirrored the struggles that Ileana had had as a freshman three years earlier — had everything to do with where the two sisters came from. And when Ivonne talked now to her friends from high school who were at other good colleges, taking freshman calculus, they were all struggling, too.

Those conversations made Ivonne feel less alone. She felt like she was part of a group, even if it was a group that was failing. But at the same time, they were deepening her doubts about her ability to bounce back in 408C. Maybe she had finally met an obstacle that all her hard work couldn't overcome. Maybe kids from the west side of San Antonio just weren't cut out for higher math.

EVERY SATURDAY, Treisman devoted four or five hours to conversations in his office with his students from 408C. He called this time "office hours," but it bore little resemblance to the way other math professors conducted their office hours. Treisman's office hours weren't by request only, and they weren't just for struggling students; he considered them more or less mandatory for every student. He and his team of five instructional assistants — an ad hoc mix of official and unofficial teaching assistants, plus former and current calculus students — went out of their way to track down students, especially those who were struggling, and schedule them into a Saturday slot. The conversations that Treisman had with students during office hours weren't mostly about calculus. They were about where students were from, where they wanted to go, and how they were feeling about their current point on that journey.

On a Saturday at the end of October, Ivonne went to see Treisman in his office on the tenth floor of the math building. It was her second round of office hours; in September, she had come in with Marcos and Malini. But this time, it seemed important for her to meet with Treisman one-on-one.

She sat down in the hard wooden chair across from Treisman's desk. Like everything else in his sparsely furnished office, it was old and battered.

"You are working so hard in this class," Treisman said. "I know you are feeling tremendously stressed, but you're not running away. Most people would run away."

"I guess I'm stubborn," Ivonne said. "I still love math."

Treisman smiled. "This is a key characteristic of a mathematician," he said. "We don't give up." He leaned forward. "But I am worried that I'm pushing you in a way that you are losing self-confidence."

"I feel like I definitely am," Ivonne said quietly.

"You shouldn't be," Treisman said. "You are by accident in a section that is really hard. If you were in one of the regular sections, you would be getting a solid A, no problem. But the difference is that this class is preparing you to be a mathematician."

Ivonne looked down and picked a little at her fingernails.

"My problem," Treisman continued, "is that I have a group of students in the class who did advanced AP Calculus in junior year, and they went to really rigorous high schools." He was talking about students like Marcos and Malini. "You're going to catch up with them in a few weeks or in a month. But because you always did well, and now you're struggling, you're saying to yourself, 'Maybe I'm not good enough to be here.' Is that in your head?"

"It pops up once in a while," Ivonne said with a little smile of understatement. "It's stressful. I feel like I'm falling behind because I'm not getting the full concept. I know if I put my effort in, I eventually will get it, but I feel like by that time it will be too late."

"It *won't* be too late," Treisman said forcefully. "You have to trust me. I've been teaching for fifty years. More than a hundred of my Latino students have gone on to get PhDs. You are not in any way unable to do this work. I know it. I know that *you* don't completely believe it yet, but I do."

Ivonne nodded her head. He was right. She didn't believe him.

"I trust you, though," she said. "In high school, math was never really challenging. This is a good change for me."

"This question of how to teach this class so that everybody struggles, without students losing their confidence — this is *my* struggle," Treisman said. "Because you guys are such incredible students. You're really accomplished. You're hardworking and serious. And I have to push you so that you can learn, but I have to get better at making sure you don't come out of this and say, 'Struggle means I'm not good.' We can't lose you. We need more mathematicians. We need more *women* mathematicians. And it wouldn't hurt to have more Latina mathematicians."

THE THIRD BIG TEST of Math 408C — the second midterm — came in the middle of November. In the days leading up to it, Ivonne spent all her time studying calculus. She worked alone; she worked with her study group; she attended all the Monday and Wednesday discussion sections, which were led by Erica Winterer, Treisman's lead teaching assistant; and she went to the long review sessions that Treisman held in the petroleum engineering building every Sunday. She wrote formulas with Expo markers on the mirror on the door of her closet at home so that she would see them every morning. And she tried to stay optimistic. She wanted to believe Professor Treisman that things suddenly were going to come into focus for her and she would catch up to everybody else. But it just didn't feel like that was happening, no matter how hard she worked.

The night before the midterm, when she was hoping that everything would magically fall into place, the opposite happened. Problems she had been able to do a day earlier were suddenly impenetrable. She felt like she was somehow going backward. She was convinced that she was going to fail. On the bus on the way to campus the next morning, the hopeless feeling of the previous night didn't fade; it grew stronger. She started crying, staring out the window so no one on the bus would see her tears.

Then, on the walk through campus from the bus stop to the math building, her phone rang. It was her mother. Ivonne picked up.

"Why does it sound like you're crying?" her mother asked.

"I have a math test, and I don't feel prepared," Ivonne replied.

Her mother tried to comfort Ivonne: If life at UT is too hard, she said, you can just come home. You can transfer to the university here in San Antonio or go to community college. You can live with us. I'll cook for you.

Ivonne knew that her mother was just trying to tell her that she loved her. But in that moment, it sounded to Ivonne like her mother didn't believe in her. Ivonne did something she never does: she hung up on her mom.

Ivonne was always one of the first students to arrive at math class each morning, and the morning of the second midterm was no exception. It was too early to be let into the auditorium, so she sat alone on a chair near the door, her eyes still red and watery.

Erica Winterer, the lead TA, spotted Ivonne and went over to make sure she was OK. But as soon as she asked Ivonne how she was doing, Ivonne started crying again for real, and Winterer led Ivonne outside, behind the math building, to sit on a bench and talk.

Through her tears, Ivonne told Winterer that she was sure she was going to fail the midterm. And there on the bench, she let out all the fears that had been building up in her talks with her sister and in her study sessions with Marcos and Malini: that the problem wasn't just this test, and it wasn't just calculus. It was *her*, Ivonne, and where she was from—her family and her neighborhood and her high school. She said she had always thought of higher education as the thing that makes everyone equal in America, the thing that gives everyone the same opportunity to succeed. But now that she was here, it didn't feel that way at all.

It was an emotional conversation for Winterer, too. She was a white

Anglo who grew up in a blue-collar family in Houston; like Ivonne, she had always loved math, and like Ivonne she graduated second in her class from a big public high school where teachers sometimes left in the middle of the school year. She got a scholarship to Tulane, where she studied engineering. She struggled at first, and then she improved, but it wasn't until her senior year that it occurred to her that she might actually be smart. After college, she had stayed in New Orleans to teach math in high schools where every student was black and poor, a system that seemed designed to set students up to fail.

There on the bench, Winterer talked to Ivonne about her own high school and the schools she'd taught in, and what she imagined Memorial in San Antonio must have been like. What she said was, in a way, not that different from what Ivonne had heard from Ileana after her last two tests: Things really *aren't* equal. They really aren't fair. You really are way behind where you deserve to be, and it really is going to be very hard to catch up.

Where Winterer's message diverged from Ileana's was in what she said to Ivonne next: Where you stand in calculus right now has nothing to do with who you really are. Who you really are is a mathematician. It's not your fault that you're behind. And it's not your destiny. It is going to be hard to erase the disparity between your math knowledge and Marcos's. But if you want that knowledge, you can get it. And if you decide you do want to get it, I'm here to help you.

3. Workshop Mode

A few years into his life as a graduate student at Berkeley, Uri Treisman finally found a problem that interested him. It wasn't a mathematical problem. He was still studying advanced math—highly abstract questions of syntactic analysis and computational linguistics—but his old doubts about the field and his place within it had not gone away. What had begun to interest him, instead, was teaching. In the Berkeley math department in the 1970s, undergraduate teach-

ing was an afterthought: as at most universities, then and now, freshman calculus was taught mostly by graduate students who were really
good at math but knew next to nothing about how best to teach it.

When Treisman expressed to Leon Henkin, the head of the math
department, that he was interested in learning how to be a better
teacher, it was such a novel concept that Henkin immediately put
Treisman in charge of the training program for all the teaching assistants in the math department. Treisman thought he must know
something about teaching—he had been doing it ever since his days
tutoring Harriet Rockmaker in Flatbush—but he had never encountered any theories or research on how to teach effectively. He had
always worked by instinct. With this new charge from Henkin, he
started spending time at the education school at Berkeley, reading
books on math pedagogy and student psychology and talking to professors, giving himself a crash course on how to teach.

As Treisman was exploring this research, a real-life teaching problem was emerging in the math department at Berkeley. A decade earlier, the university had begun to take steps to make its student body
less uniformly white. By the mid-1970s, there were 150 or so black and
Latino students in each freshman class at Berkeley, but many of them
were faltering in their studies, and almost none of them were earning degrees in math or science or engineering. Black students who
arrived at Berkeley with aspirations to enter those fields would soon
switch majors or leave the university altogether, and when Treisman
began to examine those students' records, he found that the obstacle
that was tripping up almost all of them was the first freshman calculus class, the equivalent of UT's Math 408C, which at Berkeley was
known as Math 1A. Over the previous decade, Treisman found, more
than 60 percent of the black students who enrolled in Math 1A at
Berkeley failed, and there wasn't a single year in the previous decade
when more than two black or Latino students had earned a B or better in freshman calculus.

Treisman wanted to understand why, and he set out to find an
answer. Beginning in the fall of 1975, he recruited twenty African

American students and twenty Chinese American students enrolled in freshman calculus at Berkeley; he knew, statistically, that Chinese American freshmen at Berkeley were doing much better in calculus than their black peers. He asked the students detailed questions about their study habits and practices; he followed them to the library and to their dorm rooms and watched them work; he tracked their grades in Math 1A. And by the spring of 1976, he had noticed some important differences between how the black students studied and how the Chinese American students did.

The first difference was that the black students almost always studied alone. Many of them told Treisman that they had been instructed, by their high school teachers and by their parents, to maintain a clear separation between their social life and their academic life. Studying was serious work, they were told, and it required the kind of deep concentration that came only from solitude. The Chinese American students, by contrast, tended to study with friends or in groups, sometimes sharing a meal or making a social event out of it. As they worked through homework problems, they shared notes and ideas, critiqued each other's work, and borrowed strategies from one another. Black students, working in isolation, did none of those things.

The black students also studied fewer hours each week. The rule of thumb their professors and advisers customarily gave students in Math 1A was that they should spend two hours studying for each hour in the classroom. The black students followed this directive scrupulously, studying eight hours at home each week for a four-unit calculus class. The Chinese American students, working together, concluded that eight hours wasn't enough time to master all the material they needed to cover, and they had soon increased their study time, as a group, to fourteen hours a week.

So the black students started out with poorer study strategies, they didn't have an environment where they could learn to improve those strategies, and they spent less time studying. It was no surprise to Treisman that they soon fell behind. To help students in this predicament, the university had established a number of "minority-support"

programs, but they were all presented as remedial and aimed specifically at black kids, which made them wholly unappealing to the black
calculus students at Berkeley, most of whom had been academic superstars in their high schools. Like Treisman's 408C students at UT,
they were used to being singled out for their high ability and placed
in elite and accelerated classes and after-school programs. Even when
they were struggling in freshman calculus, they couldn't imagine that
Berkeley's remedial programs were intended for them.

In 1976 Treisman was put in charge of the math component of
a special faculty-sponsored honors program at Berkeley for highly
qualified math students from low-income, predominantly minority
Bay Area high schools. It was called the Professional Development
Program, or PDP, and Treisman's job was to counteract the recurring
failure of black math students at Berkeley by engaging with potential
students well before their college careers began. Student participants
were selected in their freshman year of high school through a rigorous examination and a detailed interview; admitted students spent
three consecutive summers during high school on the Berkeley campus, taking math and science courses taught by university faculty.

In the fall of 1977, about a dozen black graduates of the PDP high
school program entered Berkeley as freshmen. Because Treisman
and the rest of the PDP staff had worked with these students in high
school, they knew they were all highly trained, academically gifted
math students. But by the fifth week of freshman calculus, all of them
seemed once again headed toward failure. Treisman, desperate to
avert this disaster, took three of them aside after the midterm and
proposed to work with them personally. He organized them into a
small informal study group that met together, with Treisman, for six
hours each week.

As he had done with Harriet Rockmaker years earlier, Treisman
was mostly winging it with these Berkeley students, trying to figure
out as he went along what might save them from failure in calculus.
But he now knew a bit more than he had back in Flatbush. He was
able to shape their group sessions based on his ed-school research,

plus some techniques he borrowed from Hashomer Hatzair, plus what he had learned from his interviews with the black and Chinese American students two years earlier. Because of what the black students had told him about the stigma attached to Berkeley's existing minority-support programs, Treisman was careful to portray the study sessions he led not as remedial but as advanced and challenging. In order to reinforce that impression, he chose particularly difficult calculus questions for the group to work through, interspersing them with more basic questions that he had designed to give students an opportunity to practice the specific theorems and methods they had not yet mastered.

It seemed to work. As the term went on, the three students improved their performance in class and gradually became more autonomous, sharing their own ideas and strategies with one another and turning to Treisman for help only occasionally. Once they made it through Math 1A, Treisman kept the group together, and they continued meeting for six hours a week through Math 1B and Math 1C, the next two courses in the Berkeley calculus sequence.

The students in that PDP cohort who hadn't been a part of Treisman's small group experienced the same dismal results as previous black math students at Berkeley. None of them received better than a C in Math 1A, and only one was able to complete the full three-course calculus sequence. But the three students in Treisman's small study group did much better, averaging a B in Math 1A and Math 1B, and improving to an A minus, on average, in Math 1C. All three remained in engineering and made it successfully through Berkeley.

Treisman began to think he might be onto something. And in the fall of 1978, he expanded his little ad hoc three-student study group into a formal program he called the Mathematics Workshop, this time enrolling forty-two minority students from Math 1A. He used the same methods — small groups working together, tackling challenging problems with limited guidance from him — and the students did even better than the previous small cohort: only one of the forty-two failed a calculus class at Berkeley, and more than half received a B minus or better in Math 1A. The following year, Treisman expanded the program again, to eighty students; again, powerful results, unlike anything Berkeley had seen before.

And just like that, Treisman had found his calling. He abandoned his mathematical studies almost entirely, and for the next several years he devoted all his time to expanding and refining the workshops. The positive results persisted. After years of overwhelming failure by black math students at Berkeley, only 3 percent of workshop students failed freshman calculus between 1978 and 1982. More than half of them earned a B minus or higher. Each year, black students who enrolled in the workshops earned grades in Math 1A that were, on average, more than a full grade point higher than black students who weren't enrolled. Forty-four percent of workshop alumni went on to graduate from Berkeley as math or science or engineering majors, compared to just 10 percent of black students who didn't take part in the workshop.

As the workshop grew, Treisman began to formalize certain practices that had begun as improvisations. He found new ways to reinforce the message that PDP was not a remedial program but a reflection of high academic achievement. Prospective workshop students were sent a formal letter the summer before their freshman year "cordially" inviting them to join a "small, intensive honors program" for "students with a deep commitment to excellence." The workshops themselves had become lively and social, a dozen or so students in the same room, mostly but not exclusively black and Latino, working together in pairs or in fluid groups of three or four. Occasionally, work would stop and a student would present an answer to the whole group. The workshop leader would circulate, offering suggestions and steering discussions but mostly operating in the background while students taught one another. The most important contribution of the workshop leader, according to Treisman, was the selection of the problems that the groups tackled in their workshop, each one carefully chosen to highlight the particular skills and methods that students were struggling to understand at that moment.

News of PDP's success spread. Claude Steele, the psychologist, visited Berkeley to observe Treisman's workshops and soon introduced a program modeled on PDP at the University of Michigan. He later cited Treisman's work at Berkeley as a major contributor to his theory of stereotype threat. Treisman was asked to visit universities across the country to speak about the workshop model, and before long, imitations and replications were popping up on campuses around the country.

Back in Berkeley, though, university administrators had begun raising questions about the fact that Treisman had been enrolled at the university as a graduate student for fifteen years without writing a PhD dissertation or progressing much at all in his official studies. In 1985 the provost imposed a firm and final deadline for Treisman to graduate, and with Henkin's help, in one harried week of all-nighters, Treisman typed out a seventy-page description of the PDP and the Mathematics Workshop and submitted it as his PhD dissertation. It was an unusual dissertation — it didn't contain a single footnote — but it finally earned Treisman his PhD, at the age of thirty-nine. In 1991 he was hired as a full professor at the University of Texas. Nine months later, he was awarded a MacArthur "genius" fellowship in recognition of his work in math education at Berkeley. That fall, he started teaching Math 408C.

HOW MUCH CAN any one professor do to help his or her students succeed? It was the question that Treisman had been asking since those earliest workshop days in Berkeley. In his national reform work, he concentrated on the structures that surrounded the classroom, from admissions to funding to curriculum. In the big picture, he was sure that those were the factors that needed to change if higher education as a whole was going to become more equitable. But he also believed there was something elemental about the interactions between a teacher and a student. One-on-one, there was no student he felt he couldn't help.

And yet this particular fall, Treisman was possessed by a nagging worry that he wasn't making enough progress with his students in 408C. He wondered if it might have something to do with his health. A year earlier, he had had open-heart surgery, and a few years before that, he had been diagnosed with Parkinson's disease. His symptoms were still mostly hard to notice—a slight tremor in his hand, the involuntary curl of his little finger. He wasn't sure if it was the Parkinson's or his overloaded schedule or just the fact that he was seventy-one now, but as the season wore on, his concern grew that he was missing something, that students who needed his help were somehow slipping past him.

Treisman held regular meetings to discuss students' progress with Erica Winterer, the lead TA, and Katie Hogan, a second teaching aide whom Treisman had recruited to work with the 408C class. Like Winterer, Hogan was a former math teacher and a current graduate student in education at UT. Since the beginning of the semester, she had been holding regular review sessions in the library three days a week for students who needed additional instruction. Her group started small, just a handful of special cases who hadn't had any calculus at all in high school. But Hogan was unusually good at explaining how to complete calculus problems, and word spread. By Thanksgiving, her group had grown to as many as two dozen students, and her study sessions now often spilled out of the small, glass-walled room she had reserved in the library.

As November gave way to December, Treisman concluded that the instruction he and Hogan and Winterer were providing students that year had fallen out of balance: too much teaching, not enough independent problem-solving. Students, he felt, were relying on him and the other instructors for strategies and answers rather than discovering them themselves and teaching them to one another. It had been the central lesson of the Berkeley workshop, but for some reason, he came to realize, he had been neglecting it with this class.

So for the last few weeks of the semester, Treisman announced, 408C was going into "workshop mode." In his lectures, Treisman still taught the way he had all year, but in his extra review sessions, he stopped doing much teaching at all. Instead, he had the students work together on problems in small groups while he circulated through the classroom, overseeing and encouraging and kibitzing, just as he had done decades earlier with the black students at Berkeley. Katie Hogan's study sessions in the library changed as well. She stopped guiding students through problems, the way she had been doing all semester, and instead organized them into pairs and groups in which they collaborated and debated and came up with solutions to problems on their own, which they would then share with the whole group.

Erica Winterer's twice-weekly discussion sections remained more or less the same, but she decided that for the last few weeks of the course she would organize a new study session for a select group of female students. At Tulane, Winterer had had plenty of opportunity to experience and observe up close how women could sometimes be intimidated or undermined — or undermine themselves — in math and science classes. The students she invited to join this new group were ones she thought were struggling not primarily with their math skills but with issues of confidence and belonging: Samantha from Houston, Isabel from La Vernia, Guiseppa from Brooklyn by way of San Antonio, and Ivonne Martinez.

Back in mid-November, when Winterer and Ivonne had their tearful conversation on the bench outside the math building, the two of them had decided that Ivonne would postpone taking the second midterm for a couple of days so that she could gather her emotions. But the extra time didn't seem to help Ivonne's grade much — she got a 55 on that midterm, which meant that despite all her hard work in 408C, she was scoring steadily worse on each big test.

At the beginning of December, Treisman informed the class (as he did near the end of the course each year) that students who had done poorly thus far would have the opportunity to replace all of their previous grades in the course with their grade on the final; get an A on the final, and you had an A in the course. The final exam was comprehensive, covering all the material from the whole semester, and it was notoriously difficult. But Ivonne realized it was her last chance. If she could master in the next few weeks not just the new material Treisman had been covering since the midterm but everything she'd been struggling with since the beginning of the course, she could still pull out a decent grade.

For Ivonne, the all-female study group that Winterer had organized felt very different from the study-group environment she was used to. Working with Marcos and Malini and Cypress, Ivonne had gotten into the habit of deferring to the others, waiting until someone else solved each problem and then trying quietly to reconstruct for herself what they had done. But Samantha and Isabel and Guiseppa didn't seem any more confident of the material than Ivonne did, so it didn't make sense to defer to them. And in these group sessions, which were held around a table on the main floor of the library, Winterer made a point of not guiding them through the answers. Instead, she would just write a problem on the top of a rolling whiteboard she had pulled over to their table and then leave it up to the four students to figure out where and how to begin.

There was, at first, a lot of silence.

"I'm not going to tell you what to do," Winterer said at the beginning of the first session. "So someone's going to have to come up with an idea."

Ivonne and the other three looked at each other.

"You can talk to each other," Winterer prodded.

They did, a bit, though tentatively at first. The four women Winterer had chosen didn't know each other well, but they had some qualities in common: they were all smart, quiet, and polite, and none of them was in the habit of speaking up or taking control in groups like this. Slowly, though, with plenty of hesitation and self-deprecating apologies and a lot of *This is probably wrong, but*, they began to share some ideas.

"Rarely is the first thing I try correct," Winterer said, trying to encourage them. "Pretty much never, in fact. I'm almost always wrong at the beginning. But it's OK to write down things that are wrong. That's why we use pencils."

That permission to make mistakes freed the students up a bit, and they started to trade suggestions and sketch out ideas more energetically. In her official discussion sections, Winterer always kept things humming along on a rigid timetable, setting the alarm on her phone for a set number of minutes for each question and then moving on to the next one as soon as her ringtone sounded. But in this new study group, she let things move much more slowly. In their second session, the four women took an hour and twenty minutes to work their way together through a single problem, calculating the volume enclosed by two overlapping spheres. But they seemed to be gaining confidence in the process.

By the end of the last session, on a Saturday two days before the final, Ivonne was standing at the whiteboard, drawing diagrams of cylinders and doughnuts and working out solutions in front of the whole group. It was something she would never have dreamed of doing when working with Marcos and Malini and Cypress. She made some mistakes as she went, and she had to start over a few times, but those mistakes didn't feel devastating.

"It felt good," she told me afterward. "I felt like I had good ideas for a change. And I wasn't afraid to not totally know how to do the problem."

After the session with Winterer ended that last Saturday afternoon, Ivonne met up with Marcos and Malini and Cypress, who had taken over a corner of the student union, and she studied with them for another few hours. For the first time, that felt good as well. Over the previous week, she had read through her entire calculus textbook again, making notes on each chapter, and now all of that information, which previously had seemed to Ivonne like a blur, was falling into place.

"It felt like things were finally making sense," she told me later. "I was answering more questions than I was asking." She even explained one problem to Cypress, working the whole thing through with her, like a teacher, and it really lifted her mood. Not because she felt smarter than Cypress — she didn't — but just because it reminded her of the warm, confident feeling she used to have in high school, when she was known at Memorial as the person to turn to if you needed help with math.

"I liked that," Ivonne said. "I just like helping people. But this year, at the beginning, I wasn't able to do that. That's what bothered me the most. I would see people feeling lost, and I would be like, 'I'm sorry, I just can't help you.' But then on Saturday, when I *could* help, I felt so much better. I felt comfortable. I finally felt happy."

THE FINAL EXAM in 408C was scheduled for 2:00 p.m. on a Monday, a week before Christmas. Ivonne had stayed up late the night before, studying calculus on her own, but she woke up on Monday morning at 6:00 a.m. and couldn't get back to sleep. She had decided already that she wouldn't study at all on the day of the exam — it would just stress her out — so to take her mind off calculus, she spent a couple of hours that morning watching makeup tutorials on YouTube and plucking her eyebrows.

Ivonne's wardrobe was always eclectic and distinctive, mostly pieced together from thrift stores in San Antonio. She knew it would give her confidence to dress well for the final, and she put a lot of thought into her outfit: an oversize white sweater with some artful rips, a long gray scarf with pom-poms, leather boots and knee socks, and around her neck, a pendant her mother had given her with an image of the Virgin of Guadalupe.

I saw Ivonne right before the final, gathering with a few other students in the lobby of the math building, and she seemed downright buoyant, happier than she had been all semester. Calculus, she told me, made sense at last. "I can see the logic of it all," she said with a grin.

Treisman had maintained the ritual throughout the semester of beginning each class with music: Linda Ronstadt one week, the Mexican rock band El Gran Silencio the next. Now, as the students filed into the auditorium for the exam, Treisman called up on YouTube a performance by the New York Philharmonic of Aaron Copland's "Fanfare for the Common Man," four majestic minutes of brass and timpani, a classic American hymn composed by another son of Jewish Brooklyn.

Ivonne took her seat in the front row, in between Marcos and Cypress, and she sat there for a few minutes, texting her sister and some friends from San Antonio, asking them each to pray for her. She turned off her phone. Then she turned it back on and made a quick call to her father. "Wish me luck," she said.

At 2:00 p.m., she opened her test paper, took a deep breath, and started in.

Two hours later, the first students began handing in their exam papers and leaving, even though there was still officially an hour left in the exam. Marcos and Malini and Cypress finished around 4:30, leaving Ivonne alone in the front row, her head bowed low, just a few inches above her paper, her mechanical pencil in one hand, her eraser in the other, her scientific calculator on her lap, and a serious look on her face.

Finally, at 4:45, after reading her answers over one last time, Ivonne decided she had done everything she could do. She closed her test, packed up her bag, and walked to the front of the auditorium, where Treisman and Hogan and Winterer were sitting in a row at a long table, greeting and congratulating students one by one as they finished.

Treisman clasped Ivonne's hand in his and looked her in the eye. "I want to make sure you understand how good you are at this," he whispered to her. "I am very, very proud of you." She smiled and thanked him, her eyes a little wet. Then she embraced Winterer and Hogan, like she was making her way down a calculus receiving line, and walked outside into the cold Texas sunshine.

Ivonne's parents drove to Austin that afternoon. They picked up Ivonne and Ileana around 9:00 p.m., and then the family drove back down Interstate 35 to San Antonio in the dark together, the car filled with warm chatter and holiday plans. A little after ten, Ivonne's phone buzzed. She saw she had an email from Professor Treisman, and she opened it.

"I wonder if you understand how talented you are, and how that talent is enriched by your amazing work ethic," it read. "You earned one of the highest grades on the final — 391 out of 400, which, of course, is a high A. It was a real privilege to have you in our course."

IN THE FALL OF 2018, as I was writing this chapter, Mitch Daniels, the president of Purdue University and the former governor of Indiana, wrote a column in the *Washington Post* about test-optional college admissions. He was against the practice, he explained. He took the straight College Board line, writing about the perils of grade inflation, citing as his only source a *USA Today* article that took as *its* only source the paper by the College Board researchers that I wrote about in chapter 5. He wrote that Purdue, which is a public university, would continue to use the SAT and the ACT in its admissions decisions because those tests provided the most accurate way to predict how students would do in college. "Accepting a high school A at face value and enrolling a student in a calculus course beyond his or her capabilities," he wrote, "does the student a serious disservice by risking an avoidable failure."

Ivonne Martinez is precisely the student Mitch Daniels was writing about. She earned a very high GPA in high school — a 3.98 out of 4 — but received only middling standardized-test scores: a 22 on the ACT and an 1120 on the SAT. She is a classic example of the deflated-SAT "discrepant" category that the College Board identified in its research — and as a Hispanic, first-generation female college student from a low-income family, Ivonne matched exactly the demographic profile that the College Board found most often went along with having a higher GPA than your SAT score would seem to predict.

As I wrote in chapter 5, the most salient effect of the use of the SAT

in admissions is to keep GPA-discrepant students like Ivonne Martinez out of elite colleges. And if Ivonne had grown up in Indiana, that
is exactly what her SAT score would have done — it would have kept
her out of Purdue (where the average incoming SAT is a 1282) and
the state's other highly selective public colleges. But because she grew
up in Texas, the Top 10 Percent Law enabled her to attend a highly
selective university that considered only her GPA, not her SAT, in its
admission decision. In fact, Texas, by law, was forced to do exactly
what Mitch Daniels warned was a "serious disservice" to students
like Ivonne: it accepted her high school A at face value. And then
Ivonne went and did exactly what Mitch Daniels advised against: she
enrolled in a high-level calculus course beyond what her SAT score
would predict she could succeed in. And just as Daniels feared, she
struggled.

But then, because she was going to the University of Texas and
not Purdue University, she got lots of thoughtful and determined
help from her professor and her TA, and she worked extraordinarily
hard, and in the end, she earned an A in freshman calculus. And then
the next semester, she went on to take Math 408D, the even-more-
challenging second half of UT's calculus sequence, and she got an A
in that class as well. And then in the fall of her sophomore year, she
took Discrete Math, covering complex set theory and number theory,
and she got a B plus. And she is now on a path to graduate from one
of the best public universities in the United States with a degree in
higher mathematics — all because the University of Texas was forced
to ignore the false signal of her SAT score, and all because she made
the choice to risk what Daniels called "an avoidable failure."

"Risking an avoidable failure." It's worth thinking about that phrase
for a while. Mitch Daniels is right that the surest way to avoid failing a rigorous class like Math 408C is simply not to take it. There is
no risk in following Daniels's approach — except for the fact that you
then cannot become an engineer or a doctor or a mathematician.

In contrast to Daniels's message, Winterer and Treisman said to
Ivonne: Yes, there is a risk in taking a highly demanding freshman

calculus course when you attended a mediocre high school and have only passable standardized test scores. The risk is that you might try something really hard and fail. But in this case, we believe that the potential reward is worth the risk. Because if you succeed, your life will change for the better — and so will your family's life, and the life of your community. And unlike Mitch Daniels, we believe that your amazing performance in high school means that you *can* succeed, with our help, if you work really hard.

Of course, it is not enough just to encourage students like Ivonne to take that risk. Daniels is right that placing students with her level of preparation into a difficult calculus course and then providing them with no support will often lead to failure. One way to avoid that failure is to steer those students away from their goal, toward less selective universities and less prestigious majors. The other way is to actually teach them calculus.

What Treisman is forced to confront anew each fall is that teaching freshman calculus, especially to students who didn't attend one of the country's gold-plated high schools, is really hard work. Even now, the task still sometimes gets the better of him. Yet Treisman never doubts its value. This is the final, unlikely element in the strange alchemy of calculus: Hundreds of years after Newton and Leibniz, this odd collection of ancient theorems and arcane tools not only helps rockets fly and self-driving cars find their destination. It can also help students like Ivonne navigate their own trajectory from America's economic margins to a life of possibility and opportunity.

IX

AFTER THE WAR

---

1. The GI Bill

In the summer of 1943, with World War II still raging in Europe and the Pacific, President Franklin Roosevelt dedicated one of his regular fireside radio chats to the question of how the United States would prepare for the end of the war. After World War I, the nation had failed to provide a decent transition to civilian life for the American soldiers who returned from the front, and Roosevelt pledged that things would be different this time. "We are, today, laying plans for the return to civilian life of our gallant men and women in the armed services," he said. "They must not be demobilized into an environment of inflation and unemployment, to a place on the bread line or on a corner selling apples. We must, this time, have plans ready."

Those plans began to take shape that autumn, as the administration made its first proposals to Congress regarding future benefits for the millions of young Americans fighting overseas. The president's initial request mainly concerned demobilization pay and unemployment insurance, but it also included a brand-new idea for veterans: educational benefits. At first, those benefits were relatively modest. Under Roosevelt's initial proposal, every service member would be eligible, after the war, for one year of higher education or training, courtesy of the federal government, and a select few "exceptionally able" veterans with "unusual promise and ability" would be funded for up to three additional years of study.

The American Legion, a veterans organization that had been founded in the aftermath of World War I, took up the cause in Congress and in the press, and over the Christmas congressional break in 1943, Legion officials, working with a small group of Democratic and Republican lawmakers, drafted a broader and more generous version of Roosevelt's proposal, giving it, for the first time, the memorable name "The GI Bill of Rights." The new bill, introduced into Congress in January 1944, now promised *four* years of higher education funding — and not just to the most academically proficient soldiers, but to any veteran who had signed up or been drafted before his twenty-fifth birthday. The federal government would cover tuition up to five hundred dollars a year and pay a monthly educational stipend of fifty dollars a month for single men and women and seventy-five dollars for those with dependents.

Despite this expanded educational benefit, the legislators debating the bill in early 1944 expected that only a small number of the returning GIs would take the government up on its offer to pay for four years of college. These might be war heroes, but they were also, for the most part, poorly educated farm boys. Fewer than 40 percent of the 16 million Americans in uniform had even graduated from high school. As John Rankin, the Mississippi Democrat who was one of the main sponsors of the legislation, put it in a speech, "The vast majority of the men who are fighting this war never saw the inside of a college and probably never will."

But after the bill passed Congress and Roosevelt signed it into law in June 1944, a chorus of concern began to sound, expressed by the leadership of some of the country's most prestigious universities. What if big numbers of GIs actually *did* show up on college campuses after the war? What then?

In December 1944 the president of the University of Chicago, Robert M. Hutchins, published a dire essay titled "The Threat to American Education" in *Collier's* magazine. "The educational provisions of the act are unworkable," Hutchins warned. If the law wasn't revised, he wrote, "unqualified veterans" would soon descend on colleges and universities where they would be unable to keep up academically— and the institutions, hooked on the federal government's tuition payments, would likely keep the failing students enrolled anyway. "Colleges and universities will find themselves converted into educational hobo jungles," Hutchins cautioned.

The solution, he wrote, was to revert to Roosevelt's original proposal: to allow access to college only to the most academically talented veterans, as measured by standardized tests. "The remedy lies in requiring the administrator to ascertain through a series of national examinations whether the veteran applying for the educational benefits has a reasonable chance of succeeding in and profiting by his proposed educational program," Hutchins concluded. "The veterans assisted to go to school should be those, and only those, for whom the schools, colleges and universities can do something now."

James Bryant Conant, the president of Harvard University, concurred with Hutchins's sentiments. He wrote in his annual letter to the university's trustees that the federal government should extend higher education benefits only to "a carefully selected group" of returning veterans "who can profit most by advanced study." He urged Congress to revise the law. "Unless high standards of performance can be maintained in spite of sentimental pressures and financial temptation," he wrote, "we may find the least capable among the war generation, instead of the most capable, flooding the facilities for advanced education in the United States."

But the law was not changed, and soon after the war ended, it became clear that Hutchins and Conant had, in one important way, been right. Veterans flocked to American campuses in much greater numbers than the government had expected. Fifty-one percent of the returning veterans enrolled in some kind of education or training, and a total of 2.2 million of them attended college or university. The

American undergraduate population more than doubled in just a few years. Universities scrambled for classrooms and professors; they set up temporary dorms in trailer parks and unused barracks. And still, the students kept coming. By 1948, 15 percent of the federal budget was devoted to the cost of the GI Bill.

But if Hutchins and Conant were right about the numbers, they were entirely wrong about how well these mostly uneducated veterans would perform in college. The veterans did not become educational hoboes; for the most part, they became excellent students. On average, veterans outperformed their civilian counterparts throughout the GI Bill era. "The G.I.'s are hogging the honor rolls and the Dean's lists," the education editor of the *New York Times* wrote in 1947. "They are walking away with the top ranks in all of their courses."

Experts had expected the returning GIs to opt for vocational or technical training to prepare themselves for a career; instead, many of them favored the liberal arts, enrolling in humanities and social science courses at a higher rate than nonveterans. "They're grinds, every one of them," a civilian senior at Lehigh University told a *New York Times Magazine* reporter in 1946. "It's books, books all the time. They study so hard, we have to slave to keep up with them."

Before the war, higher education in the United States had been the province almost exclusively of the rich and the upper middle class. But most of the students who attended college on the GI Bill came from low-income or working-class families. The bill's impact was limited by the presiding biases and divisions of the day: white students benefited more than black students, and men benefited more than women. But in the same way that the camaraderie of war had helped to blur the class divisions among soldiers on the battlefields of Europe, the postwar incursion of working-class kids onto college campuses changed the way Americans thought about college students — and the way American college students thought of themselves. Sympathetic profiles of this new generation of working-class students appeared not only in the *New York Times* but also in *Life* and the *Saturday Evening Post* and *Time,* and that coverage helped to create a new and enduring consensus in the country that the potential pool of college-ready young people was much larger than was previously thought. In the public imagination, college came to be seen, for the first time, not as an exclusive privilege of the moneyed elite but as the most promising path for ordinary Americans to reach new opportunities in life.

Suzanne Mettler, a political scientist at Cornell, conducted a detailed survey of more than a thousand World War II veterans for her 2005 book *Soldiers to Citizens*. She discovered that white male veterans who *didn't* take advantage of the educational provisions of the GI Bill experienced relatively little mobility in the postwar years; most of them took jobs in the same profession as their fathers. Among the veterans in her survey who *did* use the GI Bill to go to college, however, there were many, Mettler wrote, "who experienced breathtaking transformation in their life circumstances." In a random sampling of her respondents, she found "the postal employee's son who became a school principal, the longshoreman's son who became an attorney in private practice, the coal miner's son who became a geologist, the cobbler's son who became an engineer, and the window cleaner's son who became a chemist."

THE YOUNGEST VETERANS of World War II are now in their mid-nineties, which means that the country's firsthand memories of the war and the GI Bill era that followed it are rapidly vanishing. I wanted to hear some of those stories for myself, so on a crisp, sunny fall day, I drove to a retirement community in North Branford, Connecticut, called Evergreen Woods, where I sat for a morning and talked with a veteran named Patrick Fay. Evergreen Woods seemed a pleasant place to grow old, and Patrick Fay was doing so in good spirits and in relatively good health. The one real sadness in his life at the time was that his wife, Helen, to whom he had been married for more than seventy years, had developed dementia, and she had recently moved into a nearby facility where she could receive better care. But

Patrick was still able to spend time with her, and he had frequent visits from his children and grandchildren and great-grandchildren. As well, there were friends up and down the hall whom he would stop in regularly to see — some of them veterans like himself.

Fay was born in 1923 in Ireland, and his parents, both the children of farmers, brought him to the United States two years later. The young family settled in Weymouth, Massachusetts, a town — now a suburb — on the South Shore, twelve miles from downtown Boston, its population, at the time, a mix of Irish and Italian Catholics and English Protestants. The men in Fay's neighborhood, as he grew up, mostly made their living with their hands, including Fay's father, whose education had stopped at the sixth grade. He supported the family as a masonry contractor until the late 1930s, when he got a better-paying job building aircraft carriers and battleships for the US Navy at a shipyard in nearby Quincy.

Fay was the oldest of six children, a serious student who liked science and math. At the end of middle school, he discovered that at Weymouth High School, where he would be going the next fall, students were divided early on into four academic tracks: technical, classical, business, and general. In each class of five hundred students, there were only a few dozen with a chance of going to college after graduation, and they were the ones on the technical track, studying math and science, or the classical track, studying English and Latin. The classical and technical students tended to be the children of Weymouth's well-to-do families, the ones who owned their own homes, most of them descended from old Yankee stock. The working-class Irish kids from Fay's neighborhood were almost always steered into business or general, and away from any possibility of college.

But Fay knew he wanted to study chemistry, which meant he would need to be in technical. So that summer, before high school began, he made a special trip to his friend Lester Donovan's house, because the Donovans had a telephone. He called the school and asked if he could be placed on the technical track. The school official he spoke with agreed. Over the next four years, Fay prospered in his chemistry and math and physics classes. Outside of class, though, he didn't spend time with the other technical-track kids. His friends were all from the neighborhood, and they were all on the lower tracks.

Fay graduated from high school in 1940 and enrolled that fall at Northeastern University in Boston, then mostly a commuter college for future engineers. Early in his second year at Northeastern, in the fall of 1941, he dropped out, in part because of the expense — tuition at Northeastern was six hundred dollars a year, which was a significant sacrifice for his family — and in part because he was distracted by the approach of war. Even before the Japanese bombed Pearl Harbor that December, Fay and his four closest friends were fixated on the war. They would meet most days at the soda shop in Weymouth Square and listen to songs on the jukebox, or they'd go to the park and play touch football for a while — but wherever they went, the conversation would always turn to the war: Would they go? When would they go? Should they volunteer or wait to be drafted? What branch should they volunteer for? They followed the course of battles on radio broadcasts and in newspapers and shared with each other news of the latest troop deployments. By the end of 1942, the five of them had all enlisted: two in the Navy, one in the Air Corps, and two, including Fay, in the Army.

Fay spent his first eighteen months in uniform in the States, first in basic training and then being shuffled around from one base to another, preparing to go overseas. He was finally assigned to a combat infantry division in the summer of 1944. He landed in France that November, and his unit made its way east into Belgium. The first combat Fay saw turned out to be the largest and bloodiest battle that American troops faced in the entire war: the Battle of the Bulge, which began in December 1944 with a German surprise attack on the American positions in the Ardennes region of Belgium. "It was hell on earth," Fay told me. Nineteen thousand American troops were killed in the battle, which lasted more than a month and was fought in snow and mud and bitter cold. Another sixty thousand were wounded, including Fay, who was shot in the hand by a German sniper.

He was evacuated to a hospital in Paris, which seemed like a stroke of good fortune, despite the wound that landed him there. "To get into a bed with sheets was like going to nirvana," Fay recalled. "It was heaven." He returned to the front in February 1945, but with the Germans now in retreat, his unit didn't see combat again. He remained in Germany until the final defeat of the Nazis, spent that fall in France, and in January 1946 returned to the United States and civilian life.

His last stop on the way home to Weymouth was in Fort Devens, near Boston, where the Army sat him and thousands of other soldiers down in an assembly hall and gave them information on the GI Bill and the potential benefits it could bring them. Fay took advantage right away; within a few weeks, he had reenrolled at Northeastern. It had been more than four years since he dropped out. That summer, he married Helen, and for the next few years they lived with Helen's parents in Boston while Fay completed his bachelor's at Northeastern, majoring in chemistry.

Fay's main recollection of those years was the feeling of being in a hurry. Every student he met, it seemed, was a veteran as well, all there at Northeastern on the GI Bill, and they all felt there was no time to waste. "It was a very dedicated crowd," Fay told me. "We had lost three or four years of our lives, and now we wanted to learn. We wanted to reestablish a life and get a career. We were anxious to keep moving on everything."

Fay went on to get an MBA at Northeastern, again paid for by the GI Bill. And then he went to work. His career, from the perspective of the twenty-first-century gig economy, sounds like something out of *The Organization Man*: first, a job as a production chemist at General Chemical, then a stint for a plastics manufacturer, and finally a stable, secure three-decades-long career as a manager at General Foods. Fay and his wife had six children, and they all went to college. In fact, they all got postgraduate degrees. "Unlike my parents, who didn't understand about college, I did understand," Fay told me, "and I was very conscious of positioning my children to take advantage of their schooling." The pattern continued with his ten grandchildren, all of whom graduated from college. Now he has sixteen young great-grandchildren. "I'm not going to be around to see if they're going to make college," Fay said, "but I'm very happy to see their parents are dedicated to their education."

As I sat in Patrick Fay's living room, asking him questions and looking at his war medals and listening to his stories, I found myself thinking about all the young people I had been getting to know in my reporting. There were many echoes of his story in theirs, and vice versa — the immigrant childhood he shared with Ivonne Martinez and Taslim Mohammed; his urgent request to be placed on the more academic track in school, like KiKi Gilbert's; his family's sacrifices for his education; his eagerness to claim the opportunities to which he had been granted access.

But it was hard not to think, as well, about the differences between his story and theirs. For young Americans today, especially those from modest beginnings, the road to economic security often seems uncertain and treacherous. But for Patrick Fay, the engine of social mobility functioned almost perfectly, as it did for so many Americans of his generation. His grandfathers were farmers; his father was a manual laborer; his children and grandchildren and great-grandchildren are all highly educated and financially comfortable. He was the hinge in his family's story, the transition figure from physical work to knowledge work, and the GI Bill was what made his transformation possible, and his family's as well.

2. Playing for First

More than six decades after Roosevelt laid out the promises of the GI Bill, President Barack Obama, just a month into his first term, made a similarly bold proposal to the American people. "This country needs and values the talents of every American," Obama said in his first address to Congress, in February 2009. "That is why we will provide the support necessary for all young Americans to complete college and meet a new goal: By 2020, America will once again have the highest proportion of college graduates in the world. That is a goal we can meet."

Two months later, in a speech at the White House, Obama said it again: "By the end of the next decade, I want to see America have the highest proportion of college graduates in the world. We used to have that; we no longer do. We are going to get that lead back."

In August 2010, he delivered a particularly rousing version of his pledge before thousands of cheering college students at the University of Texas in Austin. "We are not playing for second place," Obama said. "We are the United States of America, and—like the Texas Longhorns, *you* play for first — *we* play for first."

In his speech, the president explained to those UT students the long-term context behind his promise. "America has to have the highest share of graduates compared to every other nation," he explained. "But Texas, I want you to know that we have been slipping. In a single generation, we've fallen from first place to twelfth place in college-graduation rates for young adults. Think about that. In one generation we went from number one to number twelve. Now, that's unacceptable, but it's not irreversible. We can retake the lead."

There was good reason for Obama and his education advisers to feel confident that they could achieve, in a decade, a significant improvement in the country's college-attainment rate among young adults. The United States had done it before, as the GI Bill era plainly showed. And more recently, several other countries had made rapid strides in a relatively short period. In the previous decade, while the American college-attainment rate had risen just five percentage points, South Korea had improved its rate by twenty-four points. Australia's rate had jumped fourteen points; Ireland's, fifteen points. And it wasn't just young and developing countries that were making big advances: the United Kingdom, where universities have been in business for more than eight centuries, had, during that same decade, raised its college-attainment rate by seventeen percentage points. In each country, the policy calculation driving those gains had been the same: you can't compete in a globalized and automated economy without a highly educated labor force.

In the fall of 2019, when this book is published, it will be a little more than a decade after President Obama's original pledge, and just a few months before the deadline he set for the United States to be back on top of its global competitors once again. So it is finally time to ask: How did we do?

The most recent international data came out in November 2018, and it told a singularly uninspiring story: in the decade since President Obama's challenge to America, the United States had moved from twelfth place to . . . twelfth place.

That's right: we're still in twelfth place. We're not only behind Japan and Canada and South Korea and the United Kingdom. We're behind Luxembourg. We're behind Lithuania. President Obama was right about one thing: the United States *doesn't* play for second place. We play, apparently, for twelfth.

It is possible to find economists who will tell you that our global college-attainment ranking doesn't really matter much, or that there's not much a president can do to influence it. But in fact, there were a number of specific decisions the Obama administration made — and didn't make — that had a profound effect on the nation's college-attainment rate. Consider the fate of the American Graduation Initiative.

After Obama's original announcement of his administration's 2020 goal, a small group of White House economists and policy analysts sat down and made some calculations about how to achieve it. In a private memo that went in the fall of 2009 to Lawrence Summers, then the director of Obama's National Economic Council, two White House analysts explained that in order for the United States to retake the global lead in college graduation, the administration would likely need to produce 9.3 million additional college graduates by 2020. The American Graduation Initiative, formally announced by Obama on July 14, 2009, was the first concrete step the administration took to reach that number: a $12 billion federal investment in programs to increase degree completion at the nation's community colleges.

Economists projected at the time that the American Graduation Initiative would produce five million new community college graduates by 2020 — enough to get the country more than halfway to Obama's goal. The initiative was significant not just because of the unprecedented size of the federal commitment, but also because it was targeted at community colleges, usually the most overlooked part of the higher education system. It was designed, in other words, to support young Americans like Orry and Taslim and Alicia, the students who most needed help navigating their way to a degree.

And so when the plan was unveiled in July 2009, it met with an enthusiastic reception. The White House proudly compiled a two-page roundup of some of the most glowing reviews: "An extraordinary moment . . . a red-banner day . . . the higher education equivalent of the moon shot." The administration sent its $12 billion funding request to the Democratic-controlled Congress that fall. It passed the House and was sent on to the Senate as part of the omnibus health care bill that contained the Affordable Care Act. The president's college-completion efforts were off to a powerful start.

And then, right before the health care bill was finalized, the American Graduation Initiative suddenly and quietly disintegrated. Under pressure from various factions in Congress, the White House, desperate to pass the ACA, agreed to withdraw its request for $12 billion and replace it with a much smaller request for $2 billion for job-training programs run by the Labor Department. The administration's whole community-college initiative just — *poof* — disappeared overnight.

Looking back, the oddest thing about the lonesome death of the American Graduation Initiative — and, more broadly, about the nation's failure to meet Obama's 2020 pledge — is that no one in power seemed particularly distressed. There were no public apologies. No protest marches. No indignant newspaper editorials. Not even a few mean tweets.

In fact, the only real outrage occasioned by Obama's failed promise came not because of the failure, but because of the promise. When former senator Rick Santorum was running for president in 2012, he assailed the president's 2020 plan in a campaign speech in Troy, Michigan. "President Obama once said he wants everyone in America to go to college," Santorum said, his face a mask of contempt. "What a snob! There are good, decent men and women who go out and work hard every day, that put their skills to the test, that aren't taught by some liberal college professor that's trying to indoctrinate them." The audience cheered wildly. (Santorum himself had bravely endured the snobbery of the American college campus just long enough to collect a BA, and then an MBA, and then a law degree.)

So why did Roosevelt's pledge to expand higher education to a new population succeed in such a dramatic and historical way, while Obama's simply fizzled out? I think there are some important clues in that speech by Santorum. His objection to Obama's plan was based not on his analysis of labor markets or graduation rates or test scores. It was based on his personal belief that the president was a snob. "College" has become in the United States a cultural marker, a signifier we use to divide *us* from *them*. Which means that the debates on higher education that were once conducted in the measured vocabulary of market forces and skill development now take place in the heated language of ideology and identity.

ALTHOUGH THE ERA of the GI Bill offers an intriguing contrast with the period we're now living through, there is an earlier historical comparison that might be more helpful in understanding how the national debate over college has changed. That is the period from 1910 to 1940, known to educational historians as the era of the high school movement.

In 1910 only 9 percent of American eighteen-year-olds graduated from high school; most kids left school after the sixth grade. This wasn't because they were unintelligent, or because the country was unenlightened; it was because they didn't need high school–level skills in order to hold down a job that would enable them to support a family and live a middle-class life. Work on farms and in factories and even in many offices was demanding, but it was also fairly straightforward and repetitive, performed with basic tools. It didn't require that much mental training to do it well.

But then the American workplace and the technology that powered it began to change, and, in response, the American school system changed as well. In blue-collar factories, cheap electricity and new production machines enabled more complicated and efficient manufacturing processes. Employers now wanted to hire machinists and electricians and technicians who knew algebra and geometry, who could read manuals and blueprints, who understood the basics of chemistry and electricity. In white-collar offices, new technologies like typewriters and adding machines and dictating machines made employers eager to hire clerks and bookkeepers and stenographers with the mathematical and grammar skills required to put those machines to most effective use. And if you wanted to master these new, suddenly valuable skills, a sixth-grade or even an eighth-grade education just wasn't enough. You had to go to high school.

At the beginning of the twentieth century, American families that wanted to send their children to high school generally had to pay the tuition of a private academy. But as the economy shifted, beginning around 1910, communities all over the country decided that helping their children develop the skills they needed to succeed in the modern labor market was a public good. Having more high school graduates in your town — or your state or your country — was seen as beneficial not just to the students and their families, but to everybody. So in one community and state after another, the public, through their local governments, began to build and organize and expand and staff free public high schools.

"The high school movement emerged from a grassroots desire for greater social mobility," the economists Claudia Goldin and Law-rence Katz wrote in their history of the era. "It sprung from the peo-ple and was not forced upon them by a top-down campaign." And in just a few decades, the American educational landscape was trans-formed. High school education became free and publicly available almost everywhere in the United States. By 1940, more than half of all American eighteen-year-olds were graduating from high school — five times the proportion that graduated from high school thirty years earlier.

Today, just like a century ago, technology has once again changed American workplaces, and again employers are sending a clear mes-sage to young people: if you want us to hire you and pay a decent wage, you need to get more education. There is nothing particularly ideological or cultural about this fact — or at least there shouldn't be. It is simple economics: it is now almost impossible to find a job that will let you support a family and lead a middle-class life in the United States with only a high school education.

These signals from today's marketplace are a perfect echo of the signals from a century ago: technology has changed; the labor market has changed; young people need more skills, and thus more educa-tion. The response of individual young people is much the same as it was a century ago. They *want* more education, because they know that's what it takes to live a stable middle-class life.

What is different, remarkably so, is the response of the public at large. A century ago, American communities saw that their young people needed more education in order to thrive in a changing econ-omy, and so they came together and figured out a way to provide that education and make it freely accessible. And it worked: young people got more schooling and better jobs, and their communities prospered. Now technology has changed once again, and so has the job market, and once again young people need more education in order to reach the middle class and support a family. And this time around, our message to those young people is: You're on your own.

You figure out how to get the skills you're going to need. And by the way, here's the bill.

ONE OF THE REASONS the relationship between higher education and social mobility can seem so complicated is this: When you are an eighteen-year-old student, no matter where you're going to school, college feels like a personal adventure, a process of self-discovery, what David Laude at UT likes to call "identity formation." Sometimes that adventure is fun and exciting; sometimes it is unpleasant and terrifying. But it always feels life-changing, laden with emotion, especially if you're a young person who grew up in difficult circumstances that you are eager to escape or transcend.

To an economist, though, the process of obtaining a college education is much more practical, even mercenary. Economists see college simply as a place where young people engage in "human capital formation" — where they acquire the skills they need to earn a living as adults. That is true whether those young people are studying welding at Catawba Valley Community College or philosophy at Princeton. Sitting in a Humanities Sequence precept might not resemble our conventional image of job training — that looks much more like the welding bays at CVCC — but the skills that KiKi Gilbert and her peers gained around that precept table not only legitimately count as job skills, they are job skills that are highly valued in a knowledge-based economy. (A recent analysis of US census data showed that the highest-earning 10 percent of philosophy majors will make an average of $3.5 million over the course of their careers, even more than the highest-earning 10 percent of computer science majors.)

It is certainly true that earnings are not the only important component of social mobility. And it is also true that the experience of college is about more than just gaining job skills. The process of identity formation in late adolescence is real and genuine, and how it takes place really does have a profound effect on how people's lives turn out: how happy they will be; how well they will negotiate the challenges of work and family and friendship and community. But still, it is useful, sometimes, when contemplating the meaning of college, to remember the economist's cold-eyed perspective. It lets us strip away, for a moment, all of the culturally freighted language we tend to favor, about snobbery and passion and dignity, and to remember this: the basic reason that communities and nations establish education systems is to help their young people accumulate the skills they need to succeed in life.

The decisions we make about how that system operates — how effectively it functions, who pays for it and how much they pay, how democratic or elitist its selection process is — are really decisions about how our country operates. The particular set of decisions we have made in creating our current higher education system — and those include individual decisions, institutional decisions, and public-policy decisions — have produced a mobility engine that functions incredibly well for a small number of people and quite poorly for many others. The ones who benefit most from the system tend to be wealthy and talented and well connected. The ones who benefit least tend to be from families that are deprived or isolated or fractured or all three.

There is plenty of evidence that Americans believe in the transformative power of education just as much as they did a century ago. What is different today is that we tend to consider that transformation in individual terms rather than collective ones. Over the last few decades, we have come to think of higher education principally as a competitive marketplace, one where our natural goal is to get the best that we can for ourselves or our children or our institution, even at the expense of others. When college educations are redefined as private goods, rather than public ones, the fact that they are so unequally distributed seems less jarring. Not everyone gets a big house or a sports car; not everyone gets a high-quality college education.

But at other moments in our nation's history, including the period of the high school movement and the GI Bill era, Americans have thought about the education of our young people very differently. And so we made decisions about higher education that promoted equality and shared mobility over competition and the hoarding of opportunity.

If we now want to nudge our country back in that direction, we might begin by embracing a principle that seemed self-evident to Americans a century ago, but is less widely acknowledged today: *Our collective public education benefits us all.* It's a simple idea. The primary motivating force behind the high school movement was not altruism or charity, it was collective self-interest. Americans built and funded local public high schools because they believed that a town, a city, a society where opportunity for mobility through education was widely shared was simply a better place to live.

The inequities in the American system of higher education cannot be solved by the government alone. Sure, there are regulations and policies and laws that should be reformed and improved. But in an education system as decentralized and independent as ours, pressure for change has to come from many directions at once, in individual decisions and collective ones, in what we choose to pay attention to and in how we spend our money and our time. The levers for change are all around us. We can affect them as students, as parents, as educators, and as citizens. We just need to decide which way we want to pull.

Acknowledgments

———

I'm grateful to the many people who helped bring this book into existence: my editors, my friends and colleagues, and most of all my sources and subjects.

My first debt of gratitude goes to the students who shared their thoughts and stories and reflections with me. I want to mention with special gratitude KiKi Gilbert, Shannen Torres, and Kim Henning, each of whom took great care, in multiple interviews over many years, to answer my questions thoughtfully and deeply, with candor and insight. I'm grateful as well to Orry Carriere, Matthew Rivera, Taslim Mohammed, Alicia Pollard, Ben Dormus, Amy A., Jessica, DeMarcus, Micah, Victoria, Nicolas, Clara, Ariel, Alexia White, William Walker, Erika Cabrera, Eric Sklanka, Kayle Spikes, Anthony Davis, and Anthony Mendez. An extra-special thanks to Ivonne Martinez and her fellow students in Uri Treisman's Math 408C class at the University of Texas, including Juan Villela, Bo Mannon, Sara Packard, Sydney Rabara, Joey Martinez, and Eric Zeno.

Jon Boeckenstedt shaped my understanding of how enrollment management works and the crucial role it plays in higher education. Ned Johnson gave me extraordinary access and valuable insights into his work with his students. Angel Pérez let me see up close how college admissions operates. Uri Treisman taught me a great deal about the practical mechanics and the psychological dynamics of teaching college students, even if he wasn't able to teach me much calculus. David Yeager not only guided me carefully and conscientiously through his own research, he also introduced me to and helped me make sense of a broad range of scholarship on the psychology of college students.

I'm grateful to the administrators, educators, and students at the colleges and universities where I reported, including Arrupe College (especially Father Stephen Katsouros), Austin Community College, Berea College, Catawba Valley Community College, City College of New York, Clemson University, Foothill College, Franklin & Marshall College, Georgia State University (especially Timothy Renick and Emily Buis), Indiana University, Malcolm X College (especially Omar Juarez), Miami Dade College, National Louis University, PelotonU (especially Sarah Saxton-Frump and Hudson Baird), Perimeter College (especially Cary Claibourne), Princeton University, Southern New Hampshire University, Stanford University, Trinity College, the University of Central Arkansas (especially Amy Baldwin), and the University of Maryland, Baltimore County. The institution where I reported most extensively was the University of Texas in Austin, where I'm especially grateful to David Laude, Carolyn Connerat, Katie Hogan, Erica Winterer, Cassandre Alvarado, Jenny Smith, Harrison Keller, Dena Grumbles, Gary Susswein, Maurie McInnis, and Gregory Fenves.

I'm thankful to Nicole Hurd and her colleagues at College Advising Corps for arranging a series of visits for me to high schools in North Carolina and Texas and Michigan and Pennsylvania and New York, where I was able to speak with students and advisers and deepen my understanding of the college application and admissions process. In addition, I'm grateful to the administrators and educators who welcomed me to A. Philip Randolph Campus High School in New York City; Winnfield Senior High School in Winnfield, Louisiana; Myers Park High School in Charlotte, North Carolina; Eastside College Preparatory School in East Palo Alto, California; and Cody High School in Detroit.

Researchers in a variety of fields explained their work to me with patience and clarity, often through multiple conversations. My thanks go to Joshua Angrist, David Autor, Christopher Avery, Philippe Belley, Shannon Brady, David Bressoud, Anthony Carnevale, Sheryll Cashin, Geoffrey Cohen, Tressie McMillan Cottom, Mesmin Destin, Angela Duckworth, Carol Dweck, Claudia Goldin, Valerie Purdie Greenaway, Kyla Haimovitz, Douglas Harris, Brad Hershbein, Caroline Hoxby, Anthony Abraham Jack, Kirabo Jackson, Ozan Jaquette, Lance Lochner, Hazel Markus, Mary Murphy, Sean Reardon, Lauren Rivera, Matthew Patrick Shaw, Claude Steele, Marta Tienda, and Gregory Walton. I owe an extra debt of gratitude to the scholars and researchers at the Equality of Opportunity Project at Stanford (which has since moved to Harvard and reconstituted itself as Opportunity Insights), who allowed me to embed myself in their offices and shared with me their data and their ideas. My thanks, especially, to Raj Chetty, John Friedman, Rebecca Toseland, Martin Koenen, and Michael Droste.

A number of nonprofit organizations helped me with my reporting. Leadership Enterprise for a Diverse America and its executive director, Beth Breger, invited me to spend time during two consecutive summers at LEDA's summer institute in Princeton. Sal Khan and Barb Kunz and others at Khan Academy gave me insights into the workings of Official SAT Practice. At the College Board, I'm grateful for the help of David Coleman, Aaron Lemon-Strauss, Jessica Howell, Michael Hurwitz, Emily Shaw, Steven Colón, Michael Preston, and Zachary Goldberg. At CollegePoint and America Achieves I benefited from the aid of Bryden Sweeney-Taylor, Brett Kimmel, Jon Schnur, and the virtual advisers I spoke with in Chapel Hill, including Jhenielle Reynolds. Ben Castleman shared his expertise and his data on the CollegePoint intervention. I received assistance from counselors and educators and administrators at a number of other college access and success programs, including Bottom Line, the Ron Brown Scholar Program, the IvyG Conference, Year Up, OneGoal, Duet (formerly Match Beyond), and College Access: Research & Action.

Others who spoke with me during my reporting and helped shape the thinking that went into this book include Carissa Garcia, Naiomy Guerrero, James Murphy, Jack Maguire, Richard Kahlenberg, Jim Shelton, Esther Cepeda, Dan Porterfield, Ashley Robinson, Melissa Connelly, Shirley Tilghman, Anthony Bryk, John Simpkins, Patty Diaz-Andrade, Matthew Chingos, Robert Morse, Tristan Denley, and the families of Kim Henning and KiKi Gilbert. I benefited from the recollections of a number of people who worked in the White House and the federal education department shaping higher education policy during the Obama administration, including Eric Waldo, James Kvaal, Cecelia Rouse, Ted Mitchell, Heather Higginbottom, Martha Kanter, and Rosemarie Nassif. And I'm especially grateful to Patrick Fay and other veterans of World War II who spoke with me about their experience attending college on the GI Bill, including Francis Turner, Noel Parmentel, Peter Mistretta, and Robert Simon.

Tarpley Hitt provided me with crucial early research support. Emily McCullar and Susan Banta helped fact-check the completed manuscript. Matt Klam was the first person to read each chapter, and he gave me wise and timely suggestions and direction. Ilena Silverman, Joel Lovell, and Paula Shapiro read early drafts and helped steer me toward important revisions. My agent, David McCormick, has been an invaluable adviser and advocate since the days when this book was merely hypothetical. At Houghton Mifflin Harcourt, Deanne Urmy was a tireless supporter and keen-eyed editor. Taryn Roeder, Melissa Dobson, Larry Cooper, Loren Isenberg, and Jenny Xu all gave me essential feedback and support as well. I owe a special debt of gratitude to Sara Corbett, who edited the entire manuscript after I had completed a first draft, guiding me through multiple revisions with patience and skill.

The Mesa Refuge gave me the time and space to work on my book proposal. The Spencer Foundation provided early financial support for my reporting. At the Bridgespan Group, Tod Cowen and Mike Perigo and Lija McHugh Farnham provided crucial intellectual and logistical assistance and advice. I received valuable guidance from Jeff Nelson, Nicholas Lemann, Emily Hanford, Sue Lehmann, Vera Titunik, Aaron Retica, Molly Hensley-Clancy, Chana Joffe-Walt, Charles Yao, and Misha Glouberman.

I am grateful for the support and sustenance I received along the way from friends and family, including Anne Tough, Susan Tough, Pam Shime, Elana James, Ethan Watters, Lara Cox, Evan Harris, Kate Porterfield, Kira Pollack, Jack Hitt, Michael Pollan, Kim Temple, Chris Alexander, Ira Glass, Chris Bell, Mary Poteet, Ian Brown, John Samson, and Jonathan Goldstein.

My deepest love and thanks, as always, go to Paula, Ellington, and Charles, who when I'm writing provide me with both the best reasons to keep working and the best reasons to stop. This book, in every way that matters, is for them.

Notes

I. Wanting In

The Alexis de Tocqueville quotations are from the Mentor paperback edition of *Democracy in America,* published in 1984. "Wealth circulates" is on p. 52; "New families" is on pp. 193–94; "aristocracy had made a chain" is on p. 194; and "most of the rich men" is on p. 53.

The statistic on young adults living in poverty, by education level, is from Rich Moran, Anna Brown, and Rick Fry, *The Rising Cost of* Not *Going to College* (Washington, DC: Pew Research Center, February 2014), p. 6.

The statistics on unemployment rates by education level are from "Unemployment Rates for Persons 25 Years and Older by Educational Attainment," published online by the Bureau of Labor Statistics. In March 2017 (when Shannen Torres got the news from Penn) the unemployment rate for adults with a bachelor's degree or higher was 2.4 percent, and the rate for high school graduates with no college experience was 4.9 percent.

The statistic about well-educated white men living longer is from S. Jay Olshansky et al., "Differences in Life Expectancy Due to Race and Educational Differences Are Widening, and Many May Not Catch Up," *Health Affairs* 31, no. 8 (August 2012).

The statistics about marriage and divorce rates and education levels are from Casey E. Copen et al., "First Marriages in the United States: Data from the 2006–2010 National Survey of Family Growth," *National Health Statistics Reports* 49 (March 22, 2012). Among women with a bachelor's degree, 22 percent of marriages end before their twentieth anniversary; among women with only a high school diploma, 59 percent of marriages end before their twentieth anniversary. (See Figure 5 and Table 5.)

Raj Chetty's Denmark research is included in Chetty et al., "Active vs. Passive Decisions and Crowd-out in Retirement Savings Accounts: Evidence from Denmark," *Quarterly Journal of Economics* 129, no. 3 (August 2014), available on Chetty's web page: http://www.rajchetty.com/chettyfiles/crowdout.pdf.

Chetty's Austria research is included in David Card, Raj Chetty, and Andrea Weber, "Cash-on-Hand and Competing Models of Intertemporal Behavior: New Evidence from the Labor Market" (NBER Working Paper no. 12639, National Bureau of Economic Research, Cambridge, MA, October 2006); and Card, Chetty, and Weber, "The Spike at Benefit Exhaustion: Leaving the Unemployment System or Starting a New Job?" (NBER Working Paper no. 12893, National Bureau of Economic Research, Cambridge, MA, February 2007).

The paper introducing the Mobility Report Cards is Raj Chetty et al., "Mobility Report Cards: The Role of Colleges in Intergenerational Mobility" (NBER Working Paper no. 23618, National Bureau of Economic Research, Cambridge, MA, July 2017). More detailed college mobility data is online at http://www.equality-of-opportunity.org/college/mobility_report_cards.html. The *New York Times* presented the Mobility Report Cards data on two helpful interactive pages: "Economic Diversity and Student Outcomes at America's Colleges and Universities: Find Your College," https://www.nytimes.com/interactive/projects/college-mobility/ and "Some Colleges Have More Students from the Top 1 Percent Than the Bottom 60: Find Yours," January 18, 2017, https://www.nytimes.com/interactive/2017/01/18/upshot/some-colleges-have-more-students-from-the-top-1-percent-than-the-bottom-60.html. Additional useful data and background information is at https://opportunity insights.org/. Several predoctoral fellows at the Equality of Opportunity Project (before Chetty moved to Harvard) and at Opportunity Insights (after the move to Harvard) helped me with additional analysis of the data, especially Michael Droste and Martin Koenen, and also including Sarah Merchant, Priyanka Shende, and Nick Flamang.

Further discussion of the Mobility Report Cards research is in Stephen Burd, ed., *Moving On Up? What a Groundbreaking Study Tells Us About Access, Success, and Mobility in Higher Ed* (Washington, DC: New America, 2017).

Admissions data for various selective universities in this chapter comes from "College Admissions Statistics," Top Tier Admissions, https://www.toptier admissions.com/resources/college-admissions-statistics/.

II. Getting In

The remark of a parent accused in the college-admissions scandal ("The way the world works these days is unbelievable") is from p. 68 of the "Affidavit in Support of Criminal Complaint" by Special Agent Laura Smith of the Federal Bureau of Investigation, downloaded from the website of the United States Attorney's Office for the District of Massachusetts. (The parent quoted is William E. McGlashan Jr.)

Stacy Berg Dale and Alan B. Krueger published their findings in "Estimating the Payoff to Attending a More Selective College: An Application of Selection on Observables and Unobservables," *Quarterly Journal of Economics* 117, no. 4 (November 2002), updated and expanded in "Estimating the Return to College Selectivity over the Career Using Administrative Earnings Data" (NBER Working Paper no. 17159, National Bureau of Economic Research, Cambridge, MA, June 2011).

Caroline Hoxby offered her response to the analysis of Dale and Krueger in "The Changing Selectivity of American Colleges" (NBER Working Paper no. 15446, National Bureau of Economic Research, Cambridge, MA, October 2009). Hoxby published a more accessible version of that research in "College Choices Have Consequences," *SIEPR Policy Brief* (December 2012), published by the Stanford Institute for Economic Policy Research.

The distinctions and disagreements between Dale and Krueger's and Hoxby's findings are explored in Bryan Caplan, "Hoxby vs. Dale-Krueger on the Selectivity Premium," *EconLog* (blog of the Library of Economics and Liberty), November 25, 2013.

Hoxby's research on the comparative "value-added" of colleges is in her "Computing the Value-Added of American Postsecondary Institutions" (SOI working paper, Statistics of Income, US Internal Revenue Service, 2015), a version of which was published as "The Dramatic Economics of the U.S. Market for Higher Education," *NBER Reporter* no. 3 (2016) and presented as the Eighth Annual Martin Feldstein Lecture at the National Bureau of Economic Research Summer Institute in 2016. Video is online at https://www. nber.org/feldstein_lecture_2016/feldsteinlecture_2016.html. Her slides from that presentation are available as a PDF: https://www.nber.org/feldstein_lecture_2016/hoxby_feldstein_lecture_27july2016.pdf.

One note on Hoxby's "value-added" research: I wrote that she used in her calculations information from the College Board on "where students apply"; technically, the information she used showed which colleges students had asked the College Board to send their scores to. As Hoxby explained in her 2015 paper (on p. 15), score sending is a widely used proxy for where students apply.

Hoxby's research on how much each institution spends on its students' education is in her "The Productivity of U.S. Postsecondary Institutions," published as a working paper in 2017 and included in Caroline Hoxby and Kevin M. Stange, eds., *Productivity in Higher Education,* forthcoming from NBER. She also addressed that question in her 2016 Feldstein Lecture.

Charles T. Clotfelter's research on the "inequality dividend" is in his book *Unequal Colleges in the Age of Disparity,* published in 2017 by Belknap Press, an imprint of Harvard University Press. "Inequality dividend" is on p. 113.

For the details of the Harvard fundraising campaign begun in September 2013, I relied mostly on contemporaneous reporting in *Harvard Magazine,* the *Harvard Crimson,* and the *Boston Globe.* The "running out of professors" quotation is from Andrew M. Duehren and Daphne C. Thompson, "$6.5 Billion. Now What?," *Harvard Crimson,* May 23, 2016.

Data on the family finances of Harvard's incoming freshmen is from *Harvard Crimson*'s "Class Makeup and Admissions" annual survey: https://features. thecrimson.com/2018/freshman-survey/makeup/.

Caroline Hoxby's account of the changing application patterns of high school seniors is in her "The Changing Selectivity of American Colleges" (NBER Working Paper no. 15446, National Bureau of Economic Research, Cambridge, MA, October 2009).

Caroline Hoxby's analysis of the Harvard Financial Aid Initiative is in Christopher Avery et al., "Cost Should Be No Barrier: An Evaluation of the First

Year of Harvard's Financial Aid Initiative" (NBER Working Paper no. 12029, National Bureau of Economic Research, Cambridge, MA, February 2006). Hoxby and Avery also wrote about the Harvard initiative in "The Missing 'One-Offs': The Hidden Supply of High-Achieving, Low Income Students" (NBER Working Paper no. 18586, National Bureau of Economic Research, Cambridge, MA, December 2012). "The Missing 'One-Offs'" is the main source for information about Hoxby and Avery's analysis of the college-application patterns of high-achieving low-income students.

Caroline Hoxby's packet-sending experiment with Sarah Turner, known as the Expanding College Opportunities Project, is chronicled in their paper "Expanding College Opportunities for High-Achieving, Low Income Students" (SIEPR Working Paper no. 12-014, March 2013), published by the Stanford Institute for Economic Policy Research. Their proposal to extend the project in partnership with the College Board and ACT was detailed in "Informing Students About Their College Options: A Proposal for Broadening the Expanding College Opportunities Project" (discussion paper, Hamilton Project, Brookings Institution, Washington, DC, June 2013). They also wrote about the project in "What High-Achieving Low-Income Students Know About College," *American Economic Review* 105, no. 5 (May 2015).

The early news stories reporting on Hoxby and Turner's "Expanding College Opportunities" paper are David Leonhardt, "Better Colleges Failing to Lure Talented Poor," *New York Times*, March 16, 2013, p. 1; David Leonhardt, "A Simple Way to Send Poor Kids to Top Colleges," *New York Times*, March 29, 2013; and Beckie Supiano, "The $6 Solution," *Chronicle of Higher Education*, June 16, 2014.

The *Smithsonian* profile of Hoxby is Nancy Hass, "How Do You Get Poor Kids to Apply to Great Colleges?," December 2013.

Biographical information for David Coleman was drawn from Joy Resmovits, "David Coleman, the Most Influential Education Figure You've Never Heard Of," *Forward*, August 25, 2013; Dana Goldstein, "The Schoolmaster," *Atlantic*, October 2012; and Todd Balf, "The Story Behind the SAT Overhaul," *New York Times Magazine*, March 6, 2014.

Biographical information about Caroline Hoxby is from John Cassidy, "Schools Are Her Business," *New Yorker*, October 18 and 25, 1999, and from the profile of Hoxby on the website of the American Economic Association: https://www.aeaweb.org/about-aea/committees/csmgep/profiles/caroline-hoxby.

The fact that "only about 2 percent of Yale's students come from economic backgrounds like Kim's" is from the interactive presentation of the Mobility Report Card data on the *New York Times* website, at https://www.nytimes.com/interactive/projects/college-mobility/yale-university. (According to the report cards, 2.1 percent of Yale's undergraduate student population comes from families whose income is in the bottom quintile.)

The CollegePoint intervention funded by Bloomberg Philanthropies is described in David Leonhardt, "A New Push to Get Low-Income Students Through College," *New York Times,* October 28, 2014; in Bloomberg Philanthropies, "Bloomberg Philanthropies Launches New Initiative to Help High-Achieving, Low- and Moderate-Income Students Apply to and Enroll in Top Colleges and Universities," press release, October 28, 2014; and in Michael R. Bloomberg, "The American Dream Can Only Be Fulfilled If Our Top Students Have the Opportunity to Attend Our Top Colleges," *Huffington Post,* October 29, 2014.

The fact that Bloomberg and his representatives hoped, within five years, to be persuading more than ten thousand students each year to switch to a CollegePoint target college (aka an Aspen 270 college) is in Leonhardt, "A New Push to Get Low-Income Students Through College."

The data released by CollegePoint's evaluation team in the winter of 2019 was summarized in "Class of 2018 CollegePoint Impact Evaluation," an unpublished memo produced by Ben Castleman and the staff of CollegePoint. Table 1 in the memo showed that among a control group of high school seniors who were eligible for CollegePoint but did not receive virtual advising, 53 percent of students enrolled in a CollegePoint target college. Among a treatment group who did receive CollegePoint virtual advising, 53.4 percent of students enrolled in a CollegePoint target college.

III. Fixing the Test

The history of the College Board, the SAT, and the ACT is drawn largely from Nicholas Lemann, *The Big Test: The Secret History of the American Meritocracy,* published in 1999 by Farrar, Straus and Giroux.

Information about the finances of the College Board, including executive pay, is from ProPublica's Nonprofit Explorer, which collects the tax filings and audits of nonprofit organizations. The College Board's filings are at https://projects.propublica.org/nonprofits/organizations/131623965.

Biographical information about Stanley Kaplan is from Lemann, *The Big Test*, and Malcolm Gladwell, "Examined Life," *New Yorker*, December 17, 2001.

The early competition between ACT Inc. and the College Board is covered in Daniel de Visé, "ACT or SAT? More Students Answering 'All of the Above,'" *Washington Post*, November 12, 2008.

The more recent competition between the College Board and ACT Inc. is chronicled in a number of articles by Nick Anderson in the *Washington Post*, including "SAT Revisions Follow Years of Gains for Rival ACT," March 6, 2014; "Is SAT Becoming More Like the ACT?," March 6, 2014; "SAT Usage Declined in 29 States over Seven Years," March 16, 2014; "The New SAT: Aptitude Testing for College Admissions Falls out of Favor," April 21, 2014; "Growing Number of States Fund ACT College Admission Testing for 11th-Grade Students," August 20, 2014; and "As SAT Enters a New Era This Week, Students Say the Exam Has Improved," March 3, 2016.

David Coleman's statement that "unequal test-prep access is a problem" is quoted in Todd Balf, "The Story Behind the SAT Overhaul," *New York Times Magazine*, March 6, 2014.

David Coleman's speech to college counselors during which he said that the SAT had "become captive to the advantages of wealth" was delivered on December 8, 2016, at the College Advising Corps's 2016 Adviser Summit in Washington, DC.

The College Board's data showing that "in 2013, students' SAT scores tracked their family income in a direct and linear fashion" were included as a graphic in Todd Balf, "The Story Behind the SAT Overhaul," *New York Times Magazine*, March 6, 2014.

Hoxby and Turner's prediction that the Expanding College Opportunities intervention could potentially boost the number of targeted students enrolling in selective institutions by as much as 46 percent is in their 2013 paper "Expanding College Opportunities for High-Achieving, Low Income Students," p. 48, Table 6. (The "Effect in percentage change" for the dependent variable "Enrolled in a 'Peer' Institution" is given as 46.3%.) The table shows effects for what economists call the "treatment on the treated," in this case meaning the effect the packets had on students who later said they remembered receiving one. In Hoxby and Turner's "Informing Students About Their College Options: A Proposal for Broadening the Expanding College

Opportunities Project," also from 2013, they wrote that the "treatment on the treated" estimate is "presumably closer to the effects that a trusted organization such as the College Board or ACT would experience if it were to conduct the intervention" (p. 15), and reiterated that under the treatment-on-the-treated effects, the Expanding College Opportunities intervention "caused students to enroll in colleges that were 46 percent more likely to be peer institutions" (p. 16).

The "treatment on the treated" estimates were the ones most likely to be reported in the media when Hoxby and Turner's "Expanding College Opportunities" paper was published. One article (Jay Mathews, "Admissions 101: Why Smart, Poor Students Are Dumb," *Washington Post,* April 25, 2013), for instance, stated, "The results were startling. Those who received the letters were 53 percent more likely to apply to a college that matched their high achievement level. They were 70 percent more likely to be admitted to one of those schools and 50 percent more likely to attend."

The URL that once housed the Expanding College Opportunities Project and later directed readers to Indonesian-language articles about online poker is http://expandingcollegeopps.org/.

David Coleman's description of paid tutors as "predators" and his statement "This is a bad day for them" is from Balf, "The Story Behind the SAT Overhaul."

David Coleman's 2014 SXSW speech is on YouTube at https://www.youtube.com/watch?v=MSZbPJbXwMI ("Delivering Opportunity presented by David Coleman"). The speech is covered in Tamar Lewin, "A New SAT Aims to Realign with Schoolwork," *New York Times,* March 5, 2014.

Sal Khan's personal history and the history of Khan Academy can be found in his book *The One World Schoolhouse: Education Reimagined,* published in 2012 by Twelve; in his 2011 TED talk, "Let's Use Video to Reinvent Education," https://www.ted.com/talks/salman_khan_let_s_use_video_to_reinvent_education; and in "About Khan Academy" on the Khan Academy website: https://khanacademy.zendesk.com/hc/en-us/articles/202483180-What-is-the-history-of-Khan-Academy-. See also James Temple, "Salman Khan, Math Master of the Internet," *San Francisco Chronicle,* December 14, 2009; and Claudia Dreifus, "It All Started with a 12-Year-Old Cousin," interview, *New York Times,* January 27, 2014.

The early philanthropic investments in Khan Academy are described in David A. Kaplan, "Bill Gates' Favorite Teacher," CNN Money, August 24, 2010; Salman Khan, "When Sal Khan Met Bill Gates," *Fortune,* October 9, 2012; and Tate Williams, "The Funders Pouring Money into the Khan Academy," Inside Philanthropy, June 26, 2014.

The audio for the College Board's May 2017 conference call announcing the results of Official SAT Practice to journalists is online at https://bit.ly/2Ux43ct.

Sal Khan's statement that "we're seeing that gain be consistent" is in "An Announcement from Khan Academy," on the Khan Academy YouTube channel, May 8, 2017: https://www.youtube.com/watch?v=8-pxqeO24Ww.

Thomas L. Friedman's column about the Official SAT Practice results is "Owning Your Own Future," *New York Times,* May 10, 2017.

David Coleman's "Never in my career" statement was reported in Greg Toppo, "One Million Students Now Using Free SAT Prep Materials," *USA Today,* March 9, 2016.

The Behavior Change for Good project was the subject of two Freakonomics podcasts by Stephen J. Dubner: "Could Solving This One Problem Solve All the Others?," April 5, 2017, and "How to Launch a Behavior-Change Revolution," October 25, 2017. The latter included some of the early discussion of the Behavior Change for Good project's collaboration with the College Board.

The College Board's campaign to sign testing contracts with state governments is discussed in Nick Anderson, "Michigan Picks SAT over ACT for Free College Admission Testing," *Washington Post,* January 7, 2015; and Nick Anderson, "The SAT, Now the No. 2 College Test, Pushes to Reclaim Supremacy," *Washington Post,* December 24, 2015.

The Nick Anderson profile of Coleman in the *Washington Post* is "Meet the Man Behind the New SAT: 'I'm in the Anxiety Field,'" March 4, 2016.

The College Board's improving financial fortunes are detailed in its IRS 990 forms, available online at ProPublica's Nonprofit Explorer. David Coleman's original salary was reported in Tamar Lewin, "Backer of Common Core School Curriculum Is Chosen to Lead College Board," *New York Times,* May 16, 2012.

The "daring to take seriously" remark by David Coleman that so irked Ned Johnson is from a video on the Khan Academy YouTube channel: "Sal Talks to CEO of the College Board, David Coleman," April 15, 2014, https://www.youtube.com/watch?v=Eod3b7uoxCA.

IV. Fitting In

The birth and growth of the lvyG movement is chronicled in Laura Pappano, "First-Generation Students Unite," *New York Times*, April 8, 2015; in Ishani Premaratne, "'Class Confessions' Launch Socioeconomic Discussion on Campus," *USA Today*, April 23, 2014; and in Kalpana Mohanty, "Columbia Class Confessions Opens Dialogue About First-Generation and Low-Income Students' Experiences on Campus, Students Say," *Columbia Daily Spectator*, April 10, 2015. The original Stanford Class Confessions workshop is described in "Class Confessions on Campus," an op-ed by the leadership of the Stanford First Generation and/or Low-Income Partnership (FLIP) in the *Stanford Daily*, March 1, 2013.

Anthony Marx's tenure as president of Amherst is described in David Leonhardt, "Top Colleges, Largely for the Elite," *New York Times*, May 24, 2011.

The fact that "about a third of American undergraduates" qualify for a Pell grant comes from "Undergraduate Enrollment and Percentage Receiving Pell Grants over Time" (Figure 20A), a chart on the College Board's website at https://trends.collegeboard.org/student-aid/figures-tables/undergraduate-enrollment-and-percentage-receiving-pell-grants-over-time.

Anthony Abraham Jack's *The Privileged Poor: How Elite Colleges Are Failing Disadvantaged Students* was published in 2019 by Harvard University Press. "We come here, we're so alive and full of hope" is on p. 43; "It's nice to not have to explain yourself all the time" is on p. 49; "Engaging with their peers made them feel like strangers in a place they could not fully call home" is on p. 52; "Their high schools were a preview" is on pp. 29–30; "literally déjà vu" is on p. 56; "The things that are exciting for people coming to college were very banal to me" is on p. 57; "For the Privileged Poor, it is not a matter of whether they experience culture shock, but when" is on p. 53; "Academic life at Renowned, as at every university, is inherently social" is on p. 86; "college is supposed to be about attending lectures" is on p. 81; "Trying to figure out when, how, and even why personal connections are needed can paralyze them" is on p. 81; "I don't like talking to professors one on one" is on pp. 107–8; "These kids who go to professors after class and just talk to them" is on p. 109; and "The Doubly Disadvantaged express strong faith in the idea of meritocracy" is on p. 127.

The media stories focusing on Princeton's efforts to diversify its student population are Nick Anderson, "How an Ivy Got Less Preppy: Princeton Draws Surge of Students from Modest Means," *Washington Post,* October 23, 2017; "Why Bill and Melinda Gates Put 20,000 Students Through College," *60 Minutes,* April 29, 2018; and David Leonhardt, "Princeton — Yes, Princeton — Takes on the Class Divide," *New York Times,* May 30, 2017.

Data on the variations in Pell eligibility cutoffs are from David Leonhardt, "The Methodology of Our College-Access Index," *New York Times,* September 8, 2014; and Leonhardt, "College Access Index, 2015: The Details," *New York Times,* September 16, 2015. Additional information on Pell cutoffs is in Chetty et al., "Mobility Report Cards: The Role of Colleges in Intergenerational Mobility," pp. 58–59. The "fewer than one in five students" statistic comes from that paper.

One other note on Princeton's Pell percentage: In addition to the explanations I explored in chapter 4, it is possible that the relatively high percentage of Pell-eligible freshmen admitted to Princeton in 2017 was a temporary blip. As of March 2019, the federal education department's online College Scorecard (collegescorecard.ed.gov) lists Princeton's Pell percentage as 15 percent, which is the same as Brown's, Cornell's, and Stanford's, and is seven percentage points below Columbia's.

Research on how certain colleges artificially boost their Pell percentages is from Caroline Hoxby and Sarah Turner, "Measuring Opportunity in U.S. Higher Education" (SIEPR Working Paper no. 19-001, January 2019), published by the Stanford Institute for Economic Policy Research. Hoxby's "distorted behavior" remark is from her discussion with Marty West, editor in chief of *Education Next,* on the EdNext Podcast "Identifying the Colleges That Successfully Recruit Low-Income Students," February 6, 2019, https://www.education next.org/ednext-podcast-identifying-colleges-that-successfully-recruit-low-income-students/. Some of the Pell analysis I wrote about was not included in the paper itself; Hoxby and Turner separately provided data on this "distorted" admissions behavior to journalists. See Catherine Rampell, "Colleges Have Been Under Pressure to Admit Needier Kids. It's Backfiring," *Washington Post,* January 24, 2019; and Doug Lederman, "Underrepresented Students, Underrepresented Consequences," *Inside Higher Ed,* January 28, 2019.

The family-income data for Princeton's students revealed in the Mobility Report Cards project can be found on the *New York Times* interactive page "Economic Diversity and Student Outcomes at America's Colleges and Universities: Find Your College," at https://www.nytimes.com/interactive/projects/college-mobility/princeton-university. The data on the change in the percentage of Princeton's students coming from the bottom two income quintiles can be found at http://www.equality-of-opportunity.org/college/mobility_report_cards.html; I compared the data for the cohort born in 1982 with the data for the cohort born in 1991. I received help with this analysis from Martin Koenen, a predoctoral research fellow at Opportunity Insights.

The comments by Lani Guinier and Henry Louis Gates Jr. at a 2003 reunion of black Harvard alumni are reported in Sara Rimer and Karen W. Arenson, "Top Colleges Take More Blacks, but Which Ones?," *New York Times*, June 24, 2004.

The 2007 paper following up on the comments by Gates and Guinier is Douglas S. Massey et al., "Black Immigrants and Black Natives Attending Selective Colleges and Universities in the United States," *American Journal of Education* 113, no. 2 (February 2007). That paper was featured in Cara Anna, "Among Black Students, Many Immigrants," Associated Press, April 30, 2007.

The "separate, long-term study" that looked at college enrollment patterns among students from black immigrant families and students with one black and one nonblack parent is described in Thomas J. Espenshade and Alexandria Walton Radford, *No Longer Separate, Not Yet Equal: Race and Class in Elite College Admission and Campus Life*, published by Princeton University Press in 2009; see pp. 149–50.

Shaun Harper's speech is on the National Association for College Admission Counseling YouTube channel: "2017 NACAC National Conference Keynote Speaker Shaun Harper," September 25, 2017, at https://www.youtube.com/watch?v=zcUkalvqoLA. The passage I quoted starts at about 27:00.

The fact that 15 percent of American high school graduates are black is from Common Core of Data, National Center for Education Statistics, U.S. Department of Education, "Annual Diploma Counts and the Averaged Freshmen Graduation Rate (AFGR) in the United States by Race/Ethnicity: School Years 2007–08 through 2011–12," https://nces.ed.gov/ccd/tables/AFGR0812.asp. In the most recent data, for 2012 high school graduates, 467,419 of the nation's 3,147,790 high school graduates were black.

The data showing that 8 percent of the student body is black at Princeton, Cornell, Brown, Yale, and Harvard is from the US Department of Education's online College Scorecard (collegescorecard.ed.gov), retrieved in 2018.

Jerome Karabel wrote that Harvard's freshman class in 1984 was 8 percent black on p. 525 of the paperback edition of *The Chosen: The Hidden History of Admission and Exclusion at Harvard, Yale, and Princeton,* published in 2006 by Mariner Books.

The data on black students as a proportion of Princeton's undergraduate student body in recent years is from Princeton University, Office of Institutional Research, Diversity Dashboards, https://ir.princeton.edu/university-factbook/diversity/diversity-dashboard. I set the sliders for "demographic" to "Federal Race/Ethnicity," for "Degree Level" to "Undergraduate," and for "Degree Track" to "All."

The dispute at Cornell about different cohorts within the black community was chronicled in Yvette Ndlovu, "Combating White Supremacy Should Not Entail Throwing Black Students Under the Bus," *Sunspots,* suppl. to *Cornell Daily Sun,* October 3, 2017; Marquan Jones, "We Are Not a Monolith: Nuances of Blackness at Cornell," *Cornell Daily Sun,* October 3, 2017; and Scott Jaschik, "Who Counts as a Black Student?," *Inside Higher Ed,* October 9, 2017.

Lauren Rivera's book *Pedigree: How Elite Students Get Elite Jobs* was published in paperback in 2016 by Princeton University Press. The "Iron" quotation is on p. 113; "You're one of us" is on p. 24; "you do need to be reasonably attractive" is on p. 255; and "highly correlated with parental income" is on p. 2.

I also drew on a paper by Lauren Rivera: "Ivies, Extracurriculars, and Exclusion: Elite Employers' Use of Educational Credentials," *Research in Social Stratification and Mobility* 29, no. 1 (2011). "It's light-years different" is on p. 78; "it pretty much goes into a black hole" is on p. 76; "number one people" is on p. 81; "bookworms" and "have huge glasses" are on p. 82; "drive" and "initiative" are on p. 83; "shoot the shit" is on p. 82; and "In contrast to students" is on p. 88.

My understanding of Pierre Bourdieu's work on cultural capital came from Lauren Rivera and her book *Pedigree*; from Bourdieu's book *The State Nobility,* published in English translation in 1996 by Stanford University Press; and from Shamus Rahman Khan, *Privilege: The Making of an Adolescent Elite at St. Paul's School,* published in 2011 by Princeton University Press. My interpretation of the laid-back approach to class discussion displayed by the wealthier students in KiKi Gilbert's Humanities Sequence precept at Princeton was influenced by the concept of "the ease of privilege" that Khan explores in *Privilege*.

V. Letting In

The Jack Maguire article "describing a new way of thinking about college admissions" is "To the Organized, Go the Students," *Bridge Magazine* (Fall 1976), published by Boston College.

The statistic that a quarter of private colleges are running deficits is from Jeffrey J. Selingo, "Despite Strong Economy, Worrying Financial Signs for Higher Education," *Washington Post*, August 3, 2018.

The relative weight that *U.S. News & World Report* gives to various statistical components in its rankings of American universities is analyzed in Thomas J. Webster, "A Principal Component Analysis of the *U.S. News & World Report* Tier Rankings of Colleges and Universities," *Economics of Education Review* 20 (2001).

The 2010 survey reporting what NACAC members thought of the "America's Best Colleges" list is described in *Report of the NACAC Ad Hoc Committee on U.S. News & World Report Rankings* (Arlington, VA: National Association for College Admission Counseling, September 23, 2011). See p. 8 and p. 18.

The research on the way that a change in a college's *U.S. News* ranking can affect the kind and number of applications the college will receive the following year is described in Nicholas A. Bowman and Michael N. Bastedo, "Getting on the Front Page: Organizational Reputation, Status Signals, and the Impact of *U.S. News and World Report* on Student Decisions," *Research in Higher Education* 50, no. 5 (2009).

The statistic that the average yield rate among four-year, not-for-profit colleges stands at 27 percent is from Jon Boeckenstedt. In a May 12, 2015, post, "Yes, Your Yield Rate Is Falling," on his *Higher Ed Data Stories* blog, Boeckenstedt found the average rate to be 30 percent. At my request, Boeckenstedt did an updated analysis in 2018 (based on 2016 data, the most recent available) and found that the average yield rate had fallen to 27 percent.

For the history of merit aid, I drew on Stephen Burd, "Merit Aid Madness," *Washington Monthly,* September/October 2013; and Jeffrey J. Selingo, *The Future of Enrollment: Where Colleges Will Find Their Next Students* (Washington, DC: Chronicle of Higher Education, 2017).

The statistic "89 percent of students now receive some form of financial aid" is from Joel McFarland et al., *The Condition of Education 2018* (Washington, DC: National Center for Education Statistics, May 2018), Figure 1, p. 1, "Sources of Financial Aid."

The fact that "aid goes increasingly to well-off students" is from David Radwin et al., *2015–16 National Postsecondary Student Aid Study (NPSAS:16): Student Financial Aid Estimates for 2015–16* (Washington, DC: National Center for Education Statistics, 2018); see Table 4 on p. 13. You can see similar patterns in Melissa Cominole and Jonathan Paslov, *Trends in Undergraduate Nonfederal Grant and Scholarship Aid by Demographic and Enrollment Characteristics, Selected Years: 1999–2000 to 2011–12* (Washington, DC: National Center for Education Statistics, September 2015), Table 4A, p. 25.

The statistic that "in 2018 the average tuition discount rate for freshmen at private, nonprofit universities hit 50 percent for the first time" is from "Average Freshman Tuition Discount Rate Nears 50 Percent," National Association of College and University Business Officers, press release, April 30, 2018. (I rounded up from 49.9 percent to 50 percent.) In May 2019, NACUBO reported that the average discount rate had topped 52 percent.

The fact that "the actual revenue colleges take in each year stays more or less flat" is from Slide no. 9, "What Effect Does Tuition Discounting Have on Institutional Finances?," in "Tuition Discounting: Results of the 2016 NACUBO Tuition Discounting Study," PowerPoint presentation created by NACUBO, available on the Pell Institute website at http://www.pellinstitute.org/down loads/sfarn_2017-Wyat_060917.pdf. Overall tuition revenue per full-time freshman grew 0.4 percent, in constant dollars, from 2016 to 2017.

Daniel Golden's reporting on Jared Kushner and his father appeared in Golden's *The Price of Admission: How America's Ruling Class Buys Its Way into Elite Colleges — and Who Gets Left Outside the Gates,* published in paperback in 2007 by Random House. Golden updated and reflected on his Kushner reporting in "The Story Behind Jared Kushner's Curious Acceptance into Harvard," ProPublica, November 18, 2016.

The statistic that "more than a third of legacy applicants are admitted to Harvard today" is from Delano R. Franklin and Samuel W. Zwickel, "Legacy Admit Rate Five Times That of Non-Legacies, Court Docs Show," *Harvard Crimson,* June 20, 2018.

Information on Harvard's "Z-list" is from Jamie D. Halper, "'Z-List' Students Overwhelmingly White, Often Legacies," *Harvard Crimson,* June 17, 2018; and from Anemona Hartocollis, Amy Harmon, and Mitch Smith, "'Lopping,' 'Tips' and the 'Z-List': Bias Lawsuit Explores Harvard's Admissions Secrets," *New York Times,* July 29, 2018.

The study by Lance Lochner and Philippe Belley is "The Changing Role of Family Income and Ability in Determining Educational Achievement," *Journal of Human Capital* 1, no. 1 (Winter 2007). I drew my conclusions from Figure 2a and Figure 2b, after email consultation with Lochner and Belley.

Michael Bastedo's description of enrollment managers as "faceless, pragmatic technocrats" is in his "Enrollment Management and the Low-Income Student" (paper presented at American Enterprise Institute event "Matching All Students to Postsecondary Opportunities: How College Choice Is Influenced by Institutional, State, and Federal Policy," August 4, 2015).

Jon Boeckenstedt's infographic comparing admissions data from more than a thousand colleges is "Relationship Between Freshman SAT Scores and Percent of Freshmen with Pell Grants; Colored by Diversity," in "Another 1000 Words and Ten Charts on First-Generation, Low-Income, and Minority Students," *Higher Ed Data Stories* (blog), December 17, 2014. The quote beginning "In general, the higher your freshman class SAT" is also from that post.

The fact that for universities, "higher faculty salaries and more spending on students lead directly to better rankings" on the *U.S. News* college list is explained in Robert Morse, Eric Brooks, and Matt Mason, "How U.S. News Calculated the 2019 Best Colleges Rankings," USNews.com, September 9, 2018. See the sections titled "Financial Resources" and "Faculty Resources."

The fact that "when colleges take steps to become more racially or socio-economically diverse, applications tend to go down in future years" is in Bowman and Bastedo, "Getting on the Front Page: Organizational Reputation, Status Signals, and the Impact of *U.S. News and World Report* on Student Decisions."

Jon Boeckenstedt's assertion that "Maybe — just maybe — the term 'elite' means 'uncluttered by poor people'" is from "Thinking — All Wrong — About Low-Income Students," *Admitting Things* (blog), August 26, 2014.

The data on the "apparently unbreakable relationship between family income and SAT or ACT scores" is from an unpublished analysis of 2017 College Board data by James Murphy, a tutor, testing consultant, and writer.

The Jon Boeckenstedt quote beginning "If colleges and universities are serious" is from his "Another 1000 Words and Ten Charts."

The information about "discrepant" SAT scores is from Krista D. Mattern, Emily J. Shaw, and Jennifer L. Kobrin, "A Case for Not Going SAT-Optional: Students with Discrepant SAT and HSGPA Performance," PowerPoint presentation given at the American Educational Research Association meeting in Denver on May 3, 2010. (This is the College Board study I referred to as "not one that the College Board makes public on its website these days.") Mattern, Shaw, and Kobrin published a related paper the following year: "An Alternative Presentation of Incremental Validity: Discrepant SAT and HSGPA Performance," *Educational and Psychological Measurement* 71, no. 4 (2011). There was also an earlier College Board study on discrepant SAT scores that showed similar demographic patterns (high school GPA favoring women, black and Latino students, and low-income students; SAT favoring men, white students, and high-income students). That research was published in Jennifer L. Kobrin, Wayne J. Camara, and Glenn B. Milewski, "Students with Discrepant High School GPA and SAT I Scores," in *Research Notes* (January 2002), the newsletter published by the College Board's Office of Research and Development.

The assertion that low-scoring Chicago high school students "often weren't even applying to DePaul; they assumed they wouldn't be admitted" is drawn from Jon Boeckenstedt, "A Look at Test Optional Results: Year 1," *Admitting Things* (blog), November 20, 2013.

The statistic that "about 10 percent of the students in each twenty-five-hundred-member freshman class at DePaul are now admitted without anyone at the university ever seeing their scores" is from DePaul University, *Freshman Admission Summary 2017* (Chicago: Enrollment Management and Marketing, DePaul University), p. 8.

The demographic information on DePaul applicants who choose not to submit test scores came to me from Jon Boeckenstedt and DePaul's Institutional

Research & Market Analytics office; some public data can be found on the DePaul Enrollment Management and Marketing website under the headline "DePaul Goes Test-Optional." (Click on "Preliminary results and observations.") These are also the sources of data on the academic performance of students admitted without test scores to DePaul. See also Boeckenstedt, "A Look at Test Optional Results."

The history of test-optional admissions in the United States is largely drawn from Steven T. Syverson, Valerie W. Franks, and William C. Hiss, *Defining Access: How Test-Optional Works* (Arlington, VA: National Association for College Admission Counseling, Spring 2018).

Michael Hurwitz and Jason Lee, "Grade Inflation and the Role of Standardized Testing," is in *Measuring Success: Testing, Grades, and the Future of College Admissions,* edited by Jack Buckley, Lynn Letukas, and Ben Wildavsky, published by Johns Hopkins University Press in 2018. "Fraught with equity issues" is on p. 65. "Test-optional policies may become unsustainable" is on p. 89.

"When Grades Don't Show the Whole Picture," the College Board's "sponsored content" designed to resemble an online article in the *Atlantic,* is at https://www.theatlantic.com/sponsored/the-college-board-2017/when-grades-dont-show-the-whole-picture/1479/.

The College Board's 2018 SAT validity study is Jonathan Beard and Jessica Marini, *Validity of the SAT® for Predicting First-Year Grades: 2013 SAT Validity Sample* (New York: College Board, 2018), available online at https://files.eric.ed.gov/fulltext/ED582459.pdf. The data comparing SAT scores and high school GPAs by students' household income is in Table 7.

Information on Trinity College's financial situation, including the changing demographic patterns of the Northeast, is in a draft report from the Resources Subcommittee of Trinity College's Bicentennial Strategic Planning Commission, published in 2017 on the Trinity College website, https://www.trincoll.edu/StrategicPlanning/Documents/Resources%E2%80%94Draft%20Report.pdf.

The data on Trinity College's demographics produced by Raj Chetty and his team of economists are most easily viewed on the *New York Times* interactive page "Economic Diversity and Student Outcomes at America's Colleges and Universities": information for Trinity College is at https://www.nytimes.com/interactive/projects/college-mobility/trinity-college-conn.

The problems with alcohol at Trinity College were reported in Joseph A. O'Brien Jr., "Trinity President Berger-Sweeney After a Year: Right Time, Right Place," *Hartford Courant,* August 29, 2015.

The data comparing graduation rates at Trinity College for Pell-eligible and non-Pell-eligible students are from "Common Data Set 2017–2018," under "Graduation Rates" for the Fall 2011 Cohort, line H, on p. 7, https://www.trincoll.edu/AboutTrinity/offices/InstitutionalResearchPlanning/Documents/Trinity%20College%20Common%20Data%20Set%202017-2018.pdf.

The history of early-decision admissions comes in part from Christopher Avery and Jonathan Levin, "Early Admissions at Selective Colleges," *American Economic Review* 100, no. 5 (December 2010).

The fact that "early admissions benefits affluent students more" is drawn from Avery and Levin, "Early Admissions at Selective Colleges," and from Bastedo, "Enrollment Management and the Low-Income Student."

The data about Trinity's tuition revenue, operating loss, and refinanced debt are in the draft report from the Resources Subcommittee of Trinity College's Bicentennial Strategic Planning Commission.

The fact that "on the whole, researchers have found, when colleges go test-optional it usually doesn't change the racial or economic diversity of their incoming class much at all" is from Andrew S. Belasco, Kelly O. Rosinger, and James C. Hearn, "The Test-Optional Movement at America's Selective Liberal Arts Colleges: A Boon for Equity or Something Else?," *Educational Evaluation and Policy Analysis* 37, no. 2 (2015).

VI. Staying In

The fact that 97 percent of Princeton freshmen graduate within six years is from the Graduation Dashboard on the website of Princeton's Office of Institutional Research, at https://ir.princeton.edu/data/students/graduation-dashboard. (I'm using data for the 2015 cohort year.)

The fact that "only about 60 percent of students who start a four-year degree manage to graduate in six" is from National Center for Education Statistics, Digest of Education Statistics, Table 326.10, https://nces.ed.gov/programs/digest/d17/tables/dt17_326.10.asp. (See "Graduating within 6 years after start, males and females; All 4-year institutions; 2009 starting cohort; Total.")

The fact that at two-year colleges "only three in ten students earn a degree or certificate within three years" is from National Center for Education Statistics, Digest of Education Statistics, Table 326.20, https://nces.ed.gov/programs/digest/d17/tables/dt17_326.20.asp. (See "Males and females; All 2-year institutions; 2013 starting cohort; Total.")

The turmoil at the University of Texas is described in Paul Burka, "Storming the Ivory Tower," *Texas Monthly*, October 2012. Burka wrote a series of blog posts on the magazine's website that give additional context to the dispute.

The "not customers in the traditional sense" passage is in Randy L. Diehl and Executive Leadership Team, College of Liberal Arts, *Maintaining Excellence and Efficiency at the University of Texas at Austin: A Response to the Seven "Breakthrough Solutions" and Other Proposals* (Austin: University of Texas at Austin College of Liberal Arts, July 2011).

The report of the task force "to investigate UT's lagging grad rate" is Randy Diehl, *Final Report of the Task Force on Undergraduate Graduation Rates* (Austin: University of Texas at Austin, February 15, 2012).

UT purists will tell you that the office David Laude moved into was not *in* the Tower, but in a building attached to it called Main Building. In reality, the distinction between the two buildings is mostly theoretical; they function as a single building.

Some of my reporting on David Laude, including his "massive culture shock" comment, appeared in Paul Tough, "Who Gets to Graduate?," *New York Times Magazine*, May 15, 2014. Some of my reporting on David Yeager's work was included in that article as well.

The "about $30 million" that Laude's office was given to spend on improving graduation rates was made up of a onetime $12 million grant plus a $3.8 million operating budget each year for five years.

The report that painted "two somewhat contradictory portraits of the University of Texas" is Diehl, *Final Report of the Task Force on Undergraduate Graduation Rates.*

The study that shows "only about a quarter of college students born into the bottom half of the income distribution will manage to collect a BA by age twenty-four" is Thomas G. Mortenson, "Family Income and Unequal Educational Opportunity, 1970 to 2011," *Postsecondary Education Opportunity* 245 (November 2012). (See the chart on p. 12.)

The 2015 Education Trust report on graduation rates is Andrew Howard Nichols, *The Pell Partnership: Ensuring a Shared Responsibility for Low-Income Student Success* (Washington, DC: Education Trust, September 2015), available at https://edtrust.org/resource/pellgradrates/.

The graduation-rate data for Rice University and the University of North Texas are from an Excel spreadsheet produced by the Education Trust as part of its *Pell Partnership* report. You can download it by going to https://edtrust.org/resource/pellgradrates/ and clicking on "Data File."

The fact that Trinity College's Pell-eligible students have an unusually large graduation-rate advantage over its non-Pell-eligible students comes in part from Melissa Korn, "Even at Top Colleges, Graduation Gaps Persist for Poor Students," *Wall Street Journal*, February 18, 2019. That article reported Trinity's graduation-rate gap as twelve percentage points, but Trinity's "Common Data Set for 2017–2018" reported the gap as sixteen percentage points (as noted in chapter 5).

The Pell and non-Pell graduation rates at UT are in Diehl, *Final Report of the Task Force on Undergraduate Graduation Rates,* Table 3.1.

For the history of the Top 10 Percent Rule at UT, I drew on Mark C. Long, Victor B. Saenz, and Marta Tienda, "Policy Transparency and College Enrollment: Did the Texas Top 10% Law Broaden Access to the Public Flagships?," in *Annals of the American Academy of Political and Social Science* 627, no. 1 (January 4, 2010); Douglas Laycock, "Desegregation, Affirmative Action, and the Ten-Percent Law," in *The Texas Book: Profiles, History, and Reminiscences of the University,* edited by Richard A. Holland, published in 2006 by the University of Texas Press; Sunny Xinchun Niu, Marta Tienda, and Kalena Cortes, "College Selectivity and the Texas Top 10% Law," *Economics of Education Review* 25, no. 3 (June 2006); and Sunny X. Niu and Marta Tienda, "Minority Student Academic Performance Under the Uniform Admission Law: Evidence from the University of Texas at Austin," *Educational Evaluation and Policy Analysis* 32, no. 1 (March 2010). The specific statistics on the effect that the Top 10 Percent Rule had on diversity at UT is from Long, Saenz, and Tienda, "Policy Transparency and College Enrollment."

The transformation of flagship public universities is chronicled in Stephen Burd, *Undermining Pell: How Colleges Compete for Wealthy Students and Leave the Low-Income Behind* (Washington, DC: New America Foundation, 2013), and Burd, *Undermining Pell, Volume II: How Colleges' Pursuit of Prestige and Revenue Is Hurting Low-Income Students* (Washington, DC: New America Foundation, 2014). I also drew on Stephanie Saul, "Public Colleges Chase Out-of-State Students, and Tuition," *New York Times,* July 7, 2016; and Ozan Jaquette, *State University No More: Out-of-State Enrollment and the Growing Exclusion of High-Achieving, Low-Income Students at Public Flagship Universities* (Lansdowne, VA: Jack Kent Cooke Foundation, May 2017).

The statistics on the out-of-state percentage at the University of Oregon and the University of Vermont are from Jaquette, *State University No More.*

The statistics on the percentage of students eligible for Pell grants at the University of Virginia and the University of Michigan are from Burd, *Undermining Pell.*

The data on the average family income for undergraduates at the University of Alabama are from "Economic Diversity and Student Outcomes at America's Colleges and Universities," the interactive presentation of the Mobility Report Cards data on the *New York Times* website: https://www.nytimes.com/interactive/projects/college-mobility/university-of-alabama. The data for Bryn Mawr College are from the same website.

The fact that the University of Texas admitted "politically connected but academically unqualified applicants" is from University of Texas at Austin, *Investigation of Admissions Practices and Allegations of Undue Influence: Summary of Key Findings,* a report prepared by Kroll (a corporate investigations and risk consulting firm) and submitted to the Office of the Chancellor of the University of Texas System on February 6, 2015. The report was covered in Jack Stripling, "Admissions Report Chips at Austin Chief's Uncompromising Reputation," *Chronicle of Higher Education,* February 13, 2015.

The statistics on "the biggest gains in UT's four-year graduation rate" came from the University of Texas's Institutional Reporting, Research, and Information Systems department. They were reported in "UT Austin Records Its Highest Four-Year Graduation Rate," a UT News press release issued on September 27, 2018.

The study on "the trajectories of college freshmen with SAT scores between 1000 and 1200" is included in Anthony P. Carnevale and Jeff Strohl, "How Increasing College Access Is Increasing Inequality, and What to Do About It," in *Rewarding Strivers: Helping Low-Income Students Succeed in College*, edited by Richard D. Kahlenberg, published in 2010 by the Century Foundation. (See p. 158.)

The "small but influential experiment" conducted by Duke psychology researchers Timothy D. Wilson and Patricia W. Linville is described in their "Improving the Academic Performance of College Freshmen: Attribution Therapy Revisited," *Journal of Personality and Social Psychology* 42, no. 2 (1982). A replication attempt was described in their "Improving the Performance of College Freshmen with Attributional Techniques," *Journal of Personality and Social Psychology* 49, no. 1 (1985).

The experiment by Yale researchers Gregory M. Walton and Geoffrey Cohen is described in their "A Brief Social-Belonging Intervention Improves Academic and Health Outcomes of Minority Students," *Science*, March 18, 2011.

The hypothesis "that there are certain moments in our lives, like having a first child or enrolling in college, that are so deeply disorienting" is described in Gregory M. Walton and Timothy D. Wilson, "Wise Interventions: Psychological Remedies for Social and Personal Problems," *Psychological Review* 125, no. 5 (2018).

The experiment by David S. Yeager and Gregory M. Walton involving the entire class entering UT in the fall of 2012 is described in David S. Yeager et al., "Teaching a Lay Theory Before College Narrows Achievement Gaps at Scale," *Proceedings of the National Academy of Sciences* 113, no. 24 (May 31, 2016). The data showing the effect of the intervention on first-generation and other disadvantaged students are from Table S10 on p. 41 of the appendix, available at https://www.pnas.org/content/pnas/suppl/2016/05/25/1524360113.DCSupplemental/pnas.1524360113.sapp.pdf. The fact that graduation data for the class of 2016 indicated that "the effect of the intervention had mostly faded out" came from personal communication with David Yeager in 2019.

The data on the success of the corequisite writing model at the University of Central Arkansas are from the university's Department of Student Transitions.

The fact that at Chicago's community colleges, "graduation rates are generally below 20 percent" is from the "Facts and Statistics" page of the City Colleges of Chicago website, http://www.ccc.edu/menu/pages/facts-statistics.aspx. The fact that "very few students successfully transfer to a four-year institution" is from Jenny Nagaoka, Alex Seeskin, and Vanessa Coca, *The Educational Attainment of Chicago Public Schools Students: 2016* (Chicago: University of Chicago Consortium on School Research, October 2017).

Some of the history of Arrupe College is drawn from Stephen N. Katsouros, *Come to Believe: How the Jesuits Are Reinventing Education (Again)*, published in 2017 by Orbis Books.

VII. Hanging On

The fact that most manufacturing jobs in North Carolina are nonunionized is from Katherine Peralta, "North Carolina's Union Membership Rate Is the Lowest in the Country," *Charlotte Observer*, January 28, 2015.

The Josh Mandel column, "Welders Make $150,000? Bring Back Shop Class," was published in the *Wall Street Journal* on April 21, 2014.

The essay that "upped the ante on Mandel's $150,000 welder" is Tamar Jacoby, "This Way Up: Mobility in America," *Wall Street Journal*, July 22, 2014.

Marco Rubio's comment that "welders make more money than philosophers" is on the *New Republic*'s YouTube channel: "Marco Rubio Says Welders Make More Than Philosophers," at https://www.youtube.com/watch?v=HP7vOx1ZCHE.

The *Bloomberg Businessweek* article, "Want a $1 Million Paycheck? Skip College and Go Work in a Lumberyard," by Prashant Gopal and Matthew Townsend, appeared on June 27, 2017.

The "summit meeting sponsored by the American Enterprise Institute a few weeks after the 2016 election" was "This Way Up: Economic Mobility for Poor and Middle-Class Americans," December 14–15, 2016, Washington, DC. Videos of the speeches and panel discussions are online at http://opportunityamericaonline.org/twu-summit/.

The welder from Dayton who was invited to President Trump's 2018 State of the Union address is Corey Adams. Trump spoke about Adams in that address; the clip is on the CBS News YouTube channel: "Ohio Welder, Guest at State of the Union, Praised by Trump," at https://www.youtube.com/watch?v=vInXkrmTuog.

Betsy DeVos's visits to welding classes were chronicled in Corbett Smith and Eva-Marie Ayala, "Embattled Betsy DeVos Sails Through Surprise Visit to North Texas Schools," *Dallas News,* April 5, 2018; Eric Peterson, "DeVos Visits Harper College's Manufacturing Lab, Apprenticeship Program," *Chicago Daily Herald,* October 19, 2018; Sharon Otterman, "DeVos Visits New York Schools, but Not Ones Run by the City," *New York Times,* May 16, 2018; and on Secretary DeVos's Twitter feed at https://twitter.com/betsydevosed/status/845272349725392896.

Ivanka Trump's visit to a community college near St. Louis was reported in "Ivanka Trump Tries Her Hand at Welding," CBS News, August 8, 2018.

Stuart Varney's assertion that "there's an element of snobbery in America" is from a segment of his Fox Business show *Varney & Co.,* "'Dirty Jobs' Host Mike Rowe: We Need to Encourage a Better Work Ethic," which aired March 28, 2017.

Data on the average and ninetieth-percentile salaries for welders comes from the Bureau of Labor Statistics, Occupational Employment Statistics (51-4121 Welders, Cutters, Solderers, and Brazers), https://www.bls.gov/oes/2017/may/oes514121.htm. In May 2017 the median salary for welders was $40,240 and the salary at the ninetieth percentile was $63,170. In 2014, when the *Wall Street Journal* published Josh Mandel's and Tamar Jacoby's columns, the average salary was $36,300, according to Jacoby's column.

In 2014 the poverty line (which the federal government calls the "poverty guideline") for a four-person family, as published by the US Department of Health and Human Services, was $23,850. See Office of the Assistant Secretary for Planning and Evaluation (ASPE), "Prior HHS Poverty Guidelines and Federal Register References," https://aspe.hhs.gov/prior-hhs-poverty-guidelines-and-federal-register-references.

That philosophy majors make more than welders, on average, is shown in Philip Bump, "Sorry, Marco Rubio. Philosophy Majors Actually Make Way More Than Welders," *Washington Post,* November 10, 2015.

Data on cuts in state funding for community colleges in North Carolina is from North Carolina, General Assembly, Program Evaluation Division, *Fund-*

ing for North Carolina's Community Colleges: A Description of the Current Formula and Potential Methods to Improve Efficiency and Effectiveness, Evaluation Oversight Committee Report no. 2016-09, October 10, 2016. The cut in per-student funding is on p. 5.

The fact that the cuts in North Carolina's state funding for higher education "took place during a period when state tax revenues in North Carolina actually went *up*" is from North Carolina Department of Revenue, *Statistical Abstract of North Carolina Taxes 2017,* https://www.ncdor.gov/news/reports-and-statistics/statistical-abstract-north-carolina-taxes.

The fact that "what happened in North Carolina mirrors what happened in most other states" is from Michael Mitchell, Michael Leachman, and Kathleen Masterson, *A Lost Decade in Higher Education Funding: State Cuts Have Driven Up Tuition and Reduced Quality* (Washington, DC: Center on Budget and Policy Priorities, August 23, 2017). See also David Leonhardt, "The Assault on Colleges—and the American Dream," *New York Times,* May 25, 2017.

The fact that "community college tuition in North Carolina has increased by 60 percent since 2007" is found in the ninth slide of a slide show ("Funding for North Carolina's Community Colleges: A Description of the Current Formula and Potential Methods to Improve Efficiency and Effectiveness: A presentation to the Joint Legislative Program Evaluation Oversight Committee") that accompanied the 2016 report by the Program Evaluation Division of the North Carolina General Assembly, *Funding for North Carolina's Community Colleges.*

The fact that institutions like Catawba Valley Community College have been forced to "cut budgets and cut corners" because of the cuts in state spending on higher education can be found in David J. Deming and Christopher R. Walters, "The Impacts of Price Caps and Spending Cuts on U.S. Postsecondary Attainment" (NBER Working Paper no. 23736, National Bureau of Economic Research, Cambridge, MA, August 2017).

For the history of the City College of New York, I drew on James Traub, *City on a Hill: Testing the American Dream at City College,* published in 1994 by Addison-Wesley.

The fact that City College's tuition has gone up and spending on instruction has gone down is from Michael Fabricant and Stephen Brier, *Austerity Blues:*

Fighting for the Soul of Public Higher Education, published in 2016 by Johns Hopkins University Press. (See p. 3 and p. 22.)

The fact that "City College was near the top of the list" of colleges with the highest student-mobility rates is from "Colleges with the Highest Student-Mobility Rates, 2014," *Chronicle of Higher Education,* August 19, 2018, https://www.chronicle.com/article/Colleges-With-the-Highest/244094.

The change in the college wage premium over the last few decades is from Jonathan James, "The College Wage Premium," *Economic Commentary* no. 2012-10, August 8, 2012, published by the Research Department of the Federal Reserve Bank of Cleveland.

The data on earnings for college dropouts are from Elka Torpey, "Measuring the Value of Education," in *Career Outlook* (April 2018), published by the Bureau of Labor Statistics. In 2017 the median weekly earnings for an adult with "Some college, no degree" were $774, and the median weekly earnings for an adult with "High school diploma, no college" were $712, a difference of $3,224 over a fifty-two-week year.

The fact that "engineers really do earn more than almost everyone else" is from Brad Hershbein and Melissa S. Kearney, "Major Decisions: What Graduates Earn over Their Lifetimes," a paper published by the Hamilton Project on September 29, 2014. See "Figure 2a: Median Lifetime Earnings, by College Major," a chart published online at http://www.hamiltonproject.org/assets/legacy/files/downloads_and_links/MajorDecisions-Figure_2a.pdf.

The research by the economists Tim Bartik and Brad Hershbein on how much a college degree adds to students' lifetime earnings is in their "Degrees of Poverty: Family Income Background and the College Earnings Premium," *Employment Research Newsletter* 23, no. 3 (2016), published by Upjohn Institute for Employment Research. Their definition of "lower-income" is below 185 percent of the poverty line, or about $47,000 for a family of four (as of 2019).

The NBC News/*Wall Street Journal* poll that asked young adults between the ages of eighteen and thirty-four whether a four-year college degree was worth the cost was reported in Josh Mitchell and Douglas Belkin, "Americans Losing Faith in College Degrees, Poll Finds," *Wall Street Journal,* September 7, 2017.

The fact that the "demographic group that currently harbors the most consistently negative feelings about college is old, wealthy Republicans" is from Pew Research Center, "Sharp Partisan Divisions in Views of National Institutions," July 10, 2017.

David Autor's analysis of comparative earnings for Americans with different levels of educational attainment was in "Work of the Past, Work of the Future" (NBER Working Paper no. 25588, National Bureau of Economic Research, Cambridge, MA, February 2019); see Figure 1. An earlier version of Autor's research is in his "Skills, Education, and the Rise of Earnings Inequality Among the 'Other 99 percent,'" *Science*, May 23, 2014.

The data on the increase in the size of the for-profit college sector between 2000 and 2010 are from Tressie McMillan Cottom, *Lower Ed: The Troubling Rise of For-Profit Colleges in the New Economy*, published in 2017 by the New Press. (See p. 32.)

Much of my understanding of the for-profit college sector comes from Cottom, *Lower Ed*; from Suzanne Mettler, *Degrees of Inequality: How the Politics of Higher Education Sabotaged the American Dream*, published in 2014 by Basic Books; and from Molly Hensley-Clancy, "Lower Education: How a Disgraced College Chain Trapped Its Students in Poverty," BuzzFeed News, November 13, 2014.

The statistic that "in 2012 for-profit colleges were educating just 12 percent of the nation's college students, but those students accounted for 44 percent of the nation's student-loan defaults" is from Rana Foroohar, "How the Financing of Colleges May Lead to Disaster!," *New York Review of Books*, October 13, 2016.

The fact that for-profit colleges spent twice as much on marketing and profit taking as on student instruction is from Foroohar, "How the Financing of Colleges May Lead to Disaster!"

Page citations for the quotes from Cottom, *Lower Ed* are as follows: "something more complicated than big, evil con artists" is from p. 181; "Lower Ed can exist precisely because elite Higher Ed does" is from p. 11; and "we increasingly demand more personal sacrifice" is also from p. 11. Cottom credits the phrase "the education gospel" to the economists W. Norton Grubb and Marvin Lazerson.

VIII. Getting an A

My understanding of the history of calculus came from interviews with Uri Treisman, and from David Acheson, *The Calculus Story: A Mathematical Adventure,* published in 2017 by Oxford University Press; and Silvanus P. Thompson and Martin Gardner, *Calculus Made Easy,* published in 1998 by St. Martin's Press.

Uri Treisman's statement that freshman calculus was "a burial ground" is in Treisman, "A Study of the Mathematics Performance of Black Students at the University of California, Berkeley" (PhD diss., University of California, Berkeley, 1985).

The fact that freshman calculus nationally is populated disproportionately by white and Asian students is from Table 1, p. 2, of David Bressoud, "The Calculus Students," in *Insights and Recommendations from the MAA National Study of College Calculus,* edited by David Bressoud, Vilma Mesa, and Chris Rasmussen (Washington, DC: MAA Press, 2015).

The assertion that freshman calculus students come disproportionately from well-off families is from Sarah D. Sparks, "Calculus Is the Peak of High School Math. Maybe It's Time to Change That," *Education Week,* May 22, 2018; and from p. 4 of David M. Bressoud, ed., *The Role of Calculus in the Transition from High School to College Mathematics* (report of the workshop held at the MAA Carriage House, Washington, DC, March 17–19, 2016), published by the Mathematical Association of America and the National Council of Teachers of Mathematics. (These statistics are for high school seniors taking calculus, rather than college freshmen taking calculus, but those two groups mostly overlap.)

The fact that 6,000 students were taking AP Calculus when Uri Treisman was in high school is in David M. Bressoud, "AP and the College Mathematics Curriculum," *Launchings* (monthly blog by Bressoud published by the Mathematical Association of America), May 2010.

The fact that 800,000 students now take calculus in high school each year came from Slide 2 in "The Role of Calculus in the Transition from High School to College Mathematics," a PowerPoint presentation by David Bressoud presented to the Urban Math Leadership Network in Austin on February 8, 2017, available at https://www.macalester.edu/~bressoud/talks/2017/RoleOfCalculus-UMLN.pdf.

The estimate that 650,000 students now take AP Calculus is from calculations by David Bressoud based on data from the College Board, which administers the Advanced Placement exams. According to the College Board, about 450,000 students took an AP Calculus exam in 2017. (That data can be found on the College Board website at "AP Data—Archived Data 2017," https://research.collegeboard.org/programs/ap/data/archived/ap-2017.) In a personal communication with me, Bressoud estimated, based on previous College Board data, that another 200,000 students each year take the AP Calculus course without taking an AP Calculus exam.

The fact that about a fifth of the total population of high school seniors takes calculus each year comes from Table 1-14 ("Highest-level mathematics course enrollment of high school completers, by student and family characteristics: 2013") in "Elementary and Secondary Mathematics and Science Education," part of the National Science Board's *Science & Engineering Indicators 2018* report, available online at https://www.nsf.gov/statistics/2018/nsb20181/.

The assertion that students in AP Calculus today "are usually taught a thin, flattened-out version of the subject" is from the preface to Bressoud, Mesa, and Rasmussen, eds., *Insights and Recommendations from the MAA National Study of College Calculus.*

The survey showing that "80 percent of college students who had completed AP Calculus said they took it because they thought it would look good on their college applications" is on p. 33 of Joseph G. Rosenstein and Anoop Ahluwalia, "Putting Brakes on the Rush to AP Calculus," in Bressoud, ed., *The Role of Calculus in the Transition from High School to College Mathematics.*

The fact that "highly selective colleges are much more likely to admit students who have taken AP Calculus" is from p. 100 of Kevin Eagan et al., *The American Freshman: National Norms Fall 2016* (Los Angeles: Cooperative Institutional Research Program at the Higher Education Research Institute at UCLA, 2017). (Sixty-nine percent of freshmen at "very high" selectivity private universities said they took calculus in high school.)

The fact that in 2017, "93 percent of freshmen admitted by Harvard University reported that they had taken calculus in high school" is from the *Harvard Crimson* survey of the class of 2021, https://features.thecrimson.com/2017/

freshman-survey/academics/. (Technically, that statistic refers to enrolled freshmen rather than admitted freshmen.)

The statistic that only "48 percent of high schools, nationally, offer a course in calculus" comes from Table 1-22 ("Access to high-level mathematics and sciences courses among students at low versus high black and Latino enrollment schools: 2013–14"), in "Elementary and Secondary Mathematics and Science Education," National Science Board, *Science & Engineering Indicators 2018.*

The statistic that 43 percent of schools in Texas offer a course in calculus comes from US Department of Education Office for Civil Rights, "Civil Rights Data Collection: Data Snapshot (College and Career Readiness)," Issue Brief no. 3 (March 2014), p. 22.

The fact that schools with a lot of white students are almost twice as likely to offer calculus as schools with a lot of black and Latino students is from Table 1-22 of "Elementary and Secondary Mathematics and Science Education," National Science Board, *Science & Engineering Indicators 2018.*

The statistic about students at private schools and students at public schools taking calculus at different rates is from Appendix Table 1-23 ("Highest-level mathematics course enrollment of high school completers, by student and family characteristics: 2013"), in "Elementary and Secondary Mathematics and Science Education," National Science Board, *Science & Engineering Indicators 2018.*

The statistic about "students whose families have incomes in the top quintile" taking calculus at higher rates is from Table 1-14 in "Elementary and Secondary Mathematics and Science Education," National Science Board, *Science & Engineering Indicators 2018.*

The quotation that begins "Too many students are moving too fast through preliminary courses" comes from p. 77 of Bressoud, ed., *The Role of Calculus in the Transition from High School to College Mathematics.*

The average starting salary for engineering graduates from UT Austin is from Figure 5 on p. 14 of Anthony P. Carnevale et al., *Major Matters Most: The Economic Value of Bachelor's Degrees from the University of Texas System* (Washington, DC: Georgetown University Center on Education and the Workforce, 2017).

The statistic that "40 percent of [calculus] retakers, nationally, earn a C or below" is from p. 5 of Bressoud, ed., *The Role of Calculus in the Transition from High School to College Mathematics.*

The two old books about algebra that Uri Treisman took out of the library in Brooklyn were George Chrystal, *Algebra: An Elementary Text-Book for the Higher Classes of Secondary Schools and for Colleges*, part 1, originally published in 1886; and Garrett Birkhoff and Saunders Mac Lane, *A Survey of Modern Algebra*, originally published in 1941.

My understanding of Uri Treisman's work at Berkeley came from my interviews with Treisman, and also from Rose Asera, *Calculus and Community: A History of the Emerging Scholars Program: A Report of the National Task Force on Minority High Achievement* (New York: College Entrance Examination Board, May 2001); Uri Treisman, "Studying Students Studying Calculus: A Look at the Lives of Minority Mathematics Students in College," *College Mathematics Journal* 23, no. 5 (November 1992); and Treisman, "A Study of the Mathematics Performance of Black Students at the University of California, Berkeley."

Claude Steele citing "Treisman's work at Berkeley as a major contributor to his theory of stereotype threat" can be found in Steele, "A Threat in the Air: How Stereotypes Shape Intellectual Identity and Performance," *American Psychologist* 52, no. 6 (1997); and in chapter 6 of his *Whistling Vivaldi: And Other Clues to How Stereotypes Affect Us*, published in 2010 by W. W. Norton.

The article by Mitch Daniels arguing against "accepting a high school A at face value" is "For College Admissions, Let's Value Grit over GPAs," *Washington Post*, November 28, 2018.

IX. After the War

In writing about the history of the GI Bill I relied on a number of books, most centrally Michael J. Bennett, *When Dreams Came True: The GI Bill and the Making of Modern America*, published in 1996 by Brassey's; Glenn C. Altschuler and Stuart M. Blumin, *The GI Bill: A New Deal for Veterans*, published in 2009 by Oxford University Press; Suzanne Mettler, *Soldiers to Citizens: The G.I. Bill and the Making of the Greatest Generation*, published in 2005 by Oxford University Press; and Keith W. Olson, *The G.I. Bill, the Veterans, and the Colleges*, published in 1974 by the University Press of Kentucky. I also drew on Ira Katznelson, *When Affirmative Action Was White: An Untold*

History of Racial Inequality in Twentieth-Century America, published in 2005 by W. W. Norton; Davis R. B. Ross, *Preparing for Ulysses: Politics and Veterans During World War II*, published in 1969 by Columbia University Press; Neil A. Wynn, *The Afro-American and the Second World War*, published in 1993 in a rev. ed. by Holmes & Meier; Kathleen J. Frydl, *The GI Bill*, published in 2009 by Cambridge University Press; and Joseph C. Goulden, *The Best Years: 1945–1950*, published in 1976 by Atheneum.

The quotation by Franklin Roosevelt that begins "We are, today, laying plans" is on p. 88 of Bennett, *When Dreams Came True*.

The fact that Roosevelt's initial proposal focused its attention on "exceptionally able" veterans is from p. 19 of Mettler, *Soldiers to Citizens*, and p. 132 of Bennett, *When Dreams Came True*.

In writing about the drafting of the GI Bill, I drew on, in addition to the books mentioned above, Dave Camelon, "I Saw the G.I. Bill Written," *American Legion Magazine*, September 1949.

The statistic that fewer than 40 percent of soldiers had graduated from high school comes from p. 66 of Altschuler and Blumin, *The GI Bill*.

The quotation by John Rankin that begins "The vast majority of the men" is from p. 67 of Altschuler and Blumin, *The GI Bill*.

Robert M. Hutchins, "The Threat to American Education," appeared in *Collier's Weekly*, December 30, 1944.

James Bryant Conant's comments in his letter to the trustees of Harvard University is from "Conant Suggests GI Bill Revision," *Harvard Crimson*, January 23, 1945; and from Keith W. Olson, "The GI Bill and Higher Education: Success and Surprise," *American Quarterly* 25, no. 5 (December 1973).

The statistics on the number of veterans who took advantage of the GI Bill are from p. 83 and p. 86 of Altschuler and Blumin, *The GI Bill*; and from Melissa Murray, "When War Is Work: The G.I. Bill, Citizenship, and the Civic Generation," *California Law Review* 96, no. 4 (August 2008).

The statistic that by 1948, "15 percent of the federal budget was devoted to the cost of the GI Bill," is from p. 113 of Katznelson, *When Affirmative Action Was White*.

The fact that veterans "outperformed their civilian counterparts throughout the GI Bill era" is from p. 116 of Katznelson, *When Affirmative Action Was White*; from p. 71 of Mettler, *Soldiers to Citizens*; and from Edith Efron, "The Two Joes Meet—Joe College, Joe Veteran," *New York Times Magazine,* June 16, 1946.

The quotation about the GIs "hogging the honor rolls" is from p. 41 of Olson, *The G.I. Bill, the Veterans, and the Colleges.*

The fact that veterans enrolled in humanities courses at a higher rate than nonveterans is from p. 93 of Altschuler and Blumin, *The GI Bill.*

The quotation that begins "They're grinds, every one of them" is from Efron, "The Two Joes Meet."

The fact that before the war, "higher education in the United States had been the province almost exclusively of the rich and the upper middle class" is from Daniel A. Clark, "'The Two Joes Meet. Joe College, Joe Veteran': The G.I. Bill, College Education, and Postwar American Culture," *History of Education Quarterly* 38, no. 2 (Summer 1998).

The fact that "most of the students who attended college on the GI Bill came from low-income or working-class families" is from p. 49 of Mettler, *Soldiers to Citizens.*

The idea that "the postwar incursion of working-class kids onto college campuses changed the way Americans thought about college students" is expressed in many of the sources I consulted, including on p. 174 of Clark, "'The Two Joes Meet. Joe College, Joe Veteran'"; and on p. 87 of Altschuler and Blumin, *The GI Bill.*

Suzanne Mettler's comment that there were many veterans in her survey "who experienced breathtaking transformation in their life circumstances" is on p. 95 of her *Soldiers to Citizens.* So is the longer quotation that begins "the postal employee's son."

The text of President Obama's February 2009 address to Congress is in the *New York Times,* February 24, 2009.

For President Obama's speech at the White House "two months later," see "Remarks by the President on Higher Education," April 24, 2009, Obama White

House, https://obamawhitehouse.archives.gov/the-press-office/remarks-presi
dent-higher-education.

Obama's speech in Austin in August 2010 is on YouTube ("Obama Wants US to
Be #1 in Education") at https://www.youtube.com/watch?v=XKiuAweHZHU.
The passages quoted come between 5:00 and 9:00.

The data showing the improvements that other countries made in their college-attainment rates between 1998 and 2008 come from "Population with
Tertiary Education," an interactive chart on the OECD website at https://data.
oecd.org/eduatt/population-with-tertiary-education.htm#indicator-chart.

The data showing that in November 2018 the United States was still in twelfth
place in college attainment, globally, can be found in OECD, "Population with
Tertiary Education" (set the sliders to "25–34 year-olds" and "2017").

The "private memo that went in the fall of 2009 to Lawrence Summers" was
written by Cecilia Rouse and James Kvaal; it was sent to Summers and Diana
Farrell on October 1, 2009. (A copy was provided to me by Kvaal.)

A blog post describing President Obama's announcement of the American Graduation Initiative ("Investing in Education: The American Graduation Initiative") was posted on the White House website on July 14, 2009,
and has been archived online at https://obamawhitehouse.archives.gov/
blog/2009/07/14/investing-education-american-graduation-initiative.

The eleventh-hour demise of the American Graduation Initiative is described
in Kevin Carey, "Taking an Incomplete," *New Republic*, April 12, 2010; Alan
Berube, "The End of the American Graduation Initiative," *Avenue* (Brook-
ings Institution blog), March 23, 2010; and David M. Herszenhorn and Tamar
Lewin, "Student Loan Overhaul Approved by Congress," *New York Times*,
March 25, 2010.

Rick Santorum's "snob" accusation against President Obama is on the Breitbart News YouTube channel: "Santorum on Obama 'What a Snob,'" February
25, 2012, https://www.youtube.com/watch?v=GSn3YL1hZOU.

My understanding of the history of the high school movement came mostly
from the work of the economists Claudia Goldin and Lawrence F. Katz, in
their book *The Race Between Education and Technology*, published in 2008
by Harvard University Press; and their paper "Why the United States Led in

Education: Lessons from Secondary School Expansion, 1910 to 1940" (NBER Working Paper no. 6144, National Bureau of Economic Research, August 1997). I also drew on Paul Beston, "When High Schools Shaped America's Destiny," in "The Shape of Work to Come," special issue, *City Journal*, 2017.

The growth over time in the number of high school graduates in the United States is chronicled in Table 219.10 ("High School Graduates, by Sex and Control of School: Selected Years, 1869–70 Through 2027–28") of the *Digest of Education Statistics*, published by the National Center for Education Statistics.

The "grassroots desire for greater social mobility" quotation is in Goldin and Katz, *The Race Between Education and Technology*, p. 167; "sprung from the people" is on p. 245.

The "recent analysis of US census data" showing how much top-earning philosophy majors make was described in George Anders, "Good News Liberal-Arts Majors: Your Peers Probably Won't Outearn You Forever," *Wall Street Journal*, September 11, 2016. The original analysis is on the Hamilton Project website, at "Career Earnings by College Major," http://www.hamiltonproject. org/charts/career_earnings_by_college_major/.

I borrowed the idea of "the hoarding of opportunity" from Richard V. Reeves, author of *Dream Hoarders: How the American Upper Middle Class Is Leaving Everyone Else in the Dust, Why That Is a Problem, and What to Do About It*, published in 2017 by Brookings Institution Press.

Index